Stanley Matthews was born in Stoke-on-Trent in February 1915. At the age of 15 he joined the groundstaff of Stoke City. He made his League debut for them in 1932 in the era of Dixie Dean, and played his last game at 50 in the age of George Best. He played for Stoke until 1947 when he moved to Blackpool. He reached three FA Cup finals in the next six seasons, eventually winning the competition in 1953. He returned to Stoke City in 1961 and finished his career in 1965. He won 54 caps for England between 1934 and 1957, as well as playing in 29 wartime internationals.

Stanley Matthews was the first ever Footballer of the Year (1948), and the first European Footballer of the year (1956). He was the first footballer ever to be awarded the CBE and then the first to be knighted (1965), and remains the only one to receive the award while still playing. He died peacefully on 23 February 2000.

D0238617

THE WAY IT WAS

My Autobiography

—=○=—

Stanley Matthews

HEADLINE

First published in 2000
by HEADLINE BOOK PUBLISHING

First published in paperback in 2001
by HEADLINE BOOK PUBLISHING

10 9 8 7 6 5 4 3 2 1

Cataloguing in Publication Data is available from
the British Library

ISBN 0 7472 6427 9

Typeset by Letterpart Ltd
Reigate, Surrey

Printed and bound in Great Britain by
Mackays of Chatham PLC, Chatham, Kent

HEADLINE BOOK PUBLISHING
A division of the Hodder Headline Group
338 Euston Road
London NW1 3BH

www.headline.co.uk
www.hodderheadline.com

Contents

1	If it Wasn't for my Mother	1
2	From Office Boy to International	25
3	When 149,000 Went Silent at Once	59
4	Changing the Wingers' Style	101
5	Making the Nazis Storm Out	115
6	Scotland Defeated at Last	131
7	On the Brink	147
8	The Great and Glorious of the Thirties	165
9	Corporal Matthews of the RAF	187
10	The Burnden Park Disaster	205
11	Going to the Golden Mile	227
12	The First Footballer of the Year	259
13	England's Greatest Ever Forward Line	295
14	World Cup Lessons Unlearned	317
15	Forties Favourites	345
16	Thoughts of Going Home	357
17	Through – but Phew!	381
18	Cup Fever in Blackpool	407
19	The Mortensen Final	417
20	Trying to Catch the Galloping Major	441

21 The End of my England Career   469
22 Fifties Favourites   489
23 My Final Bow   505
24 Footballing Missionary   549
25 Football in the New Millennium   577
Epilogue by Les Scott   591
Career Record   607
Index   611

My autobiography is dedicated
To my darling Mila
For whom there is no greater love

Acknowledgements

I would particularly like to express my sincere thanks and gratitude to the following, who by way of expertise, advice, access to historical data, friendship or detailed recollection where my own personal memory was sketchy, have helped me to put my story down in the way I wanted it told.

My daughter Jean, her husband Bob and my family.

Julian Alexander and all at my agents Lucas Alexander Whitley; George and Alex Best; Blackpool FC, in particular Roger Harrison; Jack Blades (South Africa); Ken and Jean Bolam; Pat Brogan; Mick Cullerton; Sir Tom Finney; the Football Association; Trevor Ford; the *Gazette* (Blackpool); Janice Hallam of Barclays Bank plc (Stafford); Dennis Herod; Nat Lofthouse; Manchester United FC, in particular Mike Mansfield; Ian Marshall and all at Headline Book Publishing; Billy Mould; Harold Naylor; Ferenc Puskas; Jack Rollin; the *Sentinel* (Stoke-on-Trent), in particular editor Sean Dooley and sports editor Alex Martin; Len Shackleton; Huston Spratt; Stoke City FC; Steve and Deb Waterall; John Whitehouse.

For Sal and Lauren.

To Les Scott

I would like to express my sincere thanks to my dear friend Les Scott who collaborated with me in the writing of my autobiography.

At the risk of appearing immodest, I could have approached many writers when I made the decision finally to commit my life to book form, but chose to work with Les, whose writing I have greatly admired for some years now.

For eighteen months, almost on a daily basis, we worked together on the manuscript. Les's expertise, knowledge and wonderful humour made the task not only easy, but highly enjoyable from my point of view.

Thanks, Les, you're a real pal.

Stanley Matthews
January 2000

1

—◦—

If it Wasn't for my Mother

I n the early fifties we were all on top money at Blackpool.
If we won, we got full whack, which in the era of the
maximum wage was £12 including our win bonus.

We collected our wages from the club office on a Friday
lunchtime. The money was for the previous week's game and
we were paid in cash. It came in a small brown envelope and
each player had to sign a chitty to say he had received his
money. We were paid in notes of the smaller denomination,
which I'm sure was a psychological ploy on the part of the
club to make it look a lot. Imagine the top players of today
picking up their wages in cash. It would be like humping a
wad the size of a bale of hay out of the club office every
week.

On this particular occasion, we'd won at home the
previous week, so I went along to collect the full amount,
£12. I signed for this princely sum and, once outside in the
club car park (a bit of a misnomer – strictly speaking, it

was the directors' car park because hardly any of the Blackpool players had cars), counted my wages and was astonished to find the envelope contained £13. We'd been playing well in front of full houses at Bloomfield Road and I had been doing OK, so I never questioned it. I simply took out the extra pound and slipped it into my wallet before taking my wages home.

We won at Chelsea the next day and the following Friday I went to pick up my wages as usual. This time when I came to count it, I discovered there was only £11 in the envelope. I immediately made a beeline for manager Joe Smith's office to point out the mistake.

Joe was a wily old bird, a great manager and a clever psychologist where the players were concerned. He had the respect of the players and we hung on his every word, so much so that if he had ever turned round and told me to 'Go to hell', I would have actually looked forward to the journey.

'You never came in complaining to me last week when we paid you a pound too much,' said Joe.

He'd caught me on the hop because I didn't think he knew about the previous week's overpayment. There was an awkward silence for a moment as I gathered my thoughts.

'Well, everyone is allowed one mistake, boss,' I said, 'but when it happened for the second week running, I thought I'd better bring it to your attention.'

— ○ —

Football is still, to use Pelé's phrase, the beautiful game. It has undergone myriad changes since I played my last league game in 1965 at the age of 50. I say league game because I actually played my last competitive match in Brazil in 1985 at the age of 70, and damaged my cartilage – a promising career cut tragically short. Football can be a cruel mistress.

Many of the changes I have witnessed have been for the good and have benefited the game; some have not. It is right that football should reflect changing society. I have always seen football as a celebration of life. Without change, life would be sterile, unchallenging, without spirit, drama and colour. Such qualities are the very essence of football. They are what make football, as Hugh McIlvanney once described it, 'life's greatest irrelevancy'.

For over 80 years football has been an intrinsic part of my life. I have loved it dearly. If longevity of career and awards are anything to go by, which I am not so sure they are, it has certainly been good to me. Football has thrown up many a challenge for me, but now in sitting down to write my autobiography I feel I am embarking upon one of the most difficult challenges of my life. Difficult? Well, yes. I wonder if you have ever tried to tell anybody who you are, what you are and what you have been. Ever since I first joined Stoke City over 70 years ago, much has been written about me. There have also been books that have carried my name, though in truth they were written by others with my consent. This is the first time that I have attempted to write the story of my life and, I have to say, I do so with some embarrassment. That I do so at all is mainly down to some warm and friendly people having persuaded me that, after 70 plus years of involvement in football, I might have a story to tell that will be of interest to you. It's true I have seen great players and great days, yet if it hadn't been for my mother, I may well have trodden a totally different sporting path.

————— ○ —————

I was born in Hanley, Stoke-on-Trent, in the heart of the Potteries on 1 February 1915, one of four brothers. My father was Jack Matthews who, in addition to owning a small barber's shop, had made something of a name for himself as a boxer.

Even as a small boy I was blessed with the ability to run fast, a fact that did not go unnoticed as far as my father was concerned. When I was six years old my father informed me he was going to take me out for some exercise. We walked from Hanley to the Victoria Ground, home of Stoke City Football Club, a distance of about two miles. This was in the summer of 1921 and at the time I had no idea why we had gone there. When the wind was in the right direction, I could hear the roar from the Victoria Ground from our backyard but this was the first time I had ever been to the stadium of one of the oldest clubs in English football. Once inside I was agog. To a six-year-old, the Victoria Ground looked gigantic with its vast open spaces of terracing now eerily mute. By the side of the pitch there was a knot of spectators and lots of boys of various ages who were busy changing into running gear. My father told me to strip to my vest and underpants and, that done, proceeded to dress me in black running pumps and a pair of shorts that had enough spare material to rig an East India-bound clipper. Then he told me what he wanted me to do.

A running track had been laid out around the pitch and he guided me to a spot some way ahead of the other boys who were by now taking up positions in their respective lanes. He said, 'Now Stanley, when you hear the man fire his gun, run like hell and don't stop running until you pass a man with a white flag.'

I stood there in my vest, the navy blue shorts my dad had given me hanging about my knees, and watched as Dad went into a huddle with a group of other men. My father produced a book and was writing things down as each man in turn spoke to him and handed him something. I didn't have a clue what was going on. I kept glancing back towards the other boys. The bigger ones were standing in a starting line next to the man with the gun.

When I heard the gun fire, I took off just as Dad had said, my little legs pounding ten to the dozen. No one overtook me. I eventually passed the man with the white flag but was so unsure of what I was doing, I just kept on going. I remember men on the sideline laughing as I passed them and my father running after me shouting, 'Stanley, Stanley, you can stop now.'

I didn't know until much later that I'd taken part in an open race for boys under 14, with a staggered start according to age. My father had run a book on me winning and after the race I remember him being as pleased as punch, ruffling my hair and saying, 'That's my boy. Well done, Stanley.'

His pocket was bulging with copper and silver coins and on the way home, we stopped off and he bought me a goldfish. He said, 'Now Stanley, if your mother asks, just say I let you run off some steam and bought you the goldfish as a present.'

At 13 I had only one thing on my mind – to be a footballer. I had one more year at school before I had to go out and make a living. My father wanted me to be a boxer. Every morning at the crack of dawn, he would get me up and supervise a rigorous workout. One morning after an hour of intensive physical training, I broke down. I ran into the kitchen and vomited. Great beads of sweat formed on my brow and eventually I collapsed on the kitchen floor. My mother put me to bed.

I could hear her downstairs in the kitchen as usual. With a husband and four hungry lads to feed, my mother seemed to spend most of her life in the kitchen; these were the days when the only thing that could stir, mix, blend and whisk was a spoon and the only things that came ready to serve were tennis balls. Eventually my father came in and asked where I was. In those days, women rarely took issue with their husbands and she had never said a word about the training. For the first time in my life, I heard my mother get on to my father.

'Ever since Stanley said he didn't want to be a boxer there has been trouble between you two,' she said.

It shocked me. It was like hearing Mother Teresa fly off the handle.

'Now it's gone too far. It's got to stop and I'm going to stop it.'

I didn't hear my father say anything. I guess like me he was shocked to hear mother being so assertive.

'Haven't you got the sense to see he wants to do one thing and you want him to do another? Stanley wants to be a footballer and you can take it from me that from now on he's getting my support and encouragement. If you have anything about you Jack Matthews, you'll get up those stairs and tell your son you love him. Tell him that you've changed your mind and you're going to do everything in your power as his father to help him realise his dream. Do that Jack Matthews and for all we have nowt, you'll make him the happiest lad in Hanley and proud to be your son.' Again there was silence.

'What would have happened if your father had wanted you to be a footballer instead of a boxer?' I heard my mother ask.

I heard my father's voice say, 'I wouldn't have let him, simple as that.'

'I know you wouldn't,' my mother said. 'You've always had a mind of your own. You were always crazy about boxing, but with Stanley, it's football. Go see him.'

The stairs creaked like the timbers on an old sailing ship as my father made his way slowly up to my bedroom. I was lying with my back to him as he entered the room but he reached out and I turned towards him.

'Listen, son,' he said. 'I've been giving this football idea of yours some thought. If you can make yourself good enough to be a schoolboy international before you leave school, go for it! Are you on?'

I immediately sat bolt upright.

'It's a bet,' I said, partly because I knew he was a betting man and partly because I didn't know what else to say.

The next morning he came into my bedroom at the crack of dawn with a football in his hand. I was back in training.

— o —

I attended Wellington Road School in Hanley. I never distinguished myself as a scholar but in many respects I suppose I was a model pupil. I listened in lessons, was fair to middling academically, enjoyed school life and was never the source of any trouble.

All the spare time I had was taken up with playing football. When the school bell rang, I'd make my way home with a stone or a ball of paper at my feet. Once home, I'd make for a piece of waste ground opposite our house where the boys from the neighbourhood gathered for a kickabout. Coats would be piled for posts and the game of football would get under way. In fine weather it would be as many as 20 a side, in bad weather a hardened dozen or so made six a side.

I firmly believe that in addition to helping my dribbling skills, these games helped all those lads to become better citizens later in life. All such kickabout football games do. My reasoning behind this is quite simple. We had no referee or linesman, yet sometimes up to 40 boys would play football for two hours adhering to the rules as we knew them. When there was a foul, there would be a free kick. When a goal was scored, the ball would be returned to the centre of the waste ground for the game to restart. We didn't need a referee; we accepted the rules of the game and stuck by them. For us not to have done so, would have spoilt the game for everyone. It taught us that you can't go about doing what you want because there are others to think of and if you don't stick to the rules, you spoil it for everyone else. Of course, that was not a conscious thought at the time, but looking back, those kickabout games on the waste ground did prepare us for life.

Today you rarely see boys playing kickabout football and perhaps that is one contributing factor to the crime we see today. Some youngsters haven't learned the principle that the game and society have rules and it is a far better life if you stick by them. Young people today, for all their awareness and sophistication with modern technical innovations, are still basically the same as youngsters in my day, no better, no worse. I am convinced that some people would benefit from taking up a sport, even a sociable kickabout with mates in the park. I've seen the value of youngsters playing football in just about every country in the world. That's why since my retirement as a player I have travelled the globe preaching the gospel of football. Even in the poorest of countries, young boys and girls have benefited from playing football. It has given them a focus, a purpose, discipline, and in many respects an escape.

Anyone who has kicked a ball about on waste ground, in a back lane or a park will, I am sure, look back fondly on such games. The boy who owned the ball was the most popular boy in our neighbourhood. The ball he owned was an old leather caseball, with shine and sheen long since gone. The leather was so lacerated that every time you headed it you were in danger of receiving 20 lashes. It was as if we were playing football on the *Bounty*. On wet days the ball was so sodden with rain it must have tripled in weight. You don't have to know much about physics to realise that when such a ball comes down from a height and makes contact with your head, there's going to be one hell of an impact. It nigh on ripped the hair from your forehead. To this day, whenever I see a bald-headed man I never think to myself, 'Now there's a chap who has known stress.' I always think, 'There's a bloke who was never afraid to get up and head a ball.'

When I wasn't playing football on the waste ground with my pals, I'd play by myself at home. I had a small rubber ball that I spent hours kicking against the backyard wall. Even at eight or nine years of age I was determined to practise at every opportunity, in the hope that the more I did it, the more I would become the ball's master. I used to place kitchen chairs in the backyard and practise dribbling the small ball in and out of them. When I felt I had become adept at that, I'd run at the chairs with the ball at my feet and flick it over each chair, catching it on my foot on the other side before spinning around and shooting into an imaginary goal. My brother Jack would tease me by saying things like, 'You're getting better, the kitchen chairs only beat you 2–1 this time.' I took it all in good humour and spent countless hours practising. Any ball control I displayed later in life as a professional footballer can be traced back to those times spent playing with that small rubber ball.

I wasn't always the master of the ball of course. On one occasion, I sliced my shot at the imaginary goal and looked on in horror as the ball crashed through the kitchen window, the remains of which were splattered with a brown liquid. The ball had landed in the stew my mother was making for dinner. I certainly got myself in a stew that day. My mother said little except that my father would take the matter up with me when he came home from work. I spent a few anguished hours sitting outside waiting for his return.

The police never had cause to visit our house, but even if

they had, nothing they could have done would compare with the wrath of my father for having the police at our door. There was pride, dignity and respect in such working-class communities in those days and every household and every father was the same. As it happened, when my father did come home from his shop, he was very understanding, probably feeling my two-hour worrying wait had been punishment enough.

I thought my father had also been understanding in saying I could carry on with football if I made the England schoolboy team, even though it was a pretty tall order. I was of the mind that to be picked for England Schoolboys was something that happened to other boys, not me.

I felt I was making good progress. I often played at centre-half for my school and in one game scored eight in a 13–2 victory. I realised what a feat this was when my headmaster, Mr Terry, said how pleased he was with the way I had played and gave me sixpence. The youngest ever professional player?

It was around this time that another teacher at the school, Mr Slack, picked me at outside-right for the school team. I felt comfortable in the position; it provided more scope for my dribbling skills but I still thought centre-half was my calling. I must have been doing something right on the wing for later that year, I was selected to play for the North against the South in an England Schoolboy trial.

Even to this day, the lads picked for England Schoolboys tend to be the ones who have physically matured quicker than others. I was only 13, so in the physical stakes I was quite some way behind lads of 14 and 15. I felt I did all right in the trial, nothing exceptional, but the selectors must have seen something because three weeks later, I played for England Boys against The Rest at Kettering Town's ground.

I never heard another thing for months and was beginning

to come to terms with the fact that at 13 I was probably a bit too young to get into the England Schoolboys team. I consoled myself with the thought that there would always be next season. I never stopped hoping, though, and I never stopped practising. I was doing so in splendid isolation, never realising that not every boy was getting up at the crack of dawn like me, going through a rigorous physical workout of sprints and shuttles and honing ball skills at every given opportunity. Such was my determination to master the ball and make it do whatever I wanted it to do.

A few months after the trial at Kettering, I was told to report to the headmaster's office. Such a call was about as bad as it could be. To be asked to report to the headmaster was a sure-fire way to immediate anxiety and guilt – a bit like your own mother saying, 'Guess what I found in your bedroom this morning.'

As I made my way to Mr Terry's office, I ran through all my recent escapades but couldn't come up with anything I'd done that merited seeing the headmaster. On entering the office my stomach was churning. He indicated I should stand before his desk and then said, 'Well, Matthews, let me congratulate you. You have been picked to play for England Schoolboys against Wales at Bournemouth's ground in three weeks' time. What do you think about that?'

I felt like saying, 'Sorry sir, could you repeat that. I didn't hear you because of the sound of angels singing.' Of course, I didn't. I just stood there dumbfounded. I could feel my face twitching, my mouth went dry and the shock made me sense I was about to embarrass myself with a bodily function. I tried to speak but the words wouldn't come. Instead, out of my mouth came the sort of noise a small frog with adenoid trouble would make – if frogs had adenoids, that is.

'I'm sorry to have given you such a shock, lad,' Mr Terry said. 'I had no idea it would upset you like this. Now come along – haven't you anything to say?'

'Urghhh, currrrrr, myk urghhhhhh, blut.'

'You'd better have a drink of water, Matthews,' said Mr Terry, pointing me in the direction of the small sink on the other side of his office. I gulped down a glass of tap water. It helped me pull myself together and I returned to my original position in front of his desk.

'Sorry, sir. Your news took me by surprise. I had no idea. It's such a shock,' I said, still reeling.

'Not to me, Matthews,' the headmaster said. 'It's all right. I can imagine how you feel. You'd better not break the news to your mother and father the way I broke it to you.'

The headmaster went on to tell me I'd been chosen to play at outside-right. Now as I say, up until a few weeks before this incident, I had played all my football at centre-half. I asked Mr Terry if he thought the position would suit me. He got up, walked across to the window and stood gazing outside with his hands clasped behind his back.

'I think it will suit you very well,' he said. 'I know you'll do your best in whatever position you're chosen to play.'

I thanked him. He continued to look out of the window and for a moment there was an awkward silence.

'Well, what are you waiting for?' he said, still with his back towards me. 'Don't you have two loving parents who would like to hear this news? Get yourself home and tell them.' I thanked him again and just as I was making my way out of the door, he turned and spoke.

'Matthews. Don't forget this is your big chance. Just play your normal game and play a good clean game. Don't forget also that you have the school at the back of you. Don't let us down.' I told him I wouldn't and left his office on silver wings running home as fast as my legs could carry me.

Once home, I flung open the door. The table was set for tea and my mother and father were in the process of having theirs. Tea was a ritual in our house. Meals were more formal in those days. The main one was dinner, the cooked meal in the middle of the day. There would always be a loaf of bread on the table and I was encouraged to eat a slice with my dinner, 'to soak up the grease' according to my mother, though there was never any grease to Mother's meals. She was an excellent cook.

My explosive entrance caused some consternation.

'What on earth is the matter?' Mother asked, alarmed. I blurted it out without pausing for breath.

'Guess what. Guess what. Guess what. I'mplayingfor-EnglandagainstWalesatBournemouthinthreeweeks'timeand-I'mplayingatoutside-right. CanIbeaprofessionalfootballer-nowDadwhenIgrowup? CanIDad? Can I? SayIcanDad. You-promised.'

I finally took a breath and gazed at them expectantly. My father stood up from the table, came over and put an arm around my shoulders.

'You hear that, Mother?' Our Stanley's going to be an international. He's done it. Well, I'll be . . .'

I joined them for tea and we talked and talked about my forthcoming big day. I'll never ever forget that tea. I had three brothers, Jack, Arthur and Ron. Jack and Arthur were older than me and, although they played football, they preferred boxing and athletics. Both were good sprinters and often brought home medals from competitions. Jack was a particularly good boxer, as was my father of course, and I'd watched several of Jack's fights at the Palais de Danse in Hanley. Ron was the youngest and later proved himself to be a decent footballer, having trials with Blackpool. We were a sporting family, but this was the very first time any one of us had gained national recognition at any level. It was quite a day in the Matthews household and that night I hardly slept a wink. I lay in bed wondering what Bournemouth's Dean

Court ground would be like; who my team colleagues on the day would be; how I'd approach the game itself. I was on tenterhooks, my stomach was doing somersaults with nerves, and there were another three weeks to go!

Those three weeks were among the happiest I've known. My father and I became great pals again. He helped me with my ball practice, talked incessantly about the forthcoming England game and gave me constant good advice. He watched over my diet, supervising everything I ate, packed me off to bed early and got me up for his specialised training at dawn the following morning. Apart from that, he ignored me.

My father was also at pains to keep me level-headed. He would never tell me I'd had a good game. All he would say was, 'Not so bad. I've seen you play better and I've seen you play worse.' It was impossible to get a swollen head off the back of remarks like that but I'm glad he took such an attitude. It served me well throughout my career, helping me keep my feet firmly on the ground no matter what success came my way. I once heard the comedian George Burns say the most difficult audience to perform in front of was a Jewish audience because half of them think they can do better than you and the other half, who can't, have a nephew who can. My father was my 'Jewish' audience. He always gave short shrift to anyone who blew their own trumpet, so you can understand there was no way he would take any nonsense from me. Years on, I looked back with great gratitude at the way he steered me through what could have been some awkward years.

The day before I was to leave for my first schoolboy international match, my mother packed my bag and gave me advice on all manner of things, as mothers do when one of their brood is away from home for the very first time. I hardly slept at all. It was one of those nights when you keep saying to yourself 'I must get some sleep', but you can't. The pillows are too lumpy, the blankets get in a tangle and no matter which way you lie, you can never get comfortable. I kept getting up and opening the bedroom window to inhale a few deep breaths of air in the hope it would relax me. It didn't. I stared out across the Potteries skyline. The pottery bottle kilns that normally sent smoke billowing into the air were eerily inactive. Sombre Victorian houses flanked the cobbled streets on which the moon danced.

The better off people lived behind Regency bays. The house numbers were displayed in bold gold-leaf numerals on the window immediately above the front door. On nearly every street corner there was a shop with an enamel advertisement attached to its gable end promoting the likes of Sunlight Soap, the *News of the World* or Bisto, complete with ragamuffin Bisto kids. Dotted about were squat companionable pubs with frosted windows engraved with the names of local breweries now long gone such as Parkers, Joules or Heaths; or else their frosted windows proclaimed in exquisite and highly decorative carved glass the small comfortable niches to be found within – snug, smoke room, saloon bar.

Canal arteries meandered peacefully past red and blue brick buildings, corroded by the smoke, and what smoke emanated from those potteries and steelworks. By day, the pottery kilns belched and blew to produce a yellowy grey cloud that hung over the five towns. On winter days, a sulphurous, muggy owl light was broken occasionally by the red and golden sparky flare of fires glimpsed in passing when kiln or furnace doors were opened. It was industrial, provincial England in full cry, which even the Potteries-born novelist Arnold Bennett found difficult to capture. As he once said, 'It is impossible to describe in full the hellish inferno of the Potteries industrial scene. Dante was born too early.'

For all that, at the time life in the Potteries was tempered by an individuality and demureness of style. It was communal, social, labour intensive and dirty, a staggered hotchpotch of houses cheek by jowl with pits, potteries and belching bottle kilns and chimneys. It was home. Even at 13, I was acutely aware that as well as representing my country, I was representing the people of my smoky home town, and I was determined not to let them down.

The next morning it was a very excited schoolboy international debutant who caught the train from Stoke station to London. I was to join the England team at their hotel that day, with the party travelling down to Bournemouth the next morning for the game.

It was my first visit to London. The streets were busier than I could ever have imagined. Full of trams and, even in 1928, alive with the throng of horse-drawn carts, the absence of any ordered traffic gave a sense of chaos to every street and road I walked down. I can remember being impressed by the style of the London squares I passed through. We certainly didn't have anything as grand back in Stoke-on-Trent. The squares looked regal with their tall, elegant houses, prim iron fences and windows draped in Nottingham lace curtains. I remember thinking, 'What on earth do the people who live in such houses do for a living?'

London was the largest city I had ever been to – the only city I had ever been to! I found the sheer size and expanse of it mind-boggling, although it was a far smaller city than it is today. For instance, Wembley stadium was almost in the countryside. All round there were fields. I passed it on the train journey in. As I made my way to the hotel where I was to meet my team-mates for the first time, I stared in fascination at London landmarks, familiar from pictures in books. In reality, they seemed different. That was my first impression of London – Nelson's Column and the rest in the context of their surroundings emphasised to me that I was a stranger in a strange world.

Meeting my fellow team-mates for the first time had the same effect. Some of the boys seemed to know one another. I thought at the time this was probably down to the fact that they had played in previous schoolboy internationals or area representative games together. I was the only lad from Stoke-on-Trent. I didn't know anybody, no one knew me. It was the first time I had ever been in a hotel. A number of the other players seemed to know how to go on, but I simply hadn't a clue and was full of anxiety in case I made a dreadful *faux pas*. I had never been waited on at a table before and this made me feel awkward. I over-emphasised my thanks to everyone who placed a plate before me or took a bowl away, such was my embarrassment at having adults seemingly at my beck and call, not that I ever dared beckon or call anyone.

All of my team-mates were older than me. Although this was only a matter of a year, they all appeared so much more mature and worldly wise than me, as if they had done it all before, which several of them had. I'd always had confidence in my own ability but as I sheepishly hung on the perimeter of the social life at the hotel, I did wonder if I was going to be up to the mark. Would I cover myself in glory, or, having teamed up with those who were considered the best schoolboy footballers in England and been pitted against the best Wales had to offer, find to my horror I was totally lacking? Would it be a case of being a big fish in a small pond in Stoke, but a floundering minnow when set alongside the cream of my contemporaries? This and my natural shyness made for a very quiet, passive and unassuming schoolboy international debutant in the build-up to the game.

When I ran down the tunnel for the first time in an England shirt, I was bursting with pride. The first sensation as the team emerged into the light was the noise of the supporters who had packed into the Dean Court ground. There must have been nigh on 20,000 there, which was far and away the largest crowd I had ever played in front of. I took a look around and the sight of so many people made me catch my breath. My heart was doing a passable impression of a kettledrum being played at full tempo, and as I ran around the soft turf, it was as if my boots would sink into it and never come unstuck. It was a terrific feeling, though. There and then, I knew that there couldn't be anything but a football career for me. It was one hell of a buzz and I felt so elated it was all I could do to stop myself shouting and screaming to release the excitement and emotion as I ran about in the warm-up.

I got an early touch of the ball from the kick-off and that settled me down. I started to enjoy the game and must admit I felt totally at home at outside-right. It was as if I had been born to it. We won 4–1 and, although disappointed that I didn't get on the scoresheet, I was happy enough with my overall contribution, having been involved in the build-up to a couple of our goals.

I had made a point of saying to my parents that I didn't want them to watch the game, partly because I thought it would unnerve me and partly because, with four sons to bring up, I knew they were on a tight budget and a trip to Bournemouth would have made quite a hole in my dad's weekly wage at the barber's shop. However, as I came off the field I felt sorry they weren't there. After all, you only make your debut for your country once.

In the dressing-room after the game, I was in the process of putting my boots into my bag when one of the officials came up and said there was someone outside the ground who would like a word with me. I made my way to the players' entrance and there was my father in his belted overcoat, clutching a brown paper bag in which he had his sandwich tin.

'Not so bad. I've seen you play better and I've seen you play worse,' he said. 'I've got just enough left for a cup of tea for the both of us, son. So let's have some tea, then we'll go home.'

We walked in near silence towards a nearby café and I fought to hold back my tears. He may well have had only the price of two cups of tea in his pocket, but he was walking proudly with his head held high.

══ o ══

Stoke City manager Tom Mather must have had the best groomed hair in Stoke-on-Trent. Following my successful debut for England Schoolboys, he called into my father's barber's shop every day. Father would sit him down and say, 'The usual?'

'Yes,' Tom would reply.

'I still think it's a bit early for him to think about signing for any club. As I keep telling you, he's still at school.' That was my father's stock reply to what was their 'usual' topic of conversation.

My father wouldn't be drawn on the subject of me signing for any club. What he was at pains to talk to me about was for me not to be complacent. I'd made a good showing on my schoolboy international debut, but he drummed it into me that anyone who gets complacent in life is heading for a big kick up the backside. Complacency did creep in but only in the fact that I could see nothing but a career in football in front of me. I carried on with my daily training programme and although any ideas about signing for a league club were put on the back burner, what motivated me in training was the thought that the next schoolboy international was to be Scotland against England at Hampden Park. The vision of stepping out at Hampden for England filled my head every day. I'd been excited enough to play at Bournemouth's Dean Court, but the thought of playing at Hampden, the scene of so many great internationals and Cup finals, took me into the realms of ecstasy.

Every day I trained hard, and at every opportunity I worked with a ball at my feet, spurred on by the goal of playing at outside-right for the England Schoolboy team in the game against the auld enemy. On the day the team was to be announced, my father put me through a rigorous training session that included timed sprints over short distances. That over, I repeated the exercise with the ball at my feet. When my training session was over, I turned to my father.

'They're picking the team for the Scotland game today, Dad. Will you be coming to watch me?'

My father's face said it all. He gently shook his head, and winced.

'I'll let you know when I've read this afternoon's paper, son.' He looked at his watch, looked at me, then scratched his nose with his finger. 'You know son, you've got a lot to learn about life. Never expect. Never take anything for granted. That way you'll never be too disappointed or hurt.'

That afternoon at school was the longest I had known. I kept watching the teacher, waiting for the moment he would tell me to report to the headmaster's office. He didn't. I made my way home and searched my mind for ways to remain optimistic. In the end I managed to convince myself the headmaster only summoned boys to talk the matter over with them, the first time they were picked. I went in somewhat tentatively. Mother said tea was on the table and that she was popping out to do some shopping. My father sat by the fire reading the local paper.

'Well Dad, am I in the team?' I stammered.

My father folded the paper and put it down by his side.

'Sorry, son. They haven't picked you.'

The world slipped from under my feet. My stomach churned. I pushed my tea to one side. I had no appetite at all. My father left the room and I picked up the paper and read the team out loud. Tears rolled down my cheeks. I felt badly done to. A great surge of self-pity swept through me and after a few minutes it was replaced by bitterness. Then I exploded with emotion and cried my heart out. When the crying subsided and gave way to intermittent gulping sobs my father came back.

'Never expect,' he said, putting a comforting arm around my shoulder. 'You'll be all right now, son. Take my word for it. You're always going to be all right.'

He never spoke a truer word.

⟶ ○ ⟶

I was coming on 15 and due to leave school. The disappointment of not being picked for the Scotland–England schoolboy international had long since gone. Older, somewhat wiser, I had in the intervening two years established my reputation in junior football, though I never again played for the England Schoolboys. Tom Mather still had the best groomed hair in the city, but word had it that other clubs were now interested in me, including Wolves, Birmingham City, Aston Villa and West Brom, all top sides of the day. My father had resisted all advances, but with my schooldays nearing an end, I hoped a decision would be taken soon.

One Saturday morning I had been to the shops for my mother. I was wearing a brand new pair of shoes. Now these shoes were special. In the first place, they had been bought for me to wear when I left school, a special pair of shoes for whatever work I would undertake. Secondly, these shoes fitted. It was quite common for mothers on a tight budget to buy their children shoes a size too big so you grew into them. The slack inside was taken up by wearing an extra, sometimes two extra, pairs of socks. As your feet grew, you simply shed the socks, like a snake would its skin. You became a man the day you wore shoes that fitted you straightaway.

That was a working-class custom borne out of necessity. Others were less practical, 'Don't eat an orange in the cinema in case you swallow a pip and a tree grows inside your stomach' and 'Never pick dandelions because they'll make you wet the bed' for example. Working-class mothers of the time had a whole list of such strange beliefs and sayings, most designed to deter children from doing something and, in particular, from asking questions.

Me: Who was that at the door, Mum?
Mother: Him off the Quaker Oats packet.

Me: What colour's your new coat, Mum?
Mother: Sky blue pink with yellow dots on.

Me: Who are you and Auntie Emma talking about, Mum?
Mother: Him with the nose on his face.

Me: What time is it, Mum?
Mother: Time you learned to say 'please'.

Me: What time is it, Mum, please?
Mother: Time you stopped asking so many questions.

Me: What's sex, Mum?
Mother: Ask your father.

I was only yards from our house when I saw a group of

friends playing football on the waste ground. They beckoned me to join in and, new shoes or not, the temptation to get a ball at my feet was too much. Game over, I looked down at my shoes, they didn't look special anymore. The waste ground was exactly that, not a blade of grass on it. It was pitted with stones and the odd embedded piece of glass and it had done its worst as far as my shoes were concerned.

I found a piece of newspaper in the street and with spit tried to clean them up but I made a poor job of it. I thought my father might not notice but I knew my mother would. Mothers have an instinct for such things. I could walk in the house sporting a silver top hat and having sprouted a handlebar moustache, but my mother's eyes would immediately be drawn to my shoes. Money was tight and I had wasted it by playing a kickabout game in my best shoes. There was nothing else for it but to face the music. I made for my father's shop and stood behind one of the chairs in the hope he wouldn't see my shoes.

'There's no need for you to stand behind the chair to hide your shoes,' he said. 'I know you've been playing football. We'll speak when we get home. Now get an apron on and give me a hand, we're busy.'

I worked diligently for the rest of the day in my father's shop, hoping my hard graft would lessen the admonishment I was due for ruining my new shoes. Come closing time I was just about to do the final sweep of the floor, when my father told me to put the brush to one side.

'That can wait until the morning,' he said, taking off his apron. 'There's someone waiting to see us back home, so let's get off.'

We walked home at a brisk pace and not one word was said about the shoes. Once inside, my mother put the kettle on the hob and brought out the best china. I hadn't a clue who the visitor would be, but I knew he or she was important. The best china came out only on special occasions, like Christmas, anniversaries or a Port Vale away win, for they were my childhood favourites.

Presently, a knock came on the door. My father answered and after a brief mumbled conversation he came into the living room followed by Stoke City manager Tom Mather, hair immaculate.

'Go ahead,' Father said when Tom Mather had settled down into the best chair, cup and saucer on his lap.

'Stanley, I have some good news for you,' said Mather. 'Your father has agreed to let you join the Stoke City staff on your fifteenth birthday. You'll start as an office boy, but after that, I know you'll be able to enjoy all the football you want. What do you say?'

I was back in the headmaster's study. I was so thrilled and surprised I was speechless. I took a sip of tea.

'This is the greatest day of my life,' I told them, having gathered myself. 'It's a dream come true.' And so it was.

'That's it settled then. We'll see you at the Victoria Ground on your fifteenth birthday,' Tom Mather said. 'Be there at nine in your best suit and tie and give your shoes a good polish. Those you're wearing could do with one.'

2

From Office Boy to International

The day of my fifteenth birthday, 1 February 1930, was a bitterly cold day. Birthday or not, I've always thought of February as a mean little month, hanging on to the coat tails of winter, which by then everyone has had enough of. But on this particular day, I felt as if the sun was shining brightly.

Stoke City's Victoria Ground seemed an intimidating place as I stood outside. I was filled with awe, yet full of great hope and expectation. Next to a large red and white sign proclaiming 'Stoke City Football Club' was a smaller sign above a tall narrow door. 'Staff Entrance' it said. I tried the tall narrow door, it opened and I stepped inside. At last, I was part of Stoke City FC. I was on £1 a week as an office boy, which to me was good money, though in truth I'd have gone there for nothing.

I made my way into the ground and checked my watch. It was nine o'clock on the dot. I looked around, the place was deserted. Suddenly, from out of an adjacent door a young girl of around my own age appeared. She looked me over, smiled and I smiled back.

'Hello, there,' she said pleasantly. 'Is your name Stanley Matthews?'

I nodded but still couldn't find the confidence to speak.

'I'm Betty Vallance. My father's the trainer here.'

Again I nodded and smiled. It provoked a puzzled look on her face. For fear of her thinking me a simpleton, I finally drew up the courage to speak.

'Pleased to meet you, Betty,' I said.

'And likewise,' she said. The puzzled look disappearing to be replaced by her bright smile. 'You look very nervous, Stanley. Really, there is no reason to be. You'll like it here. Everyone is nice, as you'll find out in due course.'

'I have to report to Mr Vallance,' I said, not wanting to appear late on my very first day.

'I know,' she said. 'That's why I'm here. I've come to take you to him. He's already out on the field with some of the players.'

I followed Betty through a door and down a passage. I looked around at the photographs of players and games that adorned the walls and felt at peace with the world. I'd only been in the place a few moments and already felt it was my second home. I only needed a warm welcome to ease my nerves, but I didn't get it.

Betty and I stood at the side of the Victoria Ground pitch where Jimmy Vallance was in the throws of a verbal attack on the group of players in his charge. The players didn't seem to mind. They stood hands on hips, some looking at him directly, others looking down at the turf. Their reaction to him was as if he was gently telling them the ingredients for a cake instead of questioning the status of their birth in language bluer than the Monday Club. As I say, they didn't turn a hair, but it rocked me back on my heels. It was the first time I'd been in the company of professional footballers and it came as a big culture shock to hear such hard words and rich language. I looked at Betty. She stood watching with a benign smile on her face, totally unshocked. It was as if her father's words never reached her ears but sailed over her head and were carried over the terracing by the icy wind. Jimmy Vallance seemed a hard nut, a demanding task master, but it wouldn't be long before I realised there is little sentiment in football, and a club could not remain top class unless there was strong discipline from top to bottom.

Vallance sent the players on a run around the cinder track that circled the pitch and made his way over to Betty and me.

'Hello there!' he said brightly. Was this the same man of a few moments earlier? It was as if he had undergone a change in personality of Jekyll and Hyde proportions. 'You must be young Matthews.'

'Yes, Mr Vallance,' I said nervously.

He looked me over.

'Work hard, do everything you're told and you'll be happy here,' he said. 'If you try to be a clever dick, you'll find we have a cure for that. Now go and clean out the dressing rooms and when you've done that, report back to me.'

Vallance spun away across the pitch, barking at the players. He was Mr Hyde again. Betty giggled.

'Oh, come on. He's not that bad, really he isn't,' she said reassuringly. 'Come along, Stanley, follow me. I'll show you where the dressing rooms are.'

I followed Betty in silence. What a start to a football career, I thought. Cleaning out dressing rooms and in my best clothes. It was as if I was back in my father's shop.

Betty left me at the door of the home-team dressing room and my heart sank when I saw the state of it. The floor was soaked in dirty water and littered with small clumps of soil, strips of bandage and tie-ups. Old china cups, some with tea still in them, adorned the benches. A large grey metal teapot that looked as if it could have gained a long-service medal with the Salvation Army was perched on a battered metal tea tray awash with cold tea. There was a large plunge bath sporting a dirty tide mark about 18 inches up its sides, and the base of the bath had more silt than the Nile Delta.

I sat down on one of the benches, cupped my chin in my hand and laughed. When you want to learn a profession, you must start at the bottom and there was no doubting, I was at the bottom. I grabbed a brush, pan and bucket of soapy water and started in earnest to ensure that dressing room was like a new pin. Once finished I stood and admired my handiwork before reporting to Mr Vallance and telling him the dressing room was spick and span.

'Have you done them both?' he asked.

'Both, Mr Vallance?' I inquired.

'Both,' he repeated. 'We have two, you know. Where do you think the opposition get changed? With us?'

I returned to another scene of bedlam but set about cleaning the away dressing room with equal vigour. No sooner had I finished when the door opened and in walked Vallance. He looked around the room, checked the large plunge bath and the toilet.

'You'll do for me, son,' he said. 'Looks as if you enjoyed doing that job. Did you?'

I hadn't really, but I wanted to show my eagerness to do well.

'I'll always try and do whatever you tell me to the best of my ability, Mr Vallance,' I said.

'Then you'll be all right here, son,' he said. 'How would you like to get changed into some kit and come and join the training with the rest of the boys? I'd like to see if you can take orders on the field as well as off it.'

I needed no second asking. Within minutes I'd donned some old football kit, laced my boots and was soon in my element playing a practice game with other youngsters and a smattering of reserve-team players. I walked back home from Stoke to Hanley, the happiest lad in the city.

Once home, my father and mother wanted to hear everything about my first day at Stoke City. I left no detail out and when I had finished my parents expressed their delight at the fact that my heart and soul was in my new job.

From that day on, I immersed myself in my work at the club. No matter what job I was given I applied myself to it fully. I worked as an office boy in Tom Mather's office where my duties included licking stamps, answering the telephone and filing paperwork. When not in the office, I cleaned the dressing rooms and swept the terracing and stands.

I'd been at Stoke City for some months and was now in my first full season, 1930–31, though still only 15. I had got into the habit of looking at the noticeboard on a Thursday morning. The various teams for the Saturday games were pinned up there. You couldn't turn professional until you were 17 in those days and the reserve team was made up entirely of pros. Stoke, like many other clubs of its size, had as many as 40 full-time professionals on the books. So you can imagine my surprise when I checked the noticeboard and saw my name down to play for Stoke City reserves against Burnley reserves that Saturday. I never for a moment expected such an elevation so early and couldn't wait to finish for the day to tell my father the good news.

As I was off to find him, I bumped into Betty and told her I'd made it into the reserves. She was delighted for me and told me she would be there to cheer me on. I smiled at her and told her I'd be in great need of her support because I was very anxious about pitting myself against seasoned professionals. Father was at the shop and looked up in surprise when I went in.

'What are you doing here at this time?' he asked, in the middle of his umpteenth short back and sides of the day. There were no hair styles in those days. Boys and men had the choice of two cuts, the pudding bowl or short back and sides. The story went that a man came into my father's shop and said, 'I want you to cut my hair like Maurice Chevalier's.' My father gave him a short back and sides. When he had finished the man looked in the mirror and said, 'Maurice Chevalier doesn't have his hair cut like this!' 'He would do if he came in here,' my father told him.

I helped him close up and, on the walk home, told him my news. He beamed, then offered his usual caution and realism.

'You're a bit young to play for the reserves, son. I hope they know what they're doing.' We walked on in silence for a minute or so. 'I think you'd better get some practice in at sprinting with the ball at your feet when you get home,' he said. 'Never forget that once you've beaten a man, he's chasing you without a ball at his feet.'

The next day at the crack of dawn he came into my bedroom with a football under his arm. He put me through a rigorous work-out, which I needed because I'd been spending more time as an office boy than with a ball at my feet.

It may have been only Stoke and Burnley reserves in front of a couple of thousand people but that day, 27 September, I couldn't have been more excited if I was playing for England against Scotland at a packed Wembley stadium. As I ran on to the pitch, I was delighted to see, in addition to Betty, a gang of my old schoolmates who had come along to lend their support. We won the game 2–1 and I laid on the pass for Joe Mawson to score our first goal. I made plenty of mistakes but, all in all, felt I'd done well and was pleased with my overall contribution. I was on my way.

My father had taken a couple of hours off work to see the game. Once I got home, I couldn't wait to hear what he had to say.

'I've seen you play better and I've seen you play worse,' he said. 'Forget about the good things you did. Players run through games in their head and always replay the good things. If you want to be a better player, think about the mistakes you made. Study them. Ask yourself why you did such and such. Work on how not to do it again. Correct your mistakes, work on your technique and you'll not keep repeating them. Remember, a man who never makes mistakes never gets anywhere. Experience is what we call our mistakes. Have you got that, son?' I nodded to indicate the message had sunk in.

I had another run out with the reserves and come the summer had completed my first full season at the club. Apart from the camaraderie with the other players, I was leading quite a lonely life. I'd work and train at Stoke City, then go home and practise my ball skills till darkness fell. Other lads my age had started to go out at night, but I was single-minded in my desire to be a footballer and shunned a social life so I could train and practise. I never got tired of it.

During 1931–32, my second full season at the club, I was more or less a regular in the reserves, playing 22 games. I was still an amateur. My wages were for my work as an office boy. However, such was the spirit and friendship in the reserve team that every time we won, the full-time pros gave me two shillings (10p) each out of their £1 bonus payment – so I got £1. It meant that when we won, I'd be taking home a total of £2, which was a grand sum in my eyes. Times were hard for a lot of people and they were to get harder still.

I gained in confidence with every reserve team game I

played to such an extent that Jimmy Vallance said to me after one game, 'You're coming on like a house on fire.' Jimmy was a great trainer, very knowledgeable about the game, a hard but fair taskmaster and a lovely man but not one given to lavish compliments. As Joe Mawson said in the dressing room one day, 'If you can get a compliment out of Jimmy, you can knit with sawdust.'

It was during this season that I solved what, up to that time, had been a problem to me in my style of play. As an outside-right, when I had the ball at my feet I had to beat the left-back to make any progress. In those days, you waited until the defender came right on top of you and then tried to jink your way around him. More often than not, I did just that, but it got me thinking about those few times when I didn't.

In a game against Manchester City reserves, I bucked the trend. I decided that instead of waiting for their left-back to approach me, I would make a beeline for him. That would surprise him for a start and he wouldn't know what on earth I was intending to do. Once on top of him, I'd put into operation the body swerve I'd been cultivating. This was throwing my body in one direction, then when the player had committed himself, swerving away in the other. Sometimes all it needed was a drop of a shoulder to pass this off.

I tried it against the Manchester City left-back and it worked a treat. The ball came to me out on the wing and I ran straight at him. He looked absolutely dumbfounded. Once close up on him, I swayed, he went the same way, committed himself to a tackle and then I swayed the other way and moved off the way I had intended. I tried the move several times during that game and it worked a treat every time.

It wasn't until I read the match report in the local and

Sunday papers that it dawned on me what effect my body swerve technique had had. Such paper talk could have made a young lad swollen-headed, but with my father's down-to-earth realism instilling itself in me, I happily kept my feet, for once, firmly planted on terra firma.

When my father read the match reports, he was far from happy, telling me overpraise and extreme flattery could ruin me. Sports reporters have to write something and even as a reserve I was becoming good copy. Thankfully I took heed of my father's words. As in most cases, it was excellent advice which was to stand me in good stead for the rest of my life. With my father and Jimmy Vallance watching over me, there was no way such journalistic flattery would go to my head. For Jimmy's part, he would look at the match report, hold the paper aloft and say, 'Today it says this, tomorrow it'll be wrapped around a haddock and chips.'

I signed as a full-time professional for Stoke City on my seventeenth birthday in 1932. The weeks preceding my birthday were among the longest I have experienced. Time just couldn't pass quickly enough for me, such was my great desire to become a professional footballer and shed the office duties. I was very happy at Stoke and Jimmy Vallance had helped me tremendously, often supervising extra training sessions for me. I had matured physically and mentally. Several clubs were chasing my signature and in the weeks coming up to my birthday my father was a busy man. A bevy of managers visited him at his shop in the hope of persuading him to allow me to sign for their respective club. Tom Mather was aware of all this and visited my father's shop every day, sometimes twice a day. The national press became aware of me and were predicting a great future for the young Stanley Matthews. My father was at pains to keep all the managers away from me and rightly so; at that age, I could have easily fallen prey to a silver tongue. I had every confidence in my father, however, and knew he'd sort things out for me, his experience as a boxer standing him in good stead when it came to negotiations.

Just before my birthday, my mother told me my father wanted to have a chat with me. She discreetly told me she had to go out to visit a neighbour. When my father arrived back from the shop he sat down in his favourite chair by the fire and beckoned me to sit opposite. He told me he had been talking to a lot of managers and the time had come for me to be brought into the situation. He informed me of every club that was interested in my signature and what they were willing to offer in pay and accommodation. I listened agog and not a little disbelief as the famous names tripped off his tongue – Wolverhampton Wanderers, Birmingham City, Aston Villa, Leicester City, FA Cup holders West Bromwich Albion, Bolton Wanderers, Newcastle United and Huddersfield Town.

'And of course there's Stoke City as well,' he said. 'I've purposefully left them till last. Mr Mather is worried, he thinks he might lose you. Now you've heard of all the interest and the details, let's hear your point of view.'

I started to speak but my mind was racing through everything he had just told me and my conversation started to meander. My father held his hand up.

'Think it over, son. I'm going for a walk around the block. Let me know your thoughts when I get back.'

He left the room and I was left to mull over all he had said. I picked up a pencil and paper and started to list the clubs and what they had been offering. I got halfway through the list then threw the pencil to one side. There was only one club for me. When my father returned, I told him I wanted to sign for Stoke City.

'I like it at Stoke City and I think I'll be happy there,' I told him.

'Well, Stoke City it is then,' my father said. 'I'll slip round to Mr Mather's house and tell him.'

———— o ————

These were the days when players and managers lived in the same city or town as the club that employed them. Hardly anyone had a car, so they tried to get fixed up as near to the ground as possible. Tom Mather was no exception. It made for more contact between supporters and players. As a result, they understood one another; there was a greater bond between the two. Players were ever mindful of how much football and the club meant to the fans because they lived cheek by jowl with one another. I feel there was a greater determination from the players to win for the supporters than there is today, and greater loyalty and commitment to the club itself.

These days top players live in secluded houses, mansions in some cases, miles from the club for which they play, and have little or no contact with their supporters. Even on matchdays, many Premiership players arrive at their clubs with the fans held back behind metal barriers some yards away, almost as if they are film stars arriving for a movie premiere. Little wonder there is a lack of understanding on the part of many players today where true loyal supporters are concerned.

My father went and told Tom Mather the news. Tom was Stoke's manager from 1923 to 1935, a 12-year stint. That was not uncommon for a manager in those days. He was a Lancastrian who oddly had no background as a player. He started out in football as an assistant secretary at Manchester City before moving on to Bolton where he eventually had what today would be thought of as a strange hybrid role of manager secretary. After World War One, he joined Southend as manager before coming to Stoke. For all his lack of experience in playing the game, Tom Mather proved himself to be an astute manager. He won the Third Division North title with Stoke in 1927 and after a few near misses in Division Two, eventually guided Stoke to Division One in 1933. He had an eye for talent, nurturing players like Bob McGrory. 'Better than ability is the ability to spot ability,' he used to say. Many of the young players he signed, like Freddie Steele and me, were to have good careers in the game.

McGrory, who eventually succeeded Tom Mather as manager, was a hard-tackling full-back with a great positional sense and an even greater temperament. McGrory was captain of Stoke when I signed as a 17-year-old. He played his last game in 1935 at the age of 43 and he had a great influence on me both on and off the park. In many ways, Tom Mather groomed McGrory as his managerial successor. Tom Mather made a good job of that as well.

I was surprised that my decision to sign for Stoke made such big news. It was understandable that the local paper, the *Evening Sentinel*, should make a lot of the story, but overnight I found myself on the inside back pages of the nationals.

Now that my future had been settled, I felt much better in myself and started to enjoy life to the full. I was to be paid £5 a week during the season and £3 a week in the summer break. Today, there is to all intents and purposes no summer break for clubs and football is played all the year round. In my day however, many players took on another job during the summer months to replace their incomes if the summer retainer wasn't enough to keep their families. This went on until the abolition of the maximum wage for players in 1961 and gave rise to all manner of funny incidents and stories. One famous one concerned the great Len Shackleton, the 'Clown Prince of Soccer', and Dickie Davis at Sunderland in the fifties. Shack had gone to see the Sunderland manager Bill Murray to re-negotiate his contract. Murray offered Shackleton the maximum £20 a week in the winter and £15 as a retainer during the summer close-season. On leaving Murray's office Dickie Davis, a free-scoring centre-forward, asked Shack what terms he had been offered. Shack told him. When it came for Dickie to see Bill Murray he was somewhat miffed to be offered the same as Shack in the winter, £20 a week, but only £10 in the summer break. Dickie said he wasn't happy and asked why Shackleton had been offered more in the close-season.

'Because Shackleton is a better player than you,' Bill Murray told him.

'What, in the summer when we're not playing?' Dickie replied.

I was more than happy with the terms Stoke offered me. It wasn't work to me, I loved playing football and that was the best part as far as I was concerned, being paid for doing something I loved. The day I signed the contract I left Tom Mather's office and heard a familiar voice.

'May I have your autograph, please?'

I turned to see Betty Vallance. She was teasing me of course.

'Congratulations, Stanley,' she said. 'I hope you'll do well and may all your dreams come true.'

It was a lovely thing to say. I was taken with how attractive she was, that and her wonderful, warm personality.

'Thanks, Betty. I know you mean it,' I said.

'Of course I mean it. You deserve to get on and I'll be following your progress.'

I walked home. On the day I fulfilled my dream of signing as a full-time professional for Stoke City, for the first time I found myself not thinking about football. I was thinking about Betty.

———— ○ ————

If joining Stoke City as an office boy had been an eye-opener, it was nothing compared with joining the ranks of the full-time professional players.

I was on big money for a lad of 17, but because of the maximum wage limit, I was on the same money as the seasoned professionals. Stoke City were a leading Second Division club and still had around 40 full-time players at the time, which was par for the course for a club of such stature in those days.

For the vast majority of players, football as we know is a short career. Although the spirit and friendship between the Stoke players was first class, I was soon to learn that you had to look out for number one. Football was the meal ticket for every player and although they all wished me well, no one wanted to lose his place in the first team. That could well have meant a quick journey out of the club and the loss of a decent livelihood. With 40 pros on the books, the competition for places was intense. Sentiment and sympathy were thin on the ground and I was made to realise in double quick time, self-preservation was paramount in the day-to-day life of a footballer. The pressure was always on to perform because the manager had plenty of options if you didn't do the business on a Saturday, as I was soon to find out.

As well as competing with team-mates, there was the opposition and I was soon to learn that for all the good things that had been written about me in the newspapers, opposing players had scant respect for reputations, especially ones in the making. If a newspaper said I had great prospects, I found I had to work doubly hard to live up to them because there were plenty of opponents around who wanted to prove 'great prospects' were what I didn't have.

A few weeks after signing professional, one Thursday afternoon I checked the noticeboard and my heart sank. The reserves were at home to Liverpool and I wasn't in the team. I scanned the youth side, the A and B teams; my name wasn't there either. What was Tom Mather playing at? I was on the point of turning away when I suddenly glanced up at the first team who were playing at Bury on 19 March. I couldn't believe it – I was down at outside-right.

As usual, I couldn't wait to tell my parents but when I got home I found my father wanted to take up another issue with me. I blurted out the news. Dad just smiled and told me to sit down at the table. He took from his pocket ten crisp £1 notes.

'This is your signing-on fee from Stoke,' he said. 'Now, I'm delighted at your news, but first things first. We need to get your money side of things sorted out. I've been talking things over with your mother and we're not worried about the football side of things at all. But we want to instil in you a sensible head for money matters.' He handed me the £10 and told me they wanted me to take it to a bank and open up a savings account in my own name. 'Every week we want you to put half your wages into that account. The other half, give to your mother for board and lodging and I shall want to see your savings book every week.'

'Half in the bank, half to mum, which I'm happy to do. But what am I going to do for pocket money?'

'You'll have to earn it like you always have,' he said. 'You get a bonus for winning don't you?' I told him I did. 'Well, you'll just have to make sure you win every week, starting at Bury on Saturday. That'll give you a pound a week, more than enough for a lad of your age.'

'I can't win games on my own, Dad,' I said. 'What if we don't win?'

'Then you'll have to sweep up and lather a few faces for me in the shop. I'll see you all right for a shilling or two. I'm not going to let you waste money. You must learn the value of it. Now if you hurry, you'll just catch the bank.'

I duly opened my savings account, handed the money over to the cashier and got a savings book in return. Walking home I must admit to feeling a trifle disgruntled. 'I'm a professional footballer, in the Stoke first team, and I'm being treated like a young schoolboy,' I thought to myself.

When I got back home, I showed my father the savings book. He checked it, then did what for him was a rare thing – he called me Stanley.

'Stanley, as a family we've never had much. But for the first time in your life, you've got money of your own. All your mother and I are saying is look after it, son, and it will look after you. Get a few noughts after the one that's already in the book and you'll be all right in life. You may not agree with what I've made you do, but later in life, you'll not regret it.' He got up from the table and walked to the door but before leaving the room turned to me. 'Well done on getting into the first team. I hope you beat Bury. A pound is a lot of money, you know.'

At the time I did think my father had been unreasonable, but as with most things he made me do, as I was to learn in later years, he was absolutely right. It was a common-sense thing and learning not to squander money has stood me in good stead throughout my life. I learned one can be generous and charitable, but never reckless where money is concerned. A fool and his money are soon parted.

There were no luxury coaches to ferry teams to away games in 1932. Just about every team travelled by train. The rail network was widespread compared with today and journeys by road were long and tiresome. We caught the train from Stoke and changed at Manchester for the Bury train. Away travel was always a hike for the backroom staff who had to haul the large wicker skip containing the strips, boots, towels and medical equipment, by hand. On a rainy day after a game on a muddy pitch, the thick cotton shirts and shorts and woollen socks could double in weight. For the trainer and kit man, away games were anything but a pleasure trip.

When I ran out on to Gigg Lane with the rest of the Stoke team, I was as excited as I had been on my schoolboy international debut, perhaps more so. I noticed there was a cemetery backing on to one end of the ground and just hoped it wasn't an omen – the football career of Stanley Matthews was born and died here!

Within minutes of the kick-off I realised that first-team football was, quite literally, a totally different ball game. Arms were flaying when players came into close contact. Shirts were held. When I tried to get near an opponent with the ball, his arm would shoot out to keep me at bay. When standing alongside my opposite number and the ball came our way, he'd whack an arm across my chest to push me back and to lever himself forward. Whenever I saw a Bury player making progress with the ball and cut across to challenge him, one of his team-mates would run and block my way to allow him to progress. When a high ball came my way, I found I couldn't get off the ground to head it because the player marking me stood on my foot as he jumped to meet the ball with his head. Not once did the referee blow up for any of this. It was my first lesson that in professional football, such things are all part and parcel of the game. You have to accept them otherwise you just wither away. I was soon to learn that the best way of combating all this was to improve my individual skills and technique, to make it harder for my opponent to get near me and the ball. I toiled away, learning from my mistakes. It was a tight game, but then our break came and when it did, it came in the strangest of circumstances.

Walter Bussy, our inside-right, centred from the right, driving the ball across the edge of the penalty box. The Bury goalkeeper was quick to react and was out of his goal like a flash, but for some reason, instead of catching the ball, he decided he would head it to safety. Tim Maloney, our outside-left, had read the situation and nipped around the Bury keeper to pinch the ball off his head before steadying himself and side-footing it into the net.

Of all the games I played in my career, I never again saw a goalkeeper trying to clear the ball with his head. We held out for the 1–0 win and my pocket money was safe. We journeyed back on the train in high spirits. I was delighted to have made a winning debut, but conscious that I had a lot to learn about the game. This was borne out by the fact that, after making my home debut the following week against Barnsley, I didn't play for the first team again for the remainder of that season. As I say, with so many professionals on the books, Tom Mather had plenty of options if a player turned in a performance that didn't set the world on fire. I obviously hadn't, but in those two games I'd been swept along a great learning curve. I'd had my eyes opened to what playing league football really meant. It was a highly competitive jungle where no quarter was asked for or given; a microcosm of life itself.

———○———

I approached the following season, 1932–33, with great enthusiasm, determined that I would have many more first-team appearances in the colours of Stoke City. The whole of the summer break was no holiday for me. I worked tirelessly every day to make myself as fit and fast as possible. I continued to work hard in Stoke's pre-season training, and when those daily sessions were over, I spent a couple of hours on my own working on my ball skills, practising short sprints of two and three yards and turning, always with the ball at my feet. I practised my body swerve and worked at variations on it. I read as many books about football as I could lay my hands on. I thought about the game incessantly, trying to work out ways of improving my technique.

There was a small pond in a field not too far from my home. One hot summer afternoon I was sitting by it, my head full of football, when I was startled by something plopping into the still water, followed by a familiar voice laughing. It was Betty.

'I was knocking around a few golf balls in the next field when I saw you sitting there, deep in thought,' she said, holding up a No. 6 iron. 'Thought I'd chip one into the pond to bring you back to life.'

We talked about golf for a few minutes. Her father played the game and he had encouraged Betty to take it up.

'You should take it up,' Betty said. 'You'll find it's harder than football and you need something to relax you. You know what they say about all work and no play.'

Betty went on to tell me that her father wanted me to accompany him on a short golfing holiday to Scotland where he'd teach me the rudiments of the game. As Stoke City trainer, he was worried that if I continued with my incessant training programme I'd suffer a burn-out. Betty's news of the proposed holiday took me by surprise. I told her there was no way I could go.

'I'd like to play golf Betty, but I'm staying here this summer. This training programme I've set myself is something I just have to do if I'm going to break into the first team.'

She told me she understood, but I couldn't help but notice her disappointment.

It was only a matter of weeks into the 1932–33 season when I got my chance again in the first team. Stoke were going great guns in Division Two at the time, so I felt pleased that I'd made a sufficient impression in the reserves to get a place in a team playing so well. I was in and out of the side that season. At 18, Tom Mather was not of a mind to expose me to the rigours of league football week in, week out. All in all, I played 15 first-team games that season, scoring my first goal against Port Vale, ironically enough. Stoke ended as champions of Division Two, a point ahead of Tottenham who were also promoted, with Fulham missing out in third place five points adrift of Spurs. My tally of appearances was enough to earn me a Division Two winners medal. For the first time, I felt I was making an impression in the game.

Tom Mather had put together a good Stoke team, one we felt was more than capable of holding its own in Division One. The top clubs at the time included Arsenal, Everton, Sunderland, Sheffield Wednesday and Aston Villa. In the Stoke team was an inside-forward called Harry Davies. Harry had been at Stoke between 1922 and 1929 before moving on to Huddersfield Town. He returned to Stoke prior to our Second Division Championship season and proved to be a more than useful goalscorer that year. Harry possessed a lot of ability and in addition to his goal contribution was very much a creative player whose incisive passing opened up many a defence. He was, in short, a bit of a class act, which made him a firm favourite with the Stoke fans. Harry Davies was one of the first players to pen a column in a newspaper and rumour had it he was receiving sixpence a word. Considering he wrote some 200 words a week, that meant a nice little earner of around £5, which doubled his weekly income.

One day Harry received a tongue-in-cheek letter from a

Stoke supporter enclosing sixpence and saying, 'I've heard you are being paid sixpence a word. Please send me one of your words.' Harry wrote a one-word reply: 'Thanks'. That was Harry Davies – whatever he did, he did with style.

Promotion achieved and having made an initial impression in the first team, I was delighted to get another invitation to join Jimmy Vallance on a golfing holiday in Scotland. This time I said yes. Jimmy and I travelled to Girvan in Ayrshire where he set about teaching me the game of golf and I set about losing more golf balls than the holiday cost. After a week, Betty joined us.

One day we met Sam English on the course. He had been a terrific centre-forward with Glasgow Rangers and was now a golfer of some note. Sam was taking a swing with his driver and the ball flew askew and hit his caddy, who hadn't been paying attention, plumb on the back of the head. The caddy was out so cold I thought we'd have to pick him up with ice tongs.

Later, the caddy having received medical treatment, Sam suggested he, Jimmy, Betty and I make up a foursome. For all Betty was the same age as me, she was a good golfer, far better than she made out. Jimmy Vallance was playing off a low handicap and Sam English was noted for his golf, though probably not by a certain caddy. I'd been playing for a week. It was decided that as the 'rabbit', I would partner Jimmy. It shows you what an accomplished golfer Jimmy was because we won, even though my array of shots was dominated by a wicked slice that resulted in half a dozen balls being buried at sea.

Sam English had been a bright, upbeat man but the stuffing had been knocked out of him a couple of years before, following a tragic incident at Ibrox Park. Rangers were playing Celtic in September 1931. Sam was trying to beat the Celtic goalkeeper, Thomson, to a through ball.

Typically, Thomson showed no fear and dived at Sam's feet but, in doing so, he fractured his skull. Thomson was rushed to hospital but died later that night. It was a tragic end for a fine young goalkeeper who was on the verge of leaving Celtic for Arsenal. Sam English had not been to blame in any way for the terrible accident. Nevertheless he was summoned to appear before the Sheriff's Court and although the jury passed a verdict of accidental death, the whole affair had a profound effect on him. He left Rangers for Liverpool in the hope that fresh pastures would rekindle his enthusiasm for the game, but it was clear he was never going to get over the tragedy and his career fizzled out.

At Girvan, I really began to enjoy Betty's company. She was special to me and I loved the conversations we had whether we were on the golf course, taking a country walk or refreshment in the clubhouse. She inspired me, made me feel good in myself, and her warm and generous spirit lifted my heart. Romance was in the air and, like all new romances, we thought it would go on forever. It was intense, spring-like and we rejoiced in our feelings for one another.

＊

Back in Stoke, I set about immersing myself in my own training programme prior to the official pre-season training. Come the start of the 1933–34 season, I'd shed buckets of sweat and tears and was raring to go. Stoke City were in Division One and that meant the big time, the best possible stage for me to show what I could do. As a newly promoted team, Stoke did well without pulling up any trees and finishing twelfth, but the good thing from my point of view was that I was a regular in the side, playing 29 times. I felt I had arrived.

Early in 1934 the newspapers started to write very complimentary things about my play, many saying I should be given a chance in the England team!

I had been constantly working at my game, learning from every match played. My technique of running directly at full-backs, body swerving and then veering away was paying handsome rewards and was even beginning to be copied by other wingers. I learned to pace myself with the ball at my feet. Time was when the ball was played to me I'd tear off at top speed only to be caught by a defender coming across to me. I quickly developed the technique of, having taken a pass, running at half to three-quarters speed and when the defender was a yard or so from me, accelerating to top so he couldn't adjust in time. It took me past countless would-be tackles. I was learning to play football with my brain as well as my feet. Whether it was my performances for Stoke, the push from the newspapers or a combination of both I don't know, but just before my nineteenth birthday I received a letter from the England selectors to say I had been chosen to play for The Rest against England in an international trial at Sunderland's Roker Park.

England did not have a manager in those days. The team was picked by a selection committee made up largely of FA officials who were very much the old school tie and blazer crowd. In my time, I've travelled the globe and walked in parks in just about every country in the world but I've never seen a statue to a committee. That great goalkeeper Frank Swift used to say, 'Anything is possible until it goes before a committee.' In many ways he had a point, but in the 1930s, the England selection committee had respect, mainly because it was the only system of picking the England team anyone had ever known.

Needless to say I was delighted to be picked for this trial. I thought if my performances had come to the attention of the England selectors, I must be doing something right. As far as I was concerned, it was the biggest break of my career, albeit my career was still very much in the embryonic stage.

Roker Park was packed. I was on the right wing and inside me was local hero Raich Carter, who I felt was the ideal partner for me. Sunderland had a very talented team at the time and Carter was its mastermind. You would never have suspected, seeing him casually taking to the pitch, that here was a man who could lay claim to football genius. But he did and often. Carter was not a buzzing, workaholic inside-forward, far from it. At times you could be tricked into thinking he had only a passing interest in a game. He'd ghost into great positions and had that rarest of talents on receiving the ball; he could turn a game. 'Let the ball do the work,' he'd say and how miraculously it did work when guided by his touches. His ball control appeared so casual and effortless it often passed unnoticed and seemed less a matter of conscious artistry than the possession of another sense.

Raich Carter was a supreme entertainer who dodged, dribbled, twisted and turned, sending bewildered left-halves madly along false trails. Inside the penalty box with the ball at his feet and two or three defenders snapping at his ankles, he'd find the space to get a shot in at goal. 'There's no such thing as a half chance,' he once told me. 'They're all chances,' and how Carter could take them. He was stocky with hair turning silver, but he had the Midas touch on a football pitch turning many a game into a golden memory.

In front of his home-town crowd, Carter put on a masterly show. Bewilderingly clever, constructive, lethal in front of goal, yet unselfish. Time and again he'd play the ball out wide to me and with such service I was in my element. I felt I had a good game but when the England team was selected for the forthcoming international against Scotland, Derby's Sammy Crooks got the nod ahead of me. Raich Carter made it into the England team and on the strength of his performance in that trial was probably the first name the selectors wrote down. I was disappointed of course, but reasoned that at not yet 19, the selectors probably felt I wasn't quite ready for a big international match. I was, however, pleased that my temperament was now such that I could take the disappointment on the chin, maintain my great motivation for the game and look forward.

That summer in 1934 I continued with my personal training programme. I'd earned enough from football not to have to take a summer job, so I applied myself fully to working on my fitness, technique and ball skills. One morning in June, I came into breakfast having just completed my dawn training session and sensed my mother was a little distant. I asked what was worrying her.

'You are,' she said to my great surprise.

'Me?' I said, not having a clue why this should be.

'What are you playing at with Betty?' Mother asked, banging my breakfast down in front of me.

Betty and I had been seeing one another regularly ever since the golfing holiday in Girvan the previous summer. The relationship had blossomed and I was very happy with the way it had developed. My mother's attitude threw me.

'What do you mean?' I asked.

My mother shook her head sadly to indicate she felt I was not getting the point.

'Do you love her?' she asked.

I got up from the table, breakfast untouched, and started to pace the room.

'Well, I, er, I mean. I like Betty a great deal. She's wonderful and we're very happy . . .'

My mother interrupted my fudged and faltering answer.

'You know your trouble, Stanley?'

I didn't, but I had no doubt my mother was about to tell me.

'Football, football, football,' she said. 'You spend too much time on your own. Practise, train, practise, train. That's all it is with you. There are other things in life besides football.'

'So what's that got to do with Betty? I take her out often,' I said defensively.

My mother came up to me, grabbed my arm and shook it.

'When you can remember! I sat here with her last night waiting for you to turn up to take her to the pictures. You forgot all about it because you were out training for hours on end. She loves you Stanley, but if you carry on like this, you'll lose her.'

I was stunned. How could I have forgotten I'd arranged to take Betty to the cinema? It shocked me into thinking about our relationship. Our dates always had to fit around my training schedule. I was so preoccupied with working at my game, I'd put my future career before our relationship. Football was of immense importance in my life, but I realised there and then that so too was Betty. I started to make for the door.

'I'll slip round to Betty's house and tell her how sorry I am.'

'She left an hour ago to join her father in Scotland,' my mother said matter of factly.

I felt an adrenalin rush. For once in my life football was completely blanked out of my mind. I could only think of Betty, of Betty and me. I did love her. 'Don't say you've blown it, you dunderhead,' I thought to myself. I was panic-stricken at the thought of losing her and made a dash for the stairs.

'Where are you going?' Mother called as I started up them as if they were on fire.

'To pack a bag. I do love her and I'm going up to Scotland now. To ask her to marry me,' I called over my shoulder.

'Don't bother packing a bag. I've already done it.'

I made a quick about turn and headed back down the stairs.

'It's behind the door.'

I gave her a hug and picked up the bag all in one movement. I raced down to the bank, withdrew some money and ran like crazy in the direction of the station. On the way I was recognised and pointed out by a Stoke supporter to his son.

'Look, there's Stanley Matthews! That's how he keeps so fit. Running with a great big bag to weigh him down.' I managed a cringing smile and kept on running at full tilt.

The journey to Girvan seemed to take an age but I consoled myself with the thought that every inch took me an inch closer to Betty. On arriving in Girvan I hit the ground running and didn't stop until I reached Jimmy Vallance's holiday home. Betty was shocked to see me. I wasn't at my best. My shirt was clinging to my back with perspiration, my tie was askew and my hair was in such a state it would have made Don King's look like Tom Mather's.

So high were emotions running, Betty and I married in the clubhouse of the Bonnytown Golf Club near Glasgow within days. It is amazing now to think that we acted with such haste, but we were young and in love, and as all young lovers do, believed our love was the most special in the world and would simply eradicate all problems.

It was a simple ceremony with just Betty's parents present and one or two officials from the golf club. The fact that we had done it more or less on the spur of the moment and without fuss or high ceremony pleased me. Simplicity I have always liked for, more often than not, it goes hand in hand with dignity and grace – two values I have always striven to achieve. The ceremony was indeed simple, but that it was also dignified and blessed with grace there was no doubt. My happiness knew no bounds. After the ceremony, the Club President said it was a momentous day for Betty and me, but also for the Bonnytown Golf Club because no one well known had ever made such news for them and probably never would do again. In 1941, Rudolph Hess landed there near the fifth hole. The story in the clubhouse was that Hess landed right beside the club's golf fanatic who was knocking a few balls around the course on his own. He reputedly said, 'It frightened the life out of me. You don't expect to see anyone at the fifth hole at three in the morning.'

We bought a new house not too far from my parents and settled into married life straightaway. As the 1934–35 season started I was very happy and contented and for all my tender years, felt well and truly settled.

Stoke started the season well and I was in good form. We were only just over a month into the new season when I was chosen to play for the Football League against the Irish League in Belfast. These inter-league games had great importance at the time. The players were selected from the respective leagues and, although a Scot could be chosen to play for the Football League if he played his football for an English club, these games were looked upon as opportunities for players on the verge of international football to show what they could do. The games attracted huge crowds, not only for nationalistic reasons but because they were played at club grounds. In the days before television, this presented an opportunity for people to see some of the game's top names play, people they had only read about or heard described on the radio.

The Football League side were far too strong for the Irish on the day. They battled away but went down 6–1. Not only did I have a hand in a couple of our goals but I managed to get on the scoresheet myself. As a result the newspapers got busy, saying I deserved a place in the England team for the game against Wales later that month. The pro-Matthews paper talk didn't affect me. I'd heard it all before prior to the Scotland game the previous season and it hadn't persuaded the selectors to pick me then, so I was very laid back about what the newspapers were writing about me, adopting an 'I'll believe it when I see it' attitude.

A few days after the inter-league match I was sitting in my father's barber's shop when one of his friends came rushing in and said, 'Jack, your Stan's in the England team.' My father's knee-jerk reaction nearly gave a pensioner a Mohican haircut. Father caught hold of his pal by his coat lapels and said, 'You wouldn't be kidding me now, would you?'

I never heard the man's reply. I was out of the door and heading for the newspaper boy who stood on the corner a block away. Before I reached him I saw the headline on the grilled news stand by his side – 'Matthews Chosen For England'. I had a hot flush, then a cold flush. My stomach felt empty, my mouth dry. I dipped into my pocket and took hold of the first coin that came to hand, a half crown (12½p). I thrust it into the boy's inky hand and grabbed a newspaper off his stand. It was true!

'I can't change this,' the newsboy said looking down at the half crown.

'You don't have to. Keep the change,' I told him. If it had been a film he would have said, 'Thanks, guv'nor. You're a real toff, ain't no mistakin'', but it wasn't and he didn't. He just stared down at the silver coin in his grimy palm and I made my way back to my father's shop as if walking on air. Inside I held up the newspaper for my father to see.

'Well, son. You've made it. Good luck to you,' he said.

His face was beaming but as he read the names on the team and got to mine, it suddenly changed. I could be wrong, but for the first time in my life I thought my father nearly cried. You could have heard hair falling to the floor from a customer's head, so silent was it. The four or five customers waiting their turn sat looking at my father, sharing the moment of emotion with him. The customer in the chair with half a short back and sides sat patiently watching us in the mirror. It was as if all these men, fathers themselves, knew what my father must be feeling and respected his emotion.

'Thanks for everything, Dad. I'll get off and tell Betty and mother,' I said and quietly slipped out of the shop. My father was still gazing down at the team names in the newspaper.

Outside, the street was full of the hustle and bustle of daily life. Shoppers, stall holders, horses and carts and the odd car went about their daily business, the noise a sharp contrast to the silence that had suddenly befallen the little barber's shop.

I had reached the height of my ambition, to play for my country. That night Betty and I went out into Hanley to celebrate, but not before I had done my personal training session.

As I walked from our home to the Victoria Ground the next morning, I found I had, overnight, become a bit of a celebrity. It took me three times as long as usual to walk to the ground because so many people stopped me in the street to wish me well and offer their congratulations. My Stoke team-mates were delighted for me and as I read the various newspapers they had bought, I found my name was splashed over the back pages of every one. I can't deny I felt pretty good about it. I was confident I could play at such a level and what's more, perform well.

The day of the Wales game got even closer and I started to feel the nerves but I made a concerted effort to control such feelings and trained harder than ever to release the tension and pent-up emotion. I couldn't control what was happening around me or how the game itself would map out, but I realised the one thing I did have control of was myself.

On the day of the game I must have appeared keen to my England team-mates. I was changed and ready for action before any of them had started to get ready. In the week preceding the game I had read the two teams over and over again. They are imprinted on my mind to such an extent that I can still rattle them off to this day without consulting any scrapbook. We lined up as follows:

England: Hibbs (Birmingham City); Cooper (Derby County), Hapgood (Arsenal); Britton (Everton), Barker (Derby County), Bray (Manchester City); Matthews (Stoke City), Bowden (Arsenal), Tilson (Manchester City), Westwood (Bolton Wanderers), Brook (Manchester City).

Wales: John (Preston North End); Lawrence (Swansea Town), Jones (Leicester City); Murphy (West Bromwich Albion), Griffiths (Middlesbrough), Richards (Wolverhampton Wanderers); Phillips (Wolverhampton Wanderers), O'Callaghan (Tottenham Hotspur), Williams (Newcastle United), Mills (Leicester City), Evans (Tottenham Hotspur).

I was left kicking my heels as my England colleagues changed and I was glad to see a familiar face pop his head around our dressing-room door. Roy John was in goal for Wales that day and although at Preston at the time, he had only recently joined them from Stoke City. Roy had come to wish me luck, which was typical of the man. We may well have been opponents on the day, but Roy, sensing my nerves and anxiety, tried to allay my fears.

'Don't be scared, Stan,' he told me. 'These internationals are like medicine, they get better as you go on. You'll not want to come off at the finish. You're up to all this Stan, otherwise you wouldn't be sitting here. Keep your chin up.

Believe me when I say you'll do all right. You've got it in you to play at this level.'

Roy's kind words made me feel better and helped me get over the dragging nervous wait. It was a great gesture on his part and looking back, one that still makes me feel there are more good than bad people in this world. Roy suggested we swap shirts after the game. I'd wanted to keep my first-ever full England shirt, but after his kind gesture, what could I say but yes?

Roy's visit was just the tonic I needed and I took the field before a Ninian Park packed with 41,000 Welshmen, feeling confident. I wasn't the only one. England tore into Wales from the start and two goals from Manchester City's Freddie Tilson and one from his club-mate Eric Brook put us 3–0 up at half-time.

A minute after the restart, Bolton's Ray Westwood sent me a cross-field pass that gave me the chance of a lifetime. I picked the ball up on the right wing and headed for their left-back. I body swerved to the right, he lunged at me and I cut inside to my left and bore down on the Welsh goal. Roy John came rushing off his line but had left a bit of space to his right and I went for it. The net ballooned as the ball hit it and I just carried on running. I was too elated to spare a thought for my good friend Roy John as my England team-mates descended on me and slapped my back. I looked up to the heavens. It wasn't a dream. It was a stone cold fact – 19 years old and I had scored on my international debut. I felt as Christopher Columbus must have felt on realising he hadn't sailed over the edge of the world.

Back in the England dressing room after the game, I was still elated but I suppressed my feelings by saying nothing much. My father's advice was ingrained in me – 'Keep your feet on the ground.' I was towelling myself down when Roy John came in, his Welsh goalkeeper's jersey in his hand and a deadpan expression on his face.

'Here you are, Stan,' he said throwing the jersey in my direction. 'The next time I open my mouth and waste sympathy on you, do me a favour. Shut me up!' I handed him my England shirt. He smiled. 'I'm pleased for you, Stan. Well done.'

We danced a little jig together, him in his suit, me in my birthday suit. Roy John was a very good goalkeeper, but I realised that day, he was also a tremendous human being. I was leaning out of the window of the carriage door as the train pulled into Stoke station late on the Sunday afternoon. Through the billowing clouds of hissing steam that plumed across the platform I saw Betty and my mother and father waiting to greet me. They were waving frantically and the look in their eyes was wonderful. They had listened to the match on the radio and apparently, when I scored, Betty went crazy with excitement. We walked up the hill towards Hanley all linking arms and I knew that I was the happiest young man in the world. We were all so excited at one point that, with arms still linked, we ran. I was glad we didn't come across the Stoke supporter and his son who had seen me running with my bag to the station on my way to ask Betty to marry me. Heaven knows what he would have said to his son about my training methods if we had.

We sat down to tea at my parents' house with my two older brothers, Jack and Arthur, who had pursued their own separate careers, and Ron, at the time still at school. We talked of nothing but the match. There was no sibling rivalry between us; being several years younger than both Jack and Arthur, I couldn't compete with them at any level. So, with Jack having followed my father and become a boxer, and Arthur having taken up running, in football I had found a pursuit that gave me standing and status within the family. My older brothers had nothing but pride for what I had achieved. Tea over, my father and I had a moment together washing up.

'You know, son, at one time I never thought you'd make it. You were so thin and scrawny as a boy. But you have made it and I can only say that from now on, you deserve everything you want from football. Heaven knows you've worked hard enough for it.'

I was touched by what my father said. For him to be so open and praising made me feel that I had indeed achieved something. What I didn't know was that God, fate, call it what you will, had plenty more for me to achieve in my life.

3

—— ◦ ——

When 149,000 Went
Silent at Once

The alarm clock sent a fire engine clanging through my head. It went off at 7 a.m. every morning and signalled the start of not only a new day, but my personal training programme. I'd get up, open the window and take several deep breaths of fresh air before changing into my training kit. I'd begin with a series of stretching exercises on the waste ground near our home, which I still do every morning to this day. The body loosened and warmed up, I'd continue with a series of fast sprints over short distances, followed by a longer run at half to three-quarters pace, then more body exercises and sprints. The final sprint over, I'd make for home and breakfast at a very brisk walking pace. That was my early morning training programme and I always looked forward to it. It never got stale. Football was my life and having done much training under the guidance of my father from an early age, it had become sheer habit.

One October morning in 1934, still basking in the glory of my international debut against Wales, I sat down to breakfast with Betty at 8.15 on the dot, as we always did.

'Don't they announce the team for the Football League against the Scottish League today?' Betty asked.

I told her they did and that it would be in the evening paper. I was keen to make the Football League representative team, not only because the game against the Scots always had great importance, but there was a very big international against Italy coming up and although I'd made a satisfactory debut against Wales, I wanted to impress upon the selectors that it wasn't a one off.

I helped Betty with the breakfast dishes and set off for my day at Stoke City. I walked to the ground for training in great anticipation. I wanted to make that Football League team as it could be the springboard to get me on to the big international stage. In 1934, as now, they didn't come much bigger than Italy. They were considered to be one of the best teams in the world and had proved it to a large extent that year by winning the second-ever World Cup tournament – although World Cup was a bit of a misnomer because many countries hadn't entered it, England included.

Thoughts of the Football League team were soon pushed to one side as Jimmy Vallance put us through another of his rigorous training sessions. In 1934, football training was far from the exact science it is today and at most clubs consisted of a few laps of the running track, some exercises, then in for a bath and a Woodbine. Often a ball wouldn't feature at all. It was different at Stoke. Jimmy was serious about fitness and although he was my father-in-law, he did me no favours. I topped up Stoke's daily training sessions with my own, but I was happy to be at a club that didn't have a lackadaisical attitude to training. As far as First Division teams went, Stoke didn't have the quality in depth of Arsenal or Sunderland but we made up for that with our superior fitness. That and the fact Jimmy Vallance introduced a lot of ball work into his sessions stood us in good stead come matchdays against the bigger and more glamorous teams.

The morning training session over, I made for a nearby café for lunch, as was my routine. I wouldn't have much to eat, a light snack or a sandwich, just enough to put something into my stomach but not to bloat me for the ball practice which I undertook every afternoon at the Victoria Ground. It must seem quaint to today's top players, who enjoy five-star restaurant facilities at their training grounds, that my contemporaries and I made do with a local café. But that's the way it was and it continued to be so for years. The corner café near to the football ground was part of a footballer's daily life for decades and many a good story has come from such places. My favourite 'café' story concerns Mike Summerbee and the day he signed for Manchester City in the sixties.

Mike was a classy winger who had made a bit of a name for himself with Swindon Town. Manchester City, in the Second Division at the time, were considered to be a far bigger club than Swindon and were underachieving. Was it ever thus at City?

At the time, Manchester City were managed by my old England team-mate Joe Mercer. Under his guidance, and with the coaching of Malcolm Allison, City went on to have arguably the most successful period in their history. Joe was in the process of turning things around at City when he became interested in Mike Summerbee. For Summerbee's part, he saw a move to City as a big step, elevating him from a homely provincial club into the relative big time. Mike Summerbee arrived in Manchester to discuss terms with Joe expecting big things and a lot more money than he was on at

Swindon. After all, Manchester City had an illustrious history and, even mid-table in Division Two, were drawing crowds of up to 27,000.

Mike had been told to meet Joe at the restaurant opposite Maine Road and on arriving searched frantically for such a place. He walked up and down the rows of streets that lead off from Maine Road, but no restaurant was to be found, only a small greasy spoon café. Mike thought to himself, 'Surely this isn't what Joe Mercer meant when he said a restaurant?' but on peering through the steamed-up window he saw Joe seated at a table sipping a cup of tea.

Mike went inside, introduced himself and Joe told him to get a cup of tea. Mike queued up and realised what sort of place he had come to when he saw there was just one spoon and it was tied to the counter with a piece of string – only there was no spoon there. Someone had nicked it.

'How badly off do you have to be to start stealing teaspoons? The folk in this part of Manchester must be desperate,' Mike thought as he joined Joe at his table. Mike sifted some sugar direct from the bowl into his tea and searched his pocket for a pen to stir it with.

'I have my own spoon,' said Joe and promptly produced one from his pocket. Mike couldn't help but notice, the spoon had a piece of string tied to the handle.

'Times are hard,' Joe said to Mike, 'but if you sign, they'll get better.' Mike did end up signing and true enough, for City things did turn around, in a big way.

I ate hardly any of the sandwich I ordered at the café. My stomach wasn't up to it and I knew I wouldn't be settled until I'd seen the Football League team in the local evening paper. I returned to the Victoria Ground and applied myself to a ball skill session, working on what I felt to be a weakness in my play – my left foot. I stopped when it got dark, showered and made my way to my father's shop:

'You're late,' he said as I walked through the door. 'I was on the point of giving you up. Have you seen the paper?'

I told him I hadn't, I wanted to hear whatever the news was from him.

'You know, son, you're a funny one at times. I know I've drummed it into you not to expect anything from life . . .' My heart sank.

'Does that mean I didn't make the team?' I said, interrupting his flow. 'You know, I must be a funny one. All day I've been on tenterhooks and now I know I'm not selected, I'm not in torment anymore. Just relieved.'

'What are you talking about?' he said. 'Of course you're in. Here – read for yourself.'

I took the paper from him, read the team aloud and jumped for joy. We left my father's shop and made our way back to my parents' house where Betty would be joining us for tea. My father, sensing the sudden change in mood, took me by the arm.

'You know, son. I keep telling you to keep your feet on the ground whatever success comes your way. I've been forever saying you should never expect much, but by the same rule, sometimes you can get to expecting too little.'

'You mean, always hope for the best?' I asked.

'I mean, son, train your mind to take the rough with the smooth, on and off the field. Never give up. Be realistic but have confidence in yourself and your own natural ability. A player can practise all he can, receive help and advice from the best managers and trainers in football, but they can't put in what God left out.'

Betty and my mother were there to greet us at the door, the expressions on their faces said it all.

'Oh, Stanley. I'm so happy!' Betty said, giving me a big hug. She wasn't the only one.

I made the headlines in the next morning's papers. The

football columnists were writing about me in glowing terms, predicting that if I played as well for the Football League as I had against Wales, there was no way the selectors could leave me out of the Italy game. I wasn't so sure.

The Football League met the Scottish League at Stamford Bridge. We ran out 2–1 winners but it wasn't a classic game by any stretch of the imagination. I felt I had a decent game, though. The service I received was good and I used the ball well, setting up one of our goals. I left the field contented with my performance, hoping it had been enough to persuade the selectors I was ready for a truly big international occasion.

I was in my father's shop when I got the news that I was in. Not only was this a clash of two footballing giants in international terms, the game had taken on extra importance because of the political situation. It was late in 1934 and Mussolini was in power in Italy with his own brand of fascism. According to the papers, Mussolini saw the forth-coming game against England as a way of boosting the morale of the Italian people, going as far as to say a victory over England would be a victory for fascism. There were all manner of stories about Mussolini offering massive money bonuses and gifts to the Italian players if they could pull off a win. It fuelled the tension in the build-up to the match and served only to make the game take on an even greater significance.

Betty was as delighted with the news as I was. As she was preparing tea, I scanned the pages of the *Evening Sentinel* and suggested we take our minds off the Italy game by going to the pictures. As we walked through Hanley towards the cinema, we felt like salmon trying to make their way upstream. Every few yards I was stopped by well-wishers, sometimes two or three at a time. In the end such well-meaning people had to make do with a nod and a 'Thank you'; otherwise we wouldn't have made it to the cinema for the main feature, never mind the B film.

In those days, a night out at the cinema consisted of two films and a round-up of recent events courtesy of Pathé News. Pathé News was the only means of seeing film of news events and even if it was a week old, these reports still carried immediacy.

As the Italy game approached the tension escalated and the football columnists found plenty to write about. There were five Arsenal players in the original line-up but on the Saturday preceding the game, Derby's Cooper and Tilson of Manchester City were both injured and had to withdraw. The selectors opted for George Male and Ted Drake both of Arsenal as replacements, which meant England would line up with seven Arsenal players in the side, something unprecedented.

Betty, my parents and a knot of well-wishers saw me off from Stoke station on the journey to London. The game had been given a massive build-up but I felt relaxed and on the journey down read part of a book before nodding off into a deep sleep. The train was in the northern suburbs of London when I finally woke up. I seemed to be getting more attuned to the big occasion. I smiled to myself when I thought of how I had been prior to my debut against Wales, as nervous as a turkey sitting on a pile of Paxo.

However, once in the dressing room, the occasion and the importance of the game got to me. The butterflies fluttered about in my stomach and having changed first, yet again, I walked around the dressing room attempting to chat to my team-mates in an effort to ease my tension.

The teams that day were:

England: Moss; Male, Hapgood (all Arsenal); Britton (Everton), Barker (Derby County), Copping (Arsenal); Matthews (Stoke City), Bowden, Drake, Bastin (all Arsenal), Brook (Manchester City).

Italy: Ceresoli (Ambrosiana); Monzeglio (Bologna), Allemandi (Ambrosiana); Ferraris (Lazio), Monti, Bertolini (both Juventus); Guiata (Roma), Serantoni, Meazza (both Ambrosiana), Ferrari, Orsi (both Juventus).

As our captain Eddie Hapgood shook hands with Monti the Italian captain, I went across to Ted Drake who was making his international debut.

'Don't be scared, Ted,' I said. 'Like medicine, these internationals improve as you go on. You're up to it, otherwise you wouldn't be here.'

'You sound just like Roy John,' Ted said.

The game got under way and from the very first tackles, I was left in no doubt that this was going to be a rough house of a game. I wasn't wrong. After a challenge between Drake and Monti, the Italian had to leave the pitch with a broken foot after only two minutes. This only made matters worse. For the first quarter of an hour there might just as well have not been a ball on the pitch as far as the Italians were concerned. They were like men possessed, kicking anything and everything that moved bar the referee. The game degenerated into nothing short of a brawl and it disgusted me.

After a few minutes I received a pass from Wilf Copping and took off down the wing making a direct beeline for the Italian left-back Allemandi, much to his surprise. I could see the puzzled look on his face. He probably thought with me being young I didn't quite have a handle on what to do in a game. I did my body swerve, Allemandi and the crowd near that touchline went one way, I went the other. This drew three Italian defenders out of position and glancing across, I saw Eric Brook steaming in at the far post from the left wing. I put some back spin on the centre, Eric Brook met the ball on the run with the meat of his forehead and it flew past Ceresoli in the Italian goal. Highbury erupted.

Five minutes later Cliff Bastin was brought down just outside the penalty area by a tackle from Ferraris that nearly cut him in half. Eric Brook was entrusted with the free kick and with the Italians expecting a chip to the far post for the head of Ted Drake, Eric ran up and hit a thunderbolt of a shot that nigh on ripped the netting from the stanchions. Ceresoli in the Italian goal never moved a muscle. For a moment he stood looking in silent disgust at the crestfallen defenders in front of him, then he kicked up a sizeable piece of the pitch before turning to retrieve the ball from the back of the net.

Just when I thought they were about to pull a goal back, Ted Drake latched on to an ale-house long ball out of defence and broke away to score a wonderful individual goal on his international debut. He paid for it. Minutes after the game re-started I watched in sadness as Ted was carried from the field, tears in his eyes, his left sock torn apart to reveal a gushing wound.

I thought the three quick goals would calm the Italians down, showing them that rough-house play didn't pay dividends, but they got worse. I felt it was a great shame they had adopted such tactics because individually they were very talented players with terrific on-the-ball skills. They didn't have to resort to rough-house play to win games. Why they had done so this day was beyond me.

Not long after Eric Brook had put us two up, Bertolini hit Eddie Hapgood a savage blow in the face with his elbow as he walked past him. Eddie fell like a Wall Street price in 1929. The next few minutes were dreadful. Tempers flared on both sides, there was a lot of pushing and jostling and punches were exchanged. I abhor such behaviour on the field and when I saw Eddie Hapgood being led off with blood streaming down his face from a broken nose, it sickened me. I'd been really keyed up and looking forward to showing what I could do on the big international scene, but this game was turning into a nightmare.

The game got under way again and the Italians continued where they had left off. It got to a few of our players and I don't mind saying it affected me. Fortunately, we had two real hard nuts in the England side that day in Eric Brook and Wilf Copping who started to dish out as good as they got and more. Wilf was an iron man of a half-back, a Geordie who didn't shave for three days preceding a game because he felt it made him look mean and hard. It did and he was. Eric Brook received a nasty shoulder injury and continued to play manfully with his shoulder strapped up. He was in obvious pain but he just carried on, seemingly ignoring it.

Just before half-time, Wilf Copping hit the Italian captain Monti with a tackle that he seemed to launch from some-where just north of Leeds. Monti went up in the air like a rocket and down like a bag of hammers and had to leave the field with a splintered bone in his foot. Italy were starting to get the upper hand and laid siege to our goal. It was desperate stuff.

Our dressing room at half-time resembled a field hospital. We were 3–0 up but had paid a bruising price. No one had failed to pick up an injury of one sort of another. The language and comments coming from my England team-mates made my hair stand on end. I was still only 19 but came to the conclusion I'd been leading a sheltered life. I was relieved when our team trainer came into the dressing room, calmed everyone down and said that under no circumstances were we to copy the Italian tactics. We were to go out, he said, and play the way every English team had been taught to play. To do anything but, he said, would exacerbate the situation. Exacerbate the situation? It was already a bloodbath.

The crowd roared their approval when they saw Eddie Hapgood was coming back out with us for the second half. From the restart, the Italians started to dictate the game and in no time had pulled two goals back through their centre-forward Meazza. The game was now on in earnest. Italy, to be fair, played some wonderful stuff in that second half but the England defence could call upon some heroes. Brook, Copping, Hapgood and Male were outstanding and when the Italians did break through, Frank Moss in goal pulled off three fantastic saves. Eddie Hapgood was magnificent. His white England shirt crimson with blood, he worked tirelessly and I don't think he missed a tackle that entire second half. It was a marvel how he forced his tired and battered body to obey his mind. The stamina and strength of conviction of the man were amazing.

I have to admit I was suffering from nerves and shock at being involved in such a game. I felt like a small boy in such company. I remember thinking, every time I believe I have this football thing cracked, it throws up another challenge for me, another means to self-exploration. My style of play never came off in such games but fortunately I never experienced such a rough madhouse as that game against Italy. We clung on to win 3–2, but it left a very sour taste in my mouth. To be truthful, this game upset me quite a lot and even went as far as denting my great enthusiasm for football. It was to be some time before I eventually got over it.

Betty met me at the station on my return to Stoke and, but for a few bruises and cuts, I assured her I was fit and well. The selectors left me out of the next international and I didn't feature again at that level for the remainder of that 1934–35 season. Of course I was disappointed, but I still had plenty of time to stake my claim for a place in the national team.

Stoke City continued to more than hold their own in Division One, moving up to tenth place. I was enjoying my domestic football and come the end of the season, I'd managed to get the Italy game out of my system. I was already looking forward to 1935–36 and turning up the heat for Stoke to get another crack at the international stage.

I continued with my training programme during the summer of 1935 and felt in great shape when I reported back for pre-season training with the rest of my Stoke team-mates. I was now 20, a little older, a little wiser. I may well have been a big fish in Stoke but as I had discovered against Italy, I'd been a bit of a tiddler in a big international game. It was something I was determined to work at. If I wanted to fulfil my ambition, I had to work and work at my game so that I didn't just get through a game at top international level, but could stamp my authority on it. I knew I was some way off that in 1935, but I believed that by studying my own game and with much hard work on my fitness, technique and ball skills, I could reach such an elevated standard.

I always enjoyed training with the Stoke team. There was a lot of leg-pulling and wisecracking among the players and it all served to improve the team spirit.

During the 1935–36 season, a fine young player, Freddie Steele, made his mark in Stoke colours. Freddie had made his debut the previous December against Huddersfield Town and netted his first goal on the Boxing Day against West Bromwich Albion. Like me, Freddie was a Hanley lad, and he had a deep feeling for the club. He joined Stoke the year after me, in 1931, and eventually went on to play 340 games for Stoke scoring 220 goals, which is remarkable in anyone's book.

The Stoke players coined the nickname 'Nobby' for Freddie and for the life of me I can't remember why, but it wasn't because he put us to shame in the shower! Goals flowed from Freddie's boots. You hear much talk about this player or that player being a natural goalscorer, but that epithet was wholly appropriate for Freddie Steele. To say that many a defender met his Waterloo at Freddie's hands would be trite. They also met their Hastings, their Blenheim, their Saratoga. Whenever the ball came to him, the reporters in the press box sharpened their pencils in anticipation. In the penalty box he was lethal, clinical and merciless, firing in shots from the tightest of angles and the smallest of spaces. In just about every game he played for Stoke, Freddie turned in a masterpiece of strength, endurance, polish and skill that more often than not at some stage resulted in a billowing net. He was a joy to play alongside and like me was a fitness fanatic going as far as to represent the county in the 4 × 100 yards relay as well as the hurdles.

Before turning professional, Freddie worked in Tom Mather's office, just as I did. One day I was in the office while Freddie was ringing the County Football Association regarding the registration of Harry Ealing, an amateur player, on Stoke's books. The man on the other end of the phone had trouble understanding Freddie's Potteries accent and asked him to spell the surname of the player in question. Freddie duly obliged – 'E for 'Erbert, A what horses eat, L where you don't want to go when you die, I what yon youth sees with, N what lays eggs, and G what James Cagney says to his "mar".' It was such high-spirited humour in the Stoke camp. That was one of the most endearing things about the club in those days, as far as I was concerned.

Due to the fact I had missed out on a number of internationals, as the 1935–36 season got under way I found myself out of the glaring spotlight of publicity. That meant I had more chance to work on my game in my spare time, which I did tirelessly. I was very keen to work on what today seems almost a forgotten art in football, dribbling. Dribbling with the ball at my feet had always come naturally to me. I didn't even have to look down, it was as if I had another sense that told me where the ball was. I wanted to bring my dribbling to perfection. I hammered wooden stakes into the ground and dribbled the ball in and out of them as quickly as I could. The better I got at this, the closer I put the stakes together, until there was just enough space to weave in and out of them.

I practised this for hours on end, day after day, and when I could finally dribble the ball in and out of these tight spaces at speed and at any direction, I felt I had improved that aspect of my game considerably. I even went as far as soaking the ground with water to simulate muddy conditions. Such concentrated practice paid big dividends and I incorporated some element of dribbling into my daily training sessions.

Opponents were beginning to latch on to my body swerve and were less likely to fall for it so I started to work on a two-way body swerve, which I found really threw opponents; they found it hard to decide which way I was going to go. I worked on the double body swerve with the dribbling, which really paid off. My upper body was flexible enough for me to sway quickly from side to side, to feint here, then there, and all the time I could keep the ball on the end of my toe. After one game against Huddersfield Town during which I had sold their left-back a dummy, our left-half Jock Kirton came up to me and said, 'Stan, I've never seen a player sell a dummy like you did today. The crowd in the paddock had to pay to get back in!'

When I put my body swerves and dummies into action, the Stoke supporters roared their heads off. Every time I received the ball they encouraged me to run at defenders, which I invariably did with great success. I was fast becoming a favourite with supporters, but found myself equally unpopular with opposing defenders. I suppose that was no bad thing – it meant I had them rattled.

After every game I'd check back through my own performance and make copious notes of any perceived weakness and possible solutions to it that I could work on. I was really enjoying my football. I wasn't aware of it at the time, but each and every game I played in the First Division was making me stronger, fitter, more mature. My contribution to and effect on a game grew with each passing match, again something I wasn't wholly aware of at the time. Betty was delighted with my progress and we were both enjoying married life to the full. Life was good. 'It can get no better than this,' I thought at one time, but I was wrong. It was to get better still.

———— o ————

One foggy November night I arrived home to find a fire roaring up the chimney, the wireless babbling and Betty laying the table for tea. It was a cosy scene and one that I had grown to love. Tea and washing up out of the way, I was all for a quiet night by the fire chatting to Betty who had picked up some knitting.

'They picked the England team for the game against Germany today, Stanley,' Betty reminded me. 'The *Evening Sentinel* is over by the door. You haven't even looked at it to see if you've made it into the side. I think you stand a good chance, you've been playing ever so well lately.'

The game against Germany was taking place in December and to be honest I hadn't checked the paper because having been out of the international scene for 12 months, I thought there was little chance of being recalled out of the blue for such a big and important game. I looked at the back page – Middlesbrough's Ralph Birkett was in at outside-right. I put the paper to one side and picked up a novel I was reading, but after a few pages, put that to one side as well. The national papers had been saying that in addition to Birkett, three other players, Geldard, Crooks and Worrall were all ahead of me in the stakes to claim the outside-right position in the England team. My career as a future international looked bleak.

'You know Betty, love, I have a feeling that within a year or so I will be the regular choice at outside-right for England.' I said it partly to bolster my own spirits. Betty glanced up from her knitting and gave me a disbelieving look.

'I will, Betty,' I re-affirmed, 'and it will be all down to those wonderful teas you make for me.' I ducked the cushion that headed my way.

'Regular in the England team, indeed!' Betty said incredulously. I'd said it partly in jest but as it turned out, I was right.

You never know what fate has in store. Someone's unlucky break can mean luck for another and that's exactly how it turned out for Ralph Birkett and me. The game against Germany was taking place on 4 December and, like the game against Italy, the pre-match build-up was electric. As opposed to the Italy game however, for some reason the newspapers never played up the political element. Hitler and the Nazis were in jingoistic mood and in the early stages of their plan to conquer the world. One had a very uncomfortable feeling about Hitler and the situation over there, even in 1935. A win for Germany could boost Nazi fascism, but there was little or no mention of the political aspect to this game in the press. Then again, I thought, why should I worry? I wasn't going to play anyway.

It was a midweek game and on the preceding Saturday morning I was scanning the paper when I noticed a piece tucked down at the bottom of the inside back page. The columnist said he had seen me play for Stoke in recent weeks and that I was in 'sparkling form' and if this form continued, it wouldn't be long before I was 'knocking on the door of the England selectors'. This lifted my spirits. It was good to know someone was noticing the benefits of all the hard work I had been putting in. That afternoon I took to the field for Stoke, probably just as Ralph Birkett was coming out for Middlesbrough. Fate had two very different endings in store for us that day.

I had a good game for Stoke and came off the field well pleased with my performance. What I didn't know was that two England selectors were sitting up in the stand watching me. When I got home, I turned on the radio for the seven o'clock news and to my great surprise, found I had made the sporting headlines. Ralph Birkett had suffered a bad injury playing for Middlesbrough and the selectors had called me up for the game against Germany. I felt sorry for Ralph, he was a great lad and to miss his chance of playing in such a big game must have been heartbreaking for him, but you have to take your opportunities when and however they arise and I was determined to make the most of this one.

I remember thinking the events of that afternoon taught me a good lesson – every footballer has the chance to play for his country if he always gives his best, even when he feels he is right out of favour. My father's words about never giving up came back to me. I had reaped the reward by following his advice.

We'd just had a telephone put into the house and that weekend I got to know what that could mean. It never stopped ringing. First the FA, then a stream of reporters and well-wishers. My name made headlines in all the Sunday and Monday papers. I was back in the spotlight but, better still, back in the England team.

Betty waved me off on the London train from Stoke

station. I tried to read, just as I had done a year before on my way to the Italy match, and had every intention of ploughing through this novel but found myself reading on automatic pilot. I closed my eyes and hoped the rocking movement of the train would send me to sleep; not this time. My mind was jumping around and I found myself thinking about all sorts of things – the Germany game, how I would approach it, Betty, Stoke City. When I started to think about our coalman and if we needed to order extra coal over Christmas, I knew sleep was hopeless.

I felt pretty tired when I reached Euston, so went straight to the hotel for an early night. Fortunately, I slept like a log and awoke the next morning feeling refreshed, fit and up for the big game.

The venue was White Hart Lane. In the dressing room I had another attack of the butterflies, but not as bad as before. When I ran down the tunnel, I felt wonderful. White Hart Lane was packed to the rafters and I knew somewhere out there on the terraces was my father. He had borrowed a car from a pal and driven down from Stoke to London, which in those days must have been a long and tiring journey. I was glad he was there and only hoped I could repay his faith in me by turning on a good performance.

In the early stages of the game, I received a great pass from Eddie Hapgood and took off down the right wing. I saw Münzenberg the German left-back coming towards me and ran straight towards him, full of confidence. Having taken the ball right up to him, I body swerved and passed him on the outside, only I didn't have the ball at my feet anymore. I couldn't believe it. I turned quickly to see Münzenberg heading up the line with the ball at his feet and gave chase. As I reached him, he showed me too much of the ball and I put my right foot in to pinch it off him, but I swung at fresh air. Having shown me the ball, as I lunged at him, he quickly dragged the ball back with the sole of his boot before playing a pass inside.

A few minutes later, I was speeding down the wing again. I put my double body swerve into operation and opted for cutting inside this time. I was sent sprawling as a sledge-hammer tackle blocked the ball and my momentum carried my body over his outstretched leg. In that first half, I tried feinting, shifting my body, swerving, but he wasn't having any of it. In fact, I realised he wasn't watching me at all; his eyes never left the ball. I remember thinking, 'You've been kidding yourself, Stan. This player is far too quick and experienced for you.'

Münzenberg was a watershed for me. Never in my short career had I come up against a full-back of his class. For all the hours and hours of practice and training I had put in, here was a man who was my superior. What on earth had he been doing back home to reach such a standard? 'Ploughing a lone furrow,' I remember thinking, 'always results in a revelation. You either find you have been doing far more than other players and have elevated yourself above them, or you have fallen short of the mark.'

I was well short of the mark this night and it rocked me. Not only was Münzenberg getting the better of me in tackles, his positioning was superb, and when it came to a chase, I was dumbfounded to find he was quicker than me. I'd never found anyone who could outpace me in domestic football. It was a shock to my system.

In desperation I moved from the wing, inside. At one point I found myself free inside the German penalty area. I was screaming for George Male to give me the ball and when it came, glanced up to pick my spot. In the process of shooting I stubbed my toe in the ground and the ball bobbled about four yards where it was smothered by the German goalkeeper. I heard a collective groan of disappointment from the packed spectators and stood rooted to the spot not believing what I had done, or rather failed to do. There I was, the young player always striving for perfection, always believing that no one loved or was as dedicated to football as I was, having made a schoolboy error of taking my eye off the ball. My aim was perfection, but on this big stage, I was making a joke of myself. I was horrified.

I moved back out on to the wing and some of the crowd started to get on my back. Normally that didn't affect me at all, but the combination of Münzenberg and miskicking in front of goal had destroyed my confidence. I might as well have walked off there and then such was my contribution to the rest of the game. The longer the game went on, the worse I got until near the end when a pass was played to me, I failed to control it and the ball passed under my boot and out for a German throw in. The jeering whistles of the crowd said it all.

The rest of the England team didn't seem to have a problem with the Germans. We ended up winning 3–0. Although I was pleased to have won, the fact that my England colleagues sailed through the game made me feel even worse. For the first time in my life, doubts crept in about my own ability to play at the highest level. I was fine in Division One, but once again, I had failed to deliver on the international stage – big style.

The other England players tried to lift me saying Münzenberg was an experienced international defender at the peak of his career and not to worry because I had years ahead of me in which to improve. I felt so ashamed of my performance I stayed at the post-match players' get-together just long enough to be polite, then crept away. I made for Euston and the next train home.

I had a bit of a wait for the next train to Stoke, so I slipped into the buffet for a cup of tea. No sooner had I sat down when some supporters who had obviously been to the game, came in for a beer before their journey back to wherever was home for them. They chatted about the match and then one of them made reference to me.

'All right in league football,' he said to his mates, 'but Matthews hasn't got what it takes at international level. I felt sorry for the lad when he missed that chance, but that said it all didn't it? He did nowt against Italy and nowt tonight. He's not good enough, simple as that.' His mates nodded their agreement.

I picked up my bag and slunk out of the buffet. As I walked down the station platform, tears were streaming down my face. I had dedicated myself to the game, worked harder and longer than any other player I knew. Surely I deserved more than this? All my hard work and hours of practising when other players were home by the fire or in the pub. Why had fate tricked me so? I was sinking into self-pity.

To my great relief I managed to find an empty compartment on the train and made myself comfortable in the corner. A whistle blew, the train gave a sudden jerk, a hiss of steam partly obscured the wet empty platform, and I was on my way home. I thought about my father making his way home in the small car and what an arduous and disappointing journey back home he had in store. I tried to keep my mind blank but to no avail. The nightmare of the game came back to haunt me all the way home.

It was a very unhappy young footballer who walked through the empty streets of Hanley that night. When I got home, I found Betty and my mother sitting by the fire. They looked at me with a sad, pitying look in their eyes.

'Oh, Stanley,' Betty said softly as she folded her arms around me. Tears flooded my eyes again. Through blurred vision I saw my mother looking up at us. She was biting her lip.

Tired as I was, I had a very restless night, grabbing only fitful sleep. At one point in the middle of the night I got up to drink a glass of water and stood looking out of an upstairs window. The night was silent as a country churchyard, the streets deserted, and then suddenly, in the distance, I heard the sound of a solitary car approaching. The sound became louder as the car got nearer until finally it came into view. It was a small black saloon. The tyres made a hissing sound on the wet road as it passed our house. My father was at the wheel. I watched the car's tail lights get smaller until it finally turned the corner, heading in the direction of Hanley. What a miserable journey home my father must have had. His disappointment must have been as great as my own, his spirits as low. I turned to go back to bed and caught sight of myself in the mirror on the landing. The face that looked back at me was haggard and forlorn. I hardly recognised it as my own.

The next morning the sports writers went through the Germany game as a customs inspector would a suitcase from Colombia. They mulled over every aspect of it and were full of praise for England but hard on me. Two newspapers even made mention of my performance, such as it was, as part of their sub headline: STYLISH ENGLAND BEAT GERMANY — BUT MATTHEWS FAILS TO PERFORM and ENGLAND POWER SHOW — IS MATTHEWS NIGHTMARE. I could only agree.

Nobody stopped me as I walked to the Victoria Ground that morning. Heads glanced up at me, smiled then looked away. I'm not saying my own townfolk had deserted me, I just think they felt sorry for me and didn't know what to say. Well, what could they say? Certainly not 'Well done!'

When I entered the Stoke dressing room the babbling conversation stopped for a moment. All the players looked in my direction.

'Sorry I let you down, lads. I don't suppose anyone wants

an autograph?' I said, making my way over to my peg. It broke the tension and they all started laughing. Within a few minutes everything was as normal as we made our way out on to the practice pitch at the back of the ground.

At lunchtime I had a light snack in the corner café as usual and went back to the ground. I put on my training kit, grabbed a sack of footballs, my hammer and wooden stakes and made for the practice area. I thought about Rudyard Kipling's poem 'If' and the part about keeping going even when all others have their doubts about you, yet being able to allow for those doubts. I put myself through a tortuous session of sprints, dribbling and general ball skills, pushing myself to the limit in every area. I felt it helped get something out of my system. I was determined to succeed, to prove to everyone, but especially myself, that I had what it took to play at international level and not just play, but dictate the game.

Darkness was falling as I made my way back to the dressing room, but there was one more thing I had to do. I took the sack of balls on to the Victoria Ground pitch and lined them up in a similar position to where the ball had been when I miskicked against Germany. I hit those balls into the net every time. Then I lined them up again. This time I made it harder for myself. I decided not to shoot into the empty goal, but to hit the crossbar to prove my accuracy. Again I felt I had got something out of my system when five out of five rattled that crossbar.

I gathered up the balls and headed towards the tunnel. In the gathering gloom, I thought I saw someone standing by the tunnel and called out.

'It's only me, son,' my father answered back. I hadn't seen him since the Germany game and as I approached I felt awkward and didn't know what to say.

'Betty called and asked your mother and me around for

tea. So I told Mother to go along while I came up for you. I thought we could walk home together.'

'How did you know I'd be here?'

'Because I know and I know what you're going through at the moment,' he replied.

After a quick shower I joined my father and we set off for home together through the dark streets.

'What about yesterday's game?' I asked.

For a few moments my father said nothing.

'Listen, son,' he said eventually, 'I'm not worried about what you did yesterday. I'm more concerned about your next game for Stoke, then the game after that, then the next. I wish I had the command of words to tell you what I want to tell you, but I'll do my best to help straighten you out if you want me to. Your future is not about the Germany game. It doesn't depend on what sports writers write or supporters say. It depends on you and how you apply yourself from now on.'

We walked along in the dark and as we passed under a gas lamp I noticed my father's face was deep in thought.

'The way I look at it is like this. To learn a trade you must serve an apprenticeship. In the building trade, engineering, plumbing, whatever it is, a lad starts at 14 or 15 and serves until he is 21. During all those years he'll make lots of mistakes, but the craftsman he is working with will keep teaching him until he is 21. After that, if he keeps on making blunders, he may get the sack. In football, things are different, there are no such rules and guidelines. You're pitched into a major game at 19 or 20 and expected to do a craftsman's job, so to speak. You're not yet 21, so you're still an apprentice in many ways.

'I did a lot of boxing, as you know. One thing experience taught me was not to try and correct a physical mistake by physical effort if your mental outlook isn't right. When you missed that goal yesterday, it had no effect on your fitness or footballing skills whatsoever. What it did affect was your mental attitude. Your mental attitude was suffering anyway, because that German full-back was a class act and you've never come across anyone half as good.

'Because your mental attitude was wrong, you let him sense he had the better of you and so his confidence grew as the game went on. You should have applied yourself to the game. Tried different things instead of thinking, "Aye up, he's better than me at this game." He isn't, but he was last night. If you experience such a situation again in a match, be mentally strong. Use guile and know-how. Try this, then that, then something else. You have all sorts of tricks up your sleeve. I didn't see you put more than a couple into operation yesterday. Be mentally strong and with your natural playing ability, you'll reach the very top. You analyse your own game continuously. That's fine, but also learn from other top players. You can learn a lot from studying them.'

We walked on in silence for a minute or two, me running everything my father had said through my mind.

'I've never said it but I believe you have it in you to be a great footballer. But if I had let you run out for Stoke in the state of mind you were in this afternoon, you could have done yourself a lot of damage. You have to be physically fit for football, but that's only a part of it. You have to be equally mentally fit. Now play your normal game on Saturday and never again lose confidence in yourself. If you haven't confidence in yourself, how do you expect anyone else to have any?'

It couldn't have been easy for him to find such words, but what he had found so hard to say lifted me enormously. Once again, I was to reap the benefits of his advice.

When I ran out for Stoke against Arsenal on the following Saturday I had it in my mind I was going to give the opposition a torrid time. The first time I received the ball I headed off down the right wing in the direction of my England colleague Eddie Hapgood. Eddie for all his toughness wasn't the greatest tackler I had come across. His strength lay in his positional sense and the way he jockeyed wingers. He stole the ball rather than won it. That said, he was the England left-back and I welcomed such a quick opportunity to show what I could do against international class opposition. Eddie tried to jockey me out to the touchline but I took the ball right up to him. I swayed one way then the other, but the position of his body forced me out wide with my back to the touchline. I remembered what my father had said about trying this and that, so I put one of my tricks into operation. Facing infield with Eddie positioning himself side on and slightly towards his own goal, I flicked the ball with my right foot, making as if I was going to retreat away from him and the Arsenal goal. As soon as I did it, he moved. In the split second the ball left my right boot, I flicked it back with my left. I'd used my feet like the rudders in a pinball machine. I left Eddie in my wake and headed for goal. For the remainder of that half I tried an array of tricks and came off the field at half-time to rapturous applause. I glanced over to where I knew my father always stood in the crowd, clenched my fist at the side of my temple to indicate mental strength and smiled. He smiled back and held the thumb of his right hand aloft. My father had provided the answer to a problem in my game. It was to be his final lesson to me. I learned from every game I played in my long career, but that day I felt my apprenticeship was over.

The Sunday newspapers couldn't fathom me out. I'd had an awful game against Germany; against an Arsenal side littered with internationals I'd run them ragged. One reporter said he 'couldn't account for the change in me'. How could he know? It wasn't a one-off. In the ensuing months I continued to hit a great vein of form and wasn't just making goals, I was scoring them.

— o —

Just before my twenty-second birthday, for the first time in my fledgling career, I became embroiled in a disagreement with the Stoke City management and board. I've never told this story before, but it had a bearing on matters that were to occur later at the club and which would ultimately determine my future.

All in all I had been with the club for seven years, since being taken on as an amateur and an office boy in 1930. The last season, 1935–36, had been good and the current one, 1936–37, was going well. In 1935–36, Stoke finished fourth in Division One, a point behind the runners-up Derby County, the highest position in the history of the club. In 1936–37, we ended up finishing tenth, but scored 15 more goals than the previous season. The team were doing well, attendances were booming – crowds in excess of 30,000 were commonplace at the Victoria Ground. I was rarely out of the national headlines, although I hadn't got back in the England side, and I was expecting a bonus. At the time, the club rewarded players who had been with them for five years with a loyalty bonus of £500. If you had been with the club in excess of that time, the payment was £650.

Tom Mather had left Stoke to manage Newcastle United in May 1935 and had been replaced as manager by Bob McGrory. McGrory had joined Stoke in 1921 from Burnley and was to give Stoke City 31 years service as player and manager. Bob knew Tom Mather had laid good foundations and kept the same squad he had known as team-mates, only making changes some years later when older players had to be replaced.

I had to negotiate a new contract so I went to see

McGrory and also mentioned that I was due the loyalty bonus. I was disappointed when he told me the club would award me a £500 bonus for the five years I had spent at the club as a professional. They refused to take into account the two years I had been there as an amateur.

'But I was playing for the club then,' I protested. 'In the reserves perhaps, but I was playing. The wording is that the extra loyalty bonus is payable to players who have seen "five years service with the club or more". If I wasn't serving the club by playing in whichever team I was asked to and working in the office, what was I doing?'

The disagreement continued until finally McGrory said he would refer the matter to the board, which I knew was a sure sign it would drag on and on. I wasn't wrong. It wasn't resolved until the summer.

In the meantime I had my twenty-second birthday a few days later and three days after that on 4 February 1937 history was made for Stoke City Football Club when we beat West Bromwich Albion by a club record score of 10–3. I didn't get on the scoresheet that day, but it didn't bother me because I had a hand in a number of the goals. Freddie Steele scored five, a hat-trick of which came from crosses supplied by yours truly, and I also had a toe in three of our other goals. So on a personal note, I was satisfied enough.

West Brom weren't a bad team at the time, far from it – they did score three goals away from home. We had been threatening to give someone a good hiding for weeks, however, and it was West Brom's misfortune that they met a Stoke team in which every player was in inspired form on the day. Glory and golden visions were not usually associated with the grimy Potteries of 1937, but they were much in evidence this day. Time and again Freddie Steele showed just what lightning speed he possessed, leaving the West Brom centre-half trailing in his wake. Even two-footed players have one foot that is stronger and more effective than the other, but I can honestly say this was not the case with Freddie Steele. He hit the ball like a bullet with either foot, from any position, from any angle. He wasn't tall, just under five ten, but he could jump as if he had bedsprings in his boots. As a cross came towards him, he would lean back slightly in midair, his head would jerk to one side as if taking an imaginary punch, only to whip back again as the ball reached him – and kapow! His forehead, hammered flat by contact with hundreds of leather caseballs, sent the ball flying off at a perfect right angle towards goal. It is no exaggeration to say Freddie could head a ball harder than some players could kick it. He was a pleasure to play alongside and in my book, the best centre-forward cum inside-forward in the history of Stoke City.

Among the goals that day was George Antonio. George had changed his name from George Rowlands, though for the life of me I can't remember why – family reasons I think. George played alongside me at inside-right and his second goal against West Brom was a pip. He cut in from the right and as the West Brom goalkeeper, Billy Light, positioned himself to cover his near post, everyone thought George would go for the gap to the keeper's left at the far post. Instead he leaned forward making as if he was about to run that way, but with the outside of his right boot, flicked the ball up and into the space between the keeper's head and the near post. It was so audacious it took Light completely by surprise. The ball gave him a closer shave on his left cheek than my father could have managed with a cut throat. It was so unexpected the keeper didn't have time to react – his left arm flinched but such was the speed of George's flick that by then it was too late. It was as if George was taking the mickey out of the goalkeeper and the Stoke crowd thundered their approval.

George's parents were Italian but he was born in a house on the Welsh border not far from Whitchurch in Shropshire. One day he was delighted to get the news that he had been selected to play for Wales. However, a couple of days before his international debut, some official discovered that the Welsh–English border ballooned around the house where George was born and the house was actually in England. So George missed out on international football. What a difference from today! When Jack Charlton was in charge of the Republic of Ireland, word had it he only had to see a player drinking a half of Guinness and that was good enough for him, irrespective of where that player, his parents or grandparents were born.

After the match, the West Brom players showed their sportsmanship by coming to our dressing-room door and congratulating us on our terrific performance. Even Billy Light came in, despite having to pick the ball out of the net so often.

'Well done, lads. You killed us today,' he said. He was just going out of the door when he turned back. 'By the way, we didn't get the rub of the green today, your ninth was offside!'

My new style of play was paying off for me and the more it did so, the more I worked on my personal game and skills. This was Stoke's fourth season in Division One since promotion and we achieved a top-ten finish scoring 72 goals in the process with Freddie Steele finishing with a season's tally of 33, still a club record. We'd been hoping for a good run in the FA Cup but had gone out in ignominious style in round four when we were beaten 5–1 at Preston. They went on to reach Wembley that year only to be beaten by Sunderland 3–1.

That 1936–37 season rained goals. Champions Manchester City scored 107 and Everton's Dixie Dean passed the career record of Derby's Steve Bloomer to finish the season with a career total of 349 league goals. It wasn't just goals galore in the top division, either. The pattern was repeated throughout

English football. Luton Town won the Third Division South netting 103 goals; Joe Payne, who had scored a record-breaking ten in the 12–0 thrashing of Bristol Rovers the previous season, carried on where he left off and ended 1936–37 with 55 goals to his name. Today many clubs struggle to hit 55 goals as a team in a season. Such prolific goalscoring would probably induce cardiac arrests in many contemporary managers and coaches for whom the first priority is not to concede goals, but the crowds loved this open, attacking style of play and attendances soared. At Stoke City the 'house full' signs started to get weather-beaten and a club record 51,380 turned up to see us play Arsenal in March.

My form was good and I found the larger the attendance, the more I was one for the big occasion. I hit a rich vein of form and the sports writers were once again putting my name forward for the England team. I wasn't to be disappointed. In the spring of 1937, the news came that I had been selected for the forthcoming international against Scotland at Hampden Park. I was back on the international scene and determined to show once and for all that I could produce the goods at the very highest level.

My selection caused much banter within the family. Jimmy Vallance was a Scot. There was much impish humour between us in the week leading up to the game, Jimmy saying things like the best view he knew of England was in his rear-view mirror when he crossed the border into Scotland. I'd come back with jokes about the supposed meanness of the Scots, telling him the current bestselling book in Scotland was *Indoor Games For Flag Days*. It was all good natured and taken in good part by us both, so when Jimmy told me to watch out for the Hampden roar because it can get to opposing players, I didn't realise how serious he was.

Stoke was the place to be at this time – in addition to

myself, the lethal Freddie Steele and Joe Johnson, a very fast and direct left-winger, had been picked for the England team. It was the first time three Stoke players had featured together in an England side since 1892, which I felt was not only a tribute to how well the three of us had been playing, but to the Stoke team in general.

The day before a major international against the 'auld enemy', Glasgow was a fascinating place. Having checked into the team hotel, I took a walk around the city to get a taste of the pre-match atmosphere. The streets were full of light and life, its pavements packed with people released from their work and anxious to squeeze a little laughter from what was left of the day. The hard accents of the people were punctuated by the noise of tram cars, coloured in broad bands like Neopolitan ice creams, which hissed and rattled their way to Renfield Street or Sauchiehall Street. Above this I could hear the occasional bass burp of tugs on the Clyde. Glasgow then had no secrets. Its shipyards ran all the way down to Greenock and were open to the sky; some 20 ships or more were in their cradles, some just keels.

In 1937, the meeting of extremes was characteristic of Glasgow; the well-to-do and those suffering abject poverty walked side by side on the street, Scotland's anchor to reality. Everywhere I walked I heard people talking about the forthcoming game and was left in no doubt that it was an occasion of great magnitude fuelled to the hilt by patriotic fervour.

On the day of the game I was up early. The newspapers were playing up the fact that I would be up against Andy Beattie, whom they were rating the best left-back in British football. 'The Irresistible Force Meets The Immovable Object' ran one headline, devoid of anything more original to say.

Beattie had just made it into the Scotland team. In fact

this game was to be his debut. I'd heard nothing but good reports about Andy Beattie and, this being his first game and at Hampden, I knew he would be determined to do well and live up to the reputation his meteoric rise had given him. I'd asked a lot of people in the game about his style of play, his strengths and weaknesses, and having weighed him up, I decided to let him worry about how he would cope with me. That was how different my mental attitude had become since my last appearance for England against Germany. I wasn't underestimating Beattie, far from it. I knew I would have to be on my mettle but I now had belief in my own ability. I was confident I would get the better of him.

After breakfast on the day of the game, the England team gathered in a private room in our hotel where we were briefed for the match. The team was placed under the guidance of a different club manager or trainer for every game, such as Tom Whittaker of Arsenal, Jack Tresadern of Spurs or Jimmy Trotter of Charlton Athletic. The situation was far from ideal; there was no continuity or consistent system of play and it often led to a Heath Robinson approach to even the most important of games. That said, I've always believed when you have players who have reached the very highest standard in football, a manager or coach doesn't have to tell them what to do because the players know. No manager or trainer ever had to teach me how to dribble a ball or cross it so that Stan Mortensen didn't have to head the part where the laces were. At the team meeting, all we were told was to swing the ball from wing to wing to create space down the middle for Freddie Steele. It wasn't worth the cost of hiring the private room to hear. While mindful of this instruction, I decided to go out and play my natural game. I was confident it would pay dividends.

When our team bus reached Hampden, I was amazed at the massive throng of humanity that circled the stadium.

The streets were so jam-packed with Scottish supporters, some of them in kilts, that I felt the sheer force of their number might push the houses on either side back a few yards. Over 149,000 crammed into Hampden that day with an estimated 12,000 locked out and no more than a few dozen, or so it appeared, were English. For them, the hostile patriotic atmosphere must have been terrifying.

The teams were playing in numbered shirts for the very first time. As was becoming the norm before England matches, I was changed before anyone else. I'd had a light breakfast and eaten no lunch but about the only feeling I didn't have in my stomach was hunger. Right up until the late sixties, a player's pre-match meal usually consisted of a steak, which was thought to give you strength and vitality. When people became more aware of dietary matters and realised that steak can take anything up to 24 hours to digest and probably did more harm than good to a performance, it was scratched from the pre-match menu.

In the immediate build up to a really big game, your mind can play tricks on you. You become aware of every little thing about you. You play around with your socks to get them just so. Having tied your tie-ups, you feel they are not sitting comfortably about the leg, so undo them and tie them again. Then it's the boots, the studs are checked and re-checked to make sure there are no worn edges and that they are hammered well into the sole. The laces are tied and re-tied until you feel they are not too slack or too tight around your boot. The shorts are dropped slightly to enable you to smooth the shirt down over your front and back, before they are hitched back up to your waist. Each leg is waggled to make sure the shorts are not pulling. I'd button my shirt leaving the top button undone, then decide that as the game progressed that might restrict my breathing, so I'd undo the second button there and then. I'd run my fingers around the shirt collar to ensure it wouldn't chafe my neck. Then it would be down to the socks again, checking the shinpads to make sure they were sitting comfortably and offering maximum protection. It was all in the mind and totally unnecessary but it helped pass the time and you'd kid yourself you had got rid of all minor irritations that could affect your performance. As the years passed, I stopped bothering with such rituals, but when I was young, they were part and parcel of my pre-match preparation, more the result of nerves than anything else. As time went on, a really big crowd atmosphere gave an edge to my game and I thrived on it. However, one thing stuck with me for my entire career and that was vomiting. Prior to every big game until I hung up my boots, I'd be physically sick. In a perverse way, I felt it did me good, ridding my stomach of partially digested food that might lie heavy and impair my performance. Eddie Clamp, my Stoke colleague of the sixties, used to call it 'Stan's technicolour yawn'.

Having changed into our strip, we whiled away the time before we received the call to take to the field. Raich Carter, who always swallowed six sugar lumps prior to a match because he felt it gave him energy, juggled a ball with either foot before letting it settle on his right boot. He balanced it there for a few moments and then flicked it into the air and caught it on his forehead, letting it rest there before jerking his head back and catching it once more on his right boot. George Male traipsed to and fro from the toilet, many times. Freddie Steele flicked through the match programme, pausing at the team page and probably wondering how on earth his name had come to be there. Goalkeeper Vic Woodley took a ball into the bath and shower area and proceeded to throw it up against the tiled wall and catch it, simply to get a 'feel' for the ball. In a muted dressing room the noise of him doing this was uncomfortably monotonous. The referee came in with his linesman, checked every player's studs for sharp edges and, satisfied all was well, collectively wished us 'Good luck and a good game'. We returned the sentiment.

The harsh ringing of the buzzer that was the signal for us to go silenced the muted small talk between the players. We stood up, shook hands and wished one another luck before our captain George Male picked up a ball and led us out of the dressing room in crocodile fashion. As we made our way towards the officials standing ready to lead us down the tunnel, it was as if the corridor has been filled with the noise of dozens of worn tappets in a motor-car engine as our studs click-clacked along the stone floor.

With military precision we met the Scotland team who had made their way down from the opposite end of the corridor, turned the corner and fell in line behind the officials who proceeded to lead us towards a rectangle of light at the end of the tunnel. I thought I'd never reach it. We seemed to be walking in slow motion. The muscles in my thighs and calves seemed to be devoid of strength and my legs turned to jelly. My hands were cold and clammy, my stomach churned and then suddenly, just as the officials and respective captains emerged into the sunlight, an ear-splitting roar that made the hair on the back of my neck stand on end swept up the tunnel as 149,000 Scots let rip.

When eventually I emerged into the light, I took one look around and it was all I could do not to stop dead in my tracks; people were so tightly packed into Hampden there couldn't have been a fag paper's width between them. The terraces heaved and swayed like the menacing swell of an ocean from which a monster of Godzilla proportions is about to surface. For a moment it unnerved me. As the teams lined up opposite one another for the official presentations, I took a series of slow deep breaths to try to relax myself. I can't remember who George Male accompanied down the line of England players because I was taking no notice. My head was bowed, my eyes on the grass at my feet, as I tried to keep my mind focused on the task ahead. I heard George mention my name, saw a hand extended and shook it without ever taking my eyes from the ground. The presentations over, the two teams wheeled away to either end of the field for the pre-match kick in. I occupied myself with a series of short sprints, partly to get some feeling back into my legs, but also to release the tension that had built up inside me. As I did so, I caught sight of Andy Beattie. He was jiggling his legs, rolling his head and shoulders, and looked calm and relaxed, but I was sure an emotional storm must have been racing through his body. You would have to be a zombie not to have been moved and unnerved by the atmosphere inside Hampden that day.

When the referee's whistle got the game under way, the sound of a tearing hurricane swept down from the stands and terraces. I was hoping to get an early touch of the ball to calm my nerves and settle me down and, thankfully, I did. Joe Johnson played the ball inside from our left wing to Ron Starling who turned before passing to me. I brought the ball under control and set off down the wing. Andy Beattie was making his way towards me. For all my concentration I was aware that the noise had suddenly abated as the crowd anticipated the first encounter between Beattie and me. I kept Beattie in my sights. I didn't have to look down to see where the ball was, my extra sense told me it was there where it should be, dancing on the toe of my right boot. I was swaying like a bird on a twig as Beattie came steaming in. I body swerved as if going to his right; he went that way and before he could regain his balance, I swerved to his left and vanished from his sight. A uniform and disappointed sigh swept down from the terraces as I made my way down the right touchline.

In crossing the ball, one ploy I used was to hang the ball

in the air just beyond the penalty spot so that the goalkeeper would be indecisive about whether to come off his line or not. If he did decide to come out, he would have ground to make up and would be at full stretch. If our centre-forward was doing his job, the goalkeeper would be under pressure from our number nine with a yawning gap behind him. I put in the cross, Dawson in the Scottish goal came out to meet it but under pressure from Freddie Steele failed to collect. The ball ran loose and there was one almighty scramble as Raich Carter and Ron Starling battled for possession before the Scottish defenders finally managed to clear the ball upfield.

It was a good start. I had won the first tussle with Andy Beattie and for the rest of the first half, the game continued in that vein, with Beattie chasing my shadow. With five minutes to go to half-time, Ron Starling found Joe Johnson on the left. Johnson made progress down the line before cutting in and playing a pass into a space just outside the penalty area. Freddie Steele and the Scottish centre-half Simpson were shoulder to shoulder as they ran to get on the end of Joe's pass and my expectations immediately rose. I didn't think Simpson had the extra pace to beat Freddie and sure enough when Freddie hit the accelerator, he gained that vital yard. Dawson came off his line to cut down the angle of Freddie's vision of goal, but I knew Freddie. From such positions he was as deadly as a cyanide injection. He got his upper body over the ball; it left his boot like a rocket and the net jerked and ballooned as it strained to halt the ball's momentum.

I wouldn't have thought it possible for 149,000 people to be silent all at once, but it happened. For a split second the only sound in a packed Hampden was that of the wind sweeping from one end of the pitch to the other. I heard George Male's voice from somewhere behind me shout, 'It's there!' his voice as strident and piercing as a scream in a cathedral. Freddie Steele disappeared under a posse of back-slapping team-mates. We were one goal to the good.

At half-time the England dressing room was bubbling. We all felt well pleased with our first-half performance and confident we had the measure of the Scots. But as soon as we kicked off the second half the Hampden roar kicked in and didn't abate until the end of the game. From the restart, Scotland poured forward. Within two minutes, Tommy Walker received a pass from the right wing, cut inside, and slipped a pass to Frank O'Donnell who tucked the ball into the corner of the net. The air was filled with a deafening noise that could be heard for miles across the Glasgow rooftops. I wouldn't have thought it possible, but the Hampden roar gained in volume after O'Donnell's equaliser. The atmos-phere was now highly charged and there is no doubt it got to some of our players. It rattled our confidence and as the England defence came under increasing pressure, we started to make mistakes. Fifteen minutes from time, Rangers' Bob McPhail fired in from 15 yards, past Vic Woodley and Hampden erupted for the second time of asking.

We had no option but to take the game to the Scots. By now I really had the measure of Andy Beattie but for all the crosses I put into the Scottish penalty area, the equaliser would not come. With England throwing men forward, three minutes from time the Scots broke away and Bob McPhail headed a third goal to put the game beyond us. We had outplayed the Scots in the first half, but to Scotland's credit they showed great strength of character in coming back at us to win the game, although the effect of that Hampden roar had been significant. I felt we were a shade unfortunate to have lost 3–1. The next day's newspapers were full of praise for England. I was satisfied with my own performance and the newspapers said I had given Andy

Beattie 'a torrid time', so although disappointed on one front, human nature being what it is, I travelled back to Stoke a happy man. I was back on the international scene and, according to the sports writers, back in some style.

━━ ○ ━━

Come the end of the season the matter of my new contract and unpaid bonus payment was still unresolved, so once again I asked for a meeting with Bob McGrory. I was told on the issue of the bonus payment that the £500 was the only one on offer, take it or leave it. I told him I would neither take it nor leave it, that I simply wanted what was due to me as written in my contract. Even if the two years' service as an amateur didn't apply, which I still disputed, I now had in excess of five years' service as a professional. So the bonus due was £650.

McGrory shook his head and informed me that while I continued to 'take this unreasonable attitude', the club would retain my registration, there would be no new contract and therefore no wages until I came to my senses.

'I only want what is due to me as per the last contract,' I said and, with that, bade my farewell and walked out of his office not knowing if I was in fact walking out of Stoke City for good.

I spent that summer as I always did, continuing with my personal training programme. I bought a car and even though Betty and I took off for a two-week holiday in Cornwall, my training kit was packed into our bags.

A few days before the Stoke players were due to report back for pre-season training for the 1937–38 season, I was summoned by Bob McGrory who informed me that the club had agreed to the £650 bonus payment even though they believed the wording in my old contract with regard to the loyalty payment to be 'somewhat grey'. As far as I was concerned it was clear enough. I received my £650 but three months without wages made a hole in it. What's more, the belligerent attitude and hard line taken by the board put a dent in the implicit trust I had in those running the club. As far as I was concerned, I'd shown great loyalty and it had not been reciprocated. My enthusiasm to play well for Stoke City the club and its supporters was as great as ever, however, and I was looking forward to the 1937–38 season with relish, and to staking a claim for a regular place in the England team.

4

Changing the Wingers' Style

I'd scored quite a number of goals for Stoke over the last few years – 38 in four seasons – but in 1937–38 decided to make a change to my style of play. I was beginning to be tightly marked by full-backs, so I made a conscious effort to drop deeper to collect the ball in order to create more space for myself.

My goals had come from cutting inside as wingers were apt to do at the time. Having given this much thought, I decided I would be better employed taking the ball to the dead-ball line and cutting it back for our oncoming forwards who couldn't be offside if they received a backward pass or centre from me.

It worked a treat. I wasn't scoring goals for Stoke anywhere like I had been, and was to score only 32 more league goals in the rest of my career, but this ploy created far more opportunities for our forwards. Of course, I had my critics who said I wasn't being direct and that taking the ball to the dead-ball line gave opposing defences the chance to regroup and cover. But Stoke were scoring goals, many of them as a direct result of my new style. At the time, I didn't think of it as innovative, although it was a totally different approach to wing play, which had remained basically unchanged for decades. When I went on such runs and took the ball to the dead-ball line, I found that two, sometimes three, defenders would come with me. This created space in the penalty area not only for our forwards but also for our half-backs, pushing up from deep.

Many people believe that in today's game with teams being so well organised, especially defensively, players are more tightly marked than ever before. It's a view I don't go along with. I would often be confronted with two or three defenders when I had the ball. Man-for-man marking was very much the order of the day in football in the late thirties. The opposing left-back stuck to me tighter than bark on a tree, but players in general were tightly marked. Today, a team losing possession will fall back to get players behind the ball thus allowing the opposition a free hand to come at them, the defending being done just outside the penalty area.

Irrespective of who their manager is – Don Howe, George Graham or Arsène Wenger – Arsenal have in essence defended this way for years. Arsenal's tactic of relinquishing space in midfield when the opposition have the ball in order to re-group and do their defending in and around the penalty area has been the key to their success over the years. The Arsenal defence has emerged as their bedrock. The only time I ever saw Don Howe smile was in an Arsenal pre-season team photograph and I'm convinced that was only because he knew every Arsenal player was behind the ball.

Confronted with this tight marking, I made a conscious effort to work on my ball skills in a confined space. I often asked defenders Harry Brigham, Jim Harbot and Jock Kirton to stay behind after training to help me out. If none of my first-team colleagues was available, two or three of the youth players were always ready and willing. The constant practice of playing one against three helped me enormously to hone my close ball skills and technique. In matches, when I did manage to create a little bit of room for myself, it was all I needed to get a cross in and more often than not my Stoke team-mates took full advantage of the space the three defenders had left behind them.

Although a big fan of football today, one thing that stands out to me about the modern game is that defenders don't know how to tackle. Football is far quicker now than it was even in the seventies or eighties, and as a result of games being played at such a terrific pace, the general level of individual skill has suffered. Of course, there will always be players like David Ginola and Gianfranco Zola, skilful enough to display their talents at breakneck speed, but there are also a number of players around today, earning a good living from football, who appear to be able to trap a ball further than I could kick it. When I talk of skill I don't mean just dazzling technique or party pieces, but also those skills which are part and parcel of a footballer's trade, such as tackling.

More often than not, a team will gain possession through a wayward pass by the opposition. At the end of the 1998–99 season, the statistics showed it was Arsenal's Patrick Vieira who had committed himself to the most tackles, 146 in 34 games, an average of just over four per game. Only five teams topped 20 tackles per game – Arsenal, Everton, Manchester United, Chelsea and Leicester City. Such statistics I feel back my theory that modern teams lose possession through giving the ball away and tackling is an almost forgotten art.

It is all in sharp contrast to how football was played in the thirties, forties and fifties, when the prime way to win the ball was through tackling and where there were some fine exponents of this physical art. Wilf Copping was a fearsome left-half with Arsenal and an England team-mate of mine. Wilf started out with Barnsley and was playing for their junior side when Leeds United snapped him up. From Leeds he moved to Arsenal where he enjoyed the best football of his career in what was, in the 1930s, the top side in England. Wilf was hard. The story was the Arsenal manager George Allison hadn't signed him, he'd quarried him. Wilf was a tough, tireless and aggressive opponent. During one game between Stoke and Arsenal at Highbury, I took the ball to Wilf swaying one way then the other in an attempt to confuse him about which way I was intending to go. Thoughts flash through your mind in a split second during a game and I wondered if Wilf would commit himself to tackle to the left or right. He did neither. He came straight through me with a sledge-hammer tackle and emerged behind me with the ball on the instep of his left boot. The sheer power of the tackle whiplashed my upper body forward and my legs were left sprawling in the air behind me. He'd won the ball cleanly but the force of the tackle had jerked my knee. Having been dumped unceremoniously in the mud, I writhed and winced from the pain in my knee. Arsenal's Frank Hill came up, took one look at me and shouted, 'You'll have to hit Stan again, Wilf. He's still wriggling.' And they say 'sledging' is a modern phenomenon!

Tackling was top priority on the agenda of every defender and players such as Aston Villa's George Beeson, Wilf's team-mate at Arsenal George Male, Sunderland's Alex Hall and Horace Burrows of Sheffield Wednesday stood out as defenders who took tackling and opposing wingers like me to new heights. It was text-book stuff. They'd slide in with the full weight of the body behind the tackling foot which was turned so the instep met with the ball, and it was all done with the precise timing of a Swiss watch. It was hard, effective and the main way to win possession of the ball and set up attacks.

It was also the key to the psychological battle between two opponents. I found the first tackle a full-back ever made on me in a game was usually the hardest as he tried to unnerve me for the remainder of the match. Ernie Blenkinsop, who played for Sheffield Wednesday and later captained Liverpool, would do this. His first tackle could be a bone crusher if you weren't careful and as we both came out of it he'd say, 'That's just to let you know I'm here.' As if I needed reminding, and this from a player who had been spotted playing for his local church team in Yorkshire.

Football may have been slower than it is today, but it was tougher and more physical. The majority of injuries now are a result of the speed at which the game is played rather than bone-crunching tackles. The only way I knew of getting the upper hand over tight marking and razor-sharp tackling was to continue to work on my skills such as dribbling and speed off the mark, making it harder for opponents to cope with me. In order to get a tackle in, an opponent would have to get near me and I would have to show him the ball, so I worked tirelessly at twisting and turning in tight spaces, with my body shielding the ball from an opponent's sight. I also tried to perfect the art of making the ball dance from one foot to the other, all the time keeping it tight on the end of my toes, never allowing it to leave the boot even by a few inches.

When I received a pass, I wouldn't trap the ball dead, then turn and flick it in front of me as many wingers did. I tried to control the pass and set myself up for a run at a defender all in one movement.

When an opponent denied me space in a game, it was up to me to create it. To shake off a tight marker as the ball was about to be played in to me, I'd quickly feint to go one way, only to snap back and go the other. I found it bought me a second or two in space and more often than not, that was all I needed to set up an attack or cross to a team-mate. It all seems par for the course nowadays, but in the late thirties, such tricks were almost unknown.

Another skill I introduced proved highly effective. If a defender jockeyed me into a position whereby I had my back to him and was facing the touchline, I would shield the ball from his vision with my body, keeping it in the space between my feet. Then I'd quickly step over the ball with my left foot and make with my upper body as if I was moving off to my right, only quickly to drag my left foot back, flick the ball in the other direction with the outside of my left boot and move off into space with the defender having gone to the right. In my training sessions I practised such skills incessantly.

— ○ —

Stoke started the 1937–38 season well and my own form was pleasing not just me but the sports writers and more importantly the England selectors. I won my fifth cap that November in the 2–1 victory over Wales at Middlesbrough's Ayresome Park and the following month, played in England's 5–4 win over Czechoslovakia at White Hart Lane. My performance against Czechoslovakia gave me considerable pleasure. I mixed my new style of taking the ball to the byline and cutting it back with the more traditional style of wing play, cutting inside. The Czechs found it hard to cope with and I led them a merry dance, ending up with a hat-trick. Three goals for England! It finally erased the awful memory of my last international appearance at White Hart Lane when I had played so poorly against Germany.

My performances for Stoke and England brought me good headlines in the newspapers and I found to my utter astonishment that I was becoming well-known beyond the Potteries. Letters poured in from all parts of Britain requesting autographs or photographs, sometimes in excess of 200 a day. I've always made a point of responding in person to letters from supporters, but it was hard to find the time to reply to such a volume of mail on a daily basis. Many of the letters didn't include return postage and the cost of stamps and stationery started to eat away at our budget. I was still on £5 a week and, although I'd be the first to admit this was far more than the weekly wage of the average working person, it was nothing compared to what film stars who received similar amounts of mail were earning at the time.

The majority of the letters were from genuine football supporters wishing me well and expressing their appreciation of the way I had been playing, but there was the occasional odd one. Some asked my opinion or advice on a whole range of matters. A woman from Walsall wrote to ask my view on birth control. I was just a footballer, what advice could I give on such a personal and emotive matter? I did reply, saying I didn't think I was the right person to ask about such a thing, but reminded her that as far as children in our family were concerned, I was the third.

Stoke-on-Trent is like a big village; word gets around very quickly. In the 1930s the sense of community was very strong. Rows and rows of terraced houses meant it was very close-knit and everyone seemed to know everyone else's business. The joke was if you sneezed in the house, they said 'bless you' four doors up the street. My performances for Stoke and England had thrust me into the limelight nationally and word got around that one or two of my Stoke City team-mates had become resentful of my new status. I have to say, I never at any time found any evidence of this in the dressing room where the team spirit and camaraderie between the players was first class. I received nothing but friendship from my Stoke team-mates, but the rumour persisted and grew. Everywhere I went in Stoke people would stop and ask me how I felt about it. I kept on denying there was any truth in this story but so often was the issue brought to my attention that, being young, I did begin to wonder if in fact there may be some substance to it.

The rumour of there being an anti-Matthews clique in the Stoke dressing room and the fact I felt the board had treated me less than well over the matter of the loyalty payment began to unsettle me. A week after my twenty-third birthday on my way to the ground for training, having been stopped yet again by several Stoke supporters wanting to know if the story of unrest in the dressing room was true, I decided I didn't need this hassle and it would be better to seek pastures new. I asked to see the Stoke City directors the same day, told them I was no longer happy at the club and would they see their way to granting me a transfer. They turned me down flat.

Later that day, I told Betty about my transfer request. She was upset but said she only wanted what was best for me and would support me in any career decision I made. The next morning my transfer request made headlines in the national papers, who had obviously been told by someone about that day's events. On the way to the ground, I had to be tactful not to get into arguments with the many Stoke supporters who came up to me and expressed their opinions on the matter. I've always been a peace-loving man, at pains to avoid even the slightest air of controversy, and I remember thinking if I'd only known what upset my transfer request would cause, I wouldn't have done it.

When the *Evening Sentinel* hit the streets, there was uproar. I knew I had a great many friends and supporters in Stoke but never realised their true strength of feeling as far as I was concerned. Within hours of the local paper declaring I was not happy at Stoke, a group of local businessmen who were staunch Stoke supporters called a public meeting at the Kings Hall to discuss the matter. Everywhere I went I saw posters and newspaper hoardings declaring 'Matthews Must Not Go'. People stopped me in the streets and the phone never stopped ringing. It was all getting too much for me. For all I loved performing in the big games, off the field I've always hankered after the quiet life. I asked the Stoke City board for a few days leave of absence which was granted and made my way home, telling Betty to pack a bag as we were going to get away from it all for a few days. She thought it a good idea and when she asked, 'Where to?' I suggested Blackpool. It was a town I had never visited – Blackpool had gained promotion from Division Two the previous season and Stoke had yet to play them away from home. It seemed an ideal bolt-hole.

'No one knows me there. We'll be able to get some peace and quiet,' I said, not knowing then, of course, the irony of my words and the decisive part Blackpool would play in my future career.

Before leaving, we decided to pay my mother and father a call. My father was tying his tie, getting ready to come round to our house to discuss the matter of the transfer request with me.

'Now what's all this about?' he asked.

I just shrugged my shoulders. My father stood in front of the fireplace with his hands behind him warming the palms.

'I hope you know what you're doing,' he said, 'because I don't.'

I told him I didn't have a grudge against the club, that

there was no truth in the rumour that some of my team-mates resented my high profile, only I felt it would be beneficial for me to have a change of scene. A new club and new surroundings would give my game fresh impetus.

'And how long do you think that would last before the same problem occurred again?' he said. 'You're 23 now, old enough to make your own decisions in life. But your game wouldn't be lifted by the simple fact you are playing with a different set of players or in front of different supporters. Your roots are here. The Stoke team are largely local lads. You've grown up here with the supporters and live alongside them. They love you because you're one of them. Do you realise how valuable you are to the club? You're a star attraction. Think what you must be worth to Stoke in extra gate revenue. I know the chairman says this is not about money, it's the principle of the matter. But when a man says that, son, believe me, it's always about the money. For that alone they won't let you go and I can't blame them.'

'But surely I've got the right to make up my own mind about where I want to play my football. It's a free country,' I said.

'Up to a point,' said my father. 'Don't get me wrong, I'm not telling you what to do. I'm just seeing it from a layman's point of view. You see, your exploits on the football field have given you celebrity status. In many respects that means you're no longer your own boss, you belong to the people now. It's the price of fame. The people of Stoke and Hanley will have something to say about this, mark my words, but I know you'll sort it out and in the right way so I'm not worried about it. As you journey through your career, accept the fame as your companion, but have reason as your guide.'

Betty and I set off for Blackpool with me turning my father's advice over in my head. We booked into a modest hotel and took a walk along the promenade. It was good to take in the sea air and even better that we were able to walk unbothered by passers-by. Blackpool was out of season and I was looking forward to a few days away from the transfer furore raging back in Stoke, but I'd greatly underestimated the investigative nose of the British press.

Throughout my life I have been fortunate enough to stay in some of the greatest hotels in the world, even the palaces of kings and presidential homes, but I've always had a fondness for the homely simplicity of seaside hotels and guest houses. The strip light above the sink mirror never works. The rooms always have a wardrobe big enough to accommodate the costumes from *South Pacific* and there's usually a burn mark on the lampshade of the bedside light. But stay in a five-star hotel and they give you a bar of soap the thickness of a book of matches that is useless after one wash. Stay in a seaside hotel and you always get a proper bar of soap. For decades these places must have kept the pink candlewick bedspread industry in business; for that alone I feel they deserve our affection and custom.

The next morning Betty and I sat down to breakfast, doing what everyone in a small seaside hotel does at meal times, counting the number of guests and trying to work out how much the owners are making. I was halfway through my bacon and egg when the hotel proprietor said there was a telephone call for me. I left the table wondering who on earth it could be; we had checked into the hotel on spec, even my parents didn't know where we were. The voice on the other end said he was a sports reporter from the *Daily Mirror* and I knew there and then our escape to Blackpool was doomed. Before breakfast was over, I'd received half a dozen calls and was in a quandary about what to do. A seventh call made my mind up for me. It came from the Stoke City chairman Albert Booth who informed me he wanted to see me 'in private as soon as possible'. Betty packed our bags and we were soon on our way back to the Potteries for another round of transfer talks.

I had it in my head that the Stoke directors would grant my request for the simple reason that if a player wants away it is better to let him go because there is no way an unsettled player can give of his best in games. Not for the first or last time in my life, I was proved wrong. Mr Booth told me in no uncertain terms, I was staying. For my part, I stuck to my request to leave and so we parted in total disagreement and with no progress having been made whatsoever.

For the next few days, my name was never out of the headlines. Newspapers were saying Everton, Newcastle United, Bolton, Derby, Leicester and current champions Manchester City were all chasing my signature. The phone never stopped ringing with reporters from the nationals to local weeklies wanting a quote on the matter of my possible move from Stoke.

The protest meeting called by leading Stoke City supporters took place with 3,000 people packed into the Kings Hall and an estimated thousand locked out. The meeting was chaired by Ashley Myott who basked in the grand title of 'Chairman of the Wages and Conditions Committee of the British Industrial and Pottery Manufacturers Federation'. Talk about a title going with the job! The supporters were adamant I should not be allowed to leave, with some pottery manufacturers even going so far as to say this whole affair was affecting their output, which seemed crazy to me. The meeting ended with supporters forming a deputation with the intention of staging separate meetings with Mr Booth and myself in an attempt to 'resolve the matter', which in their book was for me to stay.

I felt it only right to meet with the people who paid my wages and to put across my reasons for wanting to leave Stoke City, so I readily agreed to their request. In their meeting with the supporters, Mr Booth and his fellow directors reiterated their stance, saying I would have to see out the 1938–39 season with Stoke at the very least. However, come my meeting, so touched was I by the strength of feeling from the Stoke supporters, who after all were my own townsfolk, I began to have misgivings about my transfer request. That coupled with the fact that I had had quite enough of the controversy surrounding it finally swayed me. I decided to stay at the Victoria Ground. The first people I told of my decision were Betty and my mother and father.

'As far as I'm concerned, it's all settled now,' I told them. 'I'm staying at Stoke. I don't want to go through all that again.'

After the announcement of my decision to stay at Stoke, I really did notice smiling faces everywhere as I made my way to the ground for morning training. I felt a huge weight had been lifted from my shoulders. I had got something out of my system that had been eating away at me for a number of months and settled down to give of my all for Stoke, doing what I thought I did best – giving opposing defenders the runaround.

The 1937–38 season in the First Division proved a remarkable one in many ways. After a top-ten finish the previous year, I was a little disappointed in Stoke's final placing of seventeenth. However, to put this into context, that season proved to be one of the tightest on record in Division One with just 16 points separating champions Arsenal from the two teams who were relegated, Manchester City and West Bromwich Albion. As the First Division entered its final week, any one of 11 teams could have been relegated, including that year's FA Cup finalists Huddersfield Town who met Manchester City in an apocalyptic clash at Leeds Road. Huddersfield won 1–0, dooming Manchester City to Division Two. That was remarkable in itself because City with 80 goals were the highest scorers in Division One that season and had been champions only 12 months before.

I was chosen to play for England against Scotland at Wembley but once again the Scots turned us over winning 1–0 and again it was Hearts' Tommy Walker who broke English hearts, scoring the only goal. I made a mental note of the young Scottish right-half who was making his international debut that day, one Bill Shankly. He came across as single-minded, boisterous, passionate and with a heart as big as a bucket in his desire to win, qualities that were never to leave him throughout his career as a player and manager.

5

Making the Nazis
Storm Out

The 1937–38 season over, I was chosen for the England summer tour of the Continent. In 1997, the football magazine *FourFourTwo* described one of the games as one of the greatest ever in the history of football – Germany v. England at the Olympic Stadium on the 14 May 1938.

European travel in the pre-war years was a matter of catching ferries and trains. In 1938, a trip to Germany for a game was arduous but for the entire journey I had only one thing on my mind – my return clash with the German full-back Münzenberg who had outplayed me when the two teams last met at White Hart Lane. I was looking forward to playing against Münzenberg again. The press hadn't made anything of it, but I felt I had something to prove to myself.

The word 'Sudetenland' was on the tip of everyone's tongue. The fear was that Nazi Germany was about to invade this German-speaking part of Czechoslovakia, having some weeks earlier occupied Austria. The headlines were along the lines of 'Storm Clouds Are Brewing Over Europe', but in truth the brewing was almost over and the pouring about to begin.

We arrived in Berlin to what can only be described as a polite but sober welcome. I don't think any of the England players knew what Nazi fascism meant but we quickly came to realise that, whatever it stood for, warm friendship and humour were not on its list of priorities. On the face of it, pre-war Berlin came across as a beautiful city, but I quickly discovered such beauty was confined to its architecture and buildings. Berlin seemed a city of gaiety, laughter wafting out from its cafés and bars, but there was an air of menace and foreboding about the place. I've always been deeply suspicious of countries where the image of the leader is forced upon the population and wherever I looked in Berlin, there was a statue, poster, flag or hoarding depicting the face of the Führer. Eddie Hapgood joked he looked just like a former girlfriend of his, only according to Eddie, the ex-girlfriend's moustache was bigger.

Having booked into the hotel, the players had a bit of free time. I went out for a walk with Bert Sproston, a tough and uncompromising full-back with Leeds United. Bert was a down-to-earth lad who, according to the joke of the time, lived on a diet of raw meat and wingers like me. Bert and I walked around the streets near our hotel, just to get our bearings, and eventually called into a small café. We had just sat down with a pot of tea between us when the other patrons suddenly leapt to their feet in great excitement. One by one the local customers and café staff all rushed to the door. Not knowing the reason for such a commotion, Bert and I stayed where we were. I was suddenly aware of a cavalcade of cars going past and, as they did so, everyone who had rushed outside raised their arm in the Nazi salute before breaking into spontaneous applause.

'Sounds like some grande fromage has just passed by,' I said to Bert.

A tall man standing by the door heard me and turning to Bert and me said in perfect English, 'You underestimate the importance of the occasion, gentlemen. That was our beloved Führer gracing us with his presence.'

Not wanting to cause a scene, Bert and I just smiled and nodded. After all, the guy had been pleasant enough. For a moment neither Bert nor I said anything as the excited café patrons took to their seats once again. Then Bert leaned across the table.

'Stan,' he whispered, 'I'm just a workin' lad from Leeds. I've not 'ad much of an education and I know nowt 'bout politics and t'like. All I knows is football. But t'way I see it, yon 'Itler fella is an evil little twat.'

The game against Germany took on a significance far beyond football. The Nazi propaganda machine saw it as an opportunity to display Third Reich superiority and played up that disconcerting theme big style in the German newspapers. The German team had spent ten days preparing for the game at a special training centre in the Black Forest, whereas after a long and tiresome train journey, we had less than two days to prepare for what we knew was going to be a game of truly epic proportions, a game which to this day is looked upon as the most infamous game England have ever been involved in and all due to one incident.

After all this time, and once and for all, I would like to set the record straight about that incident. As the players were getting changed, an FA official came into our dressing room and informed us that when our national anthem was played, the German team would salute as a mark of respect.

The FA wanted us to reciprocate by giving the raised arm Nazi salute during the playing of the German national anthem. The dressing room erupted. There was bedlam. All the England players were livid and totally opposed to this, myself included. Everyone was shouting at once. Eddie Hapgood, normally a respectful and devoted captain, wagged his finger at the official and told him what he could do with the Nazi salute, which involved putting it where the sun doesn't shine. In fact, Eddie went so far as to offer a compromise, saying we would stand to attention military style but the offer fell on deaf ears.

I sat there crestfallen, thinking what on earth my family and the people back home would think if they saw me and the rest of the England team paying lip service, so to speak, to the Nazi regime and its leaders.

The beleaguered FA official left only to return some minutes later saying he had a direct order from Sir Neville Henderson the British Ambassador in Berlin that had been endorsed by the FA secretary Stanley Rous. We were told that the political situation between Great Britain and Germany was now so sensitive that it needed 'only a spark to set Europe alight'. Faced with the knowledge of the direst consequences, we felt we had little choice in the matter and reluctantly agreed to the request. However, the game was different. We knew we had it in our power to do something about the match itself and to a man we took the field determined to do so.

All of 110,000 people were crammed into the Olympic Stadium, including Goering and Goebbels, and they roared their approval as the German team took the field. If ever men in the cause of sport felt isolated and so very far from their homes, it was the England team that day in Berlin. The Olympic Stadium was draped in red, black and white swastikas with a large portrait of Hitler above the stand where the Nazi leaders and dignitaries sat. It seemed every supporter on the massed terraces had a smaller version of the

My father Jack Matthews, boxer and barber. He started me on my physical training regime at an early age, and was the inspiration for my career. (Stanley Matthews)

Early days at Stoke. Note the string to tie up my shorts! (Colorsport)

Alongside Freddie Steele in January 1933, the year I began to establish myself in the Stoke City side. I was still a few weeks short of my eighteenth birthday. (Allsport/Hulton Getty)

Debutant Ted Drake tangles with the Italian keeper, Ceresoli, in England's 1934 game against Italy. For all that they were world champions, the game descended into some of the dirtiest play I was ever involved in. (Popperfoto)

Although we beat Germany 3–0 in our December 1935 game at White Hart Lane, I had my worst ever international playing against the German left-back, Munzenberg. Here the German goalkeeper clears from George Camsell, who scored two goals on the day. (Popperfoto)

In action for England against Wales at Ayresome Park in November 1937 when I scored my second goal for England. (Popperfoto)

The infamous Nazi salute in Berlin, May 1938. It was a shameful moment, but you can just make out that the England players are looking slightly to their left towards two fans waving a Union Jack. They helped inspire us to a thumping 6–3 victory. (Popperfoto)

Tommy Lawton scores from my cross in this 1942 wartime international against Scotland. Two of the greatest post-war managers, Bill Shankly (left) and Matt Busby (left of Lawton), were playing for Scotland. Their success as managers has meant that people have forgotten what good players they were. (Hulton Getty)

In wartime action in March 1943. Although all league matches and full internationals were abandoned, many games were played to help raise morale. (Allsport/Hulton Getty)

Moscow Dynamo come on to the pitch at Stamford Bridge bearing flowers for their Chelsea opponents. They drew huge crowds wherever they went, but sadly my game against them was all but lost in the fog. (Hulton Getty)

Picking up an award from the mayor of Stoke for passing Eddie Hapgood's record of 43 appearances for England. It was my first opportunity for public speaking – and I was dreading it. (Huston Spratt)

Len Shackleton, the clown prince of soccer, in action for Bradford Park Avenue. One of my favourite pictures – put your finger over the ball and he could be dancing. (Huston Spratt)

In the crush at Burnden Park women are passed down over people's heads to the front. Thirty-three people died in March 1946 during this Cup tie between Bolton and Stoke. It was a crime to finish the game after this. (Hulton Getty)

A real class act. Tom Finney in action for Preston North End in 1947. After England's poor showing in the 1950 World Cup, he and I were the only two who wanted to stay on to see what we could learn from the other teams. Unfortunately we were told it couldn't be arranged. (Huston Spratt)

The Stoke City team that just missed out on winning the championship in May 1947. I was missing from this picture as I had just been sold to Blackpool, as manager Bob McGrory seemed to dislike my high profile in the game. (Huston Spratt)

When Great Britain took on the Rest of Europe in May 1947 the hype was incredible – 135,000 packed into Hampden Park. Wilf Mannion (left) completes his hat-trick following a cross from me. Britain won 6–1 in what was billed as the Match of the Century. (Huston Spratt)

swastika and they held them aloft in a silent show of collective defiance as the England team ran out.

During the pre-match kick-in, I went behind our goal to retrieve a wayward ball and an amazing thing happened. As I curled my foot around the ball to steer it back towards the pitch, two lone voices called out, 'Let them have it, Stan. Come on England!'

I scanned the sea of faces and the hundreds of swastikas before I saw the most uplifting sight I have ever seen at a football ground. There, right at the front of the terracing, were two Englishmen who had draped a small Union Jack over the perimeter fencing in front of them. Whether they were civil servants from the British Embassy, on holiday or what I don't know, but the brave and uplifting words of those two solitary English supporters among 110,000 Nazis had a profound effect on me and the rest of the England team that day.

When I got back on to the pitch I pointed out the two supporters to our captain Eddie Hapgood and the word spread throughout the team. We all looked across to these two doughty men, who responded by raising the thumbs of their right hands in encouragement. As a team we were immediately galvanised, determined and uplifted by the courage of these two supporters and their small Union Jack. Up to that point, I had never given much thought to our national flag. That afternoon however, small as that particular version was, it took on the greatest of symbolism for me and my England team-mates. It seemed to stand for everything we believed in, everything we had left behind in England and wanted to preserve. Above all, it reminded me that we were not after all alone.

The photograph of the England team giving the Nazi salute appeared in newspapers throughout the world the next day to the eternal shame of every player and Britain as a whole. But look closely at the photograph and you will see the German team looking straight ahead but the England players looking off to their left. I can tell you that all our eyes were fixed upon that Union Jack from which we were drawing the inspiration that would carry us to a fantastic and memorable victory.

The England team that day was: Woodley (Chelsea); Sproston (Leeds United), Hapgood (Arsenal); Willingham, Young (both Huddersfield Town), Welsh (Charlton Athletic); Matthews (Stoke City), Robinson (Sheffield Wednesday), Broome (Aston Villa), Goulden (West Ham United), Bastin (Arsenal).

As the teams lined up for the kick-off I looked across at my adversary Münzenberg. He was without doubt a formidable man with a neck that looked like it could dent an axe. He stared across at me with an inscrutable look on his face, but his boxing-style eyeballing didn't unnerve me at all. I was licking my lips at the prospect of taking on him and his team-mates, knowing I had improved immeasurably since our last encounter.

From the kick-off we tore into the Germans. Even allowing for football's great capacity to surprise or pull the carpet from under you, there are some games you just know are going to go your way even after a few minutes because you sense every player in your team is up for it and on top form. This was one of them.

The game was a few minutes old when Bert Sproston linked up with Huddersfield's Ken Willingham to feed me the ball out on the right. With the instep of my right boot I controlled the pass and set myself up for a run at Münzenberg. I was full of confidence and eager to get at him knowing he was probably thinking he was in for an easy afternoon. That being the case, I felt I was one up on him already. I took the ball right up to him, just as I had done in our first encounter and figured Münzenberg would think I would swerve one way only to attempt to take the ball past him in the other direction. I bore down on him and timed it right, so that even another step would have shown him too much of the ball enabling him to get a tackle in. I swerved to the left, got the toe of my right boot under the ball, flicked it over his left shoulder, carried on running to my left and met the ball behind him. I ran at three-quarter pace knowing Münzenberg could turn quickly and would be hot on my heels. I could hear his studs picking out the turf behind me. He would have to adjust his position to get goal-side of me in order to make a telling tackle and sure enough I suddenly became aware he was just behind me on my left side. So I prodded the ball a couple of feet in front of me and he saw his chance of making the tackle. In the split second he took to launch himself, I accelerated full pace, pushing the ball into space in front of me and he tackled fresh air. Looking up, I saw Frank Broome making good progress down the middle and cut the ball back to him. Frank took the pass in his stride before letting loose with a piledriver that took the tips off the blades of grass only to flash narrowly wide. I looked at the German defenders who, having been caught out by the speed of our attack, had arrived late into the penalty box. Their faces had fallen. They were rattled.

We took the lead through Cliff Bastin and, although Germany equalised, England continued to dominate the first half. My confidence soared as time and again I got the better of Münzenberg. I was pulling out all the stops, he returned again and again but never once did he win the ball from me.

Halfway through the first half, with England well on top and hardly a swastika to be seen on the terraces, I received a beauty of a pass from Robinson and took off down the right, only this time I decided to cut inside and head for goal. My pace was enough to take me past two German defenders and just as I cut into the penalty area I let fly. To be truthful, I never had the hardest of shots, but with the goalkeeper expecting me to shoot across his body into the far corner, I went for the space between him and his left-hand post. He got down pretty quick, but not quick enough. I was on the scoresheet and as we trooped off at half-time, I wasn't the only England player to have found the back of the net. The scoreboard told an unbelievable story – Germany 2 England 4.

The England changing room was situated right at the very top of the main stand which meant, after a walk down a tunnel that made Wembley's seem like the lobby of a terraced house, we had to climb about 90 concrete steps before reaching it. We took to that walk as if we were a group of high-spirited lads making our way to the local pub for a night out. We were all in a buoyant and excited mood, but the best was yet to come in the form of what was probably the greatest goal I ever saw in football, courtesy of Len Goulden.

In the second half, Alf Young broke down a German attack and played the ball to Charlton's Don Welsh who was making his England debut. We came out of defence with a series of one-touch passes that left the Germans chasing shadows before the ball was finally played out to me on the right. I took off towards Münzenberg, by now run ragged. Such was my confidence that as I ran towards him, I criss-crossed my legs over the ball as I ran and, on reaching him, swept the ball past him with the outside of my right boot and followed it. I could hear Münzenberg and the German left-half panting behind me. I glanced across and saw Len Goulden steaming in just left of the centre of midfield, some 35 yards from goal. I arced around the ball in order to get some power behind the cross and picked my spot just ahead of Len. He met the ball at around knee height. My initial thought was that he'd control it and take it on to get nearer the German goal, but he didn't. Len met the ball on the run; without surrendering any pace, his left leg cocked back like the trigger of a gun, snapped forward and he met the ball full face on the volley. To use modern parlance, his shot was like an Exocet missile. The German goalkeeper may well have seen it coming, but he could do absolutely nothing about it. From 25 yards the ball screamed into the roof of the net with such power that the netting was ripped from two of the pegs by which it was tied to the crossbar. The terraces of the packed Olympic Stadium were as lifeless as a string of dead fish.

'Let them salute that one,' Len yelled as he carried on running, arms aloft.

We'd been given little chance, but when the final whistle sounded, the scoreline of Germany 3 England 6 told its own story. As well as myself, the England goals that day came from Robinson (2), Bastin, Broome and Len Goulden's Exocet. It was perhaps the finest England performance I was ever involved in. Every player was at the top of his game, to a man we played out of our skins and Len Goulden's goal will live forever in the memory. If there had been televised football in those days, Len's goal would never have been off the screens. It was truly marvellous. Only when the heat and the tiredness from travelling got to us late in the second half did we slow down, but by then Germany were a well-beaten side.

As we left the pitch I glanced over to our source of inspiration. Our two fellow countrymen had taken their Union Jack down from the perimeter fencing and were dancing a jig, manically waving it above their heads. I looked up at the VIP section of the stand and there was a row of empty seats where Goering, Goebbels and other members of the Nazi hierarchy had been sitting. We later learned that with some ten minutes remaining, and with no chance of Germany getting back into the game, they had stormed off in a strop, just as they had done two years earlier in that very same stadium when that great American athlete Jesse Owens put the theory of the Nazi master race in its place at the 1936 Olympics.

I sat in the dressing room watching my England team-mates cock-a-hoop, celebrating what we knew was a great victory. I didn't dance or whoop and shout. I simply sat in silence sipping my tea. After the exertions of what had been a pulsating game, I had a great feeling of quiet contentment. I felt at peace with myself, happy in the knowledge that I had proved a point; when much had been asked of me, I had not been found wanting. I was never one to go overboard in the wake of a victory, even one as momentous as this, knowing only too well that in football, like life, from the sublime to the ridiculous is usually only a matter of one single step.

— o —

England took that single step in our next match against Switzerland. Hours after the exhilaration of our victory over Germany, we boarded a train for the 13-hour rail journey to Zurich. I'm not making excuses, but it was a tiresome trip. We were physically exhausted after the game in Berlin and the euphoria following our win there put a drain on our mental strength. The game against Switzerland was, on paper, a much easier match than the one against the Germans and I think this also had a negative effect. We thought we were in for an easy ride.

I was reading a novel to pass the time when Alf Young sat down next to me. Alf had played for Huddersfield in that heartbreaking Cup final against Preston a few weeks before.

That game must have left its mark on Alf, as on every Huddersfield player, but his professionalism and indefatigable spirit were pulling him through and he seemed to be getting on with the job in hand. Alf, who was from Sunderland, had been spotted playing for Durham City in 1927 and signed for Huddersfield Town that year. He quickly graduated through the ranks at Leeds Road to become Huddersfield's captain in 1935 and a year later, following a series of outstanding performances, won his second England cap, four years after his debut, in a 6–2 win over Hungary at Highbury. Alf was what in those days was termed 'a fine pivot'. He was a colossus of a centre-half, a restless powerhouse, but a player of calm authority whose physical attributes belied a warm and friendly nature.

Alf told me I was in for the time of my life in the game against Switzerland. When I asked him, 'How come?' he went on to tell me the Swiss left-back, Lehmann, was only a part-time professional who, far from having a day job, had a night job as a dance-band leader in a Zurich hotel.

'He'll be up till just before dawn the night before the game, Stan,' Alf informed me. 'After half an hour of trying to chase you around, they'll be putting him in an oxygen tent.'

The other England players in the carriage joined in the conversation and it gave me an uneasy feeling. They were too confident.

At the Grand Dolder Hotel, which was the base for the England team for our stay in Zurich, I was interviewed by the sports journalist Ivan Sharpe, a former professional player of some note. Ivan took me out on to the lawn at the rear of the hotel and, throwing me a football, asked me to give him a demonstration of 'how I did it'. I put my foot on the ball, studied it for a moment, then flicked it in the air before catching it and throwing it back to him.

'I can't do it,' I told Ivan in all honesty, 'not in cold blood.

There has to be the pressure to perform, someone to pit my wits and skills against. Don't ask me why. It only comes to me then. It's as if it's all held in reserve until the pressure of a game and the battle against my opposite number releases it. Then I can do it.'

Zurich had had 30 hours of continuous rain prior to the game and the pitch at the Hardsturm Stadium resembled Passchendaele. The pre-match talk between the England players had been very light-hearted, in sharp contrast to the Germany game. As I got changed into my strip, I didn't feel comfortable about the game at all. As we were warming up prior to the kick-off, an aeroplane swooped low over the stadium and dropped the match ball on to the pitch. It was a novel way to start the game and why it was done I don't know, but it all added to the light-hearted approach everyone was seemingly taking to this international. I say everyone, but in truth, the laissez-faire attitude was predominantly in the England ranks, as we were to find out immediately the match got under way.

We started well, bossing the match for the first 30 minutes or so. I thought that we were in for an easy afternoon after all. I was skipping past Lehmann and supplying a steady stream of crosses into the Swiss penalty area, but for all our dominance, the scoreline remained 0–0. Just after the half-hour mark, Switzerland broke away and following a cross from their right, their left winger Aeby stole in at the far post to head them in front.

The Swiss goal put some urgency into our play and as once again we laid siege, Sheffield Wednesday's Jackie Robinson was brought down in the Swiss penalty box and Cliff Bastin tucked away the subsequent penalty with typical aplomb. Far from geeing us up and denting the enthusiasm of the Swiss, that goal served only to lull us back into our previous state of indolence. Switzerland took full advantage. Lehmann may well have got to bed at four in the morning, arms tired from conducting 'Tiger Rag' and the like, but he suddenly came to life. He started to tackle me like a tiger and I have to say, at times, he ran me ragged. In the dressing room at half-time I went across to Alf Young.

'That bandleader's moonlighting, Alf,' I told him. 'He's starting to conduct this game, doing a bit of orchestrating out there on the pitch. I don't know what he's on, but whatever it is, I wish he'd give you lot some of it.'

Alf smiled and for a moment said nothing. He was having an epic battle with Bickel, the Swiss centre-forward, a nightclub doorman.

'They're all nocturnal, Stan. The bloody daylight is putting a spring into their step. They'll tire in the second half. They've had their 15 minutes.'

From the restart we tore into the Swiss, but they were up to everything we threw at them. On three occasions, when the Swiss goalkeeper was beaten, the woodwork came to his rescue. With 17 minutes remaining, Alf Young tried to breast down a centre from the right, the ball ricocheted off his beer-barrel chest, hit a clump of mud and as he moved in towards it bounced back at him and struck him on the arm. The German referee pointed immediately to the spot with Alf imploring the handball was unintentional. Abegglen, the Swiss inside-left, tucked the penalty away and we were then batting for an equaliser against the clock. We camped out in and around the Swiss penalty area but try as we did, the equalising goal remained elusive. Switzerland ran out 2–1 winners and all credit to them. The penalty against us had been highly questionable but they had battled throughout and defended magnificently.

After the game the England dressing room was subdued to say the least. Alf Young was adamant the penalty had been a case of 'ball to hand' rather than 'hand to ball'.

'For all that, you can't take anything away from them,' I said. 'They took everything we threw at them. They defended well and their goalkeeper had a very good game.'

'Not as good as his right-hand post,' said Jackie Robinson. 'That bloody post played a blinder.'

In the post-match players' get-together, my opposite number Lehmann invited me to come and watch his band in action.

'It's a very good band. The drummer plays the drums with both sticks and our piano player can even play the black notes,' he joked.

I politely turned down his offer. The travelling on the tour was tiring enough and to stay up until four in the morning I knew would knock my body clock and metabolism out of synch for weeks. Besides, five days later we were due in Paris for a big game against France. The travelling was unrelenting.

— ○ —

The mood of the England party was somewhat subdued on the train into France. We had managed to get hold of some English newspapers and the sports writers were far from happy with the way we had approached and played the game against Switzerland. The papers were right on this score, but the Swiss defeat had shaken us up and we were determined to repeat our success over Germany against a much-fancied French side.

There was a dogged professionalism in the way we set about the game against France. The England selectors made a number of changes to the team. Charlton's Don Welsh made way for Stan Cullis of Wolves. I was moved to inside-right in place of Jackie Robinson, with Aston Villa's Frank Broome moving to the right wing and his place at centre-forward being taken by Arsenal's Ted Drake.

Ted was a big man with a big heart and he was prolific in front of goal. In 1935, he had scored all seven goals for Arsenal in a 7–1 win at Aston Villa, the most amazing thing being, he had only eight chances in the whole of that game and had put all but one of them away – the other chance hit the crossbar! It spoke volumes for his ability. The word profligacy didn't feature in his vocabulary. Ted's seven-goal haul at Aston Villa ensured his name will live long in football history, but goals apart, he turned in many better performances and the game against France was one of them.

The pressure was on England to bounce back against a French team considered to be far and away a better side than Switzerland. I relished the big-match atmosphere and as soon as the game got under way I knew I was on for the palmiest of days. Everything I did came off and my England colleagues, having shaken off the lackadaisical attitude so evident against the Swiss, set about the French with vigour. Ted Drake turned in a masterful performance. He hurled himself around in the French penalty area, his robust, barnstorming style always a source of trouble to France, and he ended the game with two goals to his name. We ran out comfortable 4–2 winners with our other goals coming from Frank Broome and Cliff Bastin.

The win in Paris restored our prestige and brought the continental tour to a close. We'd beaten two of the strongest sides in Europe, which went some way towards putting the Swiss débâcle into perspective, though the easy attitude with which some of the England players approached the Swiss game disappointed me greatly. To represent your country is the highest honour that can be bestowed upon a player. National pride is at stake and irrespective of the opposition, every international match must be taken seriously and tackled with the utmost professionalism. We'd redeemed ourselves in Paris but a defeat against one of the so-called weaker continental sides tarnished the great work and effort put in against Germany and France.

Throughout the tour, even though my mind had been totally focused on football, I had written home every day. Once the game against France was done and dusted, I was smitten with homesickness and couldn't wait to get back to my family and friends in Stoke. The journey seemed interminable – train from Paris to Calais, ferry across the Channel, bus ride to Dover station, train from Dover to London, underground across London to Euston, train to Stoke changing at Nuneaton. When my train finally pulled into Stoke, I had the carriage door open before it stopped. There on the platform to greet me were Betty and my mother and father.

We talked excitedly as we walked home and after tea, when my mother and father had gone home, Betty and I sat down by the fire. I told her all about the England tour. I wished she had been there with me. She would have loved seeing Paris and Zurich. Although I had enjoyed the experience, it was one-dimensional. I would have enjoyed it far more if she had been there to share it all with me. Tour talk over, I asked Betty for her news.

'Oh, you know Stoke,' she said matter of factly. 'Nothing earth shattering ever happens here. Though I do have one piece of great news.'

'Go on then,' I said, sitting up wondering what on earth it could be.

'I'm pregnant,' she said with a beaming smile on her face. I couldn't say anything. A divine mixture of happiness, excitement, wonderment, contentment, love, satisfaction and joy swept through me in one fell swoop.

'Are you pleased?' Betty asked.

Of course I was. It was the best news I'd ever had in my life.

6

---○---

Scotland Defeated
at Last

The summer of 1938 was a glorious one. The filter at Hanley swimming baths broke down in the hottest week of the year; the newspapers ran 'What A Scorcher' headlines; and the new football season kicked off on one of the hottest days of the year. Autumnal weather and rain arrived a week later, and everyone said, 'Well, I suppose that was the summer.'

For all the golden sunshine, dark clouds loomed on the political front. Neville Chamberlain returned from meeting with Daladier, Hitler and Mussolini in Munich, waving his piece of paper promising 'peace in our time', and for a while everyone was buoyed. We didn't know that 'our time' would be so short.

For all the uncertainty in Europe, I was a very happy man indeed. Betty and I were looking forward to the birth of our first child and somehow I couldn't believe that the idyllic life we were enjoying would ever end. After the

Munich agreement, I convinced myself that war was not on the agenda, no matter what happened in Germany or the countries bordering it, it would not affect Britain.

Stoke City got off to a good start and once again reaped the benefits of producing home-grown players, with Frank Baker and Billy Mould really coming into their own during this season. For a time there was even talk of us being dark horses for the championship. Freddie Steele continued to score freely, I was playing well but in the end Stoke had to settle for a respectable seventh position, well adrift of the eventual champions Everton. Their young centre-forward, Tommy Lawton, did his utmost to do what sports writers thought was the impossible – fill the boots of the legendary Dixie Dean.

I was picked to play for England against Wales on 22 October and managed to score on my international return to Cardiff, but we went down 4–2 to a strong Welsh side inspired by Aston Villa's Dai Astley, who scored twice, and Idris Hopkins. England went on to beat the Rest of Europe 3–0 at Highbury before crushing Norway 4–0 at Newcastle on 9 November. I felt I was giving a good account of myself at international level and a week later I was selected to play for the Football League against the Scottish League at Molineux, the home of Wolverhampton Wanderers. The game was due to be played just seven days before a full international between England and Ireland at Old Trafford and was considered a last chance for players to stake a claim for a place in the England team. In addition to my club football, that was four full internationals and one league representative game in less than a month, and you hear today's top players complaining about having to play too many games at the top level!

In the thirties, no matter how well a player had played for England in previous internationals, that counted for nothing when the team for the next game was chosen. The selectors went on club form in between internationals and if you had a poor match for your club on the day the selectors came to see you, hard cheese, you were out. That's the way it was, a far cry from today when a player can be picked for his country even when he is unable to get into his club side. A prime example of this is Kevin Keegan's first game in charge of England for the European Championship qualifier against Poland in 1999. Steve McManaman, then with Liverpool, played even though he had not been in the Liverpool side for some time. Anyone who can remember that game will recall McManaman's performance as less than flattering to the lad. We've all had games like that, but how a player not currently considered good enough for his club side can be thought good enough for international football is beyond me.

The Football League outplayed the Scottish League at Molineux. Our dominance was greater than the 3–1 winning scoreline suggested. I was happy enough with my performance; the ball flowed freely to me out on the right wing and I provided a constant supply of crosses for our forwards. My inside partner for this game was Tottenham's Willie Hall. Willie was a grand lad and a bit of an all-round sportsman. In addition to being a stylish inside-forward, adept at taking chances, he was also an accomplished tennis player and golfer.

Willie and I chatted away in the dressing room after the game, both knowing we had turned in good performances and that, all things being equal, we would line up together the following week for England's game against Ireland. When we were leaving, we shook hands, Willie saying what a pleasure it had been to play alongside me and me saying likewise. I made the short journey from Wolverhampton back to Stoke in a very happy frame of mind, thinking what a friendly and generous chap Willie Hall was. At breakfast the next day I opened my morning paper to read the report of the previous night's game and was shocked at the headline: MATTHEWS STARVES HALL OUT OF ENGLAND TEAM. I couldn't believe it. I was so angry I wanted to ring the newspaper concerned to take up the issue with the journalist responsible for writing such tosh, but thankfully I thought better of it. I wondered what Willie Hall was thinking. He had left Molineux believing he had a good game, which he had. Surely he wouldn't go along with this nonsense?

When I arrived for morning training at the Victoria Ground, everyone had seen the story. Over the years I have learned not to take what the newspapers say to heart, even when they are at their most complimentary. That day, however, I did take it seriously. They were implying I had been selfish and ignored Willie Hall in order to further my own claim for a place in the England team. Nothing could have been further from the truth.

I spent a miserable 24 hours and when the news came through from the FA that I had been picked to play against Ireland my first reaction was to ask if Willie Hall had made the team. When I was informed he had, I felt a great weight lift from my shoulders. The press gave little column space to the story in the days leading up to the Ireland match, but as the England team assembled in Manchester, I was determined to bury it forever by providing Willie with the sort of service that would give him a game to remember for the rest of his life.

On arriving at England's hotel, one of the first players I met was Willie Hall. He told me he was as surprised and shocked as anyone at the allegations in the press. He was adamant it had nothing to do with him and I had no reason to doubt him. When Willie asked for the room placings to be changed so that he and I could be room-mates, I knew he was as keen to scotch the ugly story as I was.

For all this, I knew that once the game against Ireland got under way, there would be certain sports writers keeping a keen eye on my service to Willie. I shouldn't have let it be an issue in my initial thinking because as it turned out, I was on top form that day and so too was Willie Hall. From the kick-off Willie and I read each other like well-worn books. He knew when to push on, when to drop back and when to come on the outside of me. We had a field day and I felt sorry for the Irish left-back, Everton's Billy Cook, because Willie and I tore him and the Irish defence apart that afternoon. Willie scored five times, a record for an international match.

During the second half, after I'd once again taken the ball past Billy Cook to lay on a centre for the England forwards, Billy grabbed hold of me by the arm.

'Stan, if you bring that ball near me once more, I'll wring your neck,' Billy said. 'You've twisted and turned me so many times, I've been drilled into the ground up to my knees. You're just making me look silly now, so why don't you give me a break and bugger off across to the other wing.'

I burst out laughing and Billy patted me on the shoulder. He was what in those days was referred to as a dapper man, but he was also a great sport. I just can't imagine a player of today responding in such a good-humoured way to such a roasting.

Seven minutes from the end I produced a bit of a party piece. Receiving the ball just inside the England half, I headed for the Irish goal on a corkscrew dribble that took me past five Irish players. As I reached the penalty area, Billy Cook came towards me. I slipped the ball between his legs, ran round him and took off again with the ball at my feet and Billy in my wake. Twomey, the Irish goalkeeper who played for Leeds United, came off his line. I shimmied one way, he went that way and I went the other before sidefooting the ball into the empty net. Old Trafford was filled with a resounding roar and a sight now long since disappeared from football grounds. Thousands of caps and hats were thrown into the air.

I ran back towards my England team-mates, who were running towards me, and passed Billy Cook, standing forlorn with his hands on his hips.

'Stan, seeing that goal gave me great pleasure,' said Billy. Then he thrust his hands out in front of him, palms upturned, and asked in a bemused way, 'Why?'

Tommy Lawton got our other goal. The final score was England 7 Ireland 0. The game was Willie Hall's greatest triumph at international level. Try as I did to see certain newspapers writing that they had got it wrong following the Football League game against the Scots, I saw not a word to that effect in the next day's papers. It didn't bother me – I was happy to do my talking on the pitch.

Willie was full of emotion back in the dressing room and cried unashamedly as each of his team-mates in turn congratulated him on his outstanding performance and his England goalscoring match record. He was the most un-assuming of men, modest to a fault. His unselfish play and great contribution to a game was never truly appreciated by the sports writers of the day.

Eight years later, following World War Two, Willie had his right foot amputated. Some 12 months after that, thrombosis meant he had to have his left leg amputated. On a post-war trip to London for a game, I took time out to pay him a visit. He met me at the door on crutches with a beaming smile on his face. I smiled back but inside my heart bled to see such a tremendous sportsman and warm-hearted human being in such circumstances. As he made his ungainly way back into his lounge, telling me how delighted he was to see me, I asked him how he was coping.

'Not so bad, Stan,' he said with typical gusto, 'not so bad at all, but there is one thing that troubles me and has started to give me sleepless nights.'

'What's that?' I asked uncomfortably.

'Every time I come across a kid's ball or a stone on the street, I can sense my left leg going to kick it and it has started to get my back up,' he said, 'because every time it happens, I find myself kicking over the top of the ball and you know me Stan, I never used to do that. I always hit it cleanly!' He roared with laughter as he settled into his armchair. He was a man of great courage and whenever I find myself worrying over small matters in life, I think back to Willie Hall – a great sportsman, a terrific inside-right, a warm and generous man who looked adversity and personal tragedy in the eye and found the courage and humour to laugh in its face; a truly remarkable guy.

=== o ===

On New Year's day 1939, I became the father of a beautiful little girl. In those days, the father's presence at the actual birth was not considered necessary and was, in fact, actively discouraged by doctors. Betty went into hospital on New Year's Eve and I remained at home on tenterhooks awaiting news. On New Year's night I sat at home listening to the radio and passers-by celebrating and eventually dozed off by the fire. I was suddenly awoken in the wee small hours by the harsh ringing of the telephone and leapt out of the chair in my haste to answer it. The voice of a nurse gave me the joyous news, 'It's a girl, Mr Matthews, and both she and your wife are healthy and well.' I thanked the voice on the end of the phone, punched the air with my fist and slumped back into my armchair a very happy man. I closed my eyes again but not to sleep; instead, I thanked God with all my heart.

We called her Jean and I was at the hospital early enough on New Year's morning to see the first cup of tea of the day being brought round. When I held Jean in my arms for the very first time, I knew I was the happiest man in the world. People say the birth of a child changes your life and you nod in agreement without ever realising just how much. For a start, your priorities change. My daily routine was turned upside down and I found myself doing things I never imagined I would do. It must have been humorous to my parents and close friends. Overnight, parenthood had taken a grip of me and my whole conversation changed. In front of Jean I started to refer to Betty as Mummy. I acquired a whole new shelf of books on baby health and development. I took two rolls of film capturing everything Jean had done and she was only a week old, and I found myself telling people what the weather had been like at half two in the morning. The first six weeks were shattering, but I wouldn't have swapped them for the world.

The 1938–39 season drew to a close. I had been playing well for Stoke City and although there had been no internationals since the Ireland game in November, England were due to play Scotland in April and I was very hopeful of retaining my place in the side. I thought Everton's young centre-forward Tommy Lawton, who finished the season as Division One's top goalscorer with 34 goals, would be selected, too. He had made his debut in the 4–2 defeat against Wales back in October and had scored four goals in his four international appearances to date.

Tommy was a model centre-forward who went on to have a chequered career, moving from club to club for what were at the time huge transfer fees. He started out at Burnley and such was his talent he made the first team at 16 becoming the youngest centre-forward to play league football. He joined Everton in 1937 as understudy to the great but ageing Dixie Dean and played a key role in helping Everton to the championship in the last full season before war intervened. Tommy possessed a rocket of a shot and, like all great players, could hit the ball equally well with either foot. He was lethal in the air and, most surprisingly for a centre-forward of the time, had all the ball skill and creative prowess of the most mercurial of inside-forwards. Tommy was a goal-getter, a towering athlete with a seemingly elasticated neck that enabled him to rise that inch or so above defenders, which he did often to devastating effect. With his shirt unbuttoned so that it appeared to be sliding off his shoulders, a sharp flint-like face, hair greased back to form a black V off his forehead and long stringy legs protruding from his baggy shorts, he cut an unmistakable figure on the pitch. Tommy was a star but without all the designer trappings of today's footballers. He'd dress in a long, belted overcoat with slightly spivvy shoulders, double-breasted pinstriped suit and immaculately polished shoes. The only indication that he was different from the fans who worshipped him from the terraces was his trademark gaudy ties, which gave him the air of a Hollywood gangster.

Tommy was a handful for defences; he put himself about, as they say. He knew a centre-forward was expected to run through a brick outerhouse if need be and he never shirked from his responsibilities. His dominance in the air was unsurpassed and he would often hurl himself at the opposing goalkeeper and centre-half when the odds were against him winning the ball. If he didn't win the ball, neither did the goalkeeper. What resulted was a scramble in the goalmouth between him and the defenders that reminded me of the scrummage to get on the last tram of the night.

When the England team to meet Scotland was announced, I was in at outside-right and Tommy was centre-forward.

The annual clash between England and Scotland was the highlight of the international season. In much the same way as a club can do anything in a season but lose the derby match to its closest and fiercest rivals, this was the one game in the season English and Scottish fans prayed their respective countries would win. I'd played twice against Scotland and been on the losing side on both occasions; the match at Hampden on 15 April was the one in which I hoped we could turn the tables. It was going to be a tall order. The Scots had the Indian sign on us, England hadn't won in Glasgow since 1927.

March had come in like a lion and gone out like a tiger. On the big day as I emerged from the tunnel behind my England team-mates a howling wind and lashing rain rudely smacked me across the face. I looked up to the vast open terraces of Hampden where great clouds of steam rose from 142,000 fans as the torrential rain evaporated from their tightly packed ranks. I remember thinking, 'What great supporters'. The weather was terrible, the conditions on the terraces uncomfortable, yet they had left the comfort of their hearths in vast numbers to come and support their team. I was left in no doubt whatsoever that the Scots are indeed football crazy.

In the short time it took the two teams to line up for the official presentation, my shirt was soaked through and clinging to my back. On my only other visit to Hampden, I had been so nervous I had taken no notice whatsoever of the dignitaries who had been paraded before the two teams. This time it was different. I stood head held high and surveyed the massed ranks. 'Sorry folks, marvellous fans that you are, I'm going to spoil your afternoon,' I said to myself, confident that this time the Hampden roar wouldn't get to me as it had done before. The Duke of Gloucester was presented to the two teams by which time the rain had given way to a violent hailstorm. To his credit, he stuck it out, shaking hands and exchanging words with every player, even though the umbrella the official from the Scottish FA was holding to protect him from the elements blew inside out seconds after it had been opened. As the two teams made their way to either end of the pitch for the pre-match warm-up – and if ever players needed to warm up it was then – I turned to Joe Mercer.

'Have you ever known weather like this?' I asked for want of something to say. 'I didn't sleep too well because the wind was whistling all through the night.'

'Did it whistle any other Welsh hymns, Stan?' Joe asked. I burst out laughing.

It was typical Joe. There we were, moments away from playing in the most important game on the international calendar in front of 142,000 fervent supporters all of whom were against us and he was able to crack a joke and defuse the tension. My laughter served to rid me of all remaining nerves. As we kicked off I felt relaxed and was looking forward to what I knew would be an epic tussle.

— o —

As the game got under way, the weather made things tricky for both teams. It was evident that the pitch was going to cut up and before long resemble a glue pot. Thick, dark clouds the colour of a well-used frying pan scudded low over the stadium, the rain lashing out of them in torrential streams. The wind swept down the pitch in a whining frenzy, blasting the players and making our shirts billow. Playing in rain or even snow never bothered me, but the one thing that every player finds difficult to cope with is a strong and blustery wind. We were playing into the wind and it was making life very difficult. Long balls were out of the question – they would arc back towards our own goal – so we tried to keep the ball down on the cloying pitch as much as we could.

After 20 minutes of trying to battle our way out of our half of the field, we gifted the Scots a goal. Bill Morris attempted a back pass to Vic Woodley but didn't put enough behind it. The ball stuck fast in the mud and before Vic could make up the ground, Jimmy Dougall did a bit of classic poaching, got to the ball first, took it to one side and slammed it low into the net. When a goal is scored before such a massive crowd, the effect down on the pitch is of delayed reaction. When Dougall put the ball in our net, the terraces behind the goal suddenly came alive with flaying humanity; for a split second they did so in silence, then an almighty roar swept down. It was deafening. To a man, the England players stood staring at our goal in dismay. We could hardly believe such misfortune could beset us after 20 minutes of Herculean effort against the rampaging Scots and the elements. So bad was the pitch that both sides changed tack having no alternative but to keep the ball in the air, which made for some desperate play at times. As England trooped off at half-time a goal down, it was obvious that stamina and fitness were the keys to the game. I felt confident.

During the interval both teams changed into clean kit, which speaks volumes for how bad the conditions were. As the game went on, the pitch was going to get worse and I hoped such a big occasion wouldn't degenerate into a farce. I wondered how well the Scots would cope when facing the driving wind and rain. We were a goal down but I felt it was a good scoreline considering the appalling conditions and perhaps the Scots were a little disappointed they hadn't made more of the advantage of having the wind at their backs in the first half.

If ever there was a game of two halves, if you'll forgive the cliché, this was it. We took the play to the Scots from the restart and they were backpeddling like crazy in an attempt to stem the white-shirted tide that swept before them. The Hampden crowd got behind them and the Scots dug deep into their reserves of strength and determination to keep us at bay. With 20 minutes remaining, our captain Eddie Hapgood, teeth gritted and fists clenched, urged us on for another assault. Eddie led by example. Shirt clinging to his body, he slammed into tackles, emerging with the ball and driving forward up our left-hand side. Eddie gave the impression he could move a mountain if he made up his mind so to do and that afternoon he was an inspiration. A warrior with endurance, fleetness of foot and sublime accuracy of ball control, he urged us on to great and even greater efforts. It was obvious Eddie had made up his mind we weren't going to lose and when Eddie was in that sort of mood, it was infectious. I've always believed that leadership is action not position and just at the point in the game when it seemed the Scots might well hold out, Eddie burst forward, a captain leading from the front.

He took the ball down our left flank before passing inside to Pat Beasley who had taken up a position to the left just inside the Scottish penalty area. Pat managed to wrestle himself away from his marker, gaining a vital couple of feet of space, and met Eddie's pass first time with his left foot, cracking it low past Jerry Dawson into the net. Suddenly the driving wind and rain were of no consequence. It might as well have been a bright sunny spring day because our spirits were lifted and our minds totally focused. From the restart we set about the Scots with renewed vigour, in search of the goal to seal a famous victory.

Both sides called upon every reserve of energy in those final stages, the Scots trying to hang on for the draw, England pushing for victory. Scotland, as ever, gave it everything they had and for a time a draw seemed the most likely result. My match body clock told me we were running out of time and when I saw the referee glance at his watch I knew there was only a minute or so to go. If we were going to do it, it would have to be something special – and quick. Just then, Len Goulden picked up a pass from Eddie Hapgood a few yards inside the Scottish half of the field and I called out to him to feed it to me. The ball duly came to my feet and I took off down our right wing for what I knew would be our last effort. I side-stepped Sandy McNab but ran straight into George Cummings. I was off balance slightly so there was nothing for it but to push the ball forward and for Cummings and I to race one another shoulder to shoulder down the wing with me edging the ball on as we did so. I was sprinting up on my toes but couldn't shake Cummings off. He stuck like glue on the goal side of me, forcing me wide and I was in imminent danger of running out of space. Cummings was forcing me in the direction the corner flag; I was heading away from goal and the chance of getting in a telling cross was slim. Some three yards from the flag, I momentarily stopped the run of the ball with the studs on my toe of my right boot, then quickly dragged my right foot back and flicked the ball on again with my toe. It all happened in a split second but it was enough to make Cummings think I was grinding to a halt and about to turn and face him. Still upright, he slid to a momentary halt and I pushed the ball into the space in front of the corner flag. The ball stuck in the mud and for an instant I thought I was going to overrun it. I managed to glance across to the penalty area and saw Tommy Lawton steaming in from a central position, just inside the area. The angle seemed impossible but I gave it all I had. As the momentum of my run carried me forward over the ball, using my left leg as a pivot I twisted my body to face goalwards and managed to get my right boot under the ball and hook it back in the direction of Tommy as I fell towards the corner flag.

It was far from being a textbook cross but it was a cross of sorts, the best I could muster under the circumstances. As Tommy ran in, it appeared I'd got too much lift on the ball and the cross was going to be too high for him to make contact. It was then that Tommy Lawton proved just what a great centre-forward and header of the ball he was. Seated in the mud on my backside, I watched him rise majestically, the sinews in his neck bulging like strands of cooked spaghetti as he strained to make the height of the ball. He heaved a groan as he stretched his body in the air, his head lolled to one side and rested for a second on his right shoulder as if he was about to take a nap then violently snapped back and in a silent Hampden I heard the dull thud as his forehead hammered the ball towards Jerry Dawson's goal. A shower of sweat and rain arced from Tommy's head, his arms shot out to either side as he tried to balance himself on the way back down, but not for an instant did Tommy take his eyes off that ball. It flew into the net and I watched a thousand tiny raindrops fall in unison on to the Hampden turf at the back of Jerry Dawson's goal. I took to my feet and as Tommy ran towards me, small rivulets of brown water ran down his face.

'Stan, just for your future reference,' Tommy said, shaking my hand and patting my shoulder, 'I'm six feet tall, not six feet two.'

At long last we had stunned and subdued Hampden into silence. England had done it but we had left it late. There was barely time for the Scots to kick off when the referee sounded his whistle for the end of the game. It's amazing what effect victory can have on players. Both teams had given their all, but there was a sharp contrast in how we left the field. There was no tiredness in the England ranks; we were back-slapping and chatting in great mood, excited in the wake of victory. The Scots were despondent. All their efforts had come to nothing and they staggered off the pitch as a defeated army staggers away from the field of battle. For all my elation, I spared a thought for them. I knew what they were going through because I'd been there myself.

7

— ○ —

On the
Brink

They didn't know it at the time, but when Portsmouth beat Wolves 4–1 in the 1939 FA Cup final, they became the Cup holders for the next seven years. The 1938–39 season had been full of goals and the public continued to roll up in their tens of thousands to enjoy the feast. One of the season's big talking points was transfer fees which, surprise, surprise, the press reported as having 'gone through the roof'. Arsenal manager George Allison paid £14,000 to Wolves for Welsh international Bryn Jones and the consensus of opinion among most football fans was that football had gone crazy. It was a record transfer fee at the time and sparked off all manner of estimations of what other players were worth. I was surprised and flattered to see my name mentioned but totally embarrassed when one newspaper put my worth at £20,000, another at £30,000 and another at a staggering £50,000. Of course, this was just newspaper talk and in reality I could never see a club, even one as big as Arsenal, paying those ridiculous amounts of money for my signature. Besides, there was a maximum wage so if a player was on top money at an unfashionable club, there was little to be gained financially by moving to one of the glamour teams.

In the summer of 1939, I was named in the England squad for the tour of Europe which was to include matches against Yugoslavia, Romania and World Cup holders Italy. The tour took place against a mounting backdrop of discontent on the Continent with talk of a major war so strong that for a time it was touch and go whether the tour would go ahead.

But go ahead it did and once again I was a member of an England party making long and tiring journeys across Europe. The first match was against the current world champions in Milan. We set off by train from London, caught the Calais ferry at Dover and took the famous Orient Express to Italy. Due to the political situation and, to a lesser extent, the bad feeling between the two teams when last we had met in London, I expected a hostile reception. As it turned out, it was anything but.

In Milan we were met by a huge crowd of local well-wishers. They started to sing as we got off the train. Outside the marbled Milan station I couldn't believe the sight that met my eyes. Thousands of Italian football fans packed the adjacent streets. So great was their number that the two-minute walk to our team hotel, the Piazza Duca d'Aosta, took us over half an hour. Once inside, there was still no let-up. The crowds massed on the street outside and refused to move so we were asked to wave to them from a balcony. When we appeared, the crowd cheered and sang again. I was left wondering if this was the same country where, only the day before, Mussolini had been in Turin breast-beating and shouting, 'We will march with Germany to give Europe peace and justice.'

Prior to the game, I was taking tea in the hotel lounge when a man approached me asking if I was Stanley Matthews. When I told him I was, he informed me he was Maltese and had just arrived from Valletta with a large party of compatriots who had come to support England. He was a short man of slight build with brilliantined hair. He wore a white linen suit, red shirt, red and white tie and two-tone brogues. He hardly opened his mouth when he spoke, which he did in a high-pitched voice, stressing the first letter of each word. His thin smile and fawning demeanour made me uncomfortable. He went on to explain how vulnerable the Maltese people felt in the light of the Italian–Nazi axis and urged me to do my best to help England beat Italy. For my part, I assured him that to a man England would make every effort to win the game.

'At the very least, do not let them beat you,' he pleaded. He was so serious and anxious about the matter I clasped one of his hands in mine and reiterated our intention to go all out for a win. It was a sobering encounter. I was suddenly aware of the real fear of people in countries near to Italy. This was just a football match but it was evident that this man and his fellow countrymen would gain great satisfaction from seeing the jingoistic supporters of the self-proclaimed 'Il Duce' given a comeuppance.

The day before the game, the sunshine gave way to heavy rain and it was still pouring down on matchday when our coach pulled into the famous San Siro stadium. Italy had won the 1938 World Cup but the competition was still in its embryonic stages and only 36 teams had entered; England was still the yardstick by which other countries assessed their true football worth and standing. Our visit to the San Siro was thus greeted with great anticipation by the Italian supporters who saw the game as an 'undisputed' title clash.

FIFA had only 57 members, and although there had been a record number of entrants in the qualifying stages of the World Cup, England, Scotland and Wales hadn't entered. The football hierarchies in those countries thought it beneath them to enter such a commercial competition. England had been top dogs in football for decades, we invented the game, and the FA would have no truck with an emerging competition organised not by them but by the upstart world governing body. The football associations of France, Italy, Brazil and Sweden saw a great global future for football. Not for the first, or indeed last, time, our FA proved itself to be short-sighted, elitist, insular and out of step with the way football was heading.

When Italy won the World Cup for the second consecutive time by beating Hungary 4–2 in Paris, no one could doubt they were worthy winners. The side we were to meet were better than the side who had won the trophy in 1934. We were in for a very difficult game at the San Siro. Only Meazza remained from their World Cup-winning team of four years before. This Italian team were better organised, more direct and a credit to their manager/coach Vittoria Pozzo, who had introduced several young quality players to the side in the intervening years. England were known as 'the fathers of football', Italy were rising stars and very much in the ascendancy. All in all it promised to be a terrific game and I couldn't wait to get going.

The selectors made two changes to the team that had beaten Scotland at Hampden the month before – Arsenal's George Male replaced Billy Morris at right-back and Frank Broome of Aston Villa got a recall at the expense of Huddersfield's Pat Beasley.

After 36 hours of incessant rain, the San Siro pitch wasn't too far from resembling the rectangle of molasses we had played on at Hampden but we got off to a decent start. I was up against Rava, a tricky left-back. In the opening stages, he seemed not to want to wait until the end of the game to get my shirt, preferring to try to rip it off my back there and then. That apart, I felt I had the measure of him. England played some exhibition stuff for a 15-minute period but for all we gave the Italians the run-around, a goal remained elusive. Minutes before half-time I set off on a dribble that took me past three Italian defenders and I spotted Tommy Lawton making good ground up the centre of the pitch. Unlike the last-gasp winner at Hampden, on this occasion I had created the time and space for myself to send a pinpoint cross in his direction and it practically sat up and begged to be headed. Tommy needed no second chance. Meeting the ball on the run, he bowed his head as if nodding 'good morning' and it flew into the Italian goal. For a team on home soil, Italy surprised me in the first half because they were content to drop back and let us come at them, happy to try to catch us on the break. The second half was a different story.

Italy pushed men forward and gradually seized the initiative. The Italian outside-right, Biavati, got the ball deep inside his own half and set off on a run that took him to the angle of our penalty box. It was disappointing that none of our lads had managed to make a challenge of any description and we were to pay dearly for it. On reaching the angle of the box, Biavati cut inside and let rip with a seering drive that gave Vic Woodley no chance.

With the San Siro crowd roaring them on, Italy kept up the pressure and but for some top-quality defending from Joe Mercer, we could have found ourselves out of the game. Joe was everywhere, stemming the *azzuri* tide in midfield and covering for both full-backs, single-handedly keeping our creaking defence together. Just as the 70-minute mark was approaching, Italy took the lead in what were highly controversial circumstances. I had a clear view as Italy's centre-forward Piola came racing, with George Male goal-side of him, to meet a low cross from the Italian right. Piola bent forward, his left arm shot out and a clenched fist made contact with the ball sending it flying into the net only for the fist to follow through and try to make contact with the back of George's head via the front of his face. Piola wheeled away in triumph as George hit the ground, out cold. The handball and the punch that floored George were so obvious that at first none of the England players bothered to protest, but when we saw the German referee Bauwens pointing towards the centre circle for a goal, he was besieged by white shirts, to no avail. Worse still, with George back in the dressing room we were down to ten men.

As was so often the case when this England team had their backs to the wall, it was skipper Eddie Hapgood who got everybody going. Immediately we kicked off, Eddie came into his own with his trademark clenched fist and words of encouragement. With five minutes remaining, Eddie ordered Stan Cullis to join Joe Mercer and Ken Willingham in helping out our forwards as we pushed for the equaliser. Ken Willingham went into a tackle in the middle of the pitch about halfway inside the Italian half and came out with the ball at his feet. I yelled for him to pass it to me and he pushed across a delightfully weighted ball for me to run on to. I took off down the wing and heard a cockney voice shouting 'Stan, Stan, give it to me, Stan.' I looked up, saw Len Goulden, slipped the ball to him and Len let fly. His shot was on target but it was blocked by Rava. The ball cannoned off the Italian number three and before any of his team-mates could pick up the pieces, Willie Hall was on to it in a flash and sent a low drive past the Italian keeper Olivieri. The San Siro was stunned into silence.

In the England dressing room after the game the satisfaction of having come back to get a draw in a hostile atmosphere was tempered by anger over Italy's second goal. I hadn't joined the on-the-field protests to the German referee because I've always believed that no matter how unjust a decision may be, no amount of protestation will change an official's mind. Irrespective of how badly done to you have been during a game, I was always of the mind that the only way of righting such matters was to up the ante on the pitch and if possible put the opposition to the sword and win the game. We later learned that the Italian Crown Prince who had been watching the game was so incensed by the referee's decision to allow Italy's second goal that he had wanted to take to the pitch and protest to Herr Bauwens but had been persuaded not to by the FA secretary Stanley Rous.

The game had been hard but nowhere near the rough house we had experienced when beating Italy at home. Nevertheless, I came off the field with a chipped hip bone, Willie Hall had a bad ankle injury and George Male, of course, had been dispatched into the arms of Morpheus. Poor George, his eye was blackened and closed and he came in for some merciless ribbing. Trainer Tom Whittaker passed the story about that when they had got George back into the dressing room, he had held up two fingers in front of his face asking, 'How many?' to which George had replied, 'No, just the one pint for me, thanks.' I am sure that never happened, but George was reminded about it constantly, to such an extent I think some of the players convinced themselves it was true.

The England players received a little jolt during the post-match reception when during the course of conversation with the Italian captain Meazza, he informed us he was on the equivalent of £35 a week with his club. That was six times the maximum wage in England at the time and to us seemed an incredible amount of money. Even in 1939, Italy was the place to be to earn big money in the game, proof that even in the relentlessly transient world of football, some things don't change.

From Milan the England party travelled to Venice and then on to Belgrade for the second game of the tour, against Yugoslavia. After travelling all night, we arrived at Belgrade station at 6.30 a.m. and once again were taken aback by the sheer magnitude of our welcome. We hadn't expected anyone to be there at that hour of the morning and the reception we were given bowled us over.

As we alighted from the train, a very grand-looking local official approached us and unravelled a prepared speech. The speech was equally grand including such sentiments as 'Your visit cements the friendship between our two countries' and 'For the England football team to visit our country is indeed a proud day for Yugoslavia'. At the end of it, the England players gave him a round of applause. We were somewhat perplexed over why he continued to stand smiling in front of us. He extended a hand, inviting someone to join him. Stan Cullis turned to Eddie Hapgood saying he thought the official wanted to make some sort of presentation and as he was our captain, Eddie should step forward to accept it on our behalf. Eddie did step forward only to be flummoxed when the official turned to the crowded platform and said, 'The Eenlan' capitain, Meester Harp-gurd will reply on bee-arf of zee Eenlan' tim and geeve urs 'is oh-pinion on furt-boll.'

For a moment Eddie froze to the spot. He was without doubt captain courageous on the field, but he was not accustomed to official speaking, especially with nothing prepared. We all started to smile wryly at Eddie's situation, but after an awkward silence and some shuffling of his feet,

Eddie raised his hand, cleared his throat, gathered himself together and spoke.

'Sir, the England players thank you and your fellow countrymen for this marvellous reception. We feel honoured and humbled by its warmth and feel it is testimony to the friendship between our two nations. As for my opinion on football, to me it's like the dilemma of a love affair. If you don't take it seriously, you get no pleasure from it. If you do take it seriously, and as a player you have to, somewhere along the line, it will break your heart.'

I've heard literally hundreds of speeches in my time, a number from some of the most accomplished public speakers in the world, but nowhere have I seen a group of people respond so enthusiastically to a speech as the crowd on Belgrade station that morning responded to Eddie's few but heartfelt words. The station platform erupted into rapturous applause and even the England players joined in.

Our visit to Yugoslavia was off to a great start. The sad irony of that wonderful meeting was that at that very moment, unbeknown to any of us, elsewhere in Europe evil forces were putting plans in place that would soon bring untold human misery and devastation to those friendly Yugoslav people. I've always believed that the best way to learn about your home town or country is to travel away from it so you have something to compare it with. You come to realise its good and bad points and it helps you get your roots into perspective. The visit to Yugoslavia did just that. On a walk around Belgrade with some of my team-mates, I was astonished to see what meagre offerings were on hand in the food shops. Back in our hotel we sat down to lavish meals and superb cuisine and I must admit it pricked my conscience. Today we'd refer to it as a great poverty divide; in 1939 I thought it just plain unfair. So uncomfortable did it make me, I took the matter up with the hotel manager who couldn't understand why I felt so strongly about it. I was told the Yugoslav authorities considered the visit of the England team to be of such importance that special dispensation had been granted to the hotel to provide for our every need.

'Apart from that,' said the hotel manager, 'it is customary for Yugoslavs to take the food from their own table and offer it to a guest. We would be insulted if you would not accept such hospitality.'

It was an answer, but it didn't make me feel any better about it.

On one of our sightseeing trips in Belgrade, we came across Charlie. We never knew his real name or where he came from but this ebullient character attached himself to the England party as our unofficial guide. Whenever the England players appeared in the hotel lobby ready for a bit of sightseeing, Charlie was there to meet us. He knew Belgrade like the back of his hand and had a story for every street, building, park or bar we came across and the enthusiastic and humorous way he put his tales across kept us spellbound.

On one trip, Charlie took us to the Oplenae where an awe-inspiring church had been built as a memorial, he told us, to King Alexander of Yugoslavia who had been assassinated on leaving a restaurant in Marseille.

'When the King left the restaurant they shot him dead. The lesson to learn here, gentlemen,' said Charlie, 'is if you're ever in a Marseille restaurant, always leave a good tip.'

On the eve of the game as we bade our farewells to our unofficial guide, Charlie filled our heads with talk of how poor a side Yugoslavia were, saying we would win by six or seven clear goals. He left us all feeling extremely confident about the match. As it was to turn out, it was the biggest load of kiddums we were to hear. Charlie conned us into believing Yugoslavia were an easy touch; they were anything but.

I'd been having treatment for my damaged hip which had been giving me some discomfort, but on the day of the game I felt fine and told Tom Whittaker I was fit to play. With only five minutes of the game gone, I received a pass from Huddersfield's Ken Willingham, accelerated down the wing, comfortably bypassed the Yugoslav left-back Dubac but then felt a searing pain shoot down my left leg. I pulled up, wincing in pain, received some treatment but knew it was hopeless.

Substitutes were yet to be introduced in English football and injured players were simply expected to carry on as best they could. No one ever considered that in doing so you might aggravate the injury or even do permanent damage. You were expected to hobble about on the premise that if your contribution to the actual game was little or nothing, at the very least, one of the opposition would be occupied in having to mark you.

For the remainder of the game I was a passenger. Ken Willingham and George Male, as well as doing their own jobs in defence, had to push forward to give us some width on the right wing. I felt awful for having declared myself fit, feeling I'd let my team-mates and England down in a big way. Our problems were compounded when Eddie Hapgood tore his ankle ligaments. That is a serious injury today, but it was expected that Eddie would carry on and being the fully committed player he was, he did. Frank Broome dropped to left-back with Eddie taking Frank's position out on the wing, meaning England were effectively now down to nine men.

Yugoslav took a first-half lead but just after half-time, Frank Broome made a great overlapping run on our left and cut in to score a great equaliser. The nine fit England players ran themselves ragged but as the game wore on, tiredness took its toll and Yugoslavia slowly but surely gained the upper hand. Minutes from the end, Yugoslavia broke through. Perlic, their outside-left, cut in from the wing and curled a low shot past Vic Woodley and into the far corner of the net to put the match beyond us. I don't want to make excuses – Yugoslavia were, after all, a much better side than Charlie the Con Man had made out – but if Eddie Hapgood and I had been fully fit, I'm convinced we would have beaten them. However, it was not to be and a subdued England party left for Bucharest the next day.

The Romanian game didn't turn out to be an exposition of the beautiful game, but we won 2–0 with goals from West Ham's Len Goulden and the recalled Don Welsh of Charlton Athletic. It was a workmanlike win but everyone gleaned satisfaction from the result; we felt it important to finish the tour on a winning note, having up to that point drawn one game and lost one. Eddie Hapgood, Ken Willingham, Willie Hall and I were all injured and watched the game from the stand. I did so in a pretty low frame of mind. I was never a good spectator, much preferring to be out there on the pitch where I felt I could contribute to the proceedings. During the Romania game I kicked every ball from up in that stand and constantly thought what I would have done in such and such a situation. I also still felt bad about pronouncing myself fit enough to play against the Yugoslavs.

Considering the longevity of my career and the close attention paid to me, I was very lucky where injuries were concerned. I never picked up a bad injury until I played my final match at the age of 70 when I damaged a cartilage and finally decided to call it a day. I am positive all the personal training I did helped me avoid injury because it contributed in no small way to my speed, ability to twist and turn defenders and close ball skills. If I hadn't been so dedicated I am sure I would have come a cropper. For defenders to hurt me they first had to catch me, then get a tackle in. The closer they got, the harder I would work on my skills and speed to keep one step ahead. Such motivation was a constant factor in my training and if ever I did feel like having an afternoon off, the thought of being on the end of a crunching tackle from Wilf Copping or Stan Cullis focused my mind totally.

I was never booked or sent off in my entire career. As I have said, I saw no point in arguing with officials. As for being on the receiving end of a bad tackle, I never retaliated. My retaliation came the next time I took the ball down the wing in the form of wanting to take the offending defender to the cleaners. I've always believed part of a footballer's job is to retain composure and dignity even when emotions are running high. I couldn't control what an opponent would do, neither could I control how a game would pan out, but I could control myself. I felt that enabled me to contribute in a positive and telling way to the outcome of a game. That is why I was in a low frame of mind as I sat watching the Romania game.

Many players over the years have spent much of their time sitting in stands watching because their antics have got them into trouble with opponents or officials. As far as I was concerned, an arthritic octogenarian or a six-year-old boy or girl would be as good a footballer as me when I wasn't playing because they could sit in a stand and contribute the same to a match. Today's players are paid enormous amounts of money for playing football; more perplexing, they even get paid when they are suspended. Chelsea's Dennis Wise and Leeds' David Batty seemed to spend the majority of the 1998–99 season watching from the stands due to suspensions. To my mind, the contribution of those two players to their respective clubs was even less than the supporters sitting around them because at least those supporters had paid to get in.

I learned something every day in football from the first day I set foot inside Stoke City to the very last league game I played at the age of 50 and I have carried on learning to this day. Everyone makes mistakes, but it is the wise man who learns from them and a genius who makes relatively few. Some players seem never to learn from their indiscretions. Take Liverpool's Robbie Fowler. In 1999 he was involved in a controversial and silly on-the-pitch incident with Chelsea's Graeme Le Saux in which Fowler seemingly questioned Le Saux's sexuality. In the end the two players were asked to apologise to one another and no real action was taken. A few weeks later, having scored for Liverpool in a local derby against Everton, Fowler dropped to his knees in front of the Everton fans and mimicked snorting drugs. It was supposedly in response to allegations from Everton fans that Fowler was a drug user. He should have simply walked away and taken the congratulations of his team-mates, especially in the light of the recent affair with Le Saux. His goals were the perfect riposte to such scurrilous rumours. Fowler is looked up to by young people, a role model to many. What an example he set. Drugs have become a real problem in society. Government departments, health organisations and even the Premier League and Professional Footballers Association have spent millions of pounds on drug awareness but in that Merseyside derby we saw a top player making light of it all, and only weeks after having escaped disciplinary measures for another crass and unsavoury incident.

For all football has a capacity to excite, enthral and richly entertain, the antics of a certain number of star players in recent years means it now also has a great capacity to self-destruct. Fowler's gestures were not only indicative of a lack of self-control, discipline and thought, but showed that football these days can entertain and appal in equal measure. This is one of the big differences from when I played the game. In my playing days, the actions of players at worst could annoy and frustrate supporters and officialdom, but never at any time did they appal and disgust.

━━ o ━━

Before returning home, the England players visited Pelash Castle, the grand and stately home of Romania's King Carol and Madame Lupescu. On first sight, it reminded me of the castles depicted in the Frankenstein and Dracula movies of the thirties. Perched on a hill, it was grand and imposing but eerily mysterious. Several tall and pointed turrets flanked an entrance with a door that made the one at Durham Cathedral look like a cat flap. I half expected Bela Lugosi to sweep down the staircase to welcome us. The large rooms were sumptuously decorated and furnished, the pile on the carpets so thick and luxurious I could just about walk across them without the aid of snow shoes. We were left in little doubt that Pelash Castle was the home of a king.

After the guided tour, we were led out into the beautiful walled gardens at the rear. I was watching a gardener attending to the roses when suddenly a small stocky man with a moustache cut short like a worn-out brush appeared and called out to the gardener.

'Cor lumme, that ain't no way to prune roses. 'Ere, gimme those clippers and arl show yer 'ow.'

That was a surprise, so a few of us went over to make his acquaintance. It turned out he was King Carol's head gardener and originally from London's East End. He said he had answered an advert in the *Evening Standard* and ended up getting the job which he liked immensely. He asked me how West Ham had been doing in the past year and was bowled over when I introduced him to Len Goulden. It never ceases to amaze me that no matter where I travel in the world, there will be someone from Great Britain when I get there. When our party first set sight on the fairytale Pelash Castle, the last thing I expected was to be chatting away with a gardener from Forest Gate about West Ham United. Before we left, he gave us what he said were five essential tips for successful gardening.

'First thing to remember is nothing will ever turn out as beautiful as it appears on the seed packet. Second, no matter how small your lawn, it will always be bigger than your desire to mow it. Third, in a prolonged spell of dry weather, no matter how bare the lawn becomes, grass will still happily grow between the paving stones. Fourth, the only way to make sure it rains is to give the garden a good watering, and finally, no matter how poorly plants grow even when you lavish attention on them, weeds will always thrive.'

I only play at gardening, but the tips offered by that head gardener at Pelash Castle are as true today as they were back in 1939!

—— o ——

Back home, I spent the close season training as usual, but it was a subdued and tentative Stoke City squad that reported back to the Victoria Ground to prepare for the 1939–40 season, so great was the fear of war.

The season kicked off in August with the newspapers telling us Nazi Germany was on the point of invading Poland. I hoped against hope that war wouldn't come. Even when the inevitable news broke and politicians started to tell us that the piece of paper promising 'peace in our time' that Neville Chamberlain had waved on returning from Munich was worthless and meant nothing, I still remained hopeful of a last-minute negotiation for peace.

The new season was three games old. It was Sunday, 3 September and the newspapers printed the first set of league tables. Blackpool with three wins out of three topped

Division One, and Stoke, with seven goals having won one, drawn one and lost one, was in mid table. I was at home listening to the radio and Betty was in the kitchen making preparation for lunch when, like millions of other British people, I heard the Prime Minister Neville Chamberlain address the nation. He told us that from that moment, we were at war with Germany. I walked out into the back garden and at first couldn't believe what I had heard. It seemed unreal. The sun was shining, the garden was in the last throws of summer, birds were singing and to all intents and purposes it was a normal, quiet, peaceful Sunday. 'At war with Germany' – I mulled the harrowing thought over in my head and found it difficult to comprehend. A few weeks ago my life seemed mapped out and everything was wonderful. I knew where I was in life, knew my purpose, my destiny. Suddenly, like millions of other people, my future and that of my family was uncertain and riddled with anxiety of the most frightening proportion.

As I stood in the garden, my mind turned to all the people I had played football against and in front of, including the supporters who had fêted us on our tours of the Continent. I wondered what was in store for them. The words of Benjamin Franklin came to me: 'There is never a good war, or a bad peace.' I feared for the future, not only of my family, but of mankind. I suddenly felt physically sick.

At the declaration of war, the 1939–40 League programme was immediately cancelled. That in itself indicated the gravity of the situation. Even though we were to go through six or so months of phoney war before the real hostilities began, the cancellation was a major sign that what had been normal life up to that point would now cease. Life, society, the world even, would never be the same again and as football has always reflected society in general, it meant our beautiful game would irrevocably change.

8

---○---

The Great and Glorious of the Thirties

Recently, a young lady in baseball cap and jeans, approached me after a game I had been watching and asked if she could have a few words.

'Were you, Horatio Carter or Tom Finney ever in the game just for the money?' she asked at one point in our conversation.

'No,' I said, 'because there wasn't any.'

The game has changed. I may not have made a fortune from football, far from it, yet football made me the richest man alive because I was a working-class lad who realised his dream. I played in 697 league games, nigh on 1,500 in total. By and large, I played all my league football in the equivalent of the Premiership and was 50 when I played my final league match. I made 83 official and unofficial appearances for England – they are all official today – my last at the age of 42. I played in three FA Cup finals and two World Cups. I have travelled the world many times over and been awarded the occasional honour along the way. Not bad for the son of a Hanley barber. To have been paid a fortune as well would have made me incapable of looking anyone straight in the eye out of sheer embarrassment at the hand fate had dealt me.

There were many memorable games and almost as many poignant and humorous incidents. Of course, games are only memorable because of the deeds of players, and what players I had the honour to play with and against during my long career.

It was said of Whistler, probably by himself, that he mixed his paints with brains. If ever a player did that in football, it was Raich Carter of Sunderland, Derby County and Hull City. Carter was an architect who designed every game in which he played. He was blessed with such an incredible amount of talent that he could affect a game's outcome seemingly at will. Like the Australian leg-spin bowler Shane Warne, Carter was truly a connoisseur's delight.

For all his brilliance, Raich often adopted an arrogant air during games. Players trained on the club pitch in those days. The reserve teams also played their games on them, and often the juniors as well. With consistent, heavy use, come midwinter, pitches often became incredibly boggy. That is one thing that has improved over the years; most of today's pitches are still like bowling greens come the end of a season, the very antithesis of what they were like in the thirties and forties. On days of truly inclement weather, Carter would often ghost about seemingly contributing little to a game, treating even his own players with disdain, as if the slog on the mudbath was far below his dignity.

I was playing in a game for Blackpool against Derby

County. The rain was coming down like stair rods and the Bloomfield Road pitch was a quagmire. Carter was an England team-mate but I remember thinking he just wasn't up for it that day. With about five minutes remaining and the score 0–0, Derby won a corner. As the Derby players trundled into our penalty box, Harry Johnston went across to mark Carter who had taken up a position just outside the angle of the six-yard box, nearest to where the corner was being taken from. Carter stood facing the Derby winger who was taking the corner with his hands on his hips. Whenever I saw a player do that I always took it as a sign that he was banjaxed, had lost interest in the game, or both.

There was an eerie silence in the ground as the Derby player prepared to take the corner. Suddenly it was broken by a booming voice from the terracing behind our goal. 'Go home Carter! You're washed up and finished!' Even though he was an opponent of the day, I remember thinking it was a cruel thing to say. True, Raich was a great player, but on this particular day he had done nothing and the cruel shout at Carter's expense seemed to have a certain ring of truth to it. I felt sorry for him.

The corner was played in to where Carter was standing and it reached him at chest height. With a sudden but slight backward step, he cushioned the ball with his chest and it fell dead at his feet. With lightning speed, as if part of the same movement, he swivelled and with the ball at knee height hit a thunderbolt of a volley. Our goalkeeper 'Robbo' Robinson didn't have time to react and stood motionless, able only to feel the draught the ball created as it flashed past him. The far corner of the net bulged into the shape of an elbow and the ground was stunned into such a silence I actually heard the swish of the ball as it cut a furrow down the rain-soaked net to the ground. For a few seconds, the absolute silence among the rainsoaked crowd continued;

then the same booming voice came from behind our goal. 'All right then, but you're not as good as you used to be!'

Football in the thirties, forties and fifties was brimming with characters. I suppose one good point about the maximum wage was that every top club seemed to have at least one truly great player. If you were on the maximum wage at say, Middlesbrough or Preston, there was nothing to be gained from a move to Arsenal or Manchester United because you wouldn't be paid any more. That is why there were so many one-club men and great players were content to ply their trade with so-called unfashionable clubs, even world-class players such as Tom Finney at Preston and Nat Lofthouse at Bolton.

In a league career spanning about 35 years I had only two clubs, Stoke City and Blackpool. Young people today find that difficult to understand. Following a game at Old Trafford recently, a young Manchester United supporter approached me and asked me for my autograph. While I was signing his book he said, 'My dad says you were a great player. Why did you only play for Stoke and Blackpool?' I told him, 'Because I was a glory hunter.'

As I say, every club had its star performer. Wilf Mannion at Middlesbrough was the Mozart of football – stylish, graceful, courtly, showing exquisite workmanship with the ball. In the fifties there was John Charles of Leeds and later Juventus, Roma and Cardiff City. He was the 'Gentle Giant', strong as Hercules, imperious as Caesar and so bronzed and muscular he wouldn't have been out of place as the 'after' man in a Charles Atlas advert. Dominant in the air, a player of seductive passes and thunderbolt shooting, big John would shake off opponents like a dog shakes water off its back. He was a mountain of a man, hard but with an inordinate amount of self-control – the Admirable Crichton of Welsh football.

Duncan Edwards, the boy-man, made his debut for Manchester United at 17 and was an England regular at 19. You could play him anywhere and he would slot into that position as if he had been playing there season after season. For all his tender years, he was the most complete player of his time and it was a tragedy that his life was taken in the Munich air disaster of 1958. When the going was rough, Duncan would be as unmoved as a rock in a raging sea, but for all his considerable size, he possessed deft skills.

In 1957, I played for England against the Republic of Ireland at Wembley. In the second half, from deep in the England half of the field, Duncan set off on a mazy dribble that took him past five Irish players before he laid the ball off to his Manchester United team-mate Tommy Taylor. Tommy never broke step and crashed the ball first touch into the roof of the net from just outside the penalty area. One of the England reserves that day, Chelsea's Frank Blunstone, was sitting up in the Wembley stands. Frank leapt to his feet and shouted with such excited joy that his upper set of teeth shot from his mouth and disappeared six or seven rows below him. Frank never did get them back, though that mercurial Burnley, Stoke and Northern Ireland inside-forward Jimmy McIlroy reckons he recently met a man in County Cork who is still wearing them.

Great players, great days but if someone were to pin me down about which decade produced the players I most enjoyed playing with and against, it would have to be the thirties. Many of them were lost to football forever, either through being casualties of war or past their best in football terms when peace was restored and football recommenced seven years later in 1946. If the immediate post-war years can be described as the golden era of British football, the thirties were most definitely polished silver.

For all the frugality inflicted upon working people in

the thirties when depression bit hard, football enjoyed a glamorous decade. It was an era of high-scoring teams and high attendances. Football was an escape from the harsh realities of hardworking life. Supporters rarely travelled to away games because tight budgets didn't run to it, so football was in every sense a community game. There was no television so the only way anyone could see a top star from another club was when his team visited the local side. The Saturday match was a social event, an occasion, when pottery, factory, shipyard workers and miners emerged into what was for them fresh air to be entertained and to vent their frustrations and feelings. Together, men and women, boys and girls, shared the infinite pleasures and dark despair which any supporter experiences in following their team and together they watched the great players and larger-than-life characters who paraded before them every fortnight.

Everton's Dixie Dean who had scored a record 60 goals in a season in 1926 for the Merseysiders, was still a potent force for much of the thirties. In truth, Dixie's international career was almost over when the thirties got under way, but he continued to trouble defences throughout the decade. In 1936 he broke Steve Bloomer of Derby County's aggregate scoring record when he made it 352 career goals. Dixie went on to amass 379 league and Cup goals in a career spanning 437 matches which is phenomenal scoring in anyone's book.

The stories of Dixie Dean are legendary. One day when walking down a street in Liverpool he came across the Liverpool goalkeeper Elisha Scott. Dixie nodded his head in recognition and Scott instinctively flung himself to the ground in an attempt to save an imaginary ball. There was also the story of the Protestant woman who married a Catholic. On their wedding day they agreed never to have any religious artefacts in the home. After ten years of marriage the wife is said to have discovered a photograph that had been hanging in the lounge for the duration was in fact of the Pope. When asked by her mother why she had allowed it, legend has it the woman said, 'I never knew it was the Pope. My hubby always told me it was Dixie Dean wearing one of his international caps.'

So why were the England careers of such great centre-forwards relatively short-lived? The simple answer is that there were so many great centre-forwards at the time, competition for the England number nine shirt was red hot. Vying with Dixie and the like was Middlesbrough's George Camsell. In 444 league games for them and Durham City George scored 344 goals, but he made the England team just nine times between 1929 and 1937. In those nine games, he scored 18 times for England! You can't imagine a player averaging two goals a game at international level being restricted to so few appearances today, but such was the competition from a bevy of great centre-forwards at the time, George Camsell had to bide his time. George earned £5 a week when the average gate receipts for a First Division game were between £4,000 and £5,000, with the FA Cup finals and internationals at Wembley taking up to £25,000 per match. Where did that money go? Not to the players or on better facilities for supporters, that's for sure. George Camsell was a great player and the mind boggles at what value would be put on a player with that scoring rate today.

George was not alone in being a prolific goalscorer in sporadic appearances for England. Aston Villa had a superb opportunist centre-forward in Pongo Waring; he notched four goals on his five appearances for England. Manchester City's colourful and bustling Freddie Tilson produced six goals in four outings. The cavalier and fearless Ted Drake of Arsenal won five caps and scored six times and our own Freddie Steele at Stoke produced a return of eight goals for six caps. The England selectors were spoilt for choice in the thirties when it came to free-scoring centre-forwards; today you can count them on the fingers of one hand.

The careers of Billy Walker and David Jack, who scored both goals for Bolton in the very first Wembley FA Cup final in 1923 when an estimated 200,000 people descended on the new stadium, spilled over into the thirties. Perhaps the most famous player of this era was Alex James of Arsenal, he of the baggy pants and awkward shuffling gait. I'd seen James play for the Arsenal at Stoke City as a boy and was immediately taken with him. I adopted his baggy shorts and continued to sport such fashion in my own playing days with Stoke. Not only was Alex James a supreme artist with the ball, he also possessed that rarest of gifts, being able to inspire those about him to great heights.

Alex was born in North Lanarkshire, a mining area of Scotland that also produced Matt Busby, while Bill Shankly and Jock Stein came from South Lanarkshire. He began his footballing career with Raith Rovers in 1922, moved to Preston North End in 1925 and was transferred to Arsenal four years later. He began life at Arsenal as an orthodox inside-forward but whenever I played against him, he played a deep-lying role. He became what in those days was called a schemer, though to refer to James as simply that is to do him a great disservice. He scored 53 goals in 147 appearances for Preston, though the deep-lying role in Arsenal's midfield meant he didn't get into the penalty box so often which explains why he netted only 26 times in 231 games for what at the time was a free-scoring Gunners team.

Arsenal were without doubt the top side in England during the thirties, winning the League Championship four times (1931, 1933–35) and the FA Cup twice (1930 and 1936). Alex supplied the ammunition for his fellow Gunners and was widely regarded as the most astute football tactician of his time. It is no exaggeration to say that Arsenal manager Herbert Chapman built his team around him. The Arsenal of the day were a team of rare talent and Alex James was its mastermind, though you would never suspect it on seeing him. While his team-mates would run on to the pitch for a game, James would shuffle on. He was a short, squat figure with bandy legs protruding from shorts so baggy it looked as if he was wearing a large white pillow case about his midriff. Toes turned in, sleeves down but always unbuttoned at the cuff, more often than not socks about his ankles, you would never think that this was a man who laid claim to genius.

His baggy shorts which hung well below his knees became his trademark and were as popular with cartoonists as Stanley Baldwin's pipe, Neville Chamberlain's umbrella or Winston Churchill's cigar. If you really want to know what society was like in years gone by, rather than read history books, look at the cartoons of the day. In retrospect, they capture a time perfectly. No footballer was portrayed more accurately or succinctly than Alex James.

There were many who believed his carefree appearance was natural, others thought it all part of a pose, but it was in sharp contrast to one of the tidiest and sharpest football brains there has ever been. He hated wasted effort. To him it was a mark of poor technique and indicative of a poor footballing brain. For all he could be intolerant of those who did not match up to his classical artistry, he was the arch entertainer – a diminutive Scottish comic who held his audience and opponents spellbound until he delivered his killer punchline.

Under Herbert Chapman he cut out the comedy some-what and developed a taste for strategy, dominating the area of field between a resolute Arsenal defence as reluctant to push on as more contemporary Gunners defences have been, and a quicksilver forward line. Herbert Chapman's pre-match instructions to his team were as short as they were monotonous. 'Give the ball to Alex,' he would say and when they did, this unlikely looking hero single-handedly directed the Gunners offensive with seemingly consummate ease.

In 1928, Alex formed part of one of the smallest forward lines ever to take to a pitch when Scotland demolished England at Wembley. Scotland cut England to ribbons that day winning 5–1 with hat-trick hero Alex Jackson the tallest of their forwards at five foot seven. The newspapers dubbed that Scottish team the Wembley Wizards and James was their Merlin, weaving his own brand of magic to leave England, as the song goes, bewitched, bothered and bewildered but above all, well beaten.

Alex James was a formidable opponent. Trying to close him down was as difficult as trying to stand an empty sack upright and about as frustrating. When he waved his foot over the ball, we didn't know the what, when, and wherefore. All we could be certain of was that defenders would be left chasing shadows. His approach to life and football was in as sharp a contrast to that of Arsenal team-mates Eddie Hapgood or Cliff Bastin as Falstaff to Henry IV. Alex James died in 1953 some months before his fifty-second birthday but his exploits for Arsenal during the thirties have ensured his immortality.

The quality of football in this decade was high simply because every First Division team possessed a number of top-quality players who orchestrated proceedings supported by, at worst, good players. By the end of the decade, I was England's regular outside-right but I had to compete for that role with Derby County's Sammy Crooks. He was a different type of winger from me. While I worked hard at developing and changing my style, Sammy was a go-getter, fast and direct. He relished the traditional style of wing play, cutting in and going for goal, which he did to great effect. Sammy's partner on the left wing for Derby was Dally Duncan, a Scot who was so fast that Sammy reckoned on cold days they could play Duncan in his overcoat and it wouldn't make one iota of difference. Together they caused defences innumerable problems and were always a handful to play against.

Sheffield Wednesday's Alf Strange lived up to his name by converting from a free-scoring centre-forward to a formidable wing-half, a very unusual transformation in those days. Alf had considerable talent but was not averse to dishing out the rough stuff on the odd occasion. After a game between Sheffield Wednesday and Stoke at Hillsborough in which he had attempted on several occasions to sit me up in row G, he said to me, 'I always set out to play football the way it's meant to be played, Stan. But there are some games when you just have to kick everything that moves and if it doesn't move, keep kicking it until it does.' It had been one of those games and the physical effects of Alf's philosophy remained with me for some weeks after.

Peter Doherty, like Sunderland's Raich Carter, was a genius of an inside-forward who, also like Carter, lost the best years of his football career to the war. Prior to the emergence of George Best in the sixties, Doherty was to my mind the greatest footballer to come out of Northern Ireland. He began life as a bus conductor and played his football part-time for Glentoran before moving to Blackpool, then on to Manchester City. He played for Derby County with great credit in the immediate post-war years, and retired in 1953 with a career tally of 199 goals in 406 games having set up countless others for team-mates.

In one game between Stoke and Manchester City when City were heading towards the First Division Championship in 1936, Doherty had been quiet but he snapped into life, making three great passes that led to a crucial Manchester

City goal. It prompted Stoke's Jock Kirton to say, 'That's the bus conductor in you, Peter. Your team wait an hour for a telling pass from you, then three come along at once!'

For all his genius no one really warmed to Peter. In modern-day parlance you'd say he had attitude, which I am sure played a part in his meagre haul of 16 caps over 15 years for Northern Ireland. I say meagre because he was far and away the best player Northern Ireland could call upon in the thirties. A player of his quality should have been a regular at international level, especially as Northern Ireland did not have a wealth of great talent to call upon.

Peter did go on to manage Northern Ireland, taking them to the World Cup finals in 1958 and I believe if he had been able to curb his acerbity, he would have gone on to bigger and better things in management and our memory of him today would be more in keeping with the genius he displayed on the pitch.

In sharp contrast to Peter Doherty's character was that of Matt Busby. In the thirties, Manchester City were far and away the big boys in that city and Matt Busby was their prized player. It is not without irony that, when his playing days were over, Matt led City's arch-rivals Manchester United to great things, not only laying the foundations but building the first three storeys of what is today the biggest and most successful football club in the world.

Matt was a lovely man. His warmth, generosity of spirit and heart, and quiet unassuming way belied a hardness that is a necessary part of the character of all successful managers. We first met in the thirties and, I am happy to say, remained good friends until his sad passing in 1994. Matt was a classy wing-half but his talent as a player has been overshadowed by his phenomenal success as a manager.

He came from Lanarkshire, that part of Scotland which, as I have said, produced Alex James, Bill Shankly and Jock

Stein. Perhaps football was the only escape from the pit for young lads in the twenties, but why the area should have produced four of the all-time greats of British football, I don't know. Maybe their roots generated a certain kind of mentality – a great and all-consuming passion to win and succeed; an enthusiasm so great it developed into fanaticism; the ability to apply yourself to a long-term goal and the tenacity to stick at it; and great vision.

Matt joined Manchester City from the small Scottish club Denny Hibernians in 1928, originally as an inside-right, but his career blossomed when City switched him to right-half. He never had a crunching tackle, but so precise was his timing that he stole the ball off your toe. For all he was a resolute defender, he loved to get forward; in many respects he was what we would term today an attacking midfielder. Matt won an FA Cup winners medal in 1934 when Manchester City beat Portsmouth 2–1 in the final. City's teenage goalkeeper Frank Swift was so overcome with emotion he collapsed and had to be carried to the Royal Box to receive his medal. Matt moved on from City to Liverpool in 1936 for what was then a considerable fee of £8,000 and stayed at Anfield until war broke out in 1939 when, like just about every other player of the day, he joined the services. Matt did turn out for Liverpool in unofficial matches during the war years and guested for a number of clubs situated near to wherever he was stationed, but effectively his playing career ended in 1939.

One of Matt's greatest strengths as a player was his passing. Not only could he split open defences but the pass was always so beautifully timed and weighted it was perfect for City forwards such as Eric Brook, Freddie Tilson or Alex Herd to latch on to without breaking their stride. For all players were tightly marked in the thirties, Matt could overcome all that with one sweeping pass. I think his ability to pick out team-mates with superlative passing was indicative of his great vision even then.

That Matt was a visionary there is no doubt. He pioneered youth systems and took part in European football against current thinking. We all accept these as part and parcel of the modern game, but then they were radical. He built three great United teams – one in the immediate post-war years led by Johnny Carey, the Busby Babes of the fifties and United's League Championship and European Cup-winning side of the sixties that included football's holy trinity of George Best, Bobby Charlton and Denis Law.

From player in the thirties to manager in the Swinging Sixties, for all he was an innovator, he never changed his style, always holding true to a belief in sportsmanship, open entertaining football and the virtues of family life. As a manager he enjoyed patriarchal status but because of his receptiveness to new ideas was never considered old-fashioned. To this day, he is still thought of as being one of British football's foremost innovators. In creating his Busby Babes, Matt set up a network of scouts throughout the British Isles to find the very best young players. Up to that point, managers more or less just tapped into what young talent was about within a 30-mile radius of the club. Matt changed all that, but his desire to create a great team of United-bred youngsters was foiled by the Munich air disaster of 1958 in which Matt himself came close to death. Resolute and undeterred, he overcame tragedy and rebuilt. His reward came in 1968 when his League Championship side of the year before became the first English club to win the European Cup when they beat Benfica 4–1 at Wembley.

Matt had to battle with the FA and Football League to be allowed to compete in what was then an embryonic European competition. The FA and the Football League saw the First Division Championship as the main priority for English clubs and the fledgling European competitions as being unimportant sidelines. Matt told me a Football League official informed him at the time that the European Cup was nothing more than 'a gimmick that is sure to be short-lived'. Matt knew different and, as was so often the case, he was proved right. Matt told me he had the full backing of the Manchester United board in his quest for European football. 'I offer them my advice,' he said, 'then I tell them what they should be doing' – which goes a long way to indicating what a great influence he had in the club at all levels.

Matt wanted Manchester United to play European football because he foresaw a time when the balance of power would shift away from England. He had watched club sides and the national teams from Hungary, Italy, Germany, even Brazil and Uruguay, and saw the future of the game as global. He admired the superior technique and organisation of the top European sides and wanted to emulate them, to develop our domestic game and take it forward. In the wake of the 1954 World Cup, in which I had played for England, Matt wrote to me and outlined his thoughts on the future of our game:

> I watched both Hungary and Uruguay. They had strength, speed and brilliance. They attacked and defended as a single unit and there is no team in the British Isles at the moment that can come anywhere near either of them. Their height made them formidable in the air and their physical strength carried them through the rough and tumble. To gain that bit of extra speed they wear featherweight boots cut low around the ankles, and instead of a toecap stiffened with leather or metal, it's strengthened with soft rubber. Their comfort and lightness plays a big part in the deftness of their

control and swift footwork and that rubber toe lends itself to shooting with the instep as well as the meat of the foot and you know, Stan, how often a goal can be scored by a player simply passing the ball into the net.

They also wear thin short-sleeved shirts and skimpy shorts. In comparison, the shorts our players wear in England flap about the legs like divided skirts. These teams are showing us the way forward and I know it's the way we must go, because if we don't, we'll be left behind.

Matt also realised that with rapidly developing air travel, European contact would be easier and quicker. Matt saw all this when the bodies who governed football in this country couldn't see past the end of their nose.

As a manager Matt proved himself to be a master tactician but also tactful. He never gave a player a rollicking, much preferring to mask an unpleasant task, making it acceptable by turning it on its head.

When Matt stood down as manager of Manchester United, he was succeeded by one of his former Busby Babes, Wilf McGuinness. For 30-odd years Wilf had been at United, a diehard red through and through. Sadly things did not work out for Wilf and in 1970 Matt, then a board member, was given the task of relieving him of his managerial duties. To say Matt wasn't looking forward to the task is an understatement. Wilf had worked for him as a player, coach and manager since he was 15, but Matt dealt with it like the gentleman he was.

'Wilf, you've been at this club for 30 years and have given us great service and unswaying loyalty in all that time,' said Matt during the fateful meeting. 'I don't know how this club could get by without you, but we're going to give it a try.' That was Matt, sensitive, diplomatic and gentlemanly to a fault.

Matt shared my belief that when you have top-quality players in a side a manager doesn't have to tell them what to do because they will know. On one visit to Old Trafford in the sixties I sat with Matt in the directors box. Come the interval United were trailing 1–0. Matt excused himself and set off down the steps to give the team his half-time team-talk. Within minutes he was back.

'What did you say to them?' I asked, wondering why he had returned so swiftly.

'The usual,' said Matt. 'I just popped my head around the door and said, "Keep playin' fitba, lads." ' United secured another victory.

In 1967 when Manchester United beat a West Ham side including England World Cup winners Bobby Moore, Geoff Hurst and Martin Peters 6–1 at Upton Park to clinch the First Division Championship, United's directors joined the team in the dressing room to celebrate. Chairman Louis Edwards praised everyone but made particular mention of Matt Busby, ending his speech by referring to Matt as 'a truly great man'. In his response, Matt was quick to play down the esteem in which he was held by his own chairman saying, 'There are no great men, Mr Chairman, only men.'

Matt Busby may well have been only a man, but that he was a truly remarkable one there can be no doubt.

Paradoxical as it may seem, in this era noted for high goalscoring there were some very good goalkeepers, although in general goalkeepers in modern football are far and away better exponents of the art than their predecessors. It all started with Gordon Banks in the sixties. He studied and applied himself to goalkeeping in such a devoted and thorough way that he turned the art into a science. Gordon paved the way. Disciples of his style and approach took goalkeeping to new heights and British football went on to produce such great goalkeepers as Pat Jennings, Peter

Shilton, Ray Clemence and later, David Seaman, while the general standard of goalkeeping was raised immeasurably.

In the thirties five goalkeepers stood out for me – Elisha Scott, Harry Hibbs, Ted Sagar, Vic Woodley and Frank Swift. It is generally accepted that goalkeepers have to be a little crazy. I wouldn't go so far as to say that, but the position does have a habit of producing larger-than-life characters. Why anyone would wish to play in a position where just one mistake may lead to a goal for the opposition and which involves flinging yourself at the flaying boots of a barnstorming centre-forward has over the years remained a mystery to me.

Elisha Scott was in the twilight of his career when I started out at Stoke City. Born in Belfast, he made his debut for Liverpool in 1913 and remained a custodian of their net until 1934 when he returned to his homeland to manage Belfast Celtic. Of lamppost build, his square angular chin and Romanesque features gave him the look of a Hollywood film star, though I never saw any indication from him that he realised it. Scott was 40 when I encountered him during Stoke's first season back in the top flight, 1933–34, which was to be his last in a Liverpool jersey. Even at that age he was exceptionally lithe and agile. His natural ability and experience meant he read situations early and he would sally forth to great effect, seizing the initiative and putting doubt into the minds of opposing forwards. Scott saw his penalty area as his domain.

In one meeting between Stoke and Liverpool, Stoke rampaged through the opening stages, pinning Liverpool into their own half and peppering their goal with shots, to all of which Scott was equal. After 15 minutes of this onslaught, having just produced another fine save, Scott got to his feet and, ball in hand, shouted at his Liverpool team-mates, 'You lot had better start playing now, because

I'm 40 and I can't keep this up all afternoon!'

Harry Hibbs hailed from Wilnecote in Staffordshire and spent his entire career with Birmingham City. They never enjoyed the success a club of their stature merited – cue Blues fans asking 'Was it ever thus?' I played against Harry Hibbs many times in the thirties and we were England colleagues on two occasions; Harry kept goal when I made my England debut against Wales in 1934 and against Germany at White Hart Lane a year later when Münzenberg gave me the run-around. Like the great Sam Hardy who played for Liverpool, Aston Villa and England with great distinction pre and post World War One, Harry was a quiet, unassuming type of goalkeeper, unspectacular but reliable, and he possessed keen judgement and an uncanny positional sense.

My abiding memory of Harry is one day at the Victoria Ground when after cutting in from the right, I unleashed a shot at goal which veered away from him only to rebound back into play off his far post and be put behind for a corner by one of his defenders. I pursed my lips and momentarily closed my eyes in frustration at how near I had come to a goal. Harry stood rooted to the spot and seeing me do this said, 'Don't curse your bad luck, Stan. You sliced that ball, otherwise I wouldn't be standing where I am, I'd have been over there,' pointing towards his far post. He was absolutely right. I had sliced across the face of the ball. As I say, Harry Hibbs had a great sense of positioning.

With the advent of World War Two Harry Hibbs's career came to an end. Post-war, he managed Walsall until 1951 but then disappeared from the game. I never heard of him again until the newspapers carried reports of his death in 1984.

Ted Sagar kept goal for Everton and vied for the England jersey with Harry Hibbs and Preston's George Holdcroft.

George was born in Burslem and, like me, had grown up in Stoke-on-Trent. All three lost out to Chelsea's Vic Woodley. Ted was always a bit on the small side to be a truly great goalkeeper, but he made up for that with astounding agility, cat-like reflexes, courage and daring. Hull City obviously thought he was too small to make the grade because they released him as a teenager and he went into mining. Everton spotted Ted playing for a Doncaster colliery team. Hull City's loss was Everton's and Ted's gain because he went on to win championship and FA Cup winner's medals with the Merseysiders and proved that you do not necessarily have to be tall to be a goalkeeper of note.

Ted possessed a great sense of humour and win, lose or draw he was always ready with a joke or a quip. Following a game against Everton, I asked Ted about a young player whom one sports writer of the day had been bulling up, saying the lad in question was 'a very useful player with a good future ahead of him in football'.

'Played against him at Grimsby last week,' Ted informed me. 'As useful as a back pocket in a vest.'

Ted couldn't have been far wrong in his assessment because the young player in question soon faded from the scene never to be heard of again.

When football pundits and historians look back at goalkeepers of this period, Chelsea's Vic Woodley rarely gets a mention, which is a shame because he was a quality player. Perhaps this is because he wasn't flamboyant, outgoing, spectacular or a character. He was a steady goalkeeper whose consistency gave confidence to the players in front of him. His defenders were never on edge, frightened of making a mistake in case it led to a goal. He bossed the area from his line to the penalty spot and although in Alf Young and Stan Cullis England had players who could get up and head a ball, Vic would come off his line to make crosses his own. I always felt very confident with Vic as the last line of defence.

Of all the goalkeepers of that era, Frank Swift was my favourite. A large man with an even larger character, Swifty and I became great friends in the immediate post-war years when he made the England goalkeeper's jersey his own. Frank was born in Blackpool, so after my move there we had much in common. He signed for Manchester City in 1932 and made his first-team debut a year later at the age of 19. So competent a keeper was he, Frank never missed a first-team match for City for the next five years.

As opposed to Vic Woodley, Frank was so spectacular he bordered on the acrobatic. He had hands like shovels, fingers like bananas and his gorilla-like reach and spring-heeled take-off meant he could reach many shots other goalkeepers would give up on. When he left his line he'd swoop on the ball rather than bend and gather it. So enormous were his hands, he'd stand holding the ball in one hand, fingers encompassing it as if it were a grapefruit. For all his enormous size he was Swift by name and swift by nature – in midflight diving to save, Frank cut a figure as graceful as the bird. He was very much a daredevil. His indifference at meeting a rampaging forward full-on spoke volumes for his courage.

The reason for Frank Swift's popularity not only with Manchester City fans but opposing players and supporters was his ability to mix goalkeeping excellence and laughter in equal and engaging proportions to enliven even the dullest of matches. His fondness for the spectacular at times proved his undoing but more often than not he got away with it. The louder the opposition fans roared, the longer he leapt and the further he came out from his goal to clear a through ball upfield. I think it can be said that in 1937 he carried Manchester City on his broad shoulders to the First Division Championship. The following season, when Frank was plagued by injury, they were relegated. Frank was the first-ever goalkeeper to captain England and he kept goal for Manchester City for 17 highly entertaining years.

Following his retirement in 1949, Frank went to work for a Sunday newspaper, the *Empire News*, later taken over by the *People*. He died in the Munich air disaster in 1958, his tragic and untimely death, a source of deep emotion to all who knew him and a matter of sad regret to those who didn't but who appreciated football at its best and most entertaining.

The declaration of war in 1939 proved to be the most upsetting hiatus imaginable but as it turned out, in both football and my personal life, the best was yet to come. The thirties, however, left me and all football fans with a treasure trove of memories.

The aborted 1939–40 season began with players wearing numbers for the very first time in league matches for identification purposes. Even though we played just three games before the season was brought to an abrupt halt, it did prompt a wag in the Victoria Ground to shout, 'Come in number seven, your time's up' at an opposing player not having the best of games against us. The old ones may well be the best! At the time that remark was new and prompted a wave of laughter not only throughout the terraces but down on the pitch as well. In many ways, that sums up football for me in the thirties. It was physical, tough, players were very tightly marked but for all that it rained goals due to the many skilful players around at the time. Above all, it was great fun. I wonder how many of today's players will look back at Premiership football, when their playing days are over, with the first thought to come to mind being, 'It was great fun.' I'm not a betting man, but if I was my money would be on it not being many.

9

---○---

Corporal Matthews
of the RAF

There can be little doubt that World War Two took away what should have been the best years of some of the most talented players British football has ever produced. I was 24 when war was declared, past 30 when peace came; all things being equal the war should have robbed me of my prime footballing years. In a sense it did, but as fate and luck would have it, due to skills with which I had been blessed and the level of fitness maintained since childhood, once the hostilities were over I was to enjoy another 20 years in top-flight football.

Not long after war was declared, I joined the RAF and I remained in that service for the duration. Just as my football career had started out at the bottom, so did my war service. I became A/C 1361317 S. Matthews, Royal Air Force, holding the lowest rank in all of the RAF, which suited me because it evoked no jealousy or resentment on the part of my fellow servicemen.

Looking back, I think it's amazing how Blackpool played a key role in certain periods of my life. When I submitted a transfer request at Stoke City, it was to Blackpool I escaped for a few days and on joining the RAF to my delight I found I was to be stationed just outside this bright and breezy seaside town. I was told by a Commanding Officer that I was to undergo a period of basic training, and also that the War Office wanted footballers to help the war effort by continuing to play as and when circumstances allowed, to provide entertainment and a diversion from the war for both troops and the civilian population. This was music to my ears, though I was keen to serve King and country and more than willing to fight the enemy.

Training in the RAF was a bit of a misnomer. The first few weeks consisted mainly of square bashing. The services were a melting pot for the population. My fellow recruits came from just about every walk of life but I was surprised to find my NCO was Ivor Powell who had been with Queens Park Rangers. After the war, Ivor joined Aston Villa and won eight caps for Wales, but during my period of training he never made any mention of the fact that we were fellow footballers. He addressed me as he did all the other new recruits: 'Come here, you! Left–right, left–right, left–right. Don't you know your left from your right? You're supposed to be marching! Tenshun! You're a shambles but I'll knock you into shape if it takes till kingdom come.' On the parade ground, Ivor's face adopted the perpetual expression of having just smelt something burning on the back of the cooker. He was a strict NCO, as monotonous as old mutton in his delivery of orders, but he did lick us into shape. I have to admit I was one of his worst recruits.

Once the daily RAF training was over I had time to myself, and although I spent hours drilling on a parade ground, I used my free time to train and practise my ball skills. I still rose early and my daily routine would begin on the beach at six in the morning when I would go for a long run then put myself through a rigorous routine of short sprints and shuttle runs. Following the daily dose of RAF training, I'd go to a nearby sports field to do stretching exercises, then spend an hour or so on ball work before finishing with a series of sprints. In those early days in the RAF, I didn't know when I would ever get the chance to play football at any level again, but my personal training helped me psychologically. War apart, it gave me a sense of purpose.

As it happened, it wasn't long before I was donning a pair of football boots again. After a few weeks of basic training I was told to report early one morning outside the NCO billets and to bring my football kit with me. On arriving I was told a team had been selected from our barracks to play another RAF unit stationed in Yorkshire. A bus was waiting to take us to the game. Our Commanding Officer arrived, did a head count and to his chagrin found we were two players short. A quick look at the team-sheet told him the two missing players were 'Jock' Dodds, who was at Sheffield United before joining Blackpool, and Hugh O'Donnell, another Scot and a well-known left-winger with Preston North End. The pair were in digs in Blackpool, so the fuming CO ordered the bus to be driven round to their lodgings where on arrival he stormed up the garden path and proceeded to hammer on the front door. A minute or so passed with our CO continuing to bang loudly on the door before a window shot up and the sleepy head of Jock Dodds appeared.

'Shut up that racket!' shouted Jock. 'I've got a fuzzy head.'

'Fuzzy head be blowed,' shouted the CO stepping back off the doorstep so that Jock could see him. 'I'll have you by the fuzzies if you're not down here in one minute flat!'

As footballers, Jock and Hugh both had a reputation for

speed but I doubt if either ever moved as quickly as they did that morning. Within a minute they bolted through the front door hastily trying to do up their clothes as they did so and both wearing their uniforms over their pyjamas. Hugh O'Donnell had jumped out of bed in such haste he'd forgotten to bring his football boots so played the entire game in his steel-capped RAF boots. He scored the winning goal with a screamer of a shot from 20 yards. Those RAF boots took their toll on his feet, however. The pitch had been hard and bumpy and after the match when he took off his boots and football socks his toes looked like hyacinth bulbs, but he knew better than to complain.

After a time, the inter-unit matches developed into full-blown inter-service games. Jock Dodds and I were picked to play for the RAF against the Army at Elland Road and travelled to Leeds together by train. Travelling to football matches in wartime bordered on the adventurous. Having been chosen for a team, you had to apply for duty relief, which more often than not could be easily arranged. The train journeys, however, were a different matter. The railway service during wartime was erratic; trains were often re-routed and on occasions did not end up at their original destination. I thought of them as I did diets – perfectly acceptable things for other people to go on. On the journey to Leeds, a thick fog came down over the Pennines and our train when not crawling along at a snail's pace just squealed to an eerie halt. I hate being late for anything and the more time that passed the more anxious and fidgety I became. Jock tried to placate me, saying there was nothing we could do about it, but I wasn't having any. When we finally arrived at our destination there were only five minutes to kick-off time and I was all of a flutter.

'Look on the bright side,' Jock said as we sprinted out of the station in search of a cab. 'At least we're in Leeds.'

On seeing the taxi rank my heart sank. There was a massive queue and, being British, I felt there was nothing for it but to join the end of it. I've always had trouble with queues. Before Post Offices channelled us like sheep down a single route I'd always choose the queue that moved the slowest. On my rare visits to pubs, when it was my time to buy the drinks I'd find myself behind a group of women on a girls' night out all of whom insisted on buying their own instead of one of them getting a round in. At the supermarket check-out I always manage to choose the one manned by the trainee who has to ring for help in processing every other item. Queues and me just don't get on. I joined this queue with a sense of hoplessness but Jock grabbed me by the arm and dragged me to the front.

'Footballers,' he said holding up his boots to the queue as if they were a policeman's warrant card. 'We have to be at Elland Road in five minutes.'

The taxi driver's hand appeared through his open window and opened the door behind him on his side of the cab. Jock and I ran round and jumped into the back seat and we sped off in the direction of Elland Road with the line of onlookers too stupified to protest.

The RAF team were taking to the pitch with nine players as we arrived, but they held back the kick-off for a couple of minutes to allow Jock and me to do a quick change routine. We weren't the only ones to leave it late – the Army scored the winning goal in the last minute.

On another occasion, I was chosen to represent the RAF against the Army in Edinburgh. My travelling companion was Manchester City's great inside-forward Peter Doherty, not always the most congenial of people but I got on with him very well. After the game we had arranged for a taxi to take us to the station to catch a train back to Blackpool where, bright and early the next morning, we were expected to be back on regular RAF duty.

We hung around outside the football ground for 15 minutes or so before it dawned on us no taxi was coming. Peter noticed an RAF staff car in which was sitting a pretty WAAF. Peter approached her, explained our dilemma and asked if she could run us to the station. At first she told him it was out of the question as she was waiting for a Group Captain attending a meeting who was due back within the hour. Undeterred Peter turned on the Irish charm and having convinced the girl she could do the round trip in half an hour at the most, the WAAF relented and agreed to run us to the station. No sooner had we settled into the back seat, however, than the Group Captain turned up early from his meeting and in no uncertain terms ordered us out of his staff car.

A man who had been sitting on the bonnet of a small black saloon and witnessed all this called us over. Recognising Peter and me, he volunteered to run us to the station and even though he smelled of drink, such was our plight we readily accepted his kind offer. The journey from that football ground to the railway station was one of the most perilous I have ever undertaken. No sooner had we got going than we realised just how much this man had had to drink. Not only was he incapable of driving straight, he couldn't keep the car on the left-hand side of the road. We repeatedly veered towards oncoming traffic at breakneck speed only to lurch back again at the last moment. He was driving with his foot to the boards and swerved around corners so quickly that Peter and I were thrown around the back seat like corks on the ocean. After a close thing with an oncoming bus, our driver spun the steering wheel and the car swerved back to the left and mounted the pavement. It was hair-raising and on two occasions we clipped roundabouts as we sped through Edinburgh far in excess of the speed limit. As we turned the corner and on to the forecourt of the station, the car lurched violently to the right, to the left, to the right and to the left again before mounting the pavement once more and squealing to a halt. Peter and I got out shaking and ashen-faced but in good time for our train. Like gibbering wrecks we thanked the driver for the lift and offered to pay the man some money for his time and petrol which in a very slurred voice he declined.

'If I was you, I'd leave the car here and go straight home. You're in no fit state to drive, my friend. You're as drunk as a lord,' Peter said as we bade our farewell.

'Am I?' the driver asked quizzically. 'Thank heavens for that. I thought the bloody steering had gone again!'

It didn't take long before football's governing bodies, with the full backing of the government, organised an alternative programme that existed throughout the war. Due to the scarcity of fuel and the overburdened rail and road networks, regionalised competitions were introduced with many areas having their own cup competitions as well. Clubs were rarely in a position to field the same team two games running, but the problem was alleviated by the Football League's easygoing approach to guest players. A club could call upon the services of a player stationed in their area and this made for colourful if erratic team selection. The system was of particular benefit to Aldershot. As the traditional home of the British Army, this small club, having spent the majority of the thirties in the nether regions of the Third Division South, found itself at various times enjoying the services of a string of top international players.

Stoke City started the war years in fine style, topping the Western League in 1939–40, winning 13 and drawing five of the 22 matches played. I wasn't available for many games but I wasn't the only one. When war was declared, 22 of my

Stoke City team-mates were already in the Territorial Army and they were called up immediately. Frank Baker, Syd Peppitt, Billy Mould and Alex Ormston, stationed together in Northern Ireland, all won Irish Cup winners medals guesting for Linfield. Stoke City had just started to come good when war was declared and even though we showed we were a force to be reckoned with in the immediate post-war years, I'm firmly of the mind that if ever a club was robbed of honours by the hostilities, it was us.

Being stationed on the Fylde, I found myself guesting for Blackpool with increasing regularity. I was first approached by the Blackpool chairman Colonel W. Parkinson, a man as exacting as a top sergeant but one of honesty and integrity. He was held in high esteem in the town. Over the years I became good friends with Colonel Parkinson and he did me many favours, proving himself to be also the most benevolent of men.

Colonel Parkinson's connections in the services ensured Blackpool maintained a steady stream of guest players of the highest quality. Blackpool initially vied with Preston North End for the players stationed along the Fylde coast, but eventually came out as top dogs during the war years, winning the League North from 1942–44 and the League North Cup in 1942–43. To give some idea of how cosmopolitan a team could be, the Blackpool team that beat Sheffield Wednesday in 1943 to win the League North Cup, then defeated the southern Cup holders Arsenal 4–2 at Stamford Bridge in the Regional Cup decider, lined up as follows: Willy Savage (Queen of the South), 'Patty' Pope (Hearts), Sam Jones (Blackpool), George Farrow, Eric Hayward, Harry Johnston (all Blackpool), Stan Matthews (Stoke City), Ron Dix (Tottenham), Jock Dodds (Blackpool), Bob Finan (Blackpool), Eddie Burbanks (Sunderland). There was one change for the

Arsenal game – Harry Hubbick of Burnley came in at left-back for Sam Jones, which meant that six of this successful Blackpool team were in fact imports.

Blackpool's Eric Hayward was from North Staffordshire, like me. He was the elder brother of Basil Hayward who played with such distinction in that great Port Vale side of the fifties. During the war years, Eric guested for Stoke City, Wolves, West Brom, Wrexham, Walsall, Birmingham City, Northampton Town, Chesterfield and Luton Town, sometimes playing for a club one week and against them the next. Eric had an impish sense of humour. During one RAF intelligence and initiative test, we were asked to write a sentence that included the word 'archaic'. Eric's answer read, 'We can't have archaic and eat it.' If that doesn't show great initiative, what does?

The war years threw up all manner of odd footballing incidents and due to the transient composition of teams, more than its fair share of freak scorelines. On Christmas morning 1940, Brighton and Hove Albion set off from the Goldstone Ground for a South League game at Norwich with only five players. They were hoping to pick up some others on the way but with it being Christmas Day the guest players obviously opted to be with their families. Brighton ended up having to field a number of Norwich City reserve-team players and even called upon soldiers from the sparse crowd of 1,419 that had turned up to watch the game. To complete Brighton's misery, their hotchpotch makeshift side lost 18–0! On their return home, one of the Brighton five was asked by a local reporter to comment on the game. 'It was a very even game,' he said. 'They scored nine in each half.'

Peter Doherty guested twice for Port Vale in 1945 and caused a stir in one the games. He elected to take a penalty but instead of shooting for goal, he laid the ball back for a team-mate to run on to and duly score. Not many people know this is within the rules of the game and I know of only one other incident of it happening – that marvellously gifted Dutchman Johan Cruyff did exactly the same during a match in the seventies. I always fancied doing it, but no team I played for entrusted a penalty to me, which is just as well really.

During the war, players could find themselves pressed to play in positions new to them. Leslie Compton, full-back in the Arsenal reserve team pre-war, played a couple of seasons at centre-forward and ended up with 76 goals in 70 games. In February 1941, Arsenal beat Clapton Orient, formerly of the Third Division South, by the amazing scoreline of 15–2. Leslie scored ten and his brother Denis scored twice to make it a bit of a family affair.

I never expected or received any preferential treatment for being a well-known footballer; neither did I experience any resentment or petty negative attitudes towards me on the part of fellow recruits or superiors. My England team-mate Eddie Hapgood also joined the RAF and unfortunately he did. Eddie was captain of Arsenal, the top club in the thirties, and England. I'm sure he didn't expect that to cut any ice when he joined the RAF; all he wanted was to do his bit and be treated like any other recruit, but his status as a footballer did work against him occasionally. I remember Eddie telling me he had reported to RAF Cardington, a base in the south of England, a few weeks before the Battle of Britain was to take place, but was made to feel anything but 'one of the few'. On his first day, a matter-of-fact corporal read roll-call.

'Hapgood. E.A.?' bawled the corporal.

'Sir?' replied Eddie, to acknowledge his presence.

'Any relation to the Arsenal player?' asked the corporal.

'The same, sir,' replied Eddie self-consciously.

'Oh-ho,' leered the corporal. 'Well, sonny boy, you played

for a classy team, so I'm going to give you the classy jobs round here.'

The corporal disappeared for a moment and returned with a tin of floor polish which he threw at Eddie. Eddie caught the tin on his right thigh to kill the momentum of the throw, then let it fall to the floor where he caught it on his right foot before flicking it up in the air and back at the corporal. The corporal, who turned out to be a Tottenham fan, was not amused. Eddie spent the next four weeks polishing the barrack-room floor and cleaning out the toilets as part of 'doing his bit'. After a month, he ended up in sick bay with multiple septic whitlows on both hands and spent the next two and a half months having to undergo operations.

Eddie had a bit of a rough ride from small-minded immediate superiors, but found an ally when Bill Shankly was also posted to Cardington. Eddie told me he 'talked incessantly about football with all the enthusiasm of a religious fanatic,' which as far as football was concerned, Shanks was.

At another RAF camp, Eddie was confined to barracks and placed on a charge for a reason he did not know. He had been talking to a corporal about duties only for the corporal to fire up and put him on a charge. It was a Saturday morning and later that day Eddie was due to play a regional league match for Arsenal against Spurs at White Hart Lane. Eddie asked the sergeant in charge if 'something could be done about the situation'. The sergeant, an Arsenal fan, said he would have a word with the duty officer of the day which he duly did and Eddie was ushered into his presence. Eddie explained he had simply been asking the corporal about a duty roster when suddenly the man flared up and put him on a charge and he didn't know why. The duty officer leapt to his feet.

'My God, man, you're doing it now to me. How dare you!'

Eddie stunned and perplexed protested his innocence which only served to make the duty officer more irate until finally he came round his desk, took hold of Eddie's arms and pressed them into either side of his body. It turned out that Eddie, for all he had been polite and respectful, had been using his hands to emphasise certain points in the conversation. Eddie always did that but in the RAF at the time it was looked upon as gross insolence. Eddie was a conscript who, like me, knew nothing of RAF procedure and protocol. One would have thought that a simple explanation would have put Eddie right on the matter, but probably because of who he was, they came down hard on him.

Eddie, still on a charge, was allowed to turn out for Arsenal that afternoon, but he did so with a two-man escort. They not only stayed by his side as he got changed for the game, but ran up and down the touchline tracking Eddie as the game progressed for fear he'd do a runner. It was a totally absurd situation but in keeping with the mentality often shown by the forces in those days. As it turned out, the charge against Eddie was dropped the following Monday and it was back to his menial duties.

We were all there to help our country and I suppose the RAF line would be that by attending to such petty detail it formed a foundation for discipline, but you have to wonder if it was all really necessary. Eddie Hapgood had tremendous qualities of leadership, motivation and immense courage yet they were never tapped into during his early service years. Eddie moved on from menial duties to become a PT instructor and NCO in the latter years of the war. His early experience was different from my own, but I am left to reflect on how other well-known names were treated, and more to the point, how many men and women with so much to offer were never used to their full effectiveness due to service mentality at the time.

Although substitutes had never been allowed in peace-time matches, football did flirt with them during the war years. Blackpool's Stan Mortensen was an England reserve for what was considered an unofficial international against Wales played at Wembley in September 1943. Wales turned up with just the eleven and when my former NCO Ivor Powell was injured in the first half, it was agreed by both FAs that Stan Mortensen should be allowed to play the second half for Wales. Caps were not awarded for wartime internationals, which were entered in the record books as unofficial matches, but Morty must hold a unique place in British football having played for both England and Wales!

Internationals during the war were strange affairs compared with the peace-time games. It's true to say a number of players got to represent their country who probably wouldn't have done under normal circumstances; hence the games being unofficial for which no caps were awarded. They were, however, seen as being a tremendous tonic for the public, a brief diversion from the worry, anxiety and frugality of war and were taken very seriously by all the players.

The first two wartime internationals England were involved in were both played against Wales. I played in one of them. Following those two fixtures, it was arranged that England should play Scotland at St James' Park, Newcastle, with the proceeds going to wartime charities. By this time, British cities were being heavily bombed and although on the one hand the Government were keen for these matches to continue to boost public morale, they were also concerned about the risks involved in having a large crowd of people assembling in one place at the same time. In one North League game I played at Preston, we were just in the process of getting changed after the match when the sirens sounded. We quickly gathered up our clothes and headed for the shelters. As we were making our way out of the ground, Blackpool's Harry Johnston started to head back. We shouted for him to join us in making for the bomb shelter but Harry said he had to go back to the dressing room to fetch his top set of teeth. 'For God's sake, Harry, come on!' shouted team-mate Sam Jones. 'They're dropping bombs not pies!'

There was an England–Scotland match at Wembley in 1942 that was played in a blizzard and it struck me as most unusual to see Wembley under a carpet of snow. For all the inclement weather, 65,000 turned up to see the match. We beat the Scots 3–0. Wolves' Stan Cullis was outstanding in the centre of defence while Middlesbrough's Wilf Mannion and Sheffield United's Jimmy Hagan were inspirational inside-forwards on the day. Jimmy Hagan scored a wonderful individual goal to put us ahead, Arsenal's Denis Compton set up Tommy Lawton for our second and I crossed for Tommy to get his second and our third to wrap up the game. I can't recall this game in any real detail, other than the goals, but I do remember the freezing weather. In the dressing room after the game, my fingers were so numb with cold I couldn't unfasten the buttons on my shirt or undo the laces on my boots for quite some time.

'It shows you how cold it's been this afternoon,' quipped Tommy Lawton as we reached our Wembley changing room. 'I've come back into the dressing room and my suit's got my overcoat on.'

For me, the most memorable wartime international took place against Scotland at Maine Road, Manchester in October 1943. England had already beaten the Scots that year at Hampden but on this day we were inspired and irresistible, winning 8–0. That result is the biggest winning margin in the history of fixtures between the two countries to this day. Tommy Lawton, who had emerged as a diamond of a centre-forward scored four, Jimmy Hagan two, with Raich Carter and I getting a goal apiece. I derived some satisfaction from the goal I scored. I remember collecting the ball on the halfway line and setting off on a dribble that took me in and out of the Scottish defence before rounding the goalkeeper to slot the ball home. The 60,000 crowd roared their heads off but I can say in all honesty, it was just another goal to me and by the time I made that run, the Scottish team were already a well-beaten side. One newspaper said I turned in '. . . a blueprint performance that tormented the Scottish left flank from start to finish.' I'm not too sure what they meant by that, but I thought I'd done OK; besides, how could you not play well when getting service from Raich Carter and having a centre-forward as merciless and lethal as Tommy Lawton to aim for? In football, how well you play often has as much to do with the quality of players around you. In Raich Carter, Jimmy Hagan, Tommy Lawton, Denis Compton and Joe Mercer, I had the privilege that day of playing with players whose deftness of touch and adroitness in the use of the ball was matched by an unswerving reliance on playing purist football with common sense and simplicity.

Six years in the RAF resulted in a rise through the ranks to the dizzy heights of corporal, but for all my self-discipline in football I have to admit to being probably the mildest and most easygoing NCO the RAF has ever known. I just didn't have it in me to bark orders, be stern and unrelenting with recruits or come down hard on anybody. On one occasion, an aircraftman second class reported to me for punishment duty as he had been caught eating cherries that, for want of a better phrase, weren't on the official menu. When he presented himself before me I recognised him as Tom Freeman, a young sports reporter of much promise. His punishment was to accompany me on a walk around the camp during which we talked about football, offering one another our various views on the game. After the war, Tom joined my home-town newspaper the *Evening Sentinel* to cover Port Vale games before moving on to become a football writer of some note with Reuters. I often bumped into him and he would always remind me of the most informative and enjoyable 'jankers' he ever experienced in the RAF.

In January 1945, with the war slowly drawing to a close, I was in London, I think to make a radio broadcast, when I received the telephone call all offspring dread. My father was gravely ill in hospital and was asking for me. The war had meant my father and I hadn't seen much of each other in five years. My thoughts were with him and of all the help and advice he had given me, as I made a tortuous journey back to the Potteries. On arriving at Stoke station, I made straight for the hospital. His doctor told me that my father was terminally ill and only his determination to see me once more was keeping him alive. It's hard to describe the feelings that run through you on receiving news like that. The situation is numbing, yet somehow such heartbreaking circumstances elicit a strange otherwise dormant strength. When I reached the door of the ward, I paused for a brief moment, took a deep breath and tried to prepare myself for what I knew was the worst. My father seemed asleep. Betty and my mother were by his bedside. He was a shadow of the man I had known. I had last seen him some six months earlier and the deterioration shocked me. I asked my mother and Betty how he was.

'He's asleep, but he's been constantly asking for you,' Mother said, turning her tear-stained face towards me. He woke then.

'You're here at last, Stanley. What's taken you so long?' he said, his voice weak. I took his hand and explained I had been in London when I received the news he was in hospital and that I had caught the next available train. My father turned his head towards my mother. 'I told you, Mother, it wasn't like our Stanley to be late. I taught him . . .'

His voice trailed away and he turned to look at me once more. I was at a loss as to what to say and we stayed like that for some minutes, my father's face saddened. The only noise was a clock ticking on the wall. I kept smiling but I was torn apart inside, my body and mind wracked with a complete sense of hopelessness, of being incapable of doing anything to ease his pain and discomfort. It was only a couple of minutes at most but it seemed like an age before my father spoke again.

'Son, I'm no fool. I know I've had my lot,' he said in a soft husky voice, barely audible. 'I've never asked you for a thing. Not ever. But I'm going to ask you to do two things for me now.'

'You just say them and they'll be done,' I said, not knowing what he had in mind.

'Look after your mother for me when I go,' he said, finding the strength to squeeze my hand gently.

'Of course I will. But you're not on your way out yet, you're going to get better . . .' My father cut me off.

'Shush. Don't give me that. I know what's what, so don't try and kid me otherwise.'

His head sank back into the pillows and he let out a deep sigh and started to breathe slowly but deeply.

'Now Father, no more talking, take it easy,' I said, fearing this was the dreaded moment.

My mother leaned towards him and mopped his forehead with a crisp handkerchief. As she did so, I saw them gaze lovingly into one another's eyes and I suddenly realised just what they had meant to one another in life. My mother kissed him on the lips and as she pulled away I saw him looking at her, his face filled with longing and love.

By this time some other family members had come in. They had come to the hospital every day. My father turned to me again and asked to be lifted up. We managed to raise him into a sitting position. His face contorted with agony as we did so, but I saw his determination. He leaned into me. For all my closeness to him, his voice was barely audible. In a weak and husky whisper he spoke.

'Listen, son. That other thing I want you to do for me,' he said. 'I had only one more ambition for you in life. Will you do it for me?'

'Of course. Just say the word,' I replied, not having a clue what this might be.

My father then made me make one more promise, the nature of which took me aback. I heard myself acceding to a promise that in my heart of hearts I wanted to fulfil, but was not sure I could ever keep. I am not sure if any other members of the family heard what my father said; it remained a secret between us. Even though it came to pass some years later, I have not revealed it publicly until now.

They were the last words we spoke. Minutes later my father gave a weak smile, sank into his pillows and passed away.

10

The Burnden Park
Disaster

The years stationed near Blackpool with the RAF
endeared the town and its coastline to me. I decided
I preferred to live by the sea. The air suited me and
the beach was a constant source of inspiration not to
mention perfect for the daily four-mile run that still formed
an integral part of my private training. No matter what time
of year I walked or ran along the shoreline, I always found it
to be invigorating. The constant, relentless beating of the
waves on the beach had something glorious about it. Even if
I had walked along the sands the day before, there was
always something new and different to see, something of
interest. Out of the town, where the razzmatazz of the
golden mile gives way to fields and sand dunes, the wind
coming in off the sea changes the whole character of the land
from mellowness to barrenness. In late August, it punches
out the last breath of summer and in November strips the
last leaves from the bowed and crooked trees. I fell in love

with it and so did Betty. So we decided to buy a small seaside hotel and make our home there. Of course, I had one eye on the future. I had passed 30 and didn't think I had too many years left in football.

A month after my father died, I played in another wartime England–Scotland international, this time at Villa Park. England won 3–2. I had been granted a fortnight's leave and as soon as the game was over I headed north and home to Betty and Jean. The days spent with my family were a real tonic, helping me come to terms with my father's death. It was also great to be away from the daily routine of service life. Betty and I planned days out to places where Jean would enjoy herself. Some days we were content to relax at home, doing nothing much. Betty had had the strain of bringing up young Jean more or less on her own and I wanted to spend as much time as I could with our daughter, so I encouraged Betty to go into town shopping or to visit friends just to give her a break, some time to relax and do the things she wanted to do. It was a highly enjoyable fortnight.

I was back with the RAF when I received a call from Betty asking if I could meet her at a café in town for afternoon tea. I could tell straightaway by the look on her face she had good news, but she kept me waiting. We talked about this and that, how Jean had been sleeping and developing before Betty broke her news.

'Stanley, I wanted to see you because I have some great news. You're going to be a father again.'

The baby was due in November and Betty was certain it was going to be a boy. I was gloriously happy for us. I felt a second child would really make us a family.

From that day on life seemed to brighten considerably. Although there were some months to go, the nation seemed to sense that the war was at last coming to an end, with

Britain and our allies triumphant. It lifted everyone. My football fell into line with the growing optimism. I played for England against Scotland at Hampden in the April when we again drubbed the Scots, this time 6–1. In May, England beat Wales 3–2 at Cardiff and a fortnight later on 26 May drew 2–2 with a French side dubbed 'Free France' at Wembley. It was the first time I had set foot on the Wembley turf since the death of my father and even though this was an unofficial international, as the teams walked down that famous tunnel he was in my thoughts.

This was the month German forces surrendered in north west Germany, Holland and Denmark, and the Russians took Berlin. Before the month was out, Germany capitulated and the war in Europe was over. Three months later, the Americans dropped the atomic bomb on Hiroshima and on 14 August Japan signed an unconditional surrender. In my naivety, I thought that was it and I would be immediately discharged from the services, but apparently the RAF thought Corporal Matthews had played such a key role during the war I had to stay on. So they hung on to my services until the spring of 1946 when they were satisfied the skies over Britain were safe and they could get by without me.

Although it was to be another year before official league football returned to Britain, as soon as the peace was made football took off again, big style. The regional leagues continued for the 1945–46 season, but the FA Cup was re-introduced straightaway. For the best part of the season, I was still in the RAF but with the hostilities over, I found myself playing regularly once more.

In November 1945, Russia sent a team to Britain for the very first time as a goodwill gesture for the alliance between our two countries during the war. The Cold War had yet to bite and the arrival of Moscow Dynamo was greeted with great excitement and enthusiasm. Our Russian 'comrades' were regarded as friends and brothers-in-arms.

From the moment Moscow Dynamo touched down at Croydon Airport to the time they left for home, they captivated football fans the length and breadth of Great Britain. Dynamo arrived with the reputation of being a real crack side but I doubt if anyone had ever seen them play. Speculation about their quality and capabilities was rife and the sports writers had a field day.

Moscow Dynamo hadn't been in the country a day before controversy raged. Their first game was scheduled for Stamford Bridge against Chelsea on a Wednesday afternoon and the Russians were up in arms about it. Saturday was the big day for football in England, and for the game to be played midweek they felt was an insult to them. At first they refused point blank to fulfil the fixture. It was only when FA secretary Stanley Rous intervened and told them that many of England's international matches were played on a Wednesday afternoon that they relented. No sooner had that issue been settled than the Dynamo officials insisted that substitutes should be allowed during their games. Even though substitutes were not allowed in England, and wouldn't be for another 20 years, that was eventually agreed. Dynamo officials then demanded a Russian referee should officiate in at least one of their games. Not a day passed without them making headlines on the sports pages and it all served to whet the public's appetite. People couldn't wait to see if these demanding prima donnas could live up to their self-proclaimed footballing status.

I was as keen as anyone to see Moscow Dynamo play, so, with a couple of RAF pals, I went to London to watch their opening game against Chelsea. When we got near to the ground, it seemed the world and his wife wanted to be inside

Stamford Bridge that afternoon. The streets around the ground were at a standstill with thousands of people forming one seething mass around the stadium and this was at noon, two hours before kick-off. We managed to get inside just in time for the kick-off, but only just. There were 85,000 crammed into Stamford Bridge.

When Moscow Dynamo took to the pitch we all gasped in amazement. Emblazoned on the left breast of their blue shirts – Chelsea were in their change strip of red – was a large letter D in gold and there was a large golden loop circling the bottom of their blue shorts. We'd never seen such extravagance in strips but the most striking thing about their arrival on the pitch was that each player was carrying a bouquet of flowers which they proceeded to present to their opposite number in the Chelsea team.

'Bouquets of flowers. It's amazing,' I said to one of my pals.

'It is,' he replied, puffing on a Woodbine, squashed in the crush to the shape of a stick of chewing gum. 'I thought all the nurseries and allotments had been turned over to vegetables.'

At first, I thought all the big noise in the press about Moscow Dynamo being a crack side had been overdone because Chelsea raced into a 2–0 lead, but as the game progressed the Dynamos started to live up to their name. They proved themselves to be very fit and fast. They combined speed with a great amount of skill and in the end a pulsating match ended in a 3–3 draw. The scenes at the end had to be seen to be believed. The crowd were in raptures and roared their approval as the Russians left the field.

In the ensuing week, the Russians continued to make controversial headlines. Their second game was against Cardiff City at Ninian Park. At first, the Russians said they didn't want to leave London; then they felt it was demeaning for them to have to play a team who were from the Third Division South. Eventually, after much debate and negotiation between officials, the game in Wales went ahead but I reckon Cardiff manager Cyril Spiers, who had told the press his side would do what Chelsea had failed to do and beat Dynamo, wished it hadn't. Moscow Dynamo swamped them, winning 10–1 and proving their point that only the best opposition was good enough for them.

Moscow Dynamo's next game was against Arsenal, and manager George Allison had problems. A number of his top players, including Eddie Hapgood, Ted Drake, Leslie and Denis Compton, Reg Lewis and Bernard Joy, were still in the services. Lewis, Joy and Leslie Compton were actually in Germany. I'd read a newspaper report about the problem George Allison was having in raising a strong Arsenal team and was chatting about it to my Stoke team-mate Neil Franklin when a thought occurred to me. I suggested to Neil that he and I should telephone George Allison and offer our services as guest players. Neil was all for it, so having seen Stoke manager Bob McGrory and been given his permission and organised duty relief, I rang George Allison. He was delighted and accepted our offer immediately, though he later rang back to say his centre-half Bernard Joy was coming home on leave and therefore there would be no need for Neil's services in the game.

For days I looked forward to pitting my skills against Moscow Dynamo and the novelty of turning out for Arsenal. I had high hopes of it being a classic match but come the day, there was to be great disappointment. The sort of weather that inspired the song 'A Foggy Day In London Town' descended on the capital. It was a classic pea souper. Arsenal put me up in a hotel and arranged for a taxi to pick me up and take me to White Hart Lane where the game was being played. Highbury had been converted into an Air raid Patrol centre. The fog was so thick the taxi driver even stuck to the recognised route. We crawled along and I thought that with Spurs not having floodlights, like just about every other club at the time, there was no chance of the game being played.

Whether it was FA and Arsenal officials not wanting to upset the Russians or the fact that 54,000 were already crammed into White Hart Lane, I don't know, but the decision was made that the game should go ahead. It shouldn't have. Standing on the centre spot I couldn't see to the centre circle never mind the goals at either end.

To call it an Arsenal team is a bit of a misnomer; I was one of six guest players. Still, I was for the first, and as it turned out only, time wearing the famous white-sleeved red shirt of the Gunners. I was under the direction of George Allison and so as far as I was concerned, I was playing for Arsenal. For the record, Arsenal lined up as follows: Griffiths (Cardiff City – though he'd missed the earlier game); Scott, Bacuzzi (Fulham); Bastin, Joy, Halton (Bury); Matthews (Stoke City), Drury, Rooke (Fulham), Mortensen (Blackpool), Cummer.

It was a surprise to me that the game went ahead; it was even more astonishing that it went on to finish. Moscow Dynamo scored in the opening minute with their first attack but I doubt if any spectators bar those directly behind the goal saw it. At half-time with the fog if anything worse, Arsenal left the pitch leading 3–2. It had been a farce. The goals were cheered in stages by a full house unable to see what was going on. The spectators immediately behind the goal would cheer when the ball hit the back of the net, a second later they were joined by the supporters to the left and right, and the cheer would then pass around the stadium jungle telegraph style. Eventually, the supporters behind the goal at the far end cottoned on and cheered. By that time we had kicked off again. I felt sorry for the 54,000 fans who had paid over £10,000 to watch, or not watch, the game.

In the second half, Moscow Dynamo pulled back two goals and hung on to win 4–3, but the scoreline paled into insignificance in comparison with the pantomime events on the pitch. A goal down, after the interval Dynamo started to use any means, fair or foul, to get back into the game. Arsenal players were tripped as they went to meet the ball, there was a succession of late tackles and I had my shirt pulled out of my shorts on three occasions. The Russian referee did nothing to stop the rough-house play, but I'll give him the benefit of the doubt – visibility was down to a few yards and he may not have been able to see clearly what was going on. The fog had made the game a nonsense, but even so I felt there was no need for Dynamo to resort to such antics especially as in Stankevitch, Archangelski, Bobrov and Blinkov they had players of real class who, if they put their minds to it, could turn a match in their favour.

As the second half progressed, the game degenerated into something more in keeping with Hackney Empire at Christmas than White Hart Lane. The fog got worse and the crowd, frustrated and disappointed at not being able to see the game, started to boo and slow handclap. George Drury, who had been on the receiving end of some very late tackles, eventually retaliated and was given his marching orders by the referee. However, George didn't leave the field. Having been sent off, George was making his way towards the tunnel when he realised the fog was so bad the referee couldn't see him, so he just stayed out on the wing and played on! With Dynamo leading 4–3 Ronnie Rooke, guesting from Fulham, equalised but the referee disallowed it. None of the Arsenal team took issue with the referee over the decision; the fog was by then so bad the majority of us never saw Ronnie score in the first place, so we had no idea if it was a legitimate decision or not.

In the closing stages the Dynamo goalkeeper 'Tiger' Khomich pulled off a string of fine saves – at least, I think he did because we kept shooting at where we thought his goal was but the scoreline remained the same.

Back in the dressing room it was brought home to us just how much of a farce the game had been when we were informed that Moscow Dynamo had played for part of the second half with 12 men. I didn't feel badly done to. It was the 54,000 fans who had turned up expecting to see an exhibition of purist football but instead spent 90 minutes peering into the leadened gloom who had been cheated. My sympathies were with them. It was sad, though, that my one and only appearance for Arsenal was in such a pantomime of a game.

Years later at a sporting dinner I got chatting to an Arsenal fan who had been at that game. He told me he left the ground not only unsure of the final score, but unaware that I had even played. That's how bad the fog was!

Moscow Dynamo did go on to give an exhibition of their true footballing skills in a 2–2 draw with Glasgow Rangers at Ibrox in a game watched by over 90,000 people. The Dynamos were unbeaten in their short tour of Britain and lived up to the publicity, much of it self-generated, that had followed their arrival. To my mind they were a very good team bordering on great. The Russian government must have thought the same – on their arrival back in Moscow, they were made 'Heroes of the Soviet Union'.

On the domestic front, I became a father for the second time in the same month I had guested for Arsenal against Moscow Dynamo. I wouldn't go so far as to say Betty and I were relaxed about the situation, but we were not as fraught as when Jean arrived. At least, I wasn't! It was a boy and we named him Stanley.

To compensate for another year of regionalised football, the Football Association decided the 1945–46 FA Cup would be played over two legs with the exception of the semi-finals and final. These days we have become accustomed to two-legged Cup ties but in 1945 it raised more than a few eyebrows. Even though many understood the reason behind the FA's decision there was much comment in the press about the traditions of the world's oldest cup competition having been tarnished. Such arguments fell by the wayside when the tournament got under way. The re-introduction of the FA Cup was a sign that normal life was returning to Britain, and sports writers were keen to see who would win the trophy for the first time in seven years.

In January 1946, Stoke were drawn in the third round against Burnley. We won the first leg at home 3–1 and although we lost 2–1 at Turf Moor the aggregate score was enough to take us through to the fourth round where we were drawn against Sheffield United.

This was the month I was selected to play for England against Belgium in a Victory International at Wembley. My selection was something of a landmark at the time as it took me past Eddie Hapgood's record of 43 England appearances. The press made much of this milestone and the fact that another eight appearances for England would take me past the all-time British record for international appearances held by Billy Meredith of Wales. I very nearly didn't play against the Belgians. In the days leading up to the game I had been on night duty for the RAF in a spell of bitterly cold weather and eventually came down with a bout of flu. On the Thursday before the game, I decided to take a hot toddy of milk and whisky and go to bed in an attempt to sweat it out. The next morning after a hot bath I felt much better, but on the train journey down to London to join the England team I felt like the symptoms on a medicine bottle and by the time I reached Euston was so bad I had little hope of playing.

At the team hotel our trainer Bill Voisey took one look at me and confined me to bed. I felt weak and drained and within a minute or so of my head hitting the pillow I was asleep. I don't know how long I had slept, three maybe four hours, but I suddenly awoke to find Bill Voisey at my bedside with what looked like a glass of milk in his hand.

'Here Stan, take this. It's just a drop of my own medicine in a glass of milk. It'll have you back on your feet in no time,' Bill said, offering me his home-made remedy.

On my feet in no time? I took one large gulp and was nearly on my feet straightaway. I've never really drunk alcohol in any form, but I think all the forms of alcohol I have missed were contained in the glass of milk Bill gave me that evening. I managed to drink it down and no sooner had I finished than I felt my eyes bulging. I gave a shudder, let forth with a deep breath that nigh on made the varnish on the bedside table bubble, flopped back on to the bed and fell straight into a deep sleep.

I awoke in the small hours to discover my pyjamas wringing with perspiration. At first I thought someone had collapsed on the bed on top of me because I found it difficult to move. It took a moment or two to realise I was covered by half a dozen or so extra blankets. Looking across the room, I saw Bill Voisey sitting in a chair illuminated by the moonlight coming through a gap in the curtains.

'Sssh, get back to sleep, Stan. I'll stay here the night to keep an eye on you,' Bill said.

He may have said other things, too, I don't know. I was so tired, I fell back into a deep and wondrous sleep. The next morning I got out of bed feeling as if I had spent the night sleeping in a swimming pool. I took a hot bath; then Bill gave me a good massage and rub down with something that smelled not too dissimilar to what I had drunk the night before. That over, Bill asked me how I was feeling. I was feeling a whole lot better, but I was still unsure if I was fit enough to get through a full 90 minutes of football. My answer should have been no but in the light of Bill's efforts and his all-night vigil I heard myself telling him I was fit to play. He clapped his hands together and smiled broadly.

'I'll go downstairs and tell them,' he said, pleased as punch. 'I've done it again.'

'What was in that drink you gave me last night, Bill?' I asked, partly out of curiosity and partly to pander to the sense of accomplishment he was obviously feeling.

'Stan, believe me, you don't want to know,' he said. 'Put it this way, if you were a plane you'd be halfway to America by now,' and he left the room.

The England and Belgium teams were presented to the new Prime Minister, Clement Attlee, before what turned out to be an uninspired game. England won 2–0. Frank Swift must have had one of the quietest games of his career while his opposite number in the Belgian goal, Françoise Daenen, would have bankrupted the Belgian FA if he had been paid piece rate for his work that afternoon. I didn't play anywhere near my best. I was just pleased to get through the game without letting myself or anybody else down. I was always so totally focused in matches. I'd blot out anything else, including in this instance the remnants of the flu bug. As soon as the final whistle sounded, however, I felt drained and unwell and had to give the post-match banquet a miss in favour of my hotel bed, this time thankfully without having to down Bill Voisey's rocket-fuel remedy.

The following Saturday was our fourth round FA Cup tie against Sheffield United, and I was still not feeling 100 per cent. I reported to the Victoria Ground on the morning of the game although my limbs were aching and I felt as weak as a kitten. I told Bob McGrory I wasn't fit and it would be better for him to call up one of the reserves. Bob was keen for me to play, so he rang up the local infirmary and asked a specialist if he could prescribe anything that would get me through the 90 minutes. The specialist sent some pills over to the ground. They arrived around noon and the instructions were for me to take two, which I duly did. Some 30 minutes or so later, I felt a whole lot better. Bob McGrory was delighted and immediately put my name down on the team-sheet. We beat Sheffield United 2–0 that afternoon, a good scoreline to take to Bramall Lane for the second leg and I have to say, the pills did the trick because I felt strong and active, good in myself and played a decent enough game.

My usual routine following matches once the children were in bed was to sit and relax in front of the fire reading a book or the *Evening Sentinel* while listening to the radio. That night, however, even though the game against Sheffield United had been a tough one played with plenty of pace throughout, I felt I still had boundless energy. I tried sitting by the fire but couldn't. I was possessed with an urgent feeling to be on the move doing things. I went into the kitchen and washed the dishes from our evening meal. Then I set about cleaning the kitchen from top to bottom. I took all the tins and packets of food from the kitchen cabinets and cleaned all the shelves before putting them back. Not satisfied, I turned my attention to the cupboard underneath the kitchen sink. I found all the usual things there – tins of shoe polish containing a quarter-inch rim of polish that had gone rock hard; a few tiles left over from when we did the bathroom; empty jam jars that had been kept because they might come in useful one day; a cracked saucer we kept the pan scourer on; a pile of brown paper carrier bags crammed into another brown carrier bag. I threw the lot out and scoured the cupboard with Vim. Back in the lounge, I went over the carpet with the carpet sweeper, then took on the hall, stairs and landing. In the bedroom, I swept the floor, changed the bedsheets and pillow cases, dusted everywhere, even managing to remove the sticky circle on the bedside table left by the medicine bottle the contents of which I had been taking to combat the flu. Even when I'd done all that I felt I could have gone out and played another 90 minutes, so I donned some training kit and went for a run around the streets. I just kept running and running. I intended to go around the block but must have done about four miles in total. Once back home, I submerged myself in a hot bath and went to bed. At half two in the morning I was wide awake and sitting upright. Exasperated at not being able to sleep, I went downstairs and sorted out a pile of newspapers and magazines, putting the ones we no longer wanted into the dustbin. Outside, I noticed the garden path was strewn with leaves, so returning only to don a scarf and gloves, in my pyjamas and dressing-gown I proceeded to sweep the leaves into a pile before collecting them on a spade and dumping them on to the compost heap. It was only then that I stopped and thought to myself, 'Stan, it's three in the morning and you're out here sweeping leaves. What on earth is wrong with you?' I crept back to bed thankful that no one had seen me.

In the end I did manage to get to sleep and awoke the next morning feeling more like my normal self. The energy I felt the night before could only have been down to the pills. Betty and I referred to them as DAPs – Delayed Action Pills – and to this day I have no idea what they were. They must have been some sort of pep pill, illegal today. I have always treated my body with respect and taken great and meticulous care about what I eat, drink and take. When I look back on Bill Voisey's flu remedy and the specialist's DAPs, I'm horrified. For a time they turned a fitness fanatic of quiet disposition and routine ways into a cross between Mrs Mop and George Formby.

Stoke City made good progress in the FA Cup that season. We lost the return leg 3–2 at Sheffield United but again our home result was good enough to take us through to round five where we were pitted against the other side from the famous City of Steel, Sheffield Wednesday. This time a 2–0 home win and a 0–0 draw at Hillsborough not only carried us through to round six but induced a certain amount of Cup fever among Stoke City fans. When the draw was made and we came out of the velvet bag first to find we would be at home again in the first leg, this time to Bolton Wanderers, even some Stoke players started to think this indeed may be our year. Not only were we to be proved wrong, but Stoke City exited from this particular FA Cup in circumstances that no living soul could ever have imagined possible. The events of 9 March 1946 are forever ingrained in my memory. It turned into a nightmare, one that ranks alongside the Ibrox disaster, the Bradford City fire, Heysel and Hillsborough as one of football's greatest tragedies.

For all we had played poorly at the Victoria Ground in the first meeting and were two goals down, the Stoke players felt we had the measure of Bolton and so we travelled north to Burnden Park with high hopes of turning the tie around in the away leg. As I ran on to the pitch, I was amazed by the size of the crowd. Some 70,000 had crammed into Burnden Park. They were packed like sardines and during the pre-match kick-in I glanced up and saw the heaving masses on the terraces swaying like the great swell of an ocean. Even at this stage, young boys were being passed over the heads of the adults towards the relative safety of the cinder track that ran around the pitch.

The game got under way and Stoke had the better of the

play for the first ten minutes. We were looking for an early goal to lift us and unsettle the Bolton nerves. After about a quarter of an hour, a sound like muffled thunder followed by a terrific roar ripped through the ground. I glanced over my shoulder and saw the crowd swaying and tumbling towards the front of the terracing behind the goal at the far end of the pitch. People were screaming and clambering over the perimeter wall on to the cinder track and the pitch itself. I had a terrible feeling in the pit of my stomach that this wasn't just an overspill from a big crowd. Fans kept spilling on to the pitch. Gaps started to appear on the upper terracing like rotting cavities in teeth.

The referee, Mr Dutton, blew his whistle to halt the game and ran in the direction of some policemen who were making their way towards the chaos. The police managed to push the fans back over the touchline, order seemed to be restored and the game got under way again with Mr Dutton awarding a bounce up.

The game continued for five minutes or so, then Stoke skipper Neil Franklin played a ball out to me on the right wing. I was aware of someone approaching me and turned to shield the ball. Glancing up, I saw it was not a Bolton defender but a police sergeant, waving his arms frantically trying to get Mr Dutton's attention. It stopped me in my tracks. The referee stopped the game and went into a brief consultation with the sergeant and the two captains, Neil Franklin and Bolton's Harry Hubbick. Then he pointed to the tunnel, ordering both teams off the field.

We knew then the incident was a matter of great concern but no one realised that a great tragedy was unfolding before us. The tunnel was packed with supporters taking refuge and as I made my way through them an old chap in cloth cap said in a broad Lancastrian accent, "Ee lad, but that were a quick fost half." It brought me out in a shiver. He wasn't being crass; like many others he simply didn't realise the extent of what had happened.

In the dressing room, Bob McGrory was trying to keep us focused on the task in hand when George Mountford, Billy Mould and Alex Ormston who had travelled with us to Bolton as reserves came in. Their faces were ashen. They told us they had heard 'two or three people had been killed in the crush'.

Just under half an hour passed before Mr Dutton came into our dressing room. He said the Chief Constable of Bolton had ordered the game to continue. We stood up but my legs felt like lead. I didn't want to go back out; none of us did. I looked at the Bolton players as they made their way down the corridor towards the tunnel and caught the eye of Bolton's Harry Hubbick, normally a happy-go-lucky guy always ready with a quip. His face was grim. He never spoke, just shook his head slowly to indicate 'this isn't on'.

Frank Baker the Stoke outside-left was in front of me as we pushed our way through the fans bottlenecked in the tunnel. One of the fans grabbed him by the arm and angrily said, ''Tis a crime to carry on.' It was and we didn't have to be told. When we got on to the pitch, we saw fresh lines had been made with sawdust, shrinking the pitch in size to accommodate the overspill of supporters who were now ringing it.

There was play of a sort until half-time but when the referee blew his whistle for the interval, the Bolton manager Walter Rowley stepped on to the pitch and asked Mr Dutton to change straight round. So we swapped ends and recommenced playing.

Towards the end of the game, I was stopped in my tracks by a sickening sight. There had been no goals scored, players were just going through the motions, but we hit the bar and the ball was cleared by a Bolton defender for a throw in on our right-hand side. I took up a position near the right touchline and glanced towards the crowd. A shock wave went through my body and it was all I could do to prevent myself from being physically ill. Tears welled up in my eyes. There at the side of the pitch were people in body bags. I don't know how the ball was played from that throw in, I didn't care, I was elsewhere.

When the final whistle blew, we walked dejectedly from the pitch. Out of the FA Cup? That was the last thing on our minds. Football paled into significance. That night in Bolton, life came to a standstill. The pubs were deserted, the cinemas were empty, the working men's clubs silent, the music mute.

It was not until I came down to breakfast and picked up the Sunday papers that I realised the enormity of the tragedy – 33 dead, 500 injured. I tuned into the Home Service and heard on the news that Bolton had turned into a ghost town. Everyone stayed indoors. There was no way I could find to respond. How could you?

We were embarking upon what the history books refer to as the golden age of football, which is deemed to have lasted from the immediate post-war years through to the mid fifties. In many ways they are right. This period produced some of the greatest footballers ever to have graced our game. With the emphasis on skill, and players intent on providing quality and entertainment, it did provide a host of golden moments. Football was still very much a community-based game and in the aftermath of war, the public were keen to enjoy themselves. Attendances reached an all-time high. But neither football's governing bodies nor the clubs took any note of the Bolton disaster. I can't recall any real action being taken or legislation introduced to ensure such a tragedy never occurred again. World War Two had been a 'just' war; in World War One many soldiers had been simply cannon fodder. For all the wonderful football played in the golden age and for all its great characters and players, the supporters who packed into grounds the basic facilities of which had remained largely unchanged since the Victorian Age, were treated more or less as terrace fodder by the authorities and clubs.

Hindsight is a wonderful thing, but the Bolton disaster, horrendous as it was, was seen as a tragic one-off by those who ran our game and held sway in the boardrooms. In many ways Bolton begat Ibrox, which in turn begat Bradford, Heysel and Hillsborough. Forty-three years on from Bolton, it took another human tragedy at Hillsborough before football was forced to take a long, hard look at itself and how it treated its paying customers.

The experience of being at Burnden Park on that fateful day affected me deeply. For several days, I could not bring myself to train.

In my mind I kept seeing the body bags and was too distressed to even think about football. I read in the newspapers that a disaster fund had been set up for the dependants of those who lost their lives at Bolton and I immediately sent off a cheque for £30, which at the time was just over two weeks' wages. When I posted it I was torn about whether it was enough, but I knew no amount of money could ease the pain of those who had lost loved ones and friends. The Bolton disaster left me dazed. Even now it's hard to write about the day because such was the enormity of the tragedy that whatever words you summon seem trite and irrelevant. Even with the passing of time and the benefit of hindsight, I find it difficult to comment objectively because the horror scenes still remain vivid in the mind's eye, the fog is in the throat and the pen wavers.

Bolton Wanderers went on to lose 2–0 to Charlton Athletic in the semi-final, but I am sure the minds of the

Bolton players were elsewhere on the day. Following such a tragedy, football appears unimportant. Life, however, goes on and Charlton met Derby County in the first post-war FA Cup final. It went into extra time before Derby finally ran out 4–1 winners.

The game was a personal triumph for a pal of mine, Derby's Jack Stamps, who had been injured at Dunkirk and told he would never be able to play football again. Jack scored twice, made another for Peter Doherty and would have ended up with a hat-trick but for an extraordinary incident when he shot at goal only for the ball to burst and allow the Charlton goalkeeper Sam Bartram to recover and save.

Although tainted by tragedy, the FA Cup signified the resumption of normal life and following the final, the confirmation that regular league football would return in August provided a great lift to everyone. People were looking to the future, no one more so than me.

Back in March, shortly after the tragedy at Bolton, the city of Stoke-on-Trent had paid me a great honour by inviting me to the Town Hall to receive an illuminated address in recognition of passing Eddie Hapgood's record of 43 appearances for England. As I made my way to Stoke Town Hall that day I was all a quiver. I was not used to public speaking and the very thought of having to make a speech turned my legs to jelly. If I could have turned about and gone home I would have done, but this was the first honour to be bestowed upon me and my gratitude to my home-town people conquered the worries I held of not being articulate or witty enough to carry off a speech in front of the great and good of the city.

The presentation took place at 2 p.m. on the 28 March and before a packed Town Hall that included my mother and family my thoughts turned to my father who I knew would have been very proud. My nerves were tempered somewhat by the behaviour of our daughter Jean. She was fascinated by the official garb and chains that the Lord Mayor, Percy Williams, was wearing, and asked if we could have a chain like the Mayor was wearing in our toilet. It was all I could do not to burst out laughing. When the time came for me to walk up and be presented with the illuminated address, although still nervous I managed to get through my first public speech without egg on my face.

I had been discharged from the RAF in the spring and was looking forward to the 1946–47 season with great anticipation. I felt I was playing the best football of my career up to that point and believed Stoke City had a team of sufficient quality to stage a concerted effort to lift the First Division Championship. On the latter point I wasn't wrong, but as I spent the summer of 1946 training hard I had no idea that before the season was out, I'd be leaving the Victoria Ground for pastures new.

11

***

Going to the Golden Mile

A s far as league sides go, in their entire history Stoke City have had two teams I would say surpassed the very good tag but fell a little way short of being great – Tony Waddington's Stoke team of the early seventies that won the League Cup, twice went agonisingly close to FA Cup glory, flew the flag in Europe, and in 1973–74 and 1974–75 contested the championship; and the team of 1946–47.

The amazing thing about the 1946–47 Stoke City side was that they were made up almost entirely of home-grown players. On more than one occasion, Stoke fielded 11 lads who were Potteries born and bred and who had come through their junior ranks; I was one of them.

When the 1946–47 season started, I had high hopes of Stoke launching a concerted effort to take the First Division title. We had the players, albeit the war had robbed some of what would have been their best years. Two players vied for the goalkeeper's jersey – Dennis Herod, one of a number of exciting young prospects to have emerged at Stoke during the war years, and Arthur Jepson. He was a steady keeper, but I always felt a proportion of Stoke fans never really warmed to him. Why I don't know because Arthur, although at the time not in the top league, was a good shot stopper and dominated his penalty box to good effect. He was also an excellent cricketer, a hard-hitting, middle order batsman with Nottinghamshire, and he went on to become an accomplished Test umpire, retiring in 1985.

Dennis Herod wasn't the tallest of keepers but he had a pair of safe hands, tremendous courage and all the agility of a gymnast. Dennis had been badly injured in the war, though you'd never know it the way he used to fling himself about his six-yard area. In the penalty box he was the monarch of all he surveyed and, in contrast to the quiet demeanour of Arthur Jepson, he would bellow instructions to his defence and even at times to the forwards. Dennis's brave saves were not only an inspiration to us in the Stoke team but also served on numerous occasions to demoralise opposing forwards; bearing down on goal with only him to beat, not many fancied their chances of tucking the ball away.

Harry Bingham was transferred to Nottingham Forest a quarter of the way through the season and Billy Mould took over at right-back. Billy, another local lad, was equally at home at full-back or centre-half. The fact that Stoke had so many versatile players in the team at the time was to my mind one of its greatest strengths. Billy was a class player, compact and muscular, a great club man who possessed a sharp and impish wit. In February 1947, when Stoke beat Preston 5–0 at the Victoria Ground, Billy had an outstanding game. The Preston left winger never got a kick and for much of the second half resorted to hugging the touchline as the game passed him by. The Preston trainer – the team was being run by a committee – constantly encouraged the winger to 'turn on his party pieces'. On leaving the pitch, Billy passed the Preston dug-out and seeing the trainer said, 'Party pieces? You'd have been better off sending out a search party for him!'

Left-back Johnny McCue had a long and illustrious career with Stoke making 542 senior appearances as well as playing in 133 wartime matches. Johnny gained a reputation as a hard man and while he was unquestionably that, he was never a dirty player. In an age when full-backs were short squat men with prison haircuts and faces as expressionless as a smoked herring, Johnny McCue had all the right attributes. When the efforts of some full-backs in nailing a winger resembled a drunk stamping on woodlice, Johnny's high-precision and high-velocity tackling induced fear and respect in equal proportions among his opponents. I once heard him referred to as 'the poor man's Wilf Copping' but such a description did him a great disservice for, as well as being a clinical and hard full-back, he used the ball productively and was one of the finest exponents of a long pass I ever saw.

In Frank Mountford, Neil Franklin and the ageing but still eminently able Jock Kirton, a stylish and redoubtable wing-half who was a good club servant, Stoke had a half-back line as formidable as it was classy. Frank Mountford was a manager's dream; he was at home in either full-back position, at wing-half or centre-half and even proved himself to be a more than useful centre-forward. A Swiss Army knife of a footballer, Frank was a man's man, rugged and tough; no matter how cold the weather, his chest hair would protrude from his unbuttoned shirt like a burst sofa. He was a steam roller in a pair of shorts, totally committed to the cause. I never ever saw him shirk a tackle and at corners and free kicks he would sidle up to the player he was marking as watchful as a spider in its web.

Alongside Frank was perhaps the greatest centre-half I ever had the privilege of playing with, the incomparable Neil Franklin. At the time, Neil was widely considered to be the best centre-half in Britain. He had played in ten wartime and victory internationals for England and in this season went on to win the first of his 27 caps.

Neil won everything in the air, tackled with superb timing and when the ball was at his feet possessed the nous to pass it with all the guile and intelligence of the most cerebral of inside-forwards. An erect physique belied tremendous mobility and breathtaking speed over four or five yards. When it came to heading he was as dominant in the air as a Spitfire, and such was the timing of his tackling that when sliding in, his backside and tackling leg would touch the ground only momentarily before he rose majestically with the ball at his feet. Many was the game played in pelting rain on a gluepot of a pitch when all the Stoke players would leave the field covered in mud except Neil whose shirt and shorts would be just specked with splashes. The only sign he had been in the thick of it would be the brown circle of mud hammered on to his forehead.

Neil oozed class and self-control in equal measures. When his legs were kicked from under him he would rise to his feet, look pityingly at the perpetrator of the shabby assault and with a gentle, disapproving shake of the head, turn and trot away to take up his position. He used his physical strength sparingly, preferring to rely on the skills he had been blessed with. In an era of bruising, granite-like centre-halves, he was a model of restraint but could put a naughty player well and truly in his place. On the opening day of the season against Charlton Athletic, Charlton's centre-forward 'Bill' Robinson and Neil were involved in a titanic struggle in which Robinson resorted to some very late tackling.

Eventually, the referee took Robinson to one side for a talking-to only for Neil to walk up and say, 'Be lenient with him ref. His last term's report showed some improvement!'

In 1950, at the peak of his club and international career, Neil caused a sensation when he agreed to go and play abroad in Colombia, a country which at the time was outside the jurisdiction of the world football governing body FIFA. He and George Mountford, no relation to Frank, received what was an incredible offer to sign for the Bogota-based club Santa Fe, reported as signing-on fees of £3,400 each plus £170 per match, plus free accommodation and home helps thrown in for good measure and with the maximum wage in England at the time being £12 in the winter and £10 in the summer, the money promised looked like it would set up both players for life.

The national and local papers made much of the move. It was almost unheard of for British players to go and play abroad and, with the country in question being Colombia, the story was all the more exotic if not a trifle worrying for those of us who had the interests of Neil and George at heart. No one could blame them for being captivated by such an offer, but I feel they should have at least made an initial trip to check the place out before signing on the dotted line.

At first all went well, but Santa Fe were never forthcoming with the money they had promised. The country was very unstable politically and a 6.30 p.m. street curfew fuelled anxieties. Neil returned to England after two months having received only one week's wages and no signing-on fee. He had turned down the chance of playing for England in the 1950 World Cup in favour of the Colombian job, and so found himself not only out of favour but in may ways ostracised by the FA and Stoke City. Neil Franklin never played for Stoke again and some months after his return to the Potteries was transferred to Hull City, but by then what had been a glittering career was tarnished and in tatters.

George Antonio, so very nearly a Welsh international, began the season vying for the inside-right berth with Syd Peppitt who as the season progressed made the position his own. Syd was never a classy inside-forward but he was a grafter with an eye for goal and every team needs a player like that in its side.

Alongside Syd at centre-forward was Freddie Steele who started the season like a house on fire scoring 15 goals in our first ten games. In mid-season he missed a number of matches through injury but the mark of the man as a lethal centre-forward lies in the fact he still ended up with 31 goals to his name come the end of the season.

Frank Baker at inside-left was another 'play me anywhere' type of player and no matter where Frank was asked to play, half-back, on the wing or in his favoured inside-left position, he always produced the goods. He had redoubtable spirit, in his time recovering from three broken legs and, while never being a prolific goalscorer, more than made up for that by being a selfless and determined team player.

On the left wing was Alex Ormston, a small dynamo of a player who possessed more trickery than the Magic Circle and for all his diminutive size, must have had lungs like sides of beef such was his tireless workrate.

In Harry Sellars, a wing-half and inside-forward of meticulous passing, Roy Brown, another fine utility player, Freddie Steele's understudy John Jackson and George Mountford, Stoke had quality players in reserve and it was this team that went within a whisker of winning the League Championship for the first and only time in the club's history.

The season, however, started off badly. Poor results in the opening four games, when we failed to win a match, were to cost Stoke dear. I played in the opening two matches, both at home. We drew 2–2 with Charlton and lost 2–1 to Bolton Wanderers. I picked up an injury against Bolton which kept me out for the next four games.

On 21 September I came back for the game against Manchester United at the Victoria Ground. Over 40,000 saw us win 3–2 with two goals from Freddie Steele and one from George Antonio. I started well but the game ended disappointingly for me because I tweaked my ligaments. It wasn't a serious knee injury, a little aggravating, more inconvenient than anything else, but enough to sideline me once again.

In those days it was thought there was little that could be done for such knee injuries. The only treatment was rest and so I sat out Stoke's next three matches. George Mountford was my replacement at outside-right and even though Stoke hit a vein of form, winning 3–1 at Preston, 3–0 at home to Sheffield United and 5–2 at Chelsea with George doing well, I was confident that once fit again I would regain my place in the first team.

I also missed two England internationals, a 7–2 hammering of Northern Ireland and a 1–0 win over the Republic. Preston's Tom Finney played in my absence and according to reports did extremely well. Finney's performances for England didn't surprise me; I rated Tom very highly indeed.

I never took anything for granted in football; that's why I always worked so hard at my game. I wanted to regain my England place and felt, once fit again, a good run in the Stoke side would help me do that. I was 31, but fitter than just about every other player I knew and felt at the top of my game. I had it in my mind that it would be only a matter of time before a run of good club form would get me an international recall, especially as Tom Finney was so versatile he could be accommodated elsewhere in the

England forward line and perform with equal aplomb.

Following the victory over Chelsea, Stoke were due back in the capital the following Saturday for one of the most anticipated games of the season at Arsenal. I trained as normal that week at Blackpool, but came down to Stoke in midweek to play in a full-scale practice game. A player knows when he has done well; I gave my all in that practice game and felt no repercussions from the knee injury. So when manager Bob McGrory asked how I was, I had no hesitation in informing him I was 100 per cent fit. McGrory paused for a moment before saying 'Good', but his reaction told me the situation was anything but good as far as I was concerned.

Have you ever had one of those situations during a telephone conversation where you impart a piece of information or make a comment and there is a brief silence before the person on the other end of the line responds? No matter how they reply, you just know something is wrong. That's how I felt when speaking to McGrory immediately after the practice match. His demeanour told me he greeted the news that I was fit with all the enthusiasm he would a lukewarm bowl of two-day-old stew.

After training I showered, dressed and was on the point of going across the road to the café for a sandwich when McGrory appeared in the dressing room and took me to one side.

'I think it might be as well for you to have a run out with the reserves this Saturday,' he said, looking anywhere but straight at me.

I have to admit his words took me by surprise. Now it was my turn to be silent for a moment. Then I told him I couldn't take his suggestion seriously. McGrory told me he wasn't ordering me to play in the reserves merely suggesting it.

'You're the manager of this club, so manage it,' I told him, somewhat peeved. 'It's part of a manager's job to make decisions, not suggestions.'

He repeated that he was not ordering me to play in the reserves, merely suggesting it as a sensible thing to do in coming back from injury.

'I've just played a full-scale practice game and got through it no problem,' I reminded him. 'I don't need a run-out with the reserves.'

'That's as maybe, but you won't be included in the team for this Saturday's game at Arsenal,' McGrory said.

'And I won't be playing for the reserves either, so don't include me.'

I felt justified in refusing to play for the reserves – McGrory hadn't ordered me to, he had merely suggested it. As far as I was concerned, I wasn't defying him. In a backhanded way, his wishy-washy approach to man-management had given me an out and I felt secure in the knowledge I wasn't in breach of any club rules.

I don't think Bob McGrory ever warmed to me. There had been the business over the bonus payment that cost me three months' wages. Of course a manager has to answer to his board of directors, but in matters such as payment, you expect the manager to stand up for you. He knows your worth to the team and the club better than anyone. The manager should bridge differences between board and player. If he doesn't, how can he turn to you in the dressing room and say, 'I want you to go out and die for me today, son,' and expect you to give your all? Although I'd describe our relationship for the most part as amiable, I never felt Bob McGrory batted for me at the club. Even pre-war he gave the impression he was not happy with me. After a good performance, he would bull up other players but seldom mentioned me. At the time it didn't bother me; I was just happy the team were doing well and I was contributing to the success but now I started to wonder why. Bob had been a team-mate; perhaps he was a little envious of what I had gone on to achieve in the game. Whatever the reason, I felt there had been an undercurrent between us ever since I had replaced his close pal Bobby Liddle in the Stoke team when Tom Mather was manager.

On my way home I thought, 'To heck with it. I'll play in the reserves.' Just to bury the hatchet, then I thought, 'Why should I?' I was an England international, I had been included in the squad for the Northern Ireland game. Now I was fit again but not deemed good enough for my club side. To me it didn't add up.

I never mentioned the conversation between McGrory and myself to anyone, but the next morning, the story of a bust-up between us made all the newspapers. To make matters worse, one newspaper even carried the story of how a deputation of Stoke players had approached McGrory asking him not to bring me back into the first team. I couldn't believe that was true, but where did the newspaper in question get such a tale? I could only think it was from McGrory himself trying to justify his position in the light of possible criticism from the supporters. Players, managers and directors are often up in arms over what is written about them in the press, but by the same token are not averse to using the press for their own ends. I wondered at the time if this was such an instance.

Living in Blackpool, I did the majority of my training at Bloomfield Road, often just turning up at Stoke for matches. So I just continued training with the Blackpool players, as well as following my usual training schedule, busied myself with the running of our hotel and simply awaited the outcome of my disagreement with Bob McGrory.

Stoke lost 1–0 at Arsenal. It was Arsenal's first win of the season and put an end to Stoke's run of six games without defeat but I gained no satisfaction from the result at all. I was still totally committed to the Stoke cause, whether I was playing or not.

Along with the reports of the Arsenal game, the Sunday papers gave a lot of column inches to speculation about a possible transfer for me. One said I was 'Blackpool bound', another that I was on my way to Newcastle United. Others came up with Chelsea, Arsenal and Aston Villa but one constant line was that Stoke had put a £20,000 fee on my head. I never thought myself to be worth that amount of money and consoled myself that all this was just newspaper talk, but the fact that all the newspapers had quoted the same fee made me think that perhaps Stoke were planning to cash in on my services. It made me feel very restless.

On the Monday morning following Stoke's defeat at Arsenal I received a letter from the Stoke captain and my good pal Neil Franklin that gave me a tremendous lift. Neil said he was writing to me on behalf of all the Stoke first team who wanted to make it absolutely clear there had been, 'no deputation to the manager asking that I not be included in the team'. He had called a meeting of the players, asked if anyone had approached the manager and was satisfied no one had. He went on to say he would be issuing a statement to the press on behalf of the team, denying the story of an 'anti-Matthews deputation'. The problem was not resolved, but knowing that I had the support of my team-mates, including George Mountford who had replaced me, made me feel a whole lot better about the whole sorry affair.

Later in the week I received a telephone call from Bob McGrory asking me to turn up for a meeting with him and the Stoke directors the following Tuesday when 'everything would be sorted out'. I hoped that would be the case, but considering the past history of relations between McGrory and myself, and the fact that one newspaper was carrying a story that the Stoke chairman Harry Booth was going to reprimand me and insist I train at Stoke, I was sceptical about the prospect of a mutually satisfactory outcome.

I drove down to Stoke with the intention of being open-minded. I felt the whole affair had been blown up out of proportion and all I wanted was to don a red and white shirt again and prove to everyone I could still do more than a good job for Stoke and, for that matter, England.

The meeting lasted for two hours and as it went on I got the feeling that the directors were as keen as me to see the matter resolved. Bob McGrory said little, but when he did speak, went along with the sentiment being expressed by the board, which didn't surprise me. Whatever stance he took on an issue, he'd turn like a weathercock at the slightest hint of a wind of opinion from the board or supporters contrary to his own. There were no ultimatums, nothing was mentioned about me training with Blackpool rather than Stoke, so when the meeting ended with handshakes all round and a general agreement to let bygones be bygones, I asked for a week's rest which was granted.

The meeting over, the press were admitted to the boardroom and told that all problems had been resolved. Harry Booth read the following hastily prepared statement:

> The differences between the board and Stanley Matthews have been amicably settled, but because of the publicity of the past few days, Matthews [note, not Stan] has asked the board to grant him a week's holiday. The board have agreed to this request and, following this period of recuperation, hope the board of directors, manager Mr Bob McGrory, Matthews and the rest of the Stoke team can now concentrate on the job in hand of working together to bring

success to Stoke City Football Club.

For a time we did just that. During my week's holiday I missed Stoke's 3–0 defeat at home by Wolves but returned to first-team action on 2 November in a 1–0 win over Sunderland in front of 53,000 at Roker Park. In the following 19 league matches, we lost just five. The highlights were victories over Preston and Chelsea who were beaten 5–0 and 6–1 respectively, but the game against Blackpool in December when Stoke won 4–1 with goals from Freddie Steele, Syd Peppitt, Frank Baker and myself gave me more satisfaction.

The fact that I was training with Blackpool meant that I had got to know their players as well as my team-mates at Stoke and I felt my performance in this game, which many Stoke supporters have since described as my best in a Stoke shirt, proved beyond doubt where my loyalties lay. I was determined to put on a good show. For one thing, if Stoke had failed to win I would have been ribbed mercilessly by the Blackpool players in training. But I was conscious of certain rumours circulating in the city that I had divided loyalties as far as this game was concerned. This was utter nonsense and while I paid little heed to such rumours, I was keen to rubbish them all the same.

I was right on song and having had a hand in our first three goals managed to produce another party piece for the fourth. Picking up the ball on the half-way line, I waltzed through the Blackpool defence before rounding their goalkeeper to put the ball in the net. The response of the Stoke fans said it all. They roared their approval and come the final whistle both sets of players stood aside by the tunnel and applauded me off the field. It was one of those games when I was disappointed to hear the final whistle. I enjoyed our performance and victory immensely and was so fuelled up that I felt I could have gone on for another 90 minutes.

In the FA Cup, 65,681 saw us draw 2–2 at Spurs in the third round with 40,000 seeing the replay at the Victoria Ground when I managed to score the only goal of the game. We overcame Chester in round four, again after a replay, but went out in the next round to Sheffield United in controversial circumstances.

We had beaten Sheffield United 3–0 at home earlier in the season and while not underestimating their worth, I felt Stoke had sufficient quality in the side to progress to the sixth round at the first time of asking. It didn't work out that way. At the time Sheffield United, like ourselves, were in with a shout for the championship and they dug in and withstood everything we threw at them. In the second half, they won a throw-in and when the ball came back into play it was played to one of their forwards who appeared to be offside but went on to put the ball past Arthur Jepson. The Stoke supporters and my team-mates were up in arms. As usual, I accepted the official's decision to allow the goal, painful as it was.

Even at that stage of my career, I considered myself very fortunate to have had the success that had come my way in football and was of the mind that such disappointments simply had to be taken on board. It was part of my character, I suppose, that I readily accepted the rough with the smooth. In football there will be occasions when decisions go against you, but it's down to someone doing the best possible job in difficult circumstances. I maintained this attitude to referees throughout my career. In total I played 1,500 matches creating many records in the process but the fact that I was never booked or sent off is something that instils great pride in me to this day.

It was still a big disappointment to go out of the FA

Cup at home to Sheffield United. Like every other Stoke player, I wanted to see the club at Wembley and lift the famous trophy. Such disappointments, however, have to be quickly put to one side and so it was that to a man the Stoke players turned their undivided attention to winning the First Division Championship.

We bounced back in fine style. In our next game, Chelsea were beaten 6–2 at the Victoria Ground and this was followed by another highly creditable home performance when we played Arsenal off the park and ran out 3–1 winners.

The trouble between Bob McGrory and me appeared to have been forgotten. When a team are getting good results, petty differences tend to be buried, small disciplinary problems are overlooked and the mood and spirit at the club were for a time terrific. I'm not saying there was leniency at the club, more a good sense of diplomacy as shown in an incident concerning two of my team-mates and our chairman Alderman Harry Booth.

Harry Booth called in at the Victoria Ground one morning after training and spotted two Stoke players smoking while talking to pressmen and signing autographs for some young supporters. Mr Booth took a dim view of players smoking at the club but didn't wade in, admonish the players and thus make them appear small in front of the reporters and their fans. Instead he went up to the two players concerned, wished them good morning and proceeded to take two cigars from the inside pocket of his jacket.

'Lads, results are going well. Have a cigar on me,' he said. 'But I'd appreciate it if you didn't smoke them here at the ground.'

Now there was a breach of club rules dealt with smoothly and diplomatically by a tactful chairman who knew better than to throw his weight around. The message was taken on board by the players concerned; neither player felt humiliated. If anything, I dare say their respect for the chairman was all the greater for his handling of the situation and I feel there are one or two chairmen around today who would do well to take a leaf out of Harry Booth's book. One of Harry's favourite phrases when dealing with minor incidents of indiscipline at the club was, 'Let's not use a guillotine to cure dandruff.' He was one of the old school of chairmen. There's still a lot to be said for it.

Not long after I celebrated my 32nd birthday, the uneasy peace between Bob McGrory and me gave way to another fall-out which was to lead to my eventual departure from Stoke City. My performances for Stoke earned me a recall to the England team for a key game in the now defunct Home International Championship against Scotland at Wembley. My spirits rose. I felt my career was back on track and life was great. However, trouble was once again brewing in the manager's office at the Victoria Ground.

The England–Scotland game was taking place on 12 April, the Saturday following Easter weekend, which meant I would miss Stoke's game against Blackpool of all teams. Easter was a crucial time for clubs involved in chasing trophies or avoiding relegation because three games were played in four days – on Good Friday, Easter Saturday and Easter Monday. Coming as it did towards the end of a long, hard season, three games in four days took it out of you and with the England–Scotland game taking place the following weekend I had a word with Bob McGrory and asked if he would rest me for the Good Friday match away at Grimsby Town. Four big games in eight days would be too much, even for someone of my level of fitness. Bob agreed but said he would want me to play on the Saturday against Huddersfield Town and on the Monday in the return game against Grimsby, which I readily agreed to do.

Stoke won comfortably at Grimsby on the Good Friday, Freddie Steele notched another hat-trick to take his season's goal tally to 26, no mean achievement considering he had missed several games through injury. Other goals came from Syd Peppitt and Alex Ormston to secure a 5–2 victory and sustain our title challenge. The result against Grimsby had been so emphatic I drove down to Stoke on the evening of Good Friday half-expecting Bob McGrory to inform me he wanted to keep the same team and I wouldn't have blamed him if he had.

The next morning, however, I called into the manager's office at around 10.30 and was told by Bob that he had picked me for that afternoon's game against Huddersfield Town. I didn't question his decision, I happily accepted it; after all, I was keen to play.

I paid a visit to my mother and returned to the ground about an hour before kick-off. Bob McGrory had already told me I was in the team, so I started to get changed. My Stoke team-mates were happy to see me, there were the usual quips and banter and all seemed well until McGrory popped his head around the changing-room door and asked me to step outside into the corridor. Once outside, he told me he had changed his mind and he was going to stick to the same team that had won at Grimsby the day before. George Mountford was to continue at outside-right.

'Fair enough,' I said. 'I was half-expecting you to do that, but why tell me this morning that I was playing? Now I have to go back into the dressing room, take my strip off and get back into my suit.'

He mumbled a few words about it being a manager's prerogative to change his mind and while I agreed with that, for a manager to do so in such circumstances on the day of a game left me shaking my head in disbelief. If he had been straightforward and told me right away that I wasn't playing, I would have accepted my lot. But to tell me I was playing, then less than an hour before kick-off tell me I wasn't left a lot to be desired.

There are times in the career of any footballer when he doesn't agree with certain decisions a manager makes, but out of respect accepts them. Bob McGrory's behaviour not only galled me, it started to eat away at what remaining respect I had for him as a manager.

I watched the Huddersfield game from the stands. We played very well. Freddie Steele opened the scoring and further goals from Alex Ormston and Frank Baker sealed a 3–0 victory that really didn't do justice to what was a fine all-round team performance. The win was followed by a 3–0 win over Grimsby on the Easter Monday. After such a good performance against Huddersfield, I hadn't expected to play in the return game against Grimsby and was therefore not surprised when before this game Bob McGrory contacted me to say he was sticking with a winning side.

The following Saturday, while Stoke were beating Blackpool 2–0 at Bloomfield Road, I played for England in 1–1 draw against Scotland in front of 100,000 fans at Wembley. It was another epic battle. Raich Carter at his bewildering best scored England's goal with Preston's Andy McLaren replying for the Scots.

I've said before that I can't understand how a player can be picked for his country when he isn't deemed good enough to play for his club and, on the face of it, my situation at this time may have smacked of this. However, I knew I was playing some of my best football during this period and the newspapers said I was still highly prized by a bevy of top First Division clubs.

Stoke were playing well and getting good results but I felt my inclusion in the team would add to their performances. I understood that Bob McGrory didn't want to change a winning line-up, but I did wonder if he would be reluctant to do so if it was Freddie Steele, say, and not me who had been rested for a game. Freddie was a great centre-forward but was struggling with an injury in February and missed our 3–1 win over Arsenal. That match was Stoke's fourth game without defeat but Freddie pronounced himself fit for the next game against Wolves and was promptly re-instated. Quite right, too. For all Stoke were doing well, there wasn't a better centre-forward on the club's books or for that matter, Tommy Lawton excepted, in the country. Freddie Steele's immediate re-instatement after injury made me feel the basis of McGrory's decision to keep me on the sidelines was of a personal nature, a feeling reinforced by events surrounding our next game.

The Stoke centre-half and skipper Neil Franklin was also on England duty the day Stoke played Blackpool. When the teamsheet was pinned up for the next game, at home to Brentford, Neil's name was there. My name was also included, but Bob McGrory had listed six players next to which he had written 'Forwards from . . .'. As there were five berths to fill, I wasn't confident of turning out against a Brentford side that were odds-on for relegation.

When I reported to the Victoria Ground for the game I was summoned into Bob McGrory's office. He was sitting behind his desk, looking down at a pen he was twirling in the fingers of his hand, his face inscrutable, as usual. I didn't know what to expect.

'Stan, I'm recalling you at outside-right this afternoon,' he said eventually, laying the pen down and looking up at me. 'Can't have a player of your calibre, an England international, kicking his heels up in the stand. I know you can still do this club a great job so go out and prove me right. OK?'

I told him it was fine by me and that I couldn't wait to get out there against Brentford and prove he was indeed right in his assumption. I left his office in a happy frame of mind. Even when I got to the changing room and found George Mountford had been switched to inside-right instead of Albert Mitchell, a reserve-team player who had himself been a replacement for the injured Syd Peppitt at Blackpool, I was just so delighted to be back in the fold I never put two and two together.

We beat Brentford 3–1 and to top what I thought was a good personal performance, I managed to chip in with our third goal. It was only after the game that the circumstances surrounding my selection started to become clear.

I was never one to collect match programmes. I have a few. Some players collect every one, but I quite often didn't even look at it on the actual day. However, following the win over Brentford I did. As the rest of the Stoke team were changing, I picked up the match programme and was taken aback to see my name wasn't included. Match programmes in those days were printed the day before the game which meant the team news from the manager's office had to arrive at the printers on the Thursday. But with no saturation coverage of football on the radio, and television still very much in its infancy, the main sources of team news for supporters were the local newspaper and the matchday programme.

The teams listed were deemed to be wholly accurate – no listing squads of 20 players in those days. The only changes were enforced by last-minute injury. That is why on seeing George Mountford's name at outside-right, Albert Mitchell at inside-right and my own omitted, I immediately came to the conclusion that what Bob McGrory had told me in his office that morning was flannel and I had been included

Holding the first ever Footballer of the Year award in 1948. A young Stanley Jr is already keen to get a touch of the ball. (Colorsport)

Stan Mortensen crashes the ball into the top of the net to set England on their way to a 4–0 victory over Italy in May 1948. It was one of the best team performances I was ever involved in. It also gave birth to a strange story that was to follow me around the world. (Hulton Getty)

Meeting His Majesty King George VI before the 1948 FA Cup final against Manchester United. Sadly they were to beat us 4–2, thanks largely to Matt Busby's tactical awareness. (Popperfoto)

Stan Mortensen leaps for the ball in the 1951 FA Cup final against Newcastle. Yet again we were to lose in the match, and I wondered if I would ever have another chance to claim that cherished medal. (Hulton Getty)

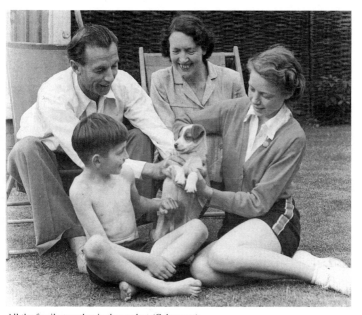

All the family together in the garden. (Colorsport)

Betty, Stanley Jr, me and Jean prepare for a game of tennis. This was to be Stanley Jr's sport. (Colorsport)

Teaching Stanley Jr early ball skills. (Popperfoto)

Harry Johnston and I are held aloft by our team-mates after Blackpool's dramatic late win against Bolton in the 1953 FA Cup final. Manager Joe Smith (right) looks on. (Allsport/Hulton Getty)

Jackie Mudie and Stan Mortensen carrying me on the Wembley turf. I hold my medal up high for my father to see. (Popperfoto)

Leaving the quagmire of Port Vale's pitch after they had knocked holders Blackpool out of the FA Cup. Not the best time to be signing autographs, but as far as I can remember I did. (Huston Spratt)

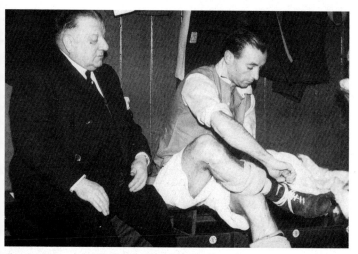

Guesting for Arsenal while George Allison looks on. Even when I was 39, his successor Tom Whittaker was still anxious to sign me for the club. (Popperfoto)

Changing times. (Above) The Hungarians celebrate yet another goal in their famous 6–3 victory at Wembley in November 1953. They were the first Continental side ever to win against England at home. (Below) Nat Lofthouse may have scored here against Uruguay in the 1954 World Cup, but we lost 4–2. The lessons of our failure in the 1950 World Cup had still not been learned. (both Hulton Getty)

Scoring a rare goal, against Tottenham, in 1956. (Popperfoto)

Slipping past a defender before preparing to cross the ball. Note the high-level security from the police (in white gloves!) in the background. (Colorsport)

Taking on Brazilian left-back Santos during our famous 4–2 victory. At 41 I felt I could still hold my own at this level – even against a side that would go on to win the World Cup in 1958. (Mirror Syndication International)

With Stanley Jr at junior Wimbledon, which he won. (Mirror Syndication International)

against Brentford only because another player had pulled out unfit at the last minute. Just to be certain, I had a word with Neil Franklin, who I knew I could trust to give me a straight answer. Neil confirmed my suspicions. Albert Mitchell was injured.

I immediately sought out the directors, who were in the boardroom for a post-match drink, and voiced my concern about the situation. They denied I had been left out of the team and only reinstated because of injury to another player. I didn't have conclusive proof, but the match programme and the conversation with Neil Franklin, of which the board were not aware, gave me ample reason to believe I was right. For the first and only time in my career, I was angry – not so much angry that the wool had been pulled over my eyes but angry that the actions of Bob McGrory and the board made me feel I had no confidence in them anymore. Every footballer has to feel he has the confidence of the directors, his manager and fellow team-mates; otherwise his own confidence is affected and he will play nowhere near to his capabilities. That is why as I journeyed back to Blackpool following our victory over Brentford, I knew the time had come for me to leave Stoke City. Where I was to go I hadn't a clue, but even at 32 I felt there would be no shortage of clubs interested in my services.

I had another meeting with the Stoke directors. Bob McGrory wasn't there. I don't know why. I told Mr Booth and his fellow board members I thought underhand work had been going on and was far from happy with my situation at the club. Mr Booth as ever tried to smooth matters over. He appeared genuinely sympathetic to my plight and offered to do whatever he could to calm the waters and iron out any differences between Bob McGrory and myself, but I felt I had heard it all before. I didn't want to blow up the difference of opinion between McGrory and myself about my suitability for the Stoke first team. I may not have agreed with Bob, but he was entitled to his opinion and he was, after all, the manager. I genuinely felt a change of club would do me the world of good, rekindle the fire within and motivate me to even greater achievement. In addition to that, the travelling between Blackpool and Stoke was starting to take its toll. War years included, I had been associated with Stoke City for 17 years and at 32 I felt that if I didn't move now, in a couple of years it might be too late to join a team of note.

At first the Stoke board refused my request for a transfer but relented when they realised how determined I was to move on. It was a condition of the transfer request being granted that no statement would be made to the press or the supporters and that I would remain with Stoke until the end of the season, when hopefully we would win the championship and negotiations for my move could begin. Mr Booth asked me if there was any club in particular I would like contacted and, having given the matter considerable thought over the previous 48 hours, I had no hesitation in replying Blackpool. For his part, Mr Booth said he would be in touch with the Blackpool chairman Colonel Parkinson and then bound everyone in the room to secrecy as he believed, rightly to my mind, that the news of my impending departure could have a detrimental effect on Stoke's run-in for the championship. I left the meeting happy with the situation. I would be on hand to help Stoke in the challenge for the championship if called upon to do so, and a new chapter in my career seemed to be taking shape.

Six men can keep a secret in football if five of them are dead, so I don't know why I was shocked the following day when the news of my transfer was splashed across the sports pages of every national newspaper. So much for Harry

Booth's pact of secrecy. I don't think it was Harry who told the press, but somebody in that meeting let the cat out of the bag, even if they didn't talk directly to the press. All I know is it wasn't me.

Less than 24 hours after my meeting with the Stoke directors, my telephone never stopped ringing with reporters wanting a quote from me about the move. I couldn't take the telephone off the hook because the summer season was just getting under way at Blackpool and it was the prime source of booking inquiries for our hotel. I simply had to endure it.

Two days later I left England for Ireland – I had been picked to represent the Football League against the League of Ireland in Dublin – but there was no escape. Reporters making the trip with the Football League party never gave me a moment's peace on the ferry and I have to say a number of them didn't give me a good press. The next day in Ireland I picked up the English newspapers and was astounded by the way events were reported. Some said I had given Stoke City an ultimatum, telling the directors that if they didn't accede to my transfer request I'd retire from football and thus deny them a five-figure windfall. Another report said I had 'grown too big for my boots' and referred to me as 'turning his back on the home-town club that had given him his chance in football'. Another accused me of bad sportsmanship. Bad sportsmanship? A player whose conduct on the pitch had never ever warranted even a talking-to by a referee? None of it was true, but I wasn't angry at such scurrilous stories, just very sad. Leaving Stoke City was a wrench for me. I loved the club and although I felt it right given the circumstances that I should move on, I did so with mixed feelings.

Following the match in Ireland, my impending move turned into a wrangle. I was training with Blackpool of course, so their manager Joe Smith knew at first-hand what I was capable of. Before Blackpool made an official offer for me, he took me to one side after training.

'Stan, regarding your possible move here. You're 32, do you think you can do a job for us for another two years?' Joe asked.

'At least two years,' I told him. 'The way I'm playing and the way I feel, I think I could go on for another five at least.'

'Me too,' said Joe. 'Players never lose skill. I still have all the skill I had when I was playing, but the legs have gone. But with you, it's different. I've seen you in training and I'd be confident of putting you up against racing pigeons.'

If I had been harbouring any doubts about whether a move to Blackpool was the right one for me, and I wasn't, Joe Smith's words of confidence in my ability to play would have erased them. I thought to myself this is a manager I want to play for.

Blackpool put in an official bid of £11,500 for my services, a pretty hefty fee in 1947, especially for a 32-year-old. Stoke City, however, were holding out for £20,000. The Blackpool chairman Colonel Parkinson took the tack that as I had requested the transfer and Stoke had granted it and contacted his club about a possible move, he wasn't prepared to pay what for them would have been a record fee. The negotiations dragged on. In the meantime, I played for Stoke in a 2–0 win at Blackburn Rovers and managed to get on the scoresheet. We followed that with another away win, this time 2–1 at Leeds. That was to be my last game in a Stoke City shirt for 14 years.

Looking back, it's incredible to think I did return to Stoke 14 years later because at the time of my move to Blackpool there were a number of people who thought I was almost finished then and I firmly believe Bob McGrory was one of them. Bob wanted me to go, of that there is little doubt. At 32, he obviously thought the £11,500 offered by Blackpool, even though it fell short of Stoke's asking price, was too good to turn down. I played 23 games for Stoke during 1946–47. Stoke won 13, drew five and lost five scoring 41 goals in the process. According to *Evening Sentinel* match reports, I had a hand in 30 of those goals, either by providing the actual pass or being involved in the final build-up. As Disraeli said, there are lies, damned lies and statistics but I feel those statistics are indicative of my contribution and commitment to the team and shoot holes in Bob McGrory's view, expressed to players like Neil Franklin and Dennis Herod, that I was playing for my own ends and no longer doing the business as far as Stoke was concerned.

My performance led me to believe I had a few more years left at the top. Of course I didn't think my best days in football were yet to come, but they were. Following the Leeds game in May, I was picked to play for Great Britain against the Rest of Europe in a prestigious fixture to celebrate the return of the four home countries to FIFA. The winter just gone had been one of the worst on record. Numerous postponements meant the domestic football season had to be extended into June. Even so, no one saw the game against the Rest of Europe as a burden upon players or an irrelevancy in the fixture list. On the contrary, in much the same way that rugby union players feel the ultimate accolade in their sport is to be picked for the British Lions, to be selected for this Great Britain team was an acknowledgement that you were the best in your position. The press built the game up not as the 'Game of the Season' but as the 'Match of the Century'. Great Britain had invented football and even though the home countries had not entered the pre-war World Cup tournaments, England in particular was still seen as the nation that every other footballing country in the world looked up to. British teams were the masters and the press worldwide saw the outcome of this match as crucial in testing that theory. A number of sports writers felt it was a belief confined to these shores.

In the days leading up to the game, the tension and atmosphere built up into a frenzy. The game was to be played at Hampden Park because at 135,000 the ground had the largest capacity of any in Britain. Even so, such was the clamour for tickets for what the *Daily Herald* described as 'The ultimate showdown of soccer styles' that it was nowhere near big enough.

I joined the Great Britain team at their headquarters in Aberfoyle, which lies at the foot of the Trossachs overlooking the picturesque Loch Ard. The time spent there came as a welcome relief from the hassle and glare of publicity surrounding my transfer. I'd rise at dawn, before any of my team-mates stirred, put myself through a training session of stretch exercises and sprints, then take a walk in the hotel grounds and surrounding countryside before breakfast. Early on the Thursday morning prior to the Hampden game, I stood totally alone by the shore of Loch Ard and watched the small waves gently breaking over brown stones. The calmness and serenity of the loch was in direct contrast to the unrest I was feeling about the transfer. Although at peace with solitude and nature, I also felt the unease of being in the public eye because I knew my name was being brandished in headlines across the back of every newspaper. I took in the soft green banks and braes, heard the whisper of woodland, and gazed at the mountains, the purple shoulders of which were draped in the ermine of white clouds. The peaks stretched away further than the eye could see. The possibilities of what lay ahead of me seemed as infinite and back at the hotel I heard on the wireless that the negotiations between Stoke and Blackpool looked like breaking down because the clubs could not agree on the fee. The weather in this part of Scotland can change in minutes. Grey clouds swung so low over the hills that it seemed possible to stand on a chair and touch them with a walking stick. Thin rain came slanting down in successive windy sheets. My mood changed accordingly. In itself, the thought of staying at Stoke City was not unappealing. I loved the club and its supporters, but the idea of playing for a manager who seemed to harbour resentment against me laid my spirits low. Later that day, however, a reporter informed me that the Stoke City president, Sir Francis Joseph, a man for whom I had a great deal of time and respect, had stepped in and persuaded the Stoke board to accept Blackpool's offer. My elation was tinged with sadness. The Great Britain team moved to Glasgow for the game and, on the night before the match, I was officially informed by those Stoke City directors who had travelled north that my move to Blackpool was on.

The match of the century attracted record receipts in excess of £30,000. It was a great honour to be chosen for the Great Britain team and I would have happily paid my own expenses and played for nothing. I am sure every other member of that team would have done the same. I believe our match fee was £14, so second-class rail fares and hotel accommodation apart, the four home Football Associations paid out a total of £154 to the British players who took part. Even allowing for fees and expenses for the Rest of Europe team, how much money did our respective footballing bodies make out of this game and, more to the point, where did it go? If only a proportion had gone to help develop the game at grass-roots level or on improved facilities at grounds for supporters I wouldn't ask such a question, but I never saw any evidence that it did.

Even in the thirties, receipts for FA Cup finals alone averaged £24,000 at a time when the maximum wage was

£5. The huge profits football's administrators were making from big names prompted Middlesbrough's Wilf Mannion, in the wake of this Great Britain game, to stage a one-man strike in protest at the maximum wage and the fees top footballers received for playing in internationals. At the time, Wilf's was a lone protesting voice. After six weeks of inactivity and with a mortgage to pay he was forced to accept defeat, return to football and accept his lot. Fifteen years later, every footballer in the land took up Wilf's stance in a move that freed players from contract slavery for ever.

Quite often a big game is so burdened by pre-publicity and hype that it is incapable of living up to expectations, but the Great Britain v. Rest of Europe match surpassed anything that had been written or said about it. For the record the teams lined up as follows:

Great Britain: Swift (England); Hardwick (England), Hughes (Wales); Macaulay (Scotland), Vernon (Northern Ireland), Burgess (Wales), Matthews, Mannion, Lawton (all England), Steel, Liddell (both Scotland).

Rest of Europe: Du Rui (France); Peterson (Denmark), Steffen (Switzerland); Carey (Republic of Ireland), Parola (Italy), Ludl (Czechoslovakia), Lambrechts (Belgium), Gren, Nordahl (both Sweden), Wilkes (Holland), Praest (Denmark).

To my mind, the rest of Europe side was not as strong as it could have been. In the aftermath of war, as their country struggled to regain its feet, key German players had not been included and a number of Italian players originally selected had for one reason or another withdrawn. That said, it was still a formidable line-up, one that it was thought would provide a stern test for the best that British football had to offer.

The 135,000 spectators who filled Hampden were treated to a classic game of football, notable for the fact that it did not contain one intentional foul. I soon had the measure of my opposite number, the Swiss left-back Steffen, and with Wilf Mannion alongside me, inspirational and irrepressible, we cut the Rest of Europe left flank to ribbons. Wilf ended the game with a hat-trick, Tommy Lawton scored twice and Billy Steel, who had played just ten Scottish league games at the time of his selection, hit an amazing goal from 35 yards to set up a 6–1 win. Even allowing for the fact that the Rest of Europe team had been drawn from nine different countries, didn't know one another and had no common language, it was an astounding margin of victory.

British football had been proved to be the best. Even the continental sports writers heaped praise on us for our performance. It was the headiest of times but in the ensuing years, while British football continued to bask in the reflections of its own glory, other footballing nations developed the game. In the fullness of time, countries as diverse as Hungary, Brazil, Germany, Spain, Yugoslavia, Italy and Uruguay gave the masters a lesson and made us students of the game we had invented.

A few hours after that memorable victory, I was joined in my Glasgow hotel by a group of directors from Stoke City and Blackpool, including Harry Booth and Colonel Parkinson, and Bob McGrory and Joe Smith. I remember the moment well. To avoid doing business in the glare of the public eye, we assembled in my room and as there was no desk, I signed the necessary forms on the dresser. Blackpool manager Joe Smith stood to my right with Bob McGrory peering over my left shoulder. There was a large mirror attached to the dresser and when I signed on the dotted line to make myself a Blackpool player, I looked into it and saw two smiling faces – Joe Smith's and my own.

The fee of £11,500, though not a record for the time, was still a considerable amount of money and it was par for the course for such weighty transfer fees to be paid in two or three instalments. I remember Harry Booth asking Colonel Parkinson how he intended to pay the fee and the surprised look on his face when the Blackpool chairman pulled a cheque book from his pocket and said, 'I assume a cheque will be acceptable?' A cheque was made out for the full amount. I was delighted everything was cut and dried and there were no loose ends. There were handshakes all round. Bob McGrory thanked me for my efforts on behalf of Stoke City and wished me luck. I reciprocated, wishing him every success, and I embarked upon a new chapter in my life, as a Blackpool player.

My joy at joining Blackpool was tempered somewhat by the fact that on the final day of the season Stoke City slipped up and missed out on the First Division Championship. Following my final game for the Potters, Stoke had drawn 0–0 with Sunderland in front of 32,000 at the Victoria Ground, followed by a 1–0 victory at Aston Villa. Liverpool beat Wolves 2–1 at Molineux to finish their season leading Division One with 57 points, but Stoke City on 55 points and with a better goal difference still had one game to play, away at Sheffield United. A win of any sort would have given Stoke the championship but again Sheffield United proved to be their undoing. While Liverpool could do nothing but sweat it out, Stoke's destiny was in their own hands but they contrived to lose 2–1 and the championship went to Merseyside.

I was disappointed for the club, its supporters and in particular the players. I would have liked to have seen out the season with Stoke. To have said farewell to the club by helping them win the championship would for me have been a fitting end to 17 years at the Victoria Ground. But who knows if my presence in the Stoke team would have swung things their way. It is not for me to say, but two of my former team-mates, Neil Franklin and Dennis Herod, had firm views. Some years later, during an interview with *Evening Sentinel* sports writer Peter Hewitt, Neil said, 'Stan was the best player I ever played with. If he had not been sold to Blackpool in 1947, I am sure Stoke would have won the First Division Championship.'

Goalkeeper Dennis Herod was even more forthright in his view and is on record in an interview he gave in 1999 as saying, 'Bob McGrory's jealousy of Stan's fame cost Stoke their best chance of the First Division title. Before our last game at Sheffield United, he sold a world-class player and we lost that match without him. I am not taking anything away from McGrory who did a great deal for Stoke City. But he wanted the limelight himself and was jealous of players like Stan and Neil Franklin. It was folly to leave Stan out and the decision to sell the best forward in the world to Blackpool was sheer stupidity.'

Whether or not my presence in the team would have aided Stoke in their quest for the championship is a matter of conjecture. Suffice to say that Stoke not winning it that season was, for me, a sad end to what had been 17 wonderful years with my home-town club.

Some consolation for Stoke lay in the fact that the £11,500 they received for me helped them make a healthy £32,000 profit on the season. The following season, the free-scoring Freddie Steele broke his leg against Charlton in September and it all but ended his career at the Victoria Ground. Stoke missed Freddie's goals and finished below halfway in Division One. Freddie's injury was a signal that the pendulum of Stoke's fortunes was about to swing the other way. Bob McGrory was replaced as manager in 1952 by Frank Taylor but they were relegated in 1953 and sadly went into decline for nigh on a decade.

12

---◦---

The First Footballer
of the Year

I couldn't wait for the start of the 1947–48 season but before I could turn my attention fully to my new club, there was England's mini-tour of the Continent which took in games against Switzerland and Portugal.

The Swiss had a very good team. The two previous meetings had resulted in a win each, the most recent being Switzerland's victory in 1938 in which I had been up against the band leader full-back. Although not considered a power in European football, the Swiss had enough quality to pull off the odd win against top international sides and this proved to be the case in our game in Zurich.

The Switzerland match was my first for England as a Blackpool player, although of course I had yet to play for my new club. Another milestone was that this was the first time an England team had travelled by air to an international match played on foreign soil. The journey was far less arduous that the network of trains and ferries we had been accustomed to. As a result, the England team arrived in Switzerland not suffering from travel fatigue. However, the relaxed mode was carried on to the pitch and despite having great players such as Frank Swift, George Hardwick, Billy Wright, Neil Franklin, Raich Carter, Tommy Lawton and Wilf Mannion, our team performance left much to be desired.

The 34,000 Swiss fans gave the England team a great reception as we took to the field, but the conviviality and friendship contrived to instil itself into our play. In the first quarter of an hour, there was a lack of sharpness and application about our game and once that is evident in a number of players, it is hard to rectify on the day. The lacklustre approach meant I wasn't getting the service I liked or normally expected, and I found myself dropping deeper and deeper in search of the ball. The Swiss scored after half an hour through their outside-left Fatton but going a goal down failed to jolt a number of the England players into action. Although we had the majority of the play in the second half, I have to say we created few real chances and the Swiss hung on for a deserved victory.

In the dressing room after the game, I was very disappointed in our performance. One of my England team-mates said the claustrophobic atmosphere of a small ground and pitch had affected him and a number of other players; they were used to playing in more spacious arenas. While he may have had a point, I didn't think it was a valid excuse. Top players should be able to perform in any arena and as far as I was concerned when I donned an England shirt, I gave my all. To be frank, some of the England players that day, although tired, just didn't have the spark and edge vital to winning games at this level.

The will to win wasn't great enough and that has to be down to a mental approach. Of course you have to be physically fit in football but you also have to be mentally fit. Perhaps some players went out thinking the game was going to be a doddle and once behind because of their relaxed mental state, couldn't lift their individual game sufficiently to claw it back.

Following the Switzerland game the English press made it quite clear they were not happy with the overall performance of the England team and one or two individuals in particular. Players don't need the press to tell them when they have been performing below par but the adverse reports of the Switzerland game did jolt one or two and when we set off for our second game in Portugal we did so with the avowed intent of redeeming English pride.

On arriving at Lisbon airport, the England party were taken in individual cars to our hotel base in Estoril about ten miles from the capital. Estoril had the reputation of being a bit of a millionaires' playground and on first sight I could understand why. An electric blue sky merged into an aqua blue sea forming a vivid and contrasting backdrop to a small town of icing sugar villas and cafés. It was so unrelentingly hot, it was as if you'd sat all day with your face an inch from one of those concertina radiators at full blast. The streets of the town were lined with palm trees and the front of every palatial white house was adorned with creeping jasmine and geraniums that ranged in colour from salmon pink to post-box red. I have often thought that if Estoril could sing, it would sound like Mario Lanza. Millionaires paid through the nose to sample its beauty. I couldn't get over the fact that I was there taking in all its splendour for free. That very fact made me appreciate this idyllic place, with its quality of light in inverse proportion to Stoke-on-Trent's.

Today, any indiscretion on the part of an England player abroad makes big headlines. In my day, there was an unwritten rule that sports journalists reported on the game and nothing else. However, such incidents as the drunken binge in the Far East prior to Euro 96 or being snapped in a nightclub at six in the morning with a beer in one hand and a cigarette in the other a week or so before France 98 far outweigh the indiscretions that we England players ran up during our time in Estoril.

Our first problem was when we all took to the beach. The England players, myself included, wore just swimming trunks or shorts and we hadn't been on the beach long before the local police approached us. We were told in the politest way that we were breaking the law as all men on the beach were required to wear at least swimming trunks and a vest. It had been a genuine mistake and no further action was taken.

Later that day, while sightseeing around the town, the England players fell foul of the local law again. I believe it was Liverpool's Phil Taylor and Arsenal's Laurie Scott who lit cigarettes only for a member of the local police to collar them both. We were all slack-jawed to discover it was against the law to use a cigarette lighter on the street without a licence because it was deemed to be detrimental to the government-controlled match-making industry. Again a protracted conversation took place with the two players involved full of apologies before both were let off with a warning.

Further on in our walkabout, we came across a set of traffic lights. As there were no cars to be seen, even though the lights indicated pedestrians should wait, a number of England players crossed the empty road. A policeman told them they had committed a jay-walking offence. The players concerned said it was quite normal to cross a British road in such circumstances without fear of retribution but offered profuse apologies for their ignorance of Portuguese law. The policeman reminded us all we were no longer in England.

These were mild indiscretions I know, but I wonder what

certain newspapers today would make of England players falling foul of the police in a foreign country three times in one day!

Once we had settled into our base in Estoril, the England players were taken to the National Stadium in Lisbon for a training session to help us get a feel for the pitch. I well recall the awe we felt on seeing the Portuguese National Stadium for the first time. It had cost £350,000 to build, which was an astronomical amount of money at the time. It was constructed almost entirely of white marble and while it was all seated, offered hardly any covered accommodation for spectators. The only covered part of the stadium was a stand with white marble pillars, a shimmering white triangular roof and sporting a long balcony ornamented with chubby-cheeked cherubims. This, we were told, was for the use of the Portuguese president and his political and military hierarchy. It seemed more in keeping with ancient Athens than a football ground, but knowing how certain governments love to construct official buildings in the image of those of ancient Greece to infer empire status, I thought this was probably the whole idea.

As we walked on to the lush pitch, it felt strangely familiar underfoot. It had a deep spring to it, the sort of turf that can quickly sap your energy if you're not careful. When I was told the pitch was of Cumberland turf imported from England, the reason for its familiar feel became immediately apparent. It was the same turf as Wembley had and, as far as I know, still has.

Soon after the war, Walter Winterbottom had been appointed England's first manager, as the FA tried to get some cohesion and leadership at the helm of our national team. The selectors, however, were reluctant to give up their control of the team entirely and still picked the side, though Walter's advice was taken on board. For the Portugal game, even though the result and performance against Switzerland had left much to be desired, only two changes were made and both of them were enforced. Liverpool's Phil Taylor and Bobby Langton of Blackburn Rovers were injured and were replaced by Stan Mortensen, winning his debut, and Tom Finney respectively. The England team lined up as follows:

Frank Swift (Manchester City); Laurie Scott (Arsenal), George Hardwick (Middlesbrough); Billy Wright (Wolves), Neil Franklin (Stoke City), Eddie Lowe (Aston Villa); Stan Matthews, Stan Mortensen (both Blackpool), Tommy Lawton (Chelsea), Wilf Mannion (Middlesbrough), Tom Finney (Preston North End).

Minutes before the kick-off, with all the England players keyed up and ready for action, we heard heated voices out in the corridor. Moments later Stanley Rous, the FA secretary, came in and told us the start of the match was to be delayed due to an argument about the size of the ball. An exasperated Rous explained that Portugal wanted to use a size four football, the same as those used in their domestic competitions, which was smaller than the balls used in British football, more in keeping with those used in schoolboy matches. Stanley Rous said the Portuguese were incensed at the thought of using a large football, which was to us normal size, because it was not conducive to skill. The matter had been referred to the match officials and while they debated the issue, he was going to go back outside for a cigarette.

'Well for heavens sake don't use a lighter or there'll be a bloody riot!' Frank Swift said. We all fell about laughing and immediately the pre-match tension and irritation we were feeling at the delayed start disappeared.

Fifteen minutes later we kicked off in front of 60,000 volatile Portuguese fans with a standard-sized football, the match officials having sided with our own FA. From the start, the ball was played by Wilf Mannion to me out on the right wing and I took off in the direction of their left-back, Feliciano. With a little drop of the shoulder I sent him the wrong way and looked up hoping to see Tommy Lawton steaming into the penalty box. Tommy didn't disappoint me. I whipped over the cross and instead of meeting it with a characteristic bullet header, Tommy casually flicked his head to one side as if taking a glance over his left shoulder at some mild commotion behind him. It was the merest of touches but enough to deflect the ball in mid flight and place it in the gap between the far post and the stranded Azevedo in the Portugal goal. There were 20 seconds on the clock and immediately 60,000 sonorous Portuguese were silent.

The Portuguese goalkeeper booted the ball towards the dugouts in disgust and when the ball was returned to the pitch it was the smaller size four version! The referee didn't seem to notice and buoyed by our excellent start, none of the England team protested. I was of the mind that they could use whatever size ball they wanted. As someone who had spent countless hours as a small boy playing with a tennis ball, the smaller size four football made not one iota of difference to me.

Seven minutes later, Wilf Mannion combined with Tom Finney on the left for Tom to find Stand Mortensen with the silkiest of passes. Morty accelerated away from a flat-footed Portuguese defence before letting rip with a shot that had the roof of the net ballooning. Four minutes later it was the turn of Tommy Lawton again. I rolled a pass inside to Tommy, who was some 30 yards from goal, and was in the process of taking off down the wing for the return when he swivelled his hips, glanced up, drew back his right leg and let fly with a shot that had Azevedo flying through the air like a trapeze artist who had missed his connecting bar.

Tom Finney may have been unaccustomed to playing at outside-left but he gave full vent to his joyous and effective artistry. You would have thought he had been born to the position. Former Stoke manager Tony Waddington once described football as the working man's ballet. On this day, Tom proved to everyone he was the *premier danseur* as time and time again he flitted through the ranks of the Portuguese defence. On 25 minutes, Tom received a pass from George Hardwick in our own half of the field and, with the ball never more than inches from the end of his toe, worked his way through the defence with all the directness of Hampton Court Maze before slamming the ball into the net, leaving a corkscrew of defenders in his wake. The Portuguese fans rose to their feet and applauded Tom all the way back to the halfway line. Stan Mortensen glanced across to the Portuguese bench.

'Sling the regular-sized ball on as well,' Stan told them. 'It'll give your lads something to play with.'

Within a minute of Stan's quip, Portugal's second-string goalkeeper Capela came on for Azevedo. There had been no arrangements made for substitutes, none of the England reserves was changed, but with a 4–0 lead we let it go. I'd heard Capela was very similar in style to Azevedo and within minutes he was doing a good impression of him, picking the ball out of the net after another fine effort from Tommy Lawton.

Portugal had been seen as much stiffer opposition for us than Switzerland and we were determined not to let up in the second half. In the dressing room at half-time, we vowed to keep the pressure up to show that the result in Switzerland had been an aberration. The heat was stifling and our thick cotton shirts, shorts and woollen socks added to our discomfort, but nothing was going to rob us of a decisive victory.

Within minutes of the restart Tom Finney rolled the ball

behind a flat Portugal defence in such a leisurely manner and with such exact appraisement of distance that the spectators in the paddock sides of the stadium could have clambered over the perimeter fencing and scored from it let alone Stan Mortensen, who did. Five minutes later I took off down the right wing and as I came up to the left-back Feliciano, he mustered token resistance. I paid him only cursory attention in bypassing him and centring for Stan Mortensen to fire home goal number seven. As I trotted back to the halfway line, Feliciano gave me a thin smile and I knew he had given up. Morty and Tommy Lawton both scored again, which gave them four goals apiece, and with Tom Finney's superb solo goal it made the score 9–0.

By this time, the Portuguese fans realised they were witnessing a performance that would have beaten any side in the world, football history in the making. They took to their feet and for the remainder of the game gave us constant and uninterrupted applause.

With minutes to go, Billy Wright sent me away down the right wing. With the game handsomely won, I decided to go it alone. I cut inside, pulled out all the tricks and found myself bearing down on Capela with the defence behind me. To be honest he made it easy for me because after initially rushing out to cut down my vision of the goal, he hesitated. It gave me the split second to pick my spot and I tapped the ball past him and into the goal to make it 10–0. I made my way back upfield and on reaching the halfway line Neil Franklin and Billy Wright trotted up.

'There, what did I tell you?' said Neil turning to Wrighty. 'Stan is just the man for a crisis!'

In addition to restoring pride after the defeat in Zurich, the victory was notable for two things. It was England's record away win and Tom Finney, in being torturer in chief, proved himself to be a footballer of world class. The Portugal team failed to turn up for the post-match buffet. At the time it perplexed me because for all we had run them ragged, Portugal had not resorted to unfair means in their attempts to stem the tide. I later learned their absence was simply down to the fact that they were so ashamed of their own performance they didn't want us to have the embarrassment of finding any comforting words for them.

Back in England, we learned that the whole team had been suspended by the Portuguese FA for what they considered an abject performance. However, I'm happy to say that when news of this reached the ears of our own FA, they protested and managed to get the ban lifted, which pleased me because for all they had been humiliated, the Portuguese team had shown great sportsmanship throughout the game and were generous in their praise of England as we left the field.

I spent the rest of the summer working at the hotel and continuing my daily training routine. When I reported to Bloomfield Road prior to the 1947–48 season, I was already at peak fitness and my new team-mates gave me a warm reception. Everyone at the club seemed delighted to see me, no one more so than manager Joe Smith. Everything was new, fresh and vibrant. I felt great and the thought of starting a new career in football at the age of 32 never bothered me at all.

I remember the first day well. We trained on the Bloomfield Road pitch. The grass had been allowed to grow a little long to minimise damage. The sun was shining, it was warm and when I finished a sprint and took in lungfuls of fresh air, I could taste the saltiness of the sea. After the disappointment and turmoil of my final weeks as a Stoke City player, Blackpool felt like my Elysium. Every player bubbled with enthusiasm and applied himself fully to all the tasks in hand.

Centre-half Eric Hayward was ribbed about his speed but took it in good part, though in truth he wasn't as slow as

Stan Mortensen and Alex Munro were trying to make out. Morty was saying the donkeys on Blackpool beach were quicker over ten yards. Towards the end of the training session there was some shooting practice for the forwards. Stan Mortensen, who had changed into a spanking new pair of boots in order to wear them in for the new season, sent his first shot high over the bar.

'Morty, if that's going to be an example of your shooting this season, you'd be better leaving that new boot on the touchline and wear the bloody box on your right foot,' said Eric by way of getting his own back.

The camaraderie and humour among the players helped me settle in straightaway. Not for one moment was I made to feel an outsider. I knew I was going to be very happy at Blackpool FC.

As 23 August and our first league fixture at home to Chelsea drew near, the marked difference between Joe Smith and Bob McGrory as managers was brought home to me when Joe took me to one side and told me how he wanted me to play.

'Play your own game, Stan,' he said. 'There are no shackles here. You have freedom of mind and style to express yourself. The grass is green, the sun is shining, go out and enjoy yourself. If we win, all well and good. If we don't, then as long as everybody has given their all, that'll be good enough for me. Rest assured, with the players you have around you here, we'll win more than we'll lose. Play your own game and whatever you do out on the pitch, do it in the knowledge that you have my full support.'

It was like a breath of fresh air off the sea. Joe was a wily old bird but he was my type of manager. He had assembled good players and believed, as I always have, that you don't have to tell good players what to do. As a manager, you must encourage them to display the gifts with which they have been blessed. In the likes of Stan Mortensen, Eddie Shimwell, Harry Johnston, Eric Hayward and Ron Suart, Blackpool had some very talented players indeed. That said, Joe's dependency on the natural talent of his players to pull Blackpool through didn't always pay off. There were occasions when just a little pre-planning could have paid significant dividends, instances when a little organisation within the side may have made the difference between us being nearlies and landing the silverware I felt our overall talent deserved. Joe's implicit belief in the ability of his players to cope with any situation and win the day was his undoing at times. You don't have to tell good players what to do, but sometimes those talents need channelling. More often than not, Joe's team-talk was brief. What to do in the game was left entirely with the players.

'Get two goals up before half-time, lads,' Joe would say, 'so I can enjoy my cigar in the second half.'

Many was the time when Joe had left the dressing room, skipper Harry Johnston would get up to say the opposition had such and such a player in their ranks and point out his weaknesses and indicate to whoever in the Blackpool team was marking him to play him in a certain way. Harry's favourite expression once Joe Smith had left us to our own devices was to say, 'We haven't a bloody clue what we're doing, have we?' Harry was right but such was the talent within the ranks we won games on sheer natural ability, with Harry taking on the manager's role on the pitch, issuing instructions as the game progressed.

If that sounds a little harsh on Joe Smith I don't intend it to. For all the emphasis was placed on the players to work things out as we went along in games, he was a marvellous manager, one for whom I had nothing but the highest respect. When Morty and I were doing well and duplicating good form with England, Joe never resented our success. In fact, he encouraged it; he believed it was good for the club and that our performances would rub off on the other Blackpool players. When things were going swimmingly for Blackpool, his only words of caution to the team prior to taking the field were, 'Don't go out with your big heads on.' We never did and I think that was one of the reasons for our success. Agony and good fortune, fame and despair, success and despondency were all met in the same steadfast, level-headed manner.

The 1947–48 season got off to a good start with a 3–0 win over Chelsea before 30,000 at Bloomfield Road. Come Christmas we were handily placed in the championship running and, in addition to filling Bloomfield Road for every home game, we were drawing massive crowds wherever we played. Although we didn't realise it at the time, our appeal was evolving into the modern-day equivalent of Manchester United. Many grounds we visited enjoyed their biggest attendance of the season – 56,000 at Aston Villa, 53,000 at Burnley, 46,000 at Bolton, 68,000 at Arsenal, 64,000 at Sunderland, 54,000 at Liverpool, 65,000 at Manchester United.

As a team, the emphasis was on entertaining. Sometimes we were brash and brassy, other times cultured and classy. When the occasion demanded, we were rough and hard-edged, but we also had great heart and tremendous feeling for the game. In many ways, we encapsulated the town of Blackpool itself. We had ball players such as myself and Alex Munro and we had hard men like Harry Johnston and Eddie Shimwell. People said as a team we were a paradox, but then so is Blackpool because the Golden Mile isn't a mile and it's debatable whether it's ever been golden. I just saw us as being balanced. If a team is to do well it must be made up of ball players, ball winners, craftsmen and runners. Joe Smith knew this and put together a team consisting of players to fulfil specific roles. I was never known for my heading ability, but Stan Mortensen was and he was the man in the middle at whom my centres were aimed. I was never a great tackler, but behind me I had Harry Johnston and Eddie Shimwell who would happily tackle a Chieftain tank in full flow. Neither Eddie nor Harry were good at taking players on and crossing the ball, but that was my job. As Joe Smith once said to me, 'Harry will keep you supplied with a constant flow of passes. He's one of the best passers of the ball over two yards in football today.' There was a glint in his eye when Joe said it, but many a true word is spoken in jest. Harry would go into a tackle, win the ball, then look up for me. I'd always be there and that ball would always come. It would be a simple two- or three-yard pass. Football is a simple game and sometimes players and coaches try to make it out to be complicated. I think they do that because they find it hard to do the simple things. Their lack of certain abilities means they have to gloss over their own shortcomings by trying to make out football is complicated and deep, when in fact it isn't.

I well recall one training session with England when manager Walter Winterbottom spent the best part of a morning running through certain complicated moves he wanted us to carry out in a game. Towards the end of the session, after countless run-throughs and the players getting fed up with being what Tom Finney used to call 'robotised', Len Shackleton turned to Walter and said, 'Boss, why don't we dump this and just do what we're good at. Billy [Wright] wins the ball and passes it to me. I give it to Stan who runs down the wing and centres for Nat [Lofthouse] who scores!'

Whatever the era, football is a game of 11 individuals playing to the best of their ability and in so doing gelling as a unit. How many supremely talented individuals there are among that 11 decrees how great a team will be – two or three and it's a good team; four or five and it's very good; more and it will embrace greatness as in the Brazil side of 1970. In winning the World Cup with such style and grace, they firmly planted their flag on football's aesthetic summit for all future generations to see and strive to emulate. Brazil of 1970, and great club sides such as Real Madrid of 1960, Ajax of the mid-seventies and Liverpool of the late seventies/ early eighties, showed true quality. Quality and class will win the day when combined with sweat and graft. That is football's simple recipe for success, always has been and always will be. Of course, other teams win sometimes but while form is temporary, class is enduring. That is why we readily recall Brazil of 1970 and Real Madrid of 1960 but no one remembers the Steaua Bucharest team that won the European Cup in 1986 and, for all their success of 1971, no one warmed to Arsenal's effective but stifling style.

Blackpool were far from being a great side, but we were a good one. Our relative success and the massive attendances we drew was attractive to would-be players. Joe Smith knew this and over the next five years he gradually brought in players of better quality. The result was Blackpool's team of 1953, their greatest ever.

Joe was always planning improvements, so I suppose you could say that first Blackpool team I played in was in a transient stage. Come the end of the season, the team showed a number of changes from the one that had kicked off the previous August.

On Boxing Day, I made a return visit to the Victoria Ground when Blackpool played Stoke City. The game ended in a 1–1 draw and was played out in front of 48,000 fans. The Stoke supporters gave me a tremendous reception when I ran on to the pitch which delighted me. As I have said, I had mixed feelings about leaving my home-town club and my relationship with what were a terrific set of supporters was always good. I certainly bore no resentment towards the club or Bob McGrory, but seemingly Bob still had an axe to grind. After this particular game, I found out that Peter Buxton a sports journalist with the *Evening Sentinel* had asked McGrory about the possibility of getting hold of a couple of tickets for some pals. Bob McGrory's response was, 'Sorry, bighead's got them all,' an oblique reference to me. The man obviously still bore a grudge. While Bob McGrory may have been happy to see the back of me, the vast majority of Stoke supporters were as sad about my departure as I had been and thought I had been forced out. A rift developed between the official supporters' club and the hierarchy at the club itself. The upshot of it all was that George Birks and his colleagues in the Supporters' Association decided to acquire a piece of land directly opposite the main entrance to the club and build their headquarters there, where it remains to this day, though of course the Victoria Ground has since been superseded by a new stadium.

In my first season, Blackpool finished in ninth place in Division One. We reached the FA Cup final but the fact that we crammed 16 games into the last two months of the season took its toll. We had a number of injuries to key players, Stan Mortensen, Eddie Shimwell, Alex Munro, Willie McIntosh and myself included, and although we had a number of very good reserve players we never had the quality in depth to sustain our title challenge. In those last two months of the season, we won only four league matches and lost six, the rest being draws.

I had built a good understanding with our two principal forwards, Willie McIntosh, who finished the season with 18 goals, and Stan Mortensen, who scored a total of 31. With some people you meet there is an immediate chemistry and you bond straightaway. With others, although you have dealings with them every day and get on perfectly well, there is nothing. With Stan Mortensen and me, the former was true. With the passing of each game, we developed a greater understanding of one another's style of play. A couple of years down the line it was as if we could read one another's minds. The on-the-field relationship was uncanny. When such a partnership is formed in football, it produces magical moments.

Later, he kindly said that his career blossomed through his on-the-pitch relationship with me. In teaming up with Morty the same can be said of my game. Whether in the shirts of Blackpool or England, we worked it the same. Wherever I was on the wing I knew where Morty would be in the middle. For a forward renowned for his goalscoring, he would often drop off quite deep to collect the ball and once he had it I'd take off down the wing. Invariably I'd never look back, the ball would be pushed in front of me to run on to, or come looping over my shoulder beautifully weighted with back spin on it so it slowed up ready for me to collect without breaking stride. Morty would head off for the left of the penalty spot, then with a burst of lightning speed head towards the near post. His change in direction and speed threw defenders and more often than not it meant he arrived at the near post in space. He wasn't the tallest of forwards and this I think helped him in his ability to swivel and turn his body for the arriving ball. He was lethal in the box and pretty lethal outside it as well. He possessed a monstrous and explosive shot with either foot. For a man of his height, five feet ten, he was a match for anyone in the air. He had the uncanny knack of all great predatory strikers of being able to predict where the ball would arrive and this meant he often met it without having an aerial duel with the towering centre-half whose job it was to mark him. Once airborne, it was as if the thumb and first finger of the right hand of the good Lord had reached down, nipped the shirt on his back and held him there because Morty seemed to defy gravity and hang in the air for ages. Denis Law in his heyday with Manchester United in the sixties is the only other player I've seen do that. Morty could despatch headers like bullets from a gun and for all he wasn't the biggest of forwards, his beer barrel chest, cornflake box shoulders and legs like bags of concrete made him a formidable opponent for the toughest of defenders. I can't ever recall him being knocked off the ball and when he went after it, he did so with demonic enthusiasm.

There were some tough centre-halves about at this time – Bill Shorthouse of Wolves, Allenby Chilton at Manchester United, 'Whacker' Hughes of Liverpool, Newcastle's Frank Brennan, Joe Kennedy of West Brom and, lest we forget, on the international front, Scotland's Willie Woodburn, a player whose exploits ended with him being banned *sine die*. Morty got stuck into them all and they into him! 'If blood be the price of Admiralty, Lord God we have paid in full,' wrote Kipling. Morty was a class act but if blood and bruises can be construed as a necessary part of winning games, then Stan Mortensen's account was paid up in full. Not once did I hear him complain about his lot. 'All part of the game, though happily the larger part is played out with the artist's brush,' he used to say and how right he was. For all he was a man of great physical strength and fortitude, more often than not his contribution to the canvas of a game had all the delicacy and elegance of a painting by Renoir.

Stan's tremendous contribution to Blackpool, England and our game in general was all the more startling for the fact he had been injured in World War Two when the bomber plane in which he was flying as a wireless operator/air gunner crashed, killing the pilot and the bomb aimer.

The navigator lost a leg and Morty was confined to hospital for a month following the incident. The injuries he received to his head meant he couldn't cope with Morse Code any more and he saw out the war confined to the ground.

His war experience had been quite traumatic all told and perhaps this had an effect on how he played the game. When decision went against him, he simply shrugged his shoulders. If he blazed over from a good position, which he rarely did, he'd stand motionless and stare, his eyes focused on the trajectory the ball had taken. Then he'd smile to himself at the absurdity of his effort. Although a formidable battler, he would never retaliate when scythed down. He had everything in perspective. He treated opponents, referees, media and supporters as he did the club's directors, with the greatest of respect. Stan Mortensen was always a gentleman. He wouldn't have understood a player wreaking havoc in a referee's room after being sent off, or inciting the wrath of rival supporters by gesticulating at them having scored a goal. To him, antics as we have seen in recent years would have been the actions of an ill-disciplined rabble. He felt that being in the public eye and a role model for youngsters, he owed much to the public who adored him.

I roomed with him when Blackpool played away or when we were together with the England team and got to know him well. He had a marvellous sense of humour and I was for ever encouraging him to tell me jokes. He was such a superb comic storyteller I still laughed even if I'd heard the tale before.

His wife's parents lived 40 yards from Bloomfield Road and he would never arrive in the dressing room until about 20 minutes before the kick-off when the rest of us were already changed. If doubts were expressed about his non-appearance, I'd say, 'Never fear, Morty will be here,' and he always was – and that applied to the penalty area as well as the dressing room.

I am proud to say we were very good friends and remained so until his sad passing in 1991. To this day I miss him dearly. He scored 225 goals in 395 league games and averaged more than a goal a game in FA Cup matches. He's the only man to score a hat-trick in a Wembley FA Cup final. In 25 games for England between 1947 and 1953 he scored 23 goals including four on his England debut in that memorable game against Portugal. I don't know if the good Lord has football teams in heaven but if He does I am sure Morty will have been handed a number nine shirt as he passed through the pearly gates and I know exactly where he will be now – waiting for me at the near post.

＊

Although our championship challenge petered out, Blackpool enjoyed a memorable FA Cup run in 1947–48. We went hell for leather from round three when we beat Leeds United 4–0 at home, followed that with a victory over Chester by the same scoreline and in round five breezed through 5–0 against that season's giant-killers Colchester United – thirteen goals in three FA Cup matches and none conceded. It was some going.

Colchester was regarded as the hardest Cup tie of those three, despite being a non-league side. They had beaten First Division Huddersfield Town, in round three. They then saw off Bradford Park Avenue who themselves had caused a big shock in the previous round by winning at Arsenal. Colchester's manager was the former West Ham United centre-half Ted Fenton. He told the press that he had studied both Huddersfield and Bradford, spotted their shortcomings and staged practice games behind closed doors with Colchester reserve players playing in the style of their opponents. The press dubbed Ted 'The Man With

The Plan' and Ted played up to them by saying he had 'The plan with which to defeat Blackpool'. All credit to Ted, who had been a fine centre-half in his day. He put Colchester on the football map and in the week preceding our fifth-round tie they were never out of the headlines.

Ted said he was bringing his players to Blackpool a couple of days before the match to acclimatise them and, as coincidence would have it, their secretary booked them into my hotel. The national press besieged the place. Ted was great copy, telling them 'Plan F' (for Fenton) would put paid to our Cup hopes. Whether he had a plan or not I have no idea, but on the day we coasted it. To be fair, Colchester kept battling to the end and did play some neat football, but plan or not, they were no match for the three Ms – Stan Mortensen, Jimmy McIntosh (two goals apiece) and Alec Munro, who got our opener. After the game, Joe Smith who had said very little in the build-up told a reporter from the *Daily Despatch*, 'Ted Fenton may well have had a team with a plan, but I had the team with Stan.'

In round six we travelled to Fulham and before a full house of 32,000 at Craven Cottage came away with a 2–0 win thanks to goals from Morty and Jimmy McIntosh.

Morty was on fire in the semi-final at Villa Park. In front of 67,500 he notched a hat-trick as we beat Tottenham 3–1. By now Morty and I had developed our understanding and he was a joy to provide crosses for. I barely had the need to look up to see where he was, whenever I got to the byline and cut the ball back he was there on the end of it and his finishing was clinical.

The final pitched us against Manchester United. It was my first appearance in a Wembley Cup final and so I was anxious to come away with a winners medal. I couldn't believe how quickly my fortunes had changed. Twelve months ago I was not considered good enough to make the

Stoke team and some sports journalists had written that I was not the player I had been and was surplus to England requirements. Yet here I was, riding high with one of the top teams in the First Division, at a Wembley Cup final and having enjoyed a super season with England. I felt great and I just knew I had many years left in me in football. The commonly held belief at the time was that once a player had passed 30 he was past his best, but my performances that season were my best to date and at 33 I felt there was even better to come. Of course, I couldn't tell anyone this. One thing I had learned was that the saying 'pride comes before a fall' was more pertinent in football than in just about any other walk of life.

I knew I was getting better as a player, my confidence was sky high and the experience I had gained from 15 years of football meant I had an old head on what were effectively still young legs. At times, I did stop to think why my performances in football were still on the upward curve. I knew this was partly down to all the training and countless hours of ball practice I had done since boyhood, but I also felt I had been blessed in some way to carry on. 'Why me?' I asked myself but I had no idea. Why did Scott Fitzgerald have a great gift for writing? Why wasn't it Bill Bloggs from Bradford? I'd come from a sporting family and although we all enjoyed football, neither my father nor my brothers had made a living out of the game even semi-professionally. It was a mystery to me why I had seemingly been given a gift of being able to excite and entertain people with a football at my feet and, if the press were to be believed, do things other players could not do.

Shortly before the 1948 FA Cup final against Manchester United, I gained an inkling of what the sporting press thought of my role in football when they voted me their very first Footballer of the Year. The award is now well established. The members of the Football Writers' Association vote for the player they think has been the best that season. To be the first winner was marvellous and I can remember being in Troon on the Friday night before England's game against Scotland at Hampden Park in April when I received the news. It was a great honour but I saw it as an award not so much for myself but for all the Blackpool team. When all is said and done, what could I have accomplished without them? How well I played was dependent on the service I received and without doubt my Blackpool team-mates played to my strengths. It was our game plan if you like, to get me involved as much as possible and I could not have grabbed the headlines without the selfless efforts of the players around me.

Today, the Footballer of the Year Award dinner takes place in May on a night that does not precede a football match of any note. In 1948, the dinner was held at the Hungaria restaurant in London on the eve of the FA Cup final! As one who has always taken to bed early, especially on the night before a game, I did wonder about the wisdom of staying out late prior to my first FA Cup final appearance at Wembley, but to be voted Footballer of the Year was such an honour I simply couldn't send my apologies.

It was a double celebration night because Stan Mortensen was runner-up but while everyone else made merry, Morty and I drank fruit juice and though delighted to be given such recognition for our efforts, spent the night with one eye on the clock.

I have the original bronze statue in my den at home. To this day I am proud to think I was the first player ever to win the award. In fact I was destined to have the great honour of winning it twice!

The average attendance at Bloomfield Road that season was over 25,000. Prior to the FA Cup final, however, I got the feeling there were 100,000 people in Blackpool who never missed a game. Everyone I met was a regular supporter who said they had attended every home match but had been unable to get a Cup final ticket. On average, I received around a hundred letters a day from football fans from all around the country, but in the week preceding the final my daily post was delivered in a mail sack. I'd open the letters and the money and cheques tumbled out, everyone asking if I could get them a ticket. I simply couldn't cope with the volume of mail and sadly many letters had to go unanswered, though everyone who had sent a cheque or money had it returned. I think I'm right in saying each player received a dozen tickets. Once family and close friends had been sorted out it meant many of the players were scrambling around themselves for the odd ticket for pals. One letter made me guffaw with laughter. Unfortunately I never kept it but it read along the following lines:

Dear Mr Matthews,

I am writing to you in the desperate hope you will be able to get me a ticket for the Cup final against Manchester United.

The ticket is not for me, but for a good friend who has done me many favours. I would not ask but this friend is an avid Blackpool supporter who has been unable to get a ticket himself and as he has helped me out on so many occasions I feel obliged to help him now but tickets are as rare as hen's teeth.

I am Blackpool through and through myself and a great fan of yours, perhaps your greatest fan. It would be wonderful if you could see your way to supplying me with a ticket for which I am only too happy to pay. Time and again I have run my legs off to get into the penalty box for one of your crosses. Even when the cross has been lousy, I've done my best to try and convert it. Do your best for me.

Yours faithfully,
Stanley Mortensen

I'd been going on about the great volume of letters I had been receiving after training one day, saying I reckoned I'd received the lion's share. Morty had taken it upon himself to write that impish letter. It was typical of his humour, but the spoof note did the trick – I never complained about the amount of letters I received again.

On the morning of the Cup final, even though I'd had what for me was a late night, I was up at the crack of dawn. We were staying at a hotel in Ascot and Cup final day or not, I put myself through my usual early morning training session of sprints and shuttle runs. Then I went for a walk around the country lanes before joining my team-mates for breakfast. The mood among the players was one of quiet confidence. Manchester United had reached the final by beating First Division opposition in every round, the first time it had ever happened. Their pedigree as finalists was not in doubt. I was up against John Aston, a classy left-back for whom I had the greatest of respect but I had done well against him in previous encounters. When we left our hotel for the coach journey to Wembley, I felt very good about our chances.

I'd played at Wembley many times for England but the atmosphere for a Cup final is totally different. To begin with, there are two separate sets of supporters; for international matches the majority are behind England. Two sets of fans in verbal opposition produces conflict and, as any writer knows, conflict is an essential ingredient of drama. That's what sets an FA Cup final apart from an international as far as I am concerned. The FA Cup final has more colour and drama than an international, even before a ball is kicked. You are also reminded of the fine tradition of the tournament. The anachronistic wording on the ticket – 'Final Tie' – which as far as I know it still says, is almost a hark back to the days of the Royal Engineers and The Wanderers.

Many a good player has reached a Wembley Cup final only to turn in a mediocre performance on his day of days because the heavy atmosphere is too much for him. Playing in a Wembley Cup final has the same effect that a school photograph has. If you appear in a school photograph as a weedy schoolboy wearing National Health specs and sporting a gormless expression, no matter if you go on to develop a body like Arnold Schwarzenegger and the brain of Stephen Fry, how you appeared in that school photograph is how you will be remembered by all those present at the time. Likewise, a player could have an outstanding season with his club, his efforts on the field may have been instrumental in getting his team to Wembley, but if he fluffs it on the day before the eyes of the nation, he'll be remembered for that and only that for the rest of his days. Ask former Brighton player Gordon Smith who fired into the body of Manchester United's goalkeeper Gary Bailey in the last minute of the 1983 Cup final and thus missed his chance to win the Cup for the south coast underdogs; or Tommy Hutchison who scored for both sides when Manchester City drew 1–1 with Spurs in 1981. A Wembley FA Cup final is the school photograph of a footballer's career.

Conversely, those 90 minutes can make lasting heroes of players whose names were almost unknown before the big day – Norman Deeley for Wolves in 1960, Sunderland's Ian Porterfield in 1973, Bobby Stokes for Southampton in 1976, Ipswich's Roger Osborne in 1978, Lawrie Sanchez of Wimbledon in 1988 to name but five. Ask yourself if you remember them for anything they did in football after the Cup final? My guess is you'd be struggling, yet when thinking of past Cup finals their names come readily to mind.

Joe Smith had played for Bolton Wanderers in the famous White Horse final in 1923, the first FA Cup final to be played at Wembley. They beat West Ham and though the official attendance was 126,047, closer to a quarter of a million gained entry. Joe knew what it took to win the Cup. He had felt the nerves himself and in his pre-match talk he made one or two funny quips to try to allay the anxieties of a few of the Blackpool team. He didn't go into detail, but then he never did. He simply asked us to go out and play our normal game.

'Play football and do your best, lads. I shall not ask for anything more,' he said. 'We're going to win, but no matter the outcome, always remember I'm proud of you all. Go out and enjoy yourselves and do your best to get two goals up at half-time so I can enjoy my cigar. Being the FA Cup final, I've treated myself to a reet good 'un. Be a pity to waste it.'

We followed him out of the dressing room and lined up in the tunnel alongside Manchester United who were led by Matt Busby. As there was deemed to be a colour clash, both teams wore their second strips. Blackpool were in white shirts and black shorts. Manchester United in blue shirts and white shorts. A steward gave both managers the nod and we started to walk. As soon as Joe and Matt emerged into the sunlight, a stentorian roar assailed our ears and swept up that tunnel like a tidal wave. As we walked on to the pitch it was as if we were gladiators entering an arena to do battle before 100,000 trumpet-tongued spectators. Even with England I had never experienced such a vociferous welcome. The teams were presented to King George VI by the captains, Harry Johnston and John Carey.

The one enforced change for Blackpool was Johnny Crosland at left-back for Ron Suart who was injured. Jimmy

McIntosh, who had done so well in the previous rounds, was omitted in a tactical change that involved Stan Mortensen moving to centre-forward and Alex Munro to inside-right with Walter Rickett filling his place on the left wing. Joe's idea was that Morty's pace would be the undoing of United's centre-half Allenby Chilton, which on a couple of occasions it was.

As the referee checked his watch and we lined up for the kick-off, I remember thinking the team that gets over the initial nerves first will take the upper hand and dictate the game. I felt there would be plenty of goals. We had scored 18 on our way to Wembley and so had United.

When two teams hell-bent on attacking meet head-on and every player plays to his form and some above it, you're in for a great game of football and this was how this final turned out. We had the better of the early exchanges and on 12 minutes got our noses in front. There didn't seem to be anything on when the United centre-half Allenby Chilton received the ball just inside the United half, but he slipped in turning and Morty struck like a viper. The higher the standard of football the fewer mistakes are made but the more those mistakes are punished. Chilton's slip showed Morty the ball for just a couple of seconds but that was enough for Stan. He was on to it in a flash and raced away towards the United goal with John Carey and Chilton hot on his heels.

I was tracking Morty from out on the wing, but I knew I was just an option for him and one he wouldn't take. With Morty in full flight and bearing down on goal, he would have one thing on his mind and that would be to go for the jugular. Morty had terrific pace and to Allenby Chilton's credit he managed to make up ground but not quite enough. Just as Morty reached the edge of the penalty area with Jack Crompton in the United goal coming out to narrow the angle, Chilton obviously thought it was do-or-die and made the tackle, but he took Morty out and not the ball. It was a difficult call for referee Mr Barrick. Ignoring United protests that contact had been made just outside the box, he pointed to the penalty spot. I had a good view from out wide and thought the referee was right in his decision. Eddie Shimwell stepped up to take the penalty. If he had any nerves they didn't show and he tucked the ball away to give us the lead.

We piled on the pressure after that but United defended well and repelled everything that came their way in the penalty box. With such pressure I was sure a second goal would be only a matter of time, but then out of the blue United broke away and our defence was caught napping. On 28 minutes there was a terrible mix-up in our defence. We failed to clear our lines and Jack Rowley practically walked the ball into the net.

Back we came at United and just before half-time we took the lead again. I was fouled out on the right and elected to take the free kick myself. As I prepared to take it, I saw Hughie Kelly drifting into the penalty area and pointing to his head. I floated the free kick in his direction, he headed on to Morty who turned and cracked the ball into the back of the net. It was Morty's tenth goal in six FA Cup matches that season and he had scored in every round, which was no mean achievement.

During the half-time interval, Joe Smith didn't say much. He just told us to keep it going. In the United dressing room Matt Busby on the other hand was busy plotting our downfall. Although Johnny Aston had played me well enough, I felt I had the beating of him but in the second half it all changed. Busby had obviously told Cockburn and Pearson to get tighter and close down Harry Johnston and Hughie Kelly because the service I received dried up. The United outside-left Charlie Mitten dropped deeper and started to tackle me whenever I got the ball. On the occasions when I did receive the ball, having two very good players such as Aston and Mitten to contend with made life difficult. However, with 20 minutes remaining and our 2–1 lead still intact I thought we would do it, but a lack of discipline in defence caught us napping for a second time.

Hughie Kelly and United's Johnny Morris got into a tangle on the edge of our penalty box. For a moment no one was sure which way the referee would give the decision. Instead of one of our defenders standing over the ball to prevent United taking a quick free kick, if that's what it was to be, our defence backed off. The referee gave the decision to United, Johnny Morris took the free kick straightaway and found the head of Jack Rowley who equalised.

That goal rocked us and filled United with confidence. We hadn't played as well in the second half as we had done in the first, but up to United's equaliser we had looked comfortable. No more. United pulled us all over the place but 12 minutes from time we had a great chance to win it. Morty had pulled wide to join me out on the right-wing and the United centre-half Allenby Chilton followed him. The ball was played out to Morty and although Chilton seemed to have it covered he misjudged the bounce. Morty needed no second asking. With me tearing down the wing and Johnny Aston in two minds about whether to stay with me or go with Morty, Morty made a beeline for the United goal. He was at an acute angle when he shot but I'd seen Morty score from tighter positions. This time he fired straight into the arms of Jack Crompton. Morty ground to a halt, his head dropped for an instant and I saw him wince. Countless centre-forwards would have failed to tuck such a chance away but by his own high standards he knew he should have done better.

Our defence had pushed up in support and no sooner had

Crompton got the ball in his hands then he let fly with a long clearance that was helped on by Anderson to Stan Pearson. Pearson veered to the right then cut inside. Our defenders, who had raced back to cover, were at sixes and sevens and could only watch as Pearson fired low past Robbo from 25 yards. The ball cracked against the post and ricocheted into the back of the net. I couldn't believe it. Seconds before with the score at 2–2, Morty had been on the point of winning the Cup for us. Now for the first time in the match and with the clock against us we were chasing the game.

Three minutes later disaster struck. United's Anderson was some 30 yards from goal when he attempted a speculative shot. Robbo in our goal seemed to have it covered, but Hughie Kelly who had moved in on Anderson to close him down couldn't get out of the way of the flight of the ball. It struck Hughie on the head and fate took it on a course far from Robbo's reach and into our net to make it 4–2 and give United the Cup.

It had been a classic Cup final – the *Sunday Chronicle* went so far as to describe it as a 'quintessential final, one that showed the art of football in its most favourable light'. When any form of art touches the quintessential level, it does so with more than a hint of pain and, having held the lead for so long only to capitulate in the late stages of the game, my Blackpool team-mates were devastated on the day. The first two post-match hours were as difficult to sit through as a performance of Kafka's *The Trial* in Latin. I was disappointed, but not gutted. Of course, I would have been delighted if we had won but I've never gone either way as far as post-match emotions are concerned. Irrespective of the result, my heart and mind always embraced the middle ground. Having reached an FA Cup final at the age of 33 and ended up on the losing side, I knew the chances of getting my hands on the medal I so dearly wanted to win were getting shorter, but even at this stage of my career I never thought it could not happen. I was in a good team and I knew I could go on playing for years to come, so I comforted myself with the thought that we would be back.

In addition, I was always of the mind that it was far better to reach the FA Cup final and lose than be knocked out in the third round. We'd had a great run, I had enjoyed it immensely and I wouldn't have had those enjoyable moments if we had gone out in the early stages of the competition. I viewed our Cup final defeat as I did all things in football, with realism and unemotional acceptance that that was what fate had in store. It wasn't Harry Johnston's or Hughie Kelly's way, but it was mine. Harry used to say I was so cool in my response to everything, he thought I had ice in my veins. I'd tell him that when surrounded by defenders in a tight corner in a big game, you needed to be that way. Hotheads are no good in such circumstances; you have to be cool and calculating. That's how I was when confronted by opponents and it was such a part of me as a person, it was how I was in victory or defeat. Many people misconstrued it. They felt that because I didn't readily display emotion, it was a sign I didn't care or that I failed to empathise with my team-mates. It's simply not true, deep down I felt the agony and ecstasy, the joy and despair, it just wasn't in me to show it. Some players are like that.

I have recognised a similar trait in others. For example, the former Watford and Liverpool winger John Barnes and the former Bolton and Everton midfielder Peter Reid hardly ever showed emotion on the pitch. Win, lose or draw they appeared stoical and inscrutable but that is not to say that inside a rollercoaster of emotion was not coursing through their veins. Two players from the old school who also had an element of unemotional bias were Bobby Charlton and

George Best. West Ham's Rio Ferdinand and Sunderland's Darren Williams appear to belong to this category, too.

I once heard a pessimist described as being 'nothing more than an optimist in full retention of the facts'. You can't be a footballer and a pessimist. You have to be optimistic every time you take to the pitch but it's as well to remember that whatever happens in football is fleeting. You can scale great heights one minute and experience the downside the next, even in the next game. By not allowing yourself to ride the emotional pendulum, you temper disappointment, disillusionment, even depression and thus keep yourself on an even keel. It's an inner defence mechanism and the more you control your emotions the more it becomes second nature. Of course, you have to have a strong element of cool in your personality in the first place to keep on a level plane of emotion even when all those around you may be sky high. I believe I did and looking back it helped me to deal with not only tension and the highs and lows of football but also with such fame that came my way.

On the day, I thought that Manchester United were deserving and worthy winners of the FA Cup and I joined my team-mates in going to their dressing room after the game and offering the players congratulations.

Without doubt, Matt Busby's half-time talk and the tactics he employed thereafter played a major part in United's success. Matt was a deep thinker where football was concerned, a good tactician and in 1948 that was somewhat innovative. Joe Smith's simple instructions for us to enjoy ourselves and play our normal game were an indication as to how many managers of that time approached games, even Cup finals. In the same way as Matt Busby did, he might have looked to counter their strengths.

In Delaney and Mitten I knew United had two wingers

that could and did cause us serious problems, yet no provision was made to deal with them. Jack Rowley was allowed far too much space in the first half, but nothing was said about it at half time and in the second half he capitalised on his freedom of movement. This being my first season I didn't think it my place to sit in the dressing room and call the shots and usurp the authority of a manager who had revitalised my career.

It had been a great first season with Blackpool but I wasn't the only one to have enjoyed the football. Attendances continued to soar with an English record crowd for a league game of 83,260 witnessing a 1–1 draw between Manchester United and Arsenal that was played at Maine Road because United's ground at Old Trafford was still under reconstruction after suffering bomb damage during the war. The fact that Manchester United never truly had home advantage in any of their games made their FA Cup win all the more remarkable. Their 'home' tie against Liverpool in round four was played on Merseyside at Goodison Park!

Arsenal once again proved to be the benchmark for all other clubs in England. They led the First Division from the start and remained there to the finish to win their sixth title in 11 seasons. Over two million people watched them play that season, which over 42 matches averages out at 54,982 a game.

Tommy Lawton caused a sensation when after only one season at Chelsea he was transferred to Notts County, a mid-table Third Division South side. County paid £20,000 for Tommy which was an astronomical amount of money at the time and beat the previous transfer record by £5,000. The deal involved County wing-half Bill Dickson joining Chelsea. Tommy was only 28 and an England regular. For him to step down two divisions was sensational news and there were all manner of stories to explain why he'd done it.

The most common was that he hadn't settled in London and that he'd had an argument with Chelsea over his contract. Tommy was a good friend of mine and he told me the move was to do with money. In addition to receiving a percentage of what was then a huge fee, a Notts County director had agreed to put Tommy on the payroll of a company he owned. The idea was that Tommy would be paid for doing promotional work on behalf of the company as well as a modicum of office work. Whether or not Tommy did any promotional work I don't know, but I do know he never went into the company's office to work! The job at the director's company was all hokum but it did mean Tommy doubled his weekly wage. Football's maximum wage was £14 and believe you me, £28 a week in 1948 was very good money indeed. So dark deeds went on in football as far as money was concerned even in those days. Tommy paid a price for stepping down to the Third Division, however. He played against Scotland at Hampden in April 1948, the first ever player from the Third Division to be capped by England, but played just two more international matches before losing his place to Newcastle's Jackie Milburn, and he never regained it.

One small but amusing incident occurred in 1948 but I was not made aware of it until I received a letter in 1999, 51 years later!

The letter came from Dr Mercia MacDermott from West Sussex who wrote that in 1948, when a student at Oxford University, she joined a Youth Brigade organised by the National Union of Students to help in the post-war reconstruction of Bulgaria. Every evening there would be an outdoor assembly at which the camp commandant would greet each international brigade and the members of the brigade would chant the name of the leader they admired most such as Stalin, Tito, Dimirov or Enver

Hoxha. The British Brigade comprised students from all political persuasions and they couldn't agree on a name acceptable to everyone. Finally, they came up with someone and for the remainder of their stay at every assembly bellowed in unison 'Stan-ley Ma-tthews, Stan-ley Ma-tthews.' I only wish I'd been there to see the reaction of the Russian, Albanian, Slavic and Bulgarian students. If they recognised my name at all, they must have wondered how I had made the quantum leap from footballer to political leader!

13

---○---

England's Greatest Ever
Forward Line

D uring the 1947–48 season, I re-established myself
in the England team. In September, I played for
England in a thrilling 5–2 victory over Belgium in
Brussels. The game was to mark the 50th anniversary of the
Belgian FA. I was credited with making every England goal
but it was down to marvellous teamwork on the day.

Over 70,000 watched the game and, as usual, I revelled in
the big-match atmosphere. Tommy Lawton and Tom Finney
scored two goals each and Morty chipped in with one to give
us a memorable victory. The newspapers were generous
about my performance, too generous I would say. They all
agreed it was my best performance to date in an England
shirt. I'd done the job I'd been selected to do and the
headlines, though welcome, were over the top. I didn't think
enough credit was given to Tom Finney or Tommy Lawton
for their decisive finishing, or Tim Ward of Derby County
or Morty, who provided me with great service throughout

the game. Joe Pannaye was left-back for Belgium and he has since told me he dined out for 42 years on his experience of playing against me that day, which was a very nice thing to say though it pains me to think I have been in some way responsible for the increasing girth of someone who was once a lithe and fleet-footed sportsman! After the match he was kind enough to say that marking me was like trying to mark a ghost, which shows how sporting players were even in defeat in those days.

I had been hoping Harry Johnston would get the nod for the eagerly anticipated Scotland game at Hampden in April. Morty and I had built up a good understanding at Blackpool and it would have meant our triangle play could continue at international level. He was in the squad but on the big day Billy Wright of Wolves was chosen at right-half, though the game did afford me the opportunity of teaming up once again with my old Stoke City skipper Neil Franklin who had been chosen at centre-half.

In the week leading up to the game, the national press gave every little story that emanated from within the England camp glaring publicity. I had a slight bruise on the ankle. It was nothing but to read about it in the press you'd think it was career-threatening. Tommy Lawton grazed his knee in training. It was so innocuous, all Tommy did was put some TCP on it but the newspapers ran with the story that Tommy 'was a doubt' and that he had been 'receiving treatment for a knee injury'. Treatment? A splash of TCP!

The players greeted such reports with good humour but in many ways this sort of reporting was an indication of things to come. On the rare occasions when an England team were given good time in which to prepare for an international, as we were this time against Scotland, reporters were assigned to the camp and they had to send copy back to their editors every day. Often there was nothing newsworthy to write about but because they had to produce a daily story they went over the top about minor things.

It's a scenario that is even more pronounced today. In my day, only one reporter per newspaper accompanied the England party and he would be the person assigned to cover the game itself. Nowadays, some newspapers send up to three reporters. As far as I can see, one is to report on the game, one to come up with daily news from the training camp and one to dig around for stories of any indiscretions. From a player's point of view, it would be far better if one reporter was flown out the day before the game to report on the match and nothing else. However, with top footballers taking on showbiz celebrity status, their newsworthiness has developed far beyond the sports pages. I feel sorry for them living under such scrutiny, but if they are happy to accept the money that goes with selling the exclusive rights to their wedding pictures or the interior of their new mansion home to magazines such as *Hello!* or *OK*, what do they expect? You can't take money for revealing aspects of your private life in certain magazines and newspapers then appeal for privacy when other reporters want a slice of the action. It's the cake-and-eat-it syndrome and it appears many top players today enjoy the overblown film-star status but not the public attention that goes hand-in-hand with such a debatable standing.

Fame in football comes quickly these days and that is part of the problem. Before the TV saturation coverage of football, a player had to perform week in, week out for a couple of seasons at least before he was held up as a star. Now a couple of telling crosses in a game or some back-to-back goalscoring and a player is hailed as a superstar. TV commentary today involves two people and there are three to four pundits in the studio – five people simply can't say the same thing. They can't all say 'So and so played all right'.

They have to come up with something different to justify being there so they heap praise and insipid superlatives on modest achievement, and because it is done before millions, the worth of what a player has done or what he has achieved is blown out of all proportion.

Tommy Lawton was banging goals in for England and Everton at 19 but only those present at matches saw him, so his fame took time in the making. Michael Owen scores one goal, albeit a wonderful goal, against Argentina in France 98 and he's a star the next day. Good luck to him, he's a fine player. Players are only great in their own time, but is Owen consistently better than Raich Carter, Peter Doherty, Wilf Mannion or even Freddie Steele were in their day? I don't think so. Who except the Stoke faithful remembers Freddie Steele today? Yet there was a player who scored a grand total of 240 goals (including wartime matches) for Stoke in the top flight and seven in six international games for England. When he eventually finished with football, Freddie went to work in a local factory. Today a player finishing with a worse record than that need never work again.

Sometimes the suddenness with which today's players are catapulted into the star bracket can be their undoing. They tend to believe what the TV pundits and tabloids say about them and often, because fame has come off the back of a few games, they have not had to work at achieving such status over seasons. The easiness with which success comes these days can make a number forget how tenuous life is for the vast majority of players. I'm convinced a number of top players think only about what football can give and not about what it can take away. That is why we have some players today acting without dignity, grace or respect for their fellow professionals and the supporters who pay their wages.

Of course, not all top players enjoy status far beyond their worth and capabilities. There are some super players about. However, it's a situation best summed up by borrowing from Cecil Beaton: 'Never has so little material been raised so high to reveal so much that needs to be covered so badly.'

Hampden Park on 10 April 1948 was its usual intimidating self – 135,000 Scots crammed in to create an atmosphere so minatory for the opposition that it caused palpitations. As the teams lined up, the blue-shirted Scotland players stared back at us with expressionless but determined faces. It was England's biennial visit to the home of our most formidable adversary and we also had the hostile atmosphere to contend with before completing our mission.

When Field Marshal Montgomery of Alamein stepped on to the pitch, 135,000 voices sounded like a million. The roar was deafening and continued for the best part of the presentation of the teams. Montgomery made a point of chatting to Tom Finney and Scotland's Willie Thornton, both of whom had served under the Field Marshal in the Eighth Army in North Africa.

For the first 20 minutes, the Scots rampaged but Frank Swift was in fine form in goal. Neil Franklin judiciously took up a position in front of him and resolutely stuck to his task, his unselfish battling in the name of his country an inspiration to us all. Such were the heroics of Swifty and Neil during those early exchanges, I felt proud just to be in the same team as the two of them. The marauding Scots threw everything at the England goal but, admirably led by Swift and Franklin, our defence held firm.

Once the initial impetus from the Scots waned somewhat, we began to make our own mark on the proceedings. Many people if asked what wins games would understandably say goals, but to my mind it's passing. Our passing was excellent, a lot of it one-touch stuff that meant we kept possession and took control of the game away from the Scots. After 35 minutes, a neat build-up involving six England players led to Tom Finney receiving the ball just outside the Scottish penalty area from where he advanced to the 18-yard line before hitting a rising drive past Black in the Scotland goal. Once again I had the rare but highly enjoyable experience of being down on the pitch before 135,000 silent Scots.

In the second half, Billy Wright continued where he had left off in the first, keeping me supplied with plenty of the ball. I made the most of the service, dribbling down the right and at every opportunity looking for Morty and Tommy Lawton in the Scottish penalty area. On 65 minutes we scored what proved to be the decisive goal. I cut the ball back from the deadball line and there was Morty as ever, poised and ready. The ball ripped into the net and there was no way back for the Scots.

The England team that day showed themselves to be as sound in temperament as in technique and although Scotland came back at us I never felt we were in danger of losing the game, although the latter stages were not without their anxieties. George Hardwick picked up an injury and played out the game limping at outside-left with Harry Cockburn filling in at left-back and Tom Finney dropping deep just in front of him. Frank Swift was bundled into the net by Billy Liddell and though suffering from a rib injury had no choice but to carry on because the one man who could have taken over in goal from Swifty was George Hardwick.

Swift's injury was bad enough to warrant an overnight stay in hospital. He and Morty were always the life and soul of the post-match banquet and his jocular presence was sorely missed. The proceedings were not totally without humour, however. The Scottish team were sporting in their congratulations to us but defeat against England was still hard to swallow for one or two of the Scottish lads. Just before the banquet Billy Wright, Morty and I were chatting to Billy Liddell and Billy Steel when the Rangers centre-half George Young appeared and was annoyed to find the two Billys chatting to us. George said as much and gave us to understand that he couldn't bring himself to go to the post-match banquet.

'For goodness sake, George, man, I play in England. I know these lads well,' Billy Liddell said. 'So we lost today, but it was only a game of football. We lost to England at Bannockburn and Culloden and they were battles.'

'Aye, that's true,' said big George, 'but after Bannockburn and Culloden we weren't asked to put our suits on and make small talk with them over bloody sandwiches!'

It was following this game that I was called before the Football Association to answer questions about the expenses I had incurred in travelling to the game. I wasn't the only England player under suspicion. Tommy Lawton and Tom Finney were hauled over the coals as well.

Looking back, the whole affair was preposterous but it was indicative of how the FA ran its affairs in those days, and of how it treated players, even those of international status. I was summoned to appear before the FA because I'd claimed expenses for a cup of tea and a scone. I had caught the train up to Scotland to join the England party, a journey which necessitated changing at Carlisle. I had a bit of a wait for my connecting train so I popped into the station buffet. I think I'm right in saying that in 1948 England players received a £14 match fee plus second-class rail fare and 'reasonable expenses', which I considered my tea and scone to be. It came to sixpence.

At FA headquarters I was confronted by two poker-faced officials. The treasurer, Mr Ewbank, was wearing a wing-collared shirt, a complete anachronism even for 1948, and an official unknown to me sat with such a sour expression on his face he looked as if he had been weaned on a lemon. Both eyed me contemptuously as I went in and took a seat when ordered to do so. Mr Ewbank was a man with the mind of an accounting ledger and a face with lines as fine as old parchment. He treated footballers as minions. Once I had taken a seat he bowed his head over what I could see was my expenses chitty for the Scotland game. He never looked in my direction, he just stared down at the expenses sheet.

'Matthews, you've been summoned to appear before me to explain the expenses you submitted for the Hampden game. In addition to your rail fare, you're claiming an extra sixpence.' His tone was that of an old headmaster about to admonish an impudent pupil. 'Perhaps you would care to offer an explanation for this sundry item of expense?'

I told him the sixpence was for the cup of tea and scone I had bought at Carlisle station en route to join the England squad. For a moment there was silence.

'The emoluments which accrue when a player has the honour of being chosen to represent England are not inconsiderable. Fourteen pounds I consider a substantial sum for 90 minutes' work and recompense enough to cover any personal expenses you see fit to incur.'

Emoluments which accrue? I felt as if I was playing out a forgotten scene from *David Copperfield*!

'Listen, Matthews,' Ewbank continued. 'If as an England player you feel a need for refreshment on your way to a game, that's your business, but it is not the business of the Football Association to pay for such.' With that he took a large blue pencil, drew a bold line through 'Sundry expenses, sixpence' and without looking up from the offending item or saying another word raised his right arm and wafted his hand towards the door to indicate the matter was over and I was dismissed. As I stood up I said, 'Thank you, gentleman,' and, 'Goodbye.' Ewbank still didn't look up. He merely nodded his head once by way of acknowledgement. The look of disdain on the face of his sidekick was such you'd have though I'd tried to fiddle them out of a million pounds and fifty caps.

I left the room wondering how on earth someone like Ewbank had reached such a position in the FA. Part of his job was the welfare of England players and to ensure they were happy in their off-the-pitch activities, yet he was the sort of person who if he went riding with the four horsemen of the apocalypse, wouldn't noticeably lighten the mood of the party.

What Tom Finney was up for I can't recall, but I have the feeling it was something similar and he didn't get any joy out of Ewbank either. As for Tommy Lawton, he hammered a few more nails into his international coffin. Tommy had added a few extra bob on the return train fare between Nottingham and Scotland, thinking Ewbank wouldn't check up on it. When Tommy presented himself, Ewbank produced the tables of train fares between Nottingham and Glasgow and pointed out there was no such fare as the one Tommy had claimed for and reprimanded him for overcharging.

That's how the FA treated the players who represented England. You just can't imagine any of today's players being reprimanded for such trivialities or being referred to at all times by surname only. The Gentlemen and Players situation still existed in cricket but the class divide was even more pronounced between the players and those who ran the game of football. Players were treated as second-class citizens. Football was a skill of the working class, but those who ran our game were anything but. Even those officials who had working-class roots were at pains to ignore or cover them up once they became part of the blazer brigade. Perhaps their backgrounds were a hindrance in getting on in a football establishment run by Old Etonians and former Oxbridge students.

It was still the case in later years. How else do you explain Alf Ramsey taking elocution lessons? Alf ended up as the England manager and we won the World Cup, so presumably as far as he and England were concerned it was money well spent.

In the forties I had the impression the FA saw the players as people who were not to be trusted and were always on the make. This wasn't the case, of course, but there were one or two naughties when it came to expenses, which didn't help our case any.

In those days, England players had to make their own way to home international matches at Wembley, Glasgow or Cardiff. I remember my England colleague Stan Cullis telling me how on one occasion when making his way to Wembley he caught a tube from Euston and had to wait in a massive queue along with spectators going to the game, who of course recognised him. In one sense it was great that players had such contact with supporters. It helped foster an understanding of how players and fans felt and thought about the game and made for a common bond. Yet for Stan Cullis to have to queue up for a tube, worrying if he was going to make it on time for a big international game is hardly ideal preparation.

Denis Compton, who played football for Arsenal and cricket for Middlesex and England, was a likeable rogue. Denis was hauled before the FA after claiming expenses for an item he classified as 'miscellaneous'. The FA official in question told Denis, 'No footballer I have come across knows what miscellaneous means. You don't even know how to spell it, so you are certainly not getting expenses for anything known as miscellaneous from this Association.'

It wasn't only certain players who tried it on; one or two

managers were not beyond making a bit on the side from expenses, my boss at Blackpool Joe Smith included. For a time in the fifties, Joe claimed expenses for entertaining a man called Willie Dugdale who Joe said was a scout attached to Glasgow Rangers. He took him to lunch every other Friday so that Willie Dugdale could keep him informed of players north of the border who were playing well and might be of interest to Blackpool. One day Joe arrived at his desk to find a memo from the Blackpool secretary saying he had checked with Glasgow Rangers who informed him they had no one by the name of Willie Dugdale working for them as a scout or in any other capacity and would Joe kindly explain. Joe sent back a memo saying, 'The man is obviously an impostor. I shall cease entertaining him immediately,' As I keep saying, Joe Smith was a wily old bird.

———— o ————

England had a history of great victories over foreign opposition but against Italy in May 1948 we reached new heights. Once again the England party enjoyed the novelty of travelling by air. On the flight, I kept thinking back to earlier encounters against the *Azzuri* at Highbury and in Milan. I knew the Italians would be as difficult to beat as ever, but the big-match occasion had got to me and I was fully motivated even on the journey. We were all determined to beat Italy in style. Money didn't come into it, but it's worth mentioning that while the England team were to receive the increased international match fee of £20, the Italians were on £100 bonus per man to beat us. That speaks volumes about how keen the Italians were to put one over on England.

The pre-match build-up was not without its problems. We were due to play Czechoslovakia prior to Italy but the game was cancelled due to internal unrest following the Communist take over. The FA tried to fix up a friendly against Spain but that fell through as well because there were insurmountable problems with currency exchange, or so we were told. Italy, on the other hand, enjoyed good wins over both Czechoslovakia and France and were training hard at their mountain retreat not far from Turin.

George Hardwick was still unfit – his place at left-back was taken by Derby County's Jack Howe – but the most surprising decision was to make Frank Swift skipper, the first time a goalkeeper had ever been given the captaincy of England. I say it was a surprise, but it was a pleasant one. I didn't think the FA selectors or Walter Winterbottom would have been so bold as to make a goalkeeper the England captain. I had no worries on this count. I knew Frank would do an excellent job.

The game was played in Turin. The Communale Stadium had a capacity of 85,000 but such was the interest in the game that the Italian FA had received over 400,000 applications for tickets. Radio commentary teams from just about every European country filed applications for seats in a press box that was already overflowing with newspaper journalists.

I relished the thought of pitting my wits against what was thought to be the best defence in European football at the time. I felt very confident about our chances. In Ballarin, Eliani, Parola and Menti Italy had top-class international defenders but I felt England had the forward line to cause them real problems. As it turned out, my optimism was not misplaced. In fact, looking back, I would go so far as to say the forward line we fielded for this game was the greatest ever to represent England. We lined up as follows:

England: Frank Swift (Manchester City); Laurie Scott (Arsenal), Jack Howe (Derby County); Billy Wright (Wolves), Neil Franklin (Stoke City), Henry Cockburn

(Manchester United); Stan Matthews, Stan Mortensen (both Blackpool), Tommy Lawton (Notts County), Wilf Mannion (Middlesbrough), Tom Finney (Preston).

Italy: Bacigalupo; Ballarin, Eliani; Annovazzi, Parola, Grezar; Menti, Loik, Gabetto, Mazzola, Carapellese.

For 24 hours prior to the game it rained incessantly but an hour or so before kick-off the clouds cleared, the sun beat down and the temperature soared into the nineties. England wore short-sleeved shirts which helped us in some small way to cope with the heat. They were made of cotton but a far cry from the airbreathe lightweight shirts worn by footballers these days.

From the start, the Italians laid siege to our goal. We managed to stem the tide and after five minutes Billy Wright brought me into the game with a pass from the edge of our penalty area, which I had dropped back to collect. A little jink took me past Carapellese, I managed to side step challenges from Grezar and Eliani and made headway down the right. My usual ploy was to get down the wing and cut the ball back from the byline, but I spotted Stan Mortensen running up from deep and switched play, hitting a long, raking, left-foot ball behind the Italian central defenders for Morty to run on to.

Morty never broke step and accelerated away but the Italian defenders regrouped quickly and forced him wide. For a moment, I thought he had run himself into an impossible position. The Italian defenders had got goalside and Morty was heading for the right touchline away from goal with Eliani and Annovazzi closing in behind him. Suddenly Morty swivelled to face the goal and from a very acute angle hit a seering shot that took Bacigalupo in the Italian goal completely by surprise. It was pure reaction stuff on the part of Bacigalupo who thrust his arms upwards, but Morty's shot flew into the roof of the net, just avoiding the angle of the post and crossbar. Morty went sprawling on the emerald green turf and in an instant the packed stadium fell silent. It was just the start we needed.

The Italians came back at us immediately and it needed some great goalkeeping from Swifty and strong refereeing from the Spanish official Signor Escartin to preserve our advantage. Italy really turned the screw. They had two goals disallowed and some of their one-touch football was a delight. I remember thinking if I had been up in the stands I would have really enjoyed watching it, but chasing about after blue shirts in 90° heat meant I wasn't fully appreciative of the dazzling array of skills on display.

The Italian pressure meant that I'd be waiting out on the wing for the ball. At one point, Henry Cockburn shouted, 'Get yourself in this bloody game. We're chasing shadows here!'

Wilf Mannion turned to Henry and said, 'You can't speak to Stan like that. Why don't you win the damn ball, give it to Stan and then you'll see him in the bloody game.'

Twenty-two minutes had elapsed before Neil Franklin stole the ball off the toe of Italy's centre-forward Gabetto and sent me away down the right wing. I looked for Morty and as ever he had made himself available. I slipped the ball to him, he took it to the byline and I remember thinking, 'Never in this world is he going to try it again.' Morty swivelled but this time, instead of chancing his arm at goal, cut the ball back to Tommy Lawton who under pressure from Parola managed to fend the Italian centre-back off with an arm to fire low past Bacigalupo's outstretched right hand. To be honest, the goal was against the run of play. Up to that point, we had been in danger of being overrun by Italy but when the half-time whistle blew, despite spending most of the first half on the rack, we found ourselves two goals to the good. Chances had been few and far between, but we had taken what had come our way and I felt confident that if we applied ourselves in a similar way in the second period, a famous victory was on the cards.

As we expected, the Italians picked up the pace from the restart. The heat was getting to both teams and at one point Italy's coach Vittorio Pozzo was running up and down the touchline squirting the Italian players with a soda siphon. During a break in play, Tommy Lawton went across to the touchline and said to Pozzo, 'Is there any whisky in that?' The Italian coach gave him a puzzled look before indignantly replying, 'Of course not!' to which Tommy responded, 'In that case, I don't want any.' The heat was on in every sense of the word, but that was Tommy; in the midst of battle he still found time to joke. He was just one of several great characters in that England team.

Minutes later, an Italian attack broke down with Swifty claiming the ball off the toes of Mazzola. He threw it out to Laurie Scott and with the Italians in retreat we worked the ball upfield before Wilf Mannion fed Tommy Lawton who in turn found Tom Finney who waltzed around Bacigalupo to make it 3–0. From leaving Swift in the England goal to hitting the back of the net, not one Italian player had touched the ball. It was as fluid and flowing a move as I can ever remember in football, a flawless counterattack.

Although the Italians had responded with character and rattled our crossbar, that third goal knocked the stuffing out of them. In the latter stages of the game, I slipped a pass to Morty who made ground before finding Tom Finney who lashed in number four. For lengthy periods of the game, we had been under bombardment. Only the calm, calculated skill of Neil Franklin and the safe hands of Swifty had saved us, but we had absorbed all Italy had thrown at us and given a perfect demonstration of counterattack.

After the game, Geoffrey Green reporting for *The Times* asked Morty if our first goal had been what he had intended to do. Morty gave him an impish smile and said, 'No. Bacigalupo got a fingertip to it and I meant it to avoid his fingers by an inch or so.' Green looked at Morty in astonishment but Morty burst out laughing and said, 'Well, you have to have a bit of luck, especially on those occasions when you hit and hope.'

Italy had been considered the best side in Europe. For England it was a famous victory and the story of one incident from the game was to follow me around the world for years, turning out to be arguably football's longest-running shaggy dog story.

Towards the end of the game, with the scoreline 4–0 in our favour, I received the ball out on the right touchline and took it towards the corner flag to kill the game and frustrate the Italians. I turned to face Italy's left-back Eliani, who was giving me a little too much space from his point of view. The heat was unbearable and the perspiration was streaming down my face, so I wiped my hand on the side of my shorts before quickly wiping away the perspiration that had gathered on the hair above my brow. It was all done in a flash. I quickly brushed my hair back with the fingertips of my right hand when I was suddenly aware of a gasp from the terraces. Believing the crowd had seen something happen off the ball, I thought nothing of it and the incident disappeared from my mind for years only to resurface some 20 years later when I was living in Malta.

I was with my second wife, Mila. It was in the late sixties and we were living in Valletta. One morning Mila said she was going to the hairdresser's and asked me to pick up some meat from a local butcher's. The butcher employed an assistant who was a football fanatic. As I entered the shop, the assistant recognised me straightaway and immediately engaged me in conversation about football. During our chat, the assistant said he had been in Turin in 1948 supporting England and the highlight of the game for him was when I took the Italian left-back to the corner flag and with the ball at my feet, produced a comb with which I proceeded to comb my hair before dribbling past my opponent.

'I have never seen such an amazing thing before or since on a football field. It was fantastic.'

I didn't have a clue what he was talking about. It was only later when thinking of the game itself that I remembered wiping the sweat from my hairline and the gasp of the crowd. It clicked that they must have thought I'd had the audacity to produce a comb and do a bit of grooming out there on the pitch against, of all teams, Italy.

Even then I thought nothing of the incident but a few weeks' later the story cropped up again. A Maltese pal of mine came to see me to say one of the ministers in the government had heard I was on the island and would like to meet me. I readily agreed to go along and meet the minister in question and during the course of our conversation he told me he had been in Turin in 1948 and I had given him his most abiding memory in football.

'What is that?' I asked, not having a clue.

'Which one?' the minister said rising to his feet with a look of amazement on his face. 'The one the whole of Malta talks about. Against that great Italian team, when you had the temerity to pull a comb from your pocket and comb your hair! What a thing to do with the ball at your feet and an Italian defender confronting you! It was fantastic.'

I attempted to play down the so-called incident but the minister interrupted.

'Stop being so modest, Mr Matthews. I see it all with my

own eyes. Are you trying to tell me my eyes deceive me. I know what I see and thousands of others see it too!'

I have to say I nodded meekly and, not wanting to further embroil myself in the tale, changed the topic of conversation.

Some years later, on another trip to the same butcher's shop, the owner's young son, now a teenager, was standing behind the counter with the assistant, whom I had got to know quite well over the years.

'Here he is!' exclaimed the assistant on seeing me. 'Stanley Matthews, the comb man!'

It was no good trying to deny the comb story to him and I was grateful that after the initial reference to it he busied himself with my order. Just as I was leaving, however, the owner's son, who if my memory serves me right was called Charlie, sidled up to me.

'Mr Matthews,' he said in a soft voice.

'Yes.'

'Is it true?'

'Is what true, Charlie?' I asked, knowing only too well what was to come.

'Is it true that once when playing for England against Italy, you stopped with the ball at your feet, pulled a comb from the pocket of your shorts and combed your hair?'

I was on the point of denying it but when I looked at the lad, his face was full of wide-eyed expectancy. I glanced over to the assistant who was smiling and nodding his head, urging me to confirm the story.

'Yes, son,' I said. 'But it was a long time ago.'

I was intending to say it was a long time ago and people's memories can play tricks but I never got the words out.

'There! What did I tell you?' the butcher's assistant blurted out and clapped his shovel-like hands together in great satisfaction. 'I was there,' he continued, suitably proud and relieved that my confirmation had released him from years of being a Walter Mitty character in the eyes of the boy. 'Against Italy I see Stan Matthews comb his hair. Now you hear it from the man himself, just like I tell you!'

It is one of the most amazing things in my life that this story, untrue as it was, followed me around the world. I was in Hong Kong in the sixties playing a series of exhibition matches and coaching local youngsters when I was asked to attend a reception held in my honour at the headquarters of the Hong Kong FA. At the start of his welcoming speech the president of the Hong Kong FA introduced me by saying, 'We have great pleasure in welcoming the man who played league football in England until he was fifty. The first footballer to receive the CBE from Her Majesty the Queen. The first to be knighted and the player who, during a game against Italy, was so particular about his appearance, he paused with the ball at his feet, to comb his hair.'

The reference to the comb made me cringe with embarrassment but in time I got used to this apocryphal tale that had attached itself to my football career. During one of my many trips to South Africa to coach youngsters, I was driven into one township in an open-topped Land Rover to be greeted by lines of schoolchildren, some of whom waved Union Jacks while others held aloft old combs.

When the time came to leave Malta, I found an old comb of mine, knocked out some of the teeth and made a last visit to the butcher's shop in Valletta. I thanked the owner, his son and their assistant for their friendship and service and said I had a special presentation to make to the assistant. I then produced a small wooden box containing the comb and handed it to him. I told him it was the comb I had used to comb my hair in the famous win against Italy in Turin in 1948. It was meant to be a bit of light-hearted fun and I never for one moment expected the effect it would have on the assistant. He gently opened the box, stared down at the comb and for a few seconds said nothing. Then his face welled up and tears came into his eyes. Still holding the box and comb in one hand, he threw his hands around me, hugged me and cried unashamedly.

'I cannot believe this,' he sobbed. 'I'm only a humble butcher's assistant but now I got a piece of football history. I will treasure it for ever. I will pass it on to my son and the son of my son and he to his son. How you say? A family heirloom, yes?'

I never expected him to take it so seriously, but there was no way I could then say it was all a joke. I had to go along with it. In true *News of the World* fashion, I hastily made an excuse and left.

Some years later a Maltese pal of mine told me the butcher's assistant had mounted the comb in a glass box and it had pride of place in his living room. As far as I know, it's still there. At the time, I did think about having a small brass plaque engraved with the message 'Parting is such sweet sorrow', which considering the present was a comb I thought appropriate. Looking back, I'm glad I didn't.

The comb story got the better of me in the end. So many people asked me about it, it was easier to go along with it and over the years I almost began to believe it actually happened – until a trip to South Africa in 1976.

I had been coaching young boys and girls in various townships including Soweto, and as with all such trips there were a number of civic and formal presentations to attend. On one such occasion I was asked to attend a dinner at a golf club not far from Johannesburg. Following the dinner, my South African hosts asked if I would pop in to the kitchen as the head chef, Carlo Loppi, was a member of the Italian squad the day England beat Italy in 1948. They felt it would be good for us to meet up again and had arranged for photographers to be present to capture the moment for the local newspapers.

Loppi was delighted to see me. It had been 30 years since the Italy game, he hadn't actually played in the match and I didn't recognise him. Despite that, we greeted one another like old friends and were soon bouncing conversation off one another about the old days.

'Valentino Mazzola, your captain that day,' I said. 'A great player and a gentleman.'

''Ee was fantastic. 'Ee could make ze ball almost talk. But what about Finney and Lawton. They were brill-i-ant. You and Mannion, too. Always a 'andful, even for as great a team as Italy.'

'Remember Gabetto's shot that hit the bar?' I reminded him.

'Si, 'ee hit it with such power, that crossbar is still shaking now. Remember Mortensen's goal? 'Ow he score from such a place I don't know. It seem impossible, but 'ee did it. A great goal.'

'Remember those two headers from Carapellese?'

'Si, we were on our feet in ze dugout. Each time we think, "Goal!" but Swift, he make two great saves. Stan, remember Menti and the goal he score?'

'A great goal, but he was offside,' I reminded him.

'So the referee say, but I dunno. Remember your battle with ze great Eliani?'

'How could I forget?' I said. 'He was one of the finest full-backs I ever played against. Great skill.'

'Si, I remember Eliani and you running the length of the pitch shoulder to shoulder, then you back heel the ball, turn and centre for Lawton who just 'ead over the bar.'

'Yes, I remember it well,' I said, aware that the conversation was becoming reminiscent of a scene from *Gigi*.

'Remember Eliani boxing me into the corner?' I ventured,

carried away with the excitement, 'and me pulling a comb from the pocket of my shorts and combing my hair?'

'That story is famous,' Loppi said. 'All round the world people talk of that. But it is rubbish. It never 'appen. Your memory is starting to play tricks on you, Stan.'

14

———◦———

World Cup Lessons
Unlearned

The 1948–49 season wasn't the most enjoyable. Blackpool stuttered and spluttered, eventually finishing a
disappointing but comfortable 16th in Division
One. I was troubled with niggling injuries and missed 17
matches. Morty, too, had injury problems. He missed eight
games, though often when he was fit I wasn't and vice versa,
which somewhat disrupted the fluidity and understanding
that had been built up in the forward line.

Throughout the season Joe Smith continued to replace
players in his quest to improve the team. Following two 3–1
defeats in September by Wolves and Derby County, we had
clocked up two wins in eight league games. Joe bought
goalkeeper George Farm for £2,700 from Hibernian. George
was to make the Blackpool goalkeeper's jersey his own and,
following his debut against Bolton Wanderers, went on to
make 188 consecutive league and Cup appearances before
missing a match in October 1952 when called up for

international duty by Scotland. George was Blackpool's regular keeper for 12 years before moving back over the border in 1960 to join the Queen of the South as player-manager. He served them admirably for a number of years. In total he played 509 games for Blackpool and must go down as one of Joe Smith's best-ever signings.

George was one of the greatest competitors I ever came across in football. Whether it was an FA Cup match or a five-a-side game in training, George went all-out to win and woe betide anyone who didn't have a similar attitude. After a defeat, George would storm into the dressing room, throw his cap and gloves across the room in the direction of his peg and let forth with a fusillade of expletives that would make Billy Connolly sound like a maiden aunt. In a five-a-side game during his last training session with us, his transfer to Queen of the South already signed and sealed, George got into an argument with Arthur Kaye and reserve-team player John Gregson over the direction of a throw-in. That's how competitive he was.

George was a fine goalkeeper with an unusual style of catching and holding the ball, one hand on the top and the other underneath it. Unfortunately, George probably had his worst game for Blackpool in our finest hour, the FA Cup final of 1953. He was a great character and his never-say-die attitude was a constant source of inspiration to us all. In 1955, during a game against Preston North End, he sustained a shoulder injury that prevented him from carrying on in goal. In these days before substitutes, one of our outfield players, I believe it was Dave Durie, replaced him in goal but George refused all pleas to leave the pitch for treatment. He carried on playing up front alongside Jackie Mudie and ended up scoring a goal.

Following his retirement he took up an unusual profession for an ex-footballer when he became a lighthouse keeper. So all of his working life he was a keeper of one sort or another. His second career was a constant source of mirth when we got together for reunions. Stan Mortensen in particular ribbed George mercilessly. On one such occasion when bidding farewell, George said to Morty that he should come and visit him at his lighthouse sometime. Morty quick as a flash replied, 'That would be great. It's a long time since I had a night out with the buoys!' George took such jests in good part, which was the mark of a man who, though totally committed, never took himself too seriously.

Joe Smith was never truly happy with the outside-left position in the team. During this season he started by playing Rickett on the left wing, then introduced Willie Wardle, brought back Rickett only to reintroduce Wardle who eventually gave way to Adams before Wardle was again recalled, then gave way to Andy McCall. While the defence remained largely unchanged, due to loss of form or injuries we rarely fielded the same forward line two games running. I'm sure the changes, whether enforced or otherwise, had an effect. But despite our mediocre league form, we did manage to pull off the occasional excellent result, most notably a 4–3 win at Manchester United in front of 55,000 and a fine 5–2 win at Aston Villa on New Year's Day in front of 49,000 at Villa Park. I got on the scoresheet against Villa, but it was one of just three goals I managed that season. By this stage of my career, I saw myself first and foremost as a provider of goals and not a scorer.

We exited from the FA Cup after a replay against Stoke City in round four. I had no complaints. We earned a creditable 1–1 draw in front of a capacity crowd of 47,000 at the Victoria Ground, but when Stoke came to Bloomfield Road they turned us over 1–0. It was good to see my old team-mates again. The atmosphere between us after the game was most convivial, though Bob McGrory was his usual self.

My stop-start season with Blackpool didn't affect my appearances for England. International games fortunately fell when I was fit and in action with the club. In September 1948, England drew 0–0 against a very highly rated Denmark team in Copenhagen. We should have won. Tommy Lawton, who by now through his move to Third Division Notts County was becoming a bit of a pariah as far as certain England selectors were concerned, missed chances. This was Tommy's last appearance in an England shirt. According to Tommy, after the game Walter Winterbottom took him aside and told him he was going to pick Newcastle's Jackie Milburn for the next international. It was a strange thing to do immediately after a game. The next international was a fortnight away and what if Tommy had banged in a hatful of goals in that time? Whether Winterbottom had had pressure put on him from above to get rid of Tommy I don't know, but after a superb performance in the memorable victory against Italy, to be told after the next international that you are finished at that level seemed crazy to me.

Two weeks' later we beat Northern Ireland 6–2 in Belfast. I scored our opener with a shot that went in off the post. Then, in what was a very good 15-minute spell for me and England, I set up two goals for Morty who went on to notch a hat-trick, and a debut goal for Jackie Milburn.

Years later, when I had returned to Stoke City in the early sixties, I teamed up with the former Burnley and Northern Ireland international Jimmy McIlroy who told me he had been a schoolboy spectator at this game. He harboured a dream that one day he might become a footballer and play in the same side as me, though with him being just 13 and me 33 he never believed it would ever happen.

'Well, 14 years on, you're 48 and I'm 28 and that dream has finally been realised,' Jimmy told me after his debut for Stoke in 1963 at Norwich. 'Another five years and it would never have happened Stan, because while you will still be playing I will have retired!'

In November 1948, England beat Wales 1–0 at Villa Park and we continued a good run of results – England lost just once in 18 internationals – when we cruised to a 6–0 victory at Highbury over Switzerland. For all England's success at international level at this time, it was amazing that only Billy Wright, Neil Franklin and myself remained from the side that achieved that tremendous win against Italy in Turin six months earlier. The times they were a-changing. Walter Winterbottom had his own ideas about what sort of player he wanted for the England team and he was beginning to persuade the England selectors to go along with him. While some of his choices were good – Jackie Milburn and Alf Ramsey for example – players who are now considered to have been great, such as Frank Swift, Laurie Scott, George Hardwick, Wilf Mannion, Len Shackleton, Jimmy Hagan and Tommy Lawton, made way in the next 12 months for the likes of Bernard Streten, Bill Ellerington, Bert Mozley, Jack Froggatt and Bobby Langton. They were all fine players in league football but do they readily come to mind when you think of the pantheon of great English footballers? In fact, this had as much to do with the way the England team was selected as it did with Winterbottom exerting his authority and ideas as manager. No matter how well someone had played in a previous international, the overriding criterion for selection for the forthcoming England game was still based on how well a player performed on the day the England selectors came to see him play for his club. If he had a stinker, he was out, which goes some way to explaining why brilliant but inconsistent players such as Len Shackleton and Jimmy Hagan were at this time giving way to what today are seen as lesser names in football. One other player found himself out in the cold from international football during 1949. Sadly, it was me, though the reasons for this were not simply down to club form.

I felt Walter Winterbottom never really appreciated my style of play. He wanted a right winger to track back, tackle and help out in defence. It wasn't my style, though I did try to help out as much as I could. I believed my contribution as a provider of goals and a creative player outweighed my so-called deficiencies in helping out in defence but for a time Walter preferred Tom Finney at outside-right. Even when I did make a return to the England team, I always had the feeling my inclusion was tenuous and my intermittent international career from 1949 until I made my final bow at this level against Denmark in 1957 seems to bear this out. All things considered, I had a good international career. At 42, I was the oldest player to represent my country and I clocked up a record 23 years as an England player. Intermittent or not, it is a record that fills me with as much pride now as I felt every time I pulled on the famous white shirt.

The England–Scotland game at Wembley in April 1949 was a triumph for the Scots who ran out 3–1 winners. On the day, they were inspired. Morton goalkeeper Jimmy Cowan and Billy Steel of Derby County, the only 'Anglo' in the Scottish side, had outstanding games. Steel and Third Lanark's Jim Mason gave the Scots a two-goal advantage and Hibernian's Laurie Reilly, a very gifted and cultured player, made it three before Jackie Milburn scored a consolation goal for England. By my own standards, I had a quiet game. Billy Steel, in addition to causing innumerable problems for the England defence, dropped back to help out the Rangers left-back Cox and along with left-half George Aitken they ensured I found little space and time to make any sort of impression on the game.

A month later, Walter Winterbottom made seven changes for the game against Sweden and I was one of them. It didn't come off, though; England lost 3–1 in Stockholm. The game marked a spell in the international wilderness for me. I was not to play in the next 11 internationals. A recall finally came against Spain in the 1950 World Cup, the game immediately following England's infamous defeat by the USA.

I felt my omission from the England team was a little harsh. I was a creative player, a provider of goals. The emphasis in English football was still very much on attacking. In 1948–49, a total of 1,303 goals was scored in Division One and Two alone, so my style was very much in keeping with how the game was being played. But I accepted my spell out of the international scene with a good grace. I simply hoped my form for Blackpool would be good enough to get me a recall one day. Even though I was now 34, I knew I was still fit enough to take on, and get the better of, the best full-backs international football had on offer.

As if to fly in the face of the England selection, Portsmouth finished the season as First Division champions without a single international player in their side, whereas Preston North End, bristling with internationals, were relegated.

The talking point of the season was the FA Cup run of non-league Yeovil Town. They created quite a stir when they beat a star-studded Sunderland side 2–1 at their famous sloping Huish Park ground. I think I am right in saying that in Alec Stock, one of a few members of that Yeovil team with experience of league football, Yeovil had the first post-war player-manager in English football.

Alec was a superb manager and a gentleman. He went on to manage Queens Park Rangers with whom he won the very first Wembley League Cup final in 1967. They also won the Third Division championship that year. After that, he had some success with Luton Town.

Alec never looked like a manager. In the late forties and fifties, managers looked much the same as they did pre-war – sombre suit, sometimes wearing a trilby, cheerless and funereal, like a magistrate or schools inspector. Match programmes never referred to a manager by his first name and surname as they do today. Instead, they would use initials with the surname, giving managers the dusty formality of Victorian cricketers. Alec was different. Immaculately dressed in tweed jacket or light sports coat, the collar of a crisp white shirt would be open and billowing out would be a scarlet cravat like a June rose in full bloom. In light cavalry twill trousers and brown brogues so highly polished you'd think they were made of glass, he looked more like the director of a local amateur dramatic society or a poet than a player-manager. In many respects his attire was fitting because Alec was an advocate of all that was quintessentially artistic in football and he spoke lyrically of the game.

Alec was a rarity among managers. He had an eye for spotting talent that never left him throughout his managerial career. Alec loved to wheel and deal, though he shied away from the limelight and was content to weave his own particular brand of magic in lower divisions. He had offers to manage in the top flight, but he liked to be his own man and felt a move to a First Division club might compromise his independence.

Throughout his managerial career, from Yeovil until his retirement at Bournemouth in 1980, he created and cultivated fine footballing teams at unfashionable clubs. His teams were made up of mavericks, eccentrics, honest journeymen and the odd ne'er-do-well. But all the players he signed had one thing in common – they could play football the way Alec liked to see it played, along the carpet with style, grace and it has to be said, at times with non-conformity, which is what you get when you sign true individuals. A team is a reflection of its manager and Alec's teams were elegant and cosmopolitan but above all endeavouring and entertaining.

He travelled far and wide watching games in the lower divisions, reserve and non-league matches in his quest for bargains and more often than not he found them. A freelance sports reporter once came across Alec sitting alone, legs crossed, arm lazily draped across the back of the empty seat next to him in a virtually deserted main stand at Craven Cottage, watching Fulham reserves on a grey Wednesday afternoon in January.

'Got your eye on anyone in particular, Alec?' The reporter asked, sensing he might be on to a story.

'No,' replied Alec, sighing to imply boredom at the game unfolding before him.

'Well, you must have some reason to come down here and watch Fulham stiffs in a game of no importance. Managers don't come here on a Wednesday afternoon for no reason at all,' the reporter said, continuing to dig.

'I do,' said Alec, sighing again. 'If you can spend a perfectly useless afternoon in a perfectly useless manner, then you have learned how to live.'

The reporter, unable to compete, gave up and wandered off. A week later, one of the Fulham reserves that day signed for Alec at Queens Park Rangers. His name was Rodney Marsh.

The 1948–49 season ended on a sad and tragic note. Many of the Italian team were killed when the plane carrying Torino back from a game in Portugal crashed into a hillside at Superga on the outskirts of the city. Eighteen Torino players lost their lives, many of whom had played for Italy against England just the year before, including their captain Valentino Mazzola. In all, 31 people died including

Torino's English manager Leslie Lievesley whom I knew well.

Torino had won four consecutive Italian League Championships. The youth team completed Torino's four remaining fixtures, their opponents also fielding their youth teams. They won every game to clinch another championship, but it was heartbreaking consolation for a club that carries its grief to this day.

———— o ————

While England set off on a tour of Scandinavia and France, I took to the boards in the summer of 1949. I'd become friends with comedian Charlie Chester who stayed at our hotel when he was appearing at the Blackpool Opera House. Charlie introduced me to Wee Georgie Wood; these days I must describe him as a vertically challenged comedian. I warmed to Charlie. Georgie it has to be said, although amiable for most of the time, could be very naughty.

My showbiz friends suggested I could boost my summer wage retainer from Blackpool by touring the variety halls doing a football entertainment act. After much discussion and not a little apprehension on my part, it was finally decided I would team up with my younger brother Ronnie. The act, such as it was, involved a tennis net being set up on stage, with Ronnie and I playing football/tennis. The gimmick was that when Ronnie returned the ball to me, I would display a few party tricks with the ball to music before sending it back over the net. It was a support act, nothing more, a little eccentric but in the days when only the well-off had television sets, I suppose it provided novelty on an entertainment bill. Ronnie and I went on stage twice nightly for about ten minutes, but injury came back to haunt me.

Today it's virtually impossible to get top players to turn out in charity football games. Managers understandably will not allow it because clubs have invested so much money in players. In 1949, however, it was different. Such requests were often left up to the player. I had struggled with injury throughout 1948–49 but agreed to turn out in a game to raise funds for a local Blackpool charity at the end of the season. I received many such requests and they were always a dilemma for me. If I did accept, I risked picking up an injury in an inconsequential game. If I declined, I risked being branded selfish and unwilling to help those less fortunate in life. On this occasion I said yes and was injured. I was taking the game less than seriously. At one point, on receiving the ball, I attempted to do a little exhibition football only to be clattered by a young full-back seemingly out to make a name for himself. My ankle blew up like a balloon and for the duration of the theatre tour it continued to dog me.

The football-tennis had its lighter moments. At one particular theatre in Southport, Ronnie and I walked into the empty auditorium prior to the show to see hanging down from the proscenium arch a fire curtain that carried the message, 'In the advent of a fire, this theatre can be cleared in ten minutes'. I turned to Ronnie and said, 'That's nothing. When they see our act, we'll clear it in five.'

I was looking forward to the 1949–50 season with great enthusiasm. My injured ankle responded to treatment during the summer and I trained as usual on my own along the sands at Blackpool. When the time came to report back to Bloomfield Road for the official pre-season training, I felt I was over the injury problems that had plagued me in the previous season and was raring to go.

The season got off to a cracking start. A 4–1 win at home over Huddersfield Town was followed by a 1–1 draw with Middlesbrough and a 3–2 win against champions Portsmouth. There followed two defeats by Middlesbrough and Wolves but from then we lost just once in our next 18 matches. The run came to an end on New Year's Day when Wolves were our undoing by a 3–0 scoreline.

Every game was like a Cup match. It appeared that every team we played raised their game when pitted against us. During this period, we were without doubt the team everyone wanted to beat. That was reflected in the attendances, for Blackpool continued to be a major draw in this post-war boom. There were 48,000 at Middlesbrough; 61,000 at Aston Villa; 65,000 at Sunderland; 58,000 at Manchester City; 67,000 at Arsenal; and 50,000 at Burnley.

In the second half of the season our results were not so good, but by any standard other than our own, not bad. From 1 January to the end of the season in May, we lost six of our 18 games and even though we were not in real contention for the title, the crowds continued to roll up to see us, including a staggering 72,000 at Everton. Blackpool's capacity at Bloomfield Road was around 32,000 and more often than not it was filled to the rafters for home games; attendances averaged 26,336, the highest in the club's history.

There was a genuine desire on the part of the players to entertain these vast crowds. To go a goal up, then sit back and kill off the game was unthinkable. If a team went two up you would hear their skipper driving them on to score a third and once that had been done, to make it four. Generally speaking, as players we were aware of the privileges we enjoyed. Many of us had grown up with the working folk who watched us and we felt morally bound to entertain and give everyone their full money's worth. Of course, winning was uppermost in our minds, but both teams would set out to achieve that in the most entertaining way possible. When I hear players or managers describing their game plan say, 'We set out to silence the crowd,' I cringe. Winning is of course important in football, but winning in an entertaining way is all-important. Look at some of the great teams – Hungary of 1953, Real Madrid 1956–60, Brazil of 1970 and Holland, or for that matter Ajax, of the Cruyff era in the early to mid seventies. Did they or any team managed by Matt Busby, Bill Nicholson or Jock Stein ever take to the pitch with the intention of silencing the crowd? Never. They were successful and they achieved their success through entertaining football. That is why such teams are all-time greats and remain a benchmark for what can be achieved in football if you go about it in the right and proper way – with style, flair, grace and a desire to be stunning in every sense of the word.

Our final position in Division One in 1949–50 was seventh, much improved on the previous season but our undoing was the number of games we drew. Out of a total of 42 matches we shared the spoils 15 times. But we finished only four points behind Portsmouth who were champions for a second successive season.

Again there was disappointment in the FA Cup when after gathering up a good head of steam we went out in round six, losing 2–0 to Liverpool in front of 54,000 at Anfield. Liverpool went on to reach the final, losing 2–0 to Arsenal. My old pal Joe Mercer, voted Footballer of the Year, had an outstanding game for Arsenal. It was interesting to note that the Arsenal team included Peter Goring, Leslie Compton, Alex Forbes and Jimmy Logie. One or two sports journalists were writing me off for the England team saying that at 35 I was too old and I believe one or two England selectors held a similar opinion.

Yet the average age of that victorious Arsenal team was over 30, as far as I can determine, they are the oldest team ever to win the FA Cup!

In addition to my brief foray into the world of variety, I had also taken up horse racing. Although not a betting man,

I always had a keen interest in horse racing and it was through Wee Georgie Wood I came to be involved in the noble sport as an owner. Georgie introduced me to a pal of his from Beverley in Yorkshire who recommended a horse by the name of Parbleu. I'd always fancied owning a racehorse to give added interest when attending meetings, so I decided to buy it knowing all too well that I wouldn't make money from its efforts. To be fair, Parbleu wasn't a bad horse. It did win quite a few races, but never when I was able to get along to watch it.

I think Parbleu and I kept Charlie Chester in gags for the two years I owned it. His favourite story was how I had shopped around for stabling and a trainer but found the costs too high. According to Charlie, at each stable I went to, when quoted the price of stabling, I said, 'Too expensive. Can you recommend a trainer who is cheaper?' Charlie's story had it that I was eventually passed down the line to a back-street trainer who quoted me 50 bob a week.

'Great!' I was reputed to have said. 'But I have one request. Can I have all the manure to put on the roses in the garden at my hotel?'

The trainer replied, 'At 50 bob a week, there ain't going to be any manure!'

This wasn't true of course, but I took all of Charlie's nonsense and jokes in good part. He was a smashing guy and I suppose his constant jokes at my expense as a race horse owner – 'Parbleu, from good stock, Stanley, out of the filly Nightnurse and that fine beast that pulls old Harry Procter on his daily milk round' – made sure I never harboured any great expectations.

Parbleu did come up trumps on the final day of the season when Blackpool visited Newcastle United, a place above us in the table. Although the race for the First Division Championship went to the very last day, it was between

Portsmouth, Wolves and Sunderland. The Blackpool–Newcastle result would not affect the outcome so our end-of-season encounter at St James' Park had a lacklustre feel to it. Parbleu was running that afternoon and I had got the nod from my trainer that it stood a very good chance of winning. Before the game, Newcastle's centre-forward Jackie Milburn popped into our dressing room for a chat and I told him that if he fancied putting a few quid in his back pocket to get a bet on Parbleu that afternoon. I had told Joe Smith and my Blackpool team-mates the same, all of whom had a flutter even those who never had a bet. Parbleu was quoted at decent odds and that afternoon every Blackpool and Newcastle player backed it. In fact, the only person in our party not to put his money on was trainer Johnny Lynas.

It may have been an end-of-season game with nothing at stake, but over 35,000 turned up at St James' Park. At one point, the ball was kicked into the crowd for a Blackpool throw-in and I went to retrieve it. As I waited for the ball to bob back down the terraces, a Geordie at the front said, 'How Stan, yor 'orse romped 'ome this affernoon. Canny odds an arl, ten to one.'

I took the throw-in and told Stan Mortensen the good news. He was at inside-right that day in a much-changed team. From our throw-in Blackpool won a corner and as I prepared to take it, Morty in the Newcastle penalty area obviously told everyone else because suddenly the players of both sides simultaneously cheered, clapped their hands and punched the air. The referee, not knowing the reason for the sudden outburst, looked on in bewilderment and the supporters on the terraces must have wondered what on earth was happening.

Needless to say, after the match there was quite a bit of celebrating on the part of both sets of players. As Jackie Milburn told his team-mates, 'We won the game. Stan's horse romped home and we don't even have to buy him a pint because Stan doesn't drink. A perfect end to a perfect day!'

= o =

England took part in the World Cup for the first time in 1950. A dispute with FIFA settled, the four home countries were eligible to participate. Qualification for the finals in Brazil was via the Home International Championship. FIFA had agreed that the champions and runners-up would qualify. England topped the table with Scotland second but for some reason known only to themselves, the Scottish FA decided they would participate only as Home International Champions, so England went alone.

I'd had a good season with Blackpool and the press were calling for my inclusion in the England squad. When the squad was announced, however, I wasn't in it. Instead, I was selected for an FA XI that was to play a series of friendly games in Canada.

I thoroughly enjoyed that trip. The people were friendly and I warmed to them, so much so that later in life I took up semi-residency in the country. When the FA party arrived in Quebec, I was besieged by pressmen wanting interviews. One of the questions asked was how much English footballers earned. When I told them, the Canadian journalists were shocked. One told me that the reserve players in their top ice-hockey and baseball teams wouldn't turn out for such a wage. It certainly got me thinking again about the esteem and worth in which footballers were held by the FA and our clubs back home, especially in light of the fact that just about every club was enjoying record attendances.

It was during this visit that I was approached about a coaching job in Canada. Out of politeness I listened to what the club had to say and was taken aback when they offered me a wage of £50 a week. Back in England, I was earning around £14 a week in the winter, less in the summer, and when called upon to play for England received a £14 fee which included expenses other than rail fare and hotel accommodation. For all that, I was still content to play my football in England because I felt I had years left at the top. Out of respect I said I would give the matter due consideration, but the following day the Canadian newspapers carried the story that I was leaving British football and taking up a coaching job in Canada. I spent the following days trying to box clever, emphasising my loyalty to Blackpool and British football in general while at the same time trying not to upset my Canadian hosts by rejecting their coaching offer outright.

The FA XI played Manchester United in an exhibition game in Toronto in front of 32,000 people, which at the time was the largest attendance for a soccer game in Canada. Exhibition game or not, I gave it my all which served to make the British press call for my inclusion in the World Cup party once again.

The FA had been dithering but the press claims for me to join the World Cup party were so vociferous that eventually they relented and, along with Johnny Aston and Henry Cockburn of Manchester United, I received a telegram telling me to fly to Brazil. It wasn't ideal preparation. The journey took us through New York, Port-of-Spain and Trinidad and we arrived in Brazil after a tiring 28 hours with only three days to go before England's curtain-raiser against Chile.

On arrival, I was made to realise how seriously the FA were taking the World Cup. Just one England selector, Arthur Drewry, had accompanied the squad and I believe he made the journey only because he wanted to exert his influence on team selection, which he invariably did.

Today international teams book into hotels or leisure

complexes away from the hustle and bustle of cities and fans so they can get some peace and quiet, and prepare in a relaxed way without interruption. Little was known about such preparation in 1950. England had been booked into the Luxor Hotel which was situated on a busy main road that ran alongside the Copacabana beach. It had no training facilities. Our stay was as peaceful as Hyde Park Corner at four o'clock on a Friday afternoon and to make matters worse, the food was unpalatable.

Consideration is given to footballers' diets these days, and quite rightly so. When travelling abroad, teams often take their own food and their own chef. The first meal we sat down to at the Luxor Hotel was cold ham and fried eggs swimming in black oil. Alf Ramsey was the first of several players to be taken ill. The food was so bad a number of us existed solely on bananas. It prompted Stan Mortensen to resurrect an old joke when he was asked by a journalist if this was an ideal diet with which to prepare for games.

'Probably not,' said Morty, 'but you should see us climb trees.' Morty added, 'I'm sticking to the bananas. What else can you do in a hotel where the food is so bad even the dustbins have ulcers.'

It was my opinion and that of many other England players that there had been too much chopping and changing in the England team since the super victory over Italy two years before. Billy Wright wrote as much in his autobiography. He said if the forward line of myself, Morty, Tommy Lawton, Wilf Mannion and Tom Finney had been kept together, England would have been a force to be reckoned with and I tend to agree. Although England had done well at international level, we weren't creating so many chances and what chances were created were not put away. Apart from the two goals scored against a mediocre Chile side, this was the case in Brazil.

The day before we were due to play Chile the England party went along to the Maracana Stadium to watch our hosts take on Mexico. It turned out to be an experience far removed from anything I had ever come across in football before. The Maracana had seating for 130,000, which in 1950 was a rarity. It also had terracing behind each goal which accommodated another 30,000 fans and every ticket for the game had been sold. Such was the traffic and congestion on the roads leading to the stadium, we had to abandon our coach and walk the rest of the way. The atmosphere inside the stadium was provocative, animated, impassioned and intoxicating. The group dynamics built up as the kick-off approached and within minutes of the teams appearing it verged on hysteria.

When the Brazilian team emerged, hundreds of fireworks were set off in the stands and great plumes of yellow smoke wafted up and drifted across the pitch. We had noticed a cannon to the right and rear of where we were sitting and as Brazil took to the field it fired. The sudden, unexpected and deafening boom made us all jump in our seats. Almost immediately, Spurs' Eddie Baily and Ted Ditchburn, who had been sitting with their backs to the cannon, made their way out to the refreshment kiosk to buy bottles of soft drinks. Laurie Scott volunteered his own theory about why Eddie and Ted had made a sharp exit which brought a moment of light relief in what was an intense and highly volatile atmosphere.

The game was a fascinating spectacle. For me, the interest lay with the Brazilians and how they played the game. Breath-taking skill on the ball was coupled with precise passing and explosive shooting. It was evident from watching Brazil and, later in the tournament, Uruguay that many of the competing teams had made tremendous progress in footballing terms. Brazil played a game that was fast and accurate with an inordinate amount of skill. Although attacking football was the order of the day in England, the fluidity with which Brazil took the game to opponents had a controlled grace and style about it I had not seen before. In England, teams loved to attack but in comparison to the Brazilians, our style came across predominantly as hell-for-leather running and chasing.

I realised that English football had no exclusivity on fitness and skill. Brazil demonstrated that our training methods had become, to be quite frank, conservative, even detrimental to a game that globally was quickly developing. I had spent all my career working with the ball but had done so in virtual isolation. Although Stoke City and Blackpool used a ball in training more than most clubs, it was still nowhere near enough as far as I was concerned; hence my private training. At some of our top clubs, players never saw a ball from one Saturday to the next, the theory being that it would make them hungry for it. I'd always believed that to be nonsense. I wouldn't have had the skills I possessed if I hadn't spent countless hours by myself with a ball at my feet.

I admired the way the Brazilians played football and was not a little envious of their constant use of the ball in training. I wasn't alone. Tom Finney shared similar views, but the people who ran our game regarded anything new with suspicion. This was, after all, the first time England had competed in the World Cup. We had been members of FIFA only since 1946 and the hierarchy in English football clung on to the old methods, still believing we were the football masters of the world. When we failed miserably in this World Cup, the disappointment was brushed aside by FA officials. They had their heads in the sand. Rather than seeing it as an opportunity to learn from other countries who were introducing new ideas into football, the attitude was that the World Cup was a gimmick, it would never catch on and all that mattered was our domestic game which they ran and ruled.

I was much taken with the quality of the Brazilian play, particularly their free kicks, bending the ball around defensive walls. It was the first time I had ever seen that done. Stan Mortensen joked there might be something in the banana diet after all, but joking apart Morty, too, was mesmerised by what he saw. We were both in awe of the skills on display. At times, Brazil bewildered Mexico with a display of football craft beyond the understanding of many, showing footballing dexterity that seemingly knew no bounds. They were a delight to watch and I left the stadium excited, my mind buzzing with new ideas and possibilities.

One of the things that had impressed me was the Brazilian kit, which was short and lightweight. Of particular interest to me were their boots which were shaped to hug the foot, light and far less cumbersome than the traditional English boot. The day after the game, I visited a Rio sports shop and bought a pair, size seven. The boots were indeed light, made of thin leather. They had no bulbous toecap and no steelplate in the sole which was also made of a thin strip of leather. The boots were streamlined in design and barely reached the ankle, unlike British boots which, in affording complete protection for not only the ankle but a couple of inches above, were weighty and not conducive to speed off the mark, especially on heavy grounds.

I was in talks with the Co-op at the time about promoting their own brand of football boots, to my knowledge the first ever commercial deal struck by a footballer (unless you count Denis Compton). I realised that with a pair of these lightweight, streamlined boots I could be even quicker, if only by inches over a yard or so, but in football that can be imperative. I wouldn't be able to buy boots like this at home, but my idea was to take the boots back to England and pay the Co-op boot factory to make me a number of pairs to my own specifications, which is exactly what I did.

When I returned to England from the World Cup, I agreed the deal with the Co-op. I was to be paid £15 a week, more than I earned with Blackpool, to lend my name and image to their football boots. In addition to endorsing the product, the deal involved making a personal appearance on a Saturday morning at a Co-op store in whichever town or City Blackpool were scheduled to play an away game. I cleared the deal with Joe Smith and eased his fears about the Saturday morning personal appearances. I always got up at 6 a.m., long before any other Blackpool player, and even allowing for a personal training session could be at a shop for 9 a.m. and back by half eleven in plenty of time for lunch and a rest before the match in the afternoon. 'Besides,' I told him, 'being in a shop for a couple of hours signing autographs will keep me occupied. You know how broody and restless I can get hanging around a hotel.'

Joe agreed to the deal and for nigh on ten years I enjoyed a happy association with the Co-op, helping them to sell literally millions of pairs of football boots. The fact that I never wore the actual boots myself did not bother me. As far as British boots went they were fine and, as most mothers discovered to their joy, very affordable.

The Saturday morning ritual of attending a shop on the day of a Blackpool away match never had a detrimental effect on my game, although I have to say I was often astounded by the numbers of people who turned up. The Co-op printed thousands of promotional photographs of me and everyone who attended the shop in question on a Saturday morning was given one, which I invariably ended up signing. Some days, even at 9 a.m., the queues went out into the street and never abated until it was time for me to take my leave. Once my promotional session was over, I would be whisked back to our team hotel by car where I would rest for an hour and a half, awaking refreshed and ready for action.

The boots I bought in Brazil I took to the Co-op boot factory in Heckmondwike in Yorkshire. I've never smoked a cigarette in my life, but I took along a box of cigarettes for the foreman as a thank-you gesture for looking after me, something I would do for the duration of the time it took to develop my perfect boot. It took a few goes before they came up with the boots I wanted, but once they were right it took only one game for me to fall in love with them. The leather was as thin as card, the boots hand-stitched. There was no bulbous toecap, no steel plate in the sole. In fact, the leather sole was so thin they had to produce special nails small enough to tack it to the upper and for the studs. The boots afforded little protection for the ankle in much the same way as boots do not today, but my theory was if a defender caught me, it was my fault for not being skilful or quick enough to evade his tackle. The boots weighed just a few ounces and were so supple and flexible I could fold them up and put them in my jacket pocket without them being cumbersome. From 1950 until my retirement from league football in 1965, I wore that style of boot in every game I played. Heaven knows how many pairs I got through; they were so light and delicate they would last for two or three games at the most, sometimes not even for a game. I always had four or five pairs in the dugout as a precaution. One pair has survived the years and looking at them now they are not far removed in design from the boots current players wear, but they were certainly revolutionary in the fifties.

Today when I hear of players being paid a million pounds a season to promote and wear a certain brand of boot, then when the deal runs out and they do not get the improved offer they want, continuing to wear the boots but blacking out the manufacturer's logo with black tape, it strikes me as selfish and petty-minded. Perhaps I was naive in paying for special boots to be made, but I felt it was money well spent. Besides, I felt very fortunate and privileged to have a commercial deal with the Co-op.

If I have one main criticism of players today, it is that many do not know how lucky they are. I knew countless players, good ones, whose careers were curtailed by injury, often one that can be treated easily today. I thank the good Lord I never sustained a bad injury. Even a damaged cartilage drew a veil over a player's career in my day and I consider myself very fortunate indeed never to have been stricken with anything like that. The boot deal with the Co-op was not the icing on the cake, the longevity of my career was. Never for one moment did I consider myself anything but a damn lucky so-and-so to reap financial benefits, such as they were, from a game I was devoted to and loved to play.

— ○ —

The team for the Chile game was primarily down to England selector Arthur Drewry, who picked it in consultation with manager Walter Winterbottom. Despite my late recall to the squad, it came as no surprise when I heard the news I wasn't in it. England gained a comfortable if unconvincing 2–0 victory against Chile which everyone believed set us up nicely for our next game against the USA. Given the footballing prowess of both countries, England were odds-on to win.

Walter Winterbottom wanted to play me against the USA because he felt I could unlock their defence, which appeared to lack technical ability and organisation. However, the stumbling block was Arthur Drewry who didn't believe in horses for courses and maintained you should never change a winning team. Stanley Rous the FA secretary apparently went to see Drewry to put the case for my inclusion in the team, but Drewry held firm.

We flew from Rio to Belo Horizonte where we stayed as guests of a British mining firm. In the light of what we had experienced at the hotel in Rio, they afforded us excellent hospitality.

We arrived at the stadium after a nerve-racking and bumpy bus journey from the mining camp courtesy of a local driver who commanded the wheel with all the calm and mental stability of Caligula. The Belo Horizonte stadium had been specially built for the World Cup but the pitch was small and the surface only marginally less bumpy than the local roads.

The USA had proved to me they would be no pushovers by giving Spain a good run for their money in their opening game, holding them at 1–1 before eventually succumbing to two late second-half goals. I still expected England to win but we huffed and puffed, conceded a goal just before half-time and for all our domination in the second half, couldn't make the necessary breakthrough. The game was purgatory to watch from the stands and come the final whistle I thanked my lucky stars I hadn't been a part of it. Whether or not I would have made any difference if I had played is debatable. All I know is England missed a hatful of chances and never looked capable of scoring even if we'd played for nine hours never mind 90 minutes. Even allowing for the uncomfortable journey to the game, the poor pitch and the fact we dominated the match it was a humiliating defeat.

We flew back to Rio in sombre mood. We had to beat Spain in order to qualify for the next stage, a group play-off. Against a resolute Spanish team it would be a tall order. I did feel confident about one thing, however – I'd get a recall.

Four changes were made to the team that had lost to the USA. I came in at outside-right for Tom Finney who switched to the left flank in place of Jimmy Mullen of Wolves. Bill Eckersley of Blackburn Rovers came in for Johnny Aston, with Eddie Baily of Spurs and Newcastle's Jackie Milburn replacing Wilf Mannion and Roy Bentley respectively.

The game was a dour affair, full of niggly fouls. The stopping and starting prevented either side from getting any sort of rhythm into their play. Jackie Milburn managed to head home from one of my crosses but the Italian referee Signor Galeati ruled it offside. To my mind it was a good goal, a view born out by photographs in the newspapers which clearly showed a Spanish defender playing Jackie onside. Such are the trials and tribulations of football, however. Spain scored just after half-time through their centre-forward Zarra and although we took the game to the Spanish for much of the second half, we never troubled them unduly. In the end the game fizzled out and we were out.

I was keen to get back home to my family, but nevertheless quite fancied staying on in Brazil, not so much to see how the World Cup would turn out, but to watch sides like Brazil and Uruguay. I felt much could be learned from them. Tom Finney quite fancied the idea as well, but we were tied to travelling home with the England party. It is one thing for players to return home, but neither Arthur Drewry nor Walter Winterbottom stayed on to study how the teams who had reached the next stage were applying themselves to the tournament. All the English sports journalists were also recalled by their newspapers, so while the game of football continued to develop with new ideas being put into practice, we all went home and, to all intents and purposes, buried our heads in the sand. Well, I tried not to. In the limited games I had seen I had picked up quite a few ideas on technique and training which I aimed to implement and packed in my bag was the pair of Brazilian boots I'd bought.

— ○ —

The FA produced a report on the World Cup that recommended the formation of a technical committee. The brief would be to study the training, technique and pre-match preparation of the Brazilians with a view to implementing such ideas in our own game. As far as I know, this committee met just once and filed a report saying that it was their considered view that such training methods would not be suited to the English game. I found that disappointing. British football could have learned much from the Brazilians and even the Uruguayans, but the sad thing was that those in authority in our game didn't want to learn. I believe that had a detrimental effect on our game at all levels for a decade and more.

From boyhood, an integral part of my game had been self-examination. I had worked hard at trying to improve my skills, technique and general play as well as working out ways to provide forwards with better service. When the German full-back Münzenberg had got the better of me as a 20-year-old at White Hart Lane, I worked at finding out why. If ever there was a time when English football should have sat down and taken a long, hard look at itself, it was in the aftermath of the 1950 World Cup. Although the fifties produced some great players and the general level of entertainment and skill was high, globally the game was changing. The standard of British football wasn't bad, in fact it was good, but other countries were catching us up; some had overtaken us. We stood still, our insular attitude reinforced by the notion we had invented the game. British football in the fifties produced some great players, but on the international front and emerging European club scene, no great teams. In the main, I believe this was down to a lack of technical awareness. We had superbly gifted individual players but little was done to form them into a unit, a team that could play to a system with players who would help one another so that individual skill and guile also became collective skill and guile.

Of course, no matter how well a team is organised you still need players who can do the unexpected, a player who can produce that moment of magical skill to unlock the most organised of defences. Often such skills are innate, no coach can put in what God left out, but the skilful player also learns from other skilful players. I had certainly learned from watching the likes of Ademir, Friaça and Jair in the Brazilian team. In fact, I couldn't wait for the 1950–51 season to start so I could incorporate some of the ideas I had picked up from the 1950 World Cup into my own game.

15

———o———

Forties
Favourites

I t is impossible to compare the forties with any other decade simply because of World War Two. The war robbed many fine players of what would have been their prime footballing years and we can only speculate about how many great careers never happened because young footballers of promise were tragically to be remembered as exactly that.

Nevertheless, the forties did produce great players – Tommy Lawton, Frank Swift, Neil Franklin, Peter Doherty and Stan Mortensen to name but a few. But no mention of the forties would be complete without including the talents of Wilf Mannion, Johnny Carey, Billy Liddell, Trevor Ford and Bill Shankly.

Wilf Mannion was a scheming inside-forward, not dissimilar to the great Alex James of the thirties. Wilf on his day was brilliant and, much to the consternation of his opponents, Wilf's day was more often than not a Saturday. A shock of long blond hair made him an unmistakable figure on the pitch, but it was his superb ball control and passing skills that really caught the eye. Like so many great players of his time, Wilf's international career was comparatively short, from 1946 to 1951. However, I'm absolutely certain that if it hadn't been for the war and a bitter wage dispute with his club Middlesbrough in 1948, in which he was branded a troublemaker by officialdom, Wilf would have won far more than the 26 England caps he has to his name.

In the immediate post-war years Wilf, Raich Carter and Tommy Lawton formed an England spearhead attack that was sagacious, inventive and above all, lethal. Playing for Great Britain against the Rest of Europe in 1947, Wilf proved himself to be a footballing craftsman of the highest calibre. Clever, ingenious, shrewd and adroit he master-minded a famous victory but it was no one-off. He turned in many such performances for his beloved Middlesbrough and one in particular sticks in my memory. Against Blackpool in November 1947 he displayed all his audacious skills in a performance that filled a treasure chest with golden memories for all those fortunate enough to have been present. I wasn't playing due to injury, but I sat in the stand mesmerised from start to finish by the brilliance of this flaxen-haired individualist.

There is a story behind Wilf's brilliant virtuoso performance on this day and it concerns a girl called Bernadette whom he was later to marry. Wilf was very sweet on Bernadette and on the day before Middlesbrough were due to entertain Blackpool, she agreed to their engagement. Bernadette knew nothing at all about football. In fact, she had never seen a game, but she agreed to go along to Ayresome Park to watch her new fiancé play to see 'what all the fuss was about'. Well, Ayresome Park turned into Awesome Park. Wilf wanted Bernadette to remember the day for ever and he turned in the performance of his life to ensure that she would.

Middlesbrough played a similar type of game to Blackpool but on this day there was one big difference, and it was Wilf. It was nip and tuck for the first half hour of what was an end-to-end game; then Wilf grabbed the proceedings by the scruff of the neck and continued to dictate for the remainder of the match. Every pass he made was perfect; in every tackle he came away with the ball. As the game progressed, he grew in confidence. Blackpool played well but on the day playing well against Wilf wasn't enough. Middlesbrough ran out 4–0 winners and only the fact that Wilf masterminded and set up their goals prevented him from being on the scoresheet himself. If greatness in football can be determined by the ability of one player not only to dominate proceedings throughout but to impose his personality on a game, then Wilf showed on this day he was indeed blessed with greatness. Tricky, elusive and chock-full of confidence, time and again he found his fellow Middlesbrough forwards with passing so cleverly veiled it had a more than competent Blackpool defence switching their heads this way and that to see what perils had developed behind them. His fiancée of 24 hours may have left Ayresome Park not knowing much more about football than when she set foot in the ground, but I am sure having watched Wilf that day she had a far greater understanding of 'what all the fuss was about'.

When his career with Middlesbrough ended in 1954, Wilf had a short spell at Hull City before hanging up his boots. He returned to his native Teeside but, sadly at a time of high employment, inexplicably found doors closed to him and work hard to come by. Wilf was reduced to knocking on doors looking for any work he could get, a belittling and humiliating experience for a truly gifted player who only years before had been fêted in Middlesbrough. Today Wilf enjoys legendary status in the town, but for years he had to scrimp and scrape a living the best way he could. It was a shocking state of affairs for a man who single-handedly put the town at the forefront of football's map and serves as a lesson on how fickle and unappreciative of talent some people can be.

John Carey won caps for the Republic of Ireland in six different positions, as well as playing for Northern Ireland, and he enjoyed a long and illustrious career with Manchester United that stretched from his signing as a 17-year-old in 1936 to his retirement in 1953. Like Paddy Crerand in that other United team of the sixties, Johnny wasn't known for his pace, and also like Crerand, he more than made up for it by an astute and intelligent use of the ball and uncanny sense of positioning. Johnny, who was balding in his twenties, always appeared to be older than his actual years. In a way, that was appropriate because even when young he used the ball with all the guile and cunning of the most experienced professional.

Johnny bowed out at the age of 34, having been the cornerstone of the first great United team built by Matt Busby. They won the First Division Championship in 1952 and beat Blackpool in my first FA Cup final appearance in 1948. He still had a few years left at the top when he decided to retire and the temptation to carry on must have been a strong one. But two considerations weighed heavy on his mind – a reluctance to carry on in the public eye for a day longer than he could guarantee a flawless performance, and a concern that, after 17 highly enjoyable years with United, to stay longer would deny similar privileges to the youngsters coming through the ranks at Old Trafford. In addition to being known for an inordinate amount of footballing talent, Johnny Carey was also renowned for his generous nature.

By retiring with his reputation at, or near, its meridian,

he escaped the jibes of those who take delight in chivvying flagging football warriors, however eminent. His versatility as a player was his strength, he turned in immaculate performances in both full-back and all three half-back positions whereas his leisurely gait when playing as a forward prompted team-mate Henry Cockburn to say, 'Johnny's pace deceives opponents. He's actually slower than he looks.'

I played against Johnny many times. Although I had much the better of him when it came to speed, his astute sense of positioning which he used to force me wide and into a position where it was difficult to make a telling pass made him a tricky adversary. He was an artistic defender whose comfort on the ball was matched by a deftness of touch, such as displayed in later years by Liverpool's Alan Hansen. He was voted Footballer of the Year in 1949, a fitting tribute to a man known by team-mates and opponents alike as 'Gentleman John'. Following his retirement from playing, he enjoyed a distinguished managerial career guiding both Blackburn Rovers and Leyton Orient to promotion to Division One and he also managed Everton and Nottingham Forest. As a manager, he was not motivated by financial reward. His enjoyment remained the same as it had been as a player – simply the thrill and excitement of being involved in a game he loved.

Billy Liddell was the original Anfield legend who, in the days when Scots were renowned for their liking of a drop of the hard stuff and a pint of Heavy, rejoiced in the middle name of Beveridge. He signed for Liverpool in 1939 and was immediately adopted by the Anfield faithful who warmed to his versatile forward play. For me, Billy was at his best when displaying his considerable skills on the left wing, but he adapted equally well to playing right-wing or centre-forward. Today, in an age when some top players are one-footed and seemingly use the other just for standing up and running, Billy would be somewhat of an anachronism; he was naturally two-footed.

Billy didn't make his league debut until 1946, aged 24, because of the war but if ever a player made up for lost time, it was Billy Liddell. His career was extraordinary by any standards. He made an immediate impact in the Liverpool team in the post-war years and continued to exert his influence until his retirement, 537 games and 229 goals later, in 1961. He won 28 caps for Scotland and a League Championship medal with Liverpool in 1947, and was unique in top-flight football because throughout a career that lasted for 15 years, he remained a part-time professional.

Billy's day job was with a Liverpool firm of accountants. Despite enjoying legendary status not only on Merseyside but in football in general, nothing could persuade him to leave the security of his accountancy job and take up football full-time. He was a warm and amiable guy with a ready wit who never thought anything untoward of his dual role at a time when football was rapidly becoming more professional. He loved his work as an accountant; he found it stimulating and interesting and often a source of humour. After one game at Anfield, I was chatting to him about his work and asked, quite genuinely because I did not know, the difference between an accountant and an auditor. 'Auditors are people who got out of accountancy because they found it too exciting,' was Billy's droll reply.

Following his retirement from football in 1961, Billy became an assistant bursar at Liverpool University but he continued to live a life of dual roles, combining his post at the University with much good work with the city's youngsters as a youth project worker. He also found the time to be a lay preacher and a Justice of the Peace. That year the Football

Writers' Association should have awarded him their Footballer of the Year honour, for at the time of his retirement there would not have been a more fitting recipient than Billy Liddell. A flying winger with an eye for goal, he worked tirelessly to repay his adopted Merseyside for the things it had given to him – a sense of standing, integrity, dignity and enjoyment of football.

In 1999, I had the great pleasure of being re-united with Trevor Ford at a sporting dinner. He was a great centre-forward with Swansea Town, Aston Villa, Sunderland and Cardiff City. He hadn't changed. His impish humour, forthright opinions and larger than life character were as infectious as ever. In the forties, Trevor made the Wales's number nine shirt his own. He was to my mind one of the best centre-forwards of the post-war era, a bustling, combative player, a real handful for defences. The game and rules being what they were then, he would often shoulder charge goalkeepers into the back of the net whether they had the ball in their hands or not. His prowess on the ground was matched by his considerable power in the air. He was not only a decent scorer of goals, 177 in 349 matches, his ability to shield and hold the ball then lay it off, set up many chances for team-mates. He won 38 caps for Wales and in scoring 23 goals shared the Welsh goalscoring record with Ivor Allchurch for three decades before it was beaten by Ian Rush.

Trevor was an honest player and he often rubbed football's establishment up the wrong way. One typical Ford fusillade in his 1957 autobiography, the appropriately entitled *I Lead The Attack*, resulted in his suspension from the English game. Trevor, undeterred, went abroad and for three years played for Dutch side PSV Eindhoven.

Invariably, after a game, conversation with Trevor would turn to the worth that footballers had for their clubs and

FAs. He believed clubs were making a fortune out of players and didn't care one iota about us really. Following one game, he told me that when he had signed for Aston Villa from Swansea Town, his transfer fee was £13,500 plus a Villa player going in the opposite direction. Trevor's cut from the deal was the princely sum of £10. Trevor went on to tell me that from this £10 he was expected to stump up the costs of finding a new home in the Birmingham area and moving house. He kicked up about it and while Swansea declined to help, Aston Villa, not wanting to have an unhappy major signing on their books, relented and came up with some money for removal expenses.

The maximum wage was still in force of course when Trevor signed for Aston Villa in 1947, but he told me how Villa got round that problem and managed to pay him bonuses for scoring goals. Whenever Trevor scored, the Villa manager, Alex Massie, would invite him for a game of snooker and bet Trevor £5 on the outcome of their game. Alex Massie always contrived to lose and that was Villa's way of getting around the maximum wage and paying Trevor his bonus.

'Villa were paranoid about being caught paying bonuses which the Football League and FA deemed illegal,' Trevor told me, 'so I had to go through this rigmarole every time I scored. What annoyed me was the feeling I had about accepting under-the-counter money. Why should I, a professional footballer, feel like a criminal for taking money for a job well done and that my skills have earned?'

He had a point then and, as I found at the sporting dinner in 1999, the years have not mellowed a man whose views are as forthright and rumbustious as ever.

Bill Shankly and I served together in the RAF during the war. He had been a regular in the Scotland team until 1939 but when peace came he was getting on for 33 and was never chosen again.

He had been a fine player with Carlisle United before being transferred to Preston North End in 1933 and he returned to the Cumberland club as player-manager in 1949. His managerial career took in Grimsby Town, Workington and Huddersfield Town before he moved to what was a forlorn and dilapidated Anfield to manage Liverpool in 1959. The rest, as they say, is history.

As a player, Bill was in much the same mould as he was as a manager – outrageous, obsessed, ironic, totally focused, honest, passionate, funny, compassionate and at times, ruthless. Football and Liverpool have had more successful managers – Bob Paisley, Shankly's successor at Anfield for example, achieved a 13-trophy haul – but never has football produced such a complex character who, at the same time, could be so straightforward and uncomplicated.

Bill and I remained good friends for over 40 years. He spanned the two great ages of football. His playing days were those of toe-capped boots, Brylcreemed hair and baggy shorts. When he enjoyed his period of imperialism as a manager, it was in the age of permed hair, tight-legged Gola tracksuits and the first of the players' agents.

One good team may make a manager's reputation, but it is continuity of achievement that proves his worth beyond doubt. Bill spanned successive decades in football with all the presence of the Humber Bridge and that is why for anyone over the age of 35, our recollections of him are so strong. As a player and manager, he built success on success, reason enough to award him the reverence of a football great. He has become, along with Matt Busby and Jock Stein, one of football's seers, the granddaddy of the elders who begat the likes of Brian Clough and Alex Ferguson.

We all know what Bill said about life and football. When he said it, it was not a smart quip to win column space in newspapers. He never had to do that; everything he came out with was eminently quotable. When he said football wasn't a matter of life and death, it was much more important than that, it was Sam Goldwyn meeting Bertrand Russell. In essence that is what Bill was – part football manager, part stand-up comic, part philosopher, with common sense embedded in barbed darts and thrown at you to see how you coped.

I knew him well but millions of others who had never met him also felt they knew the man. This was because Bill always showed himself to be human; people felt they understood him. It is one of the reasons why there are so many stories about Bill Shankly, true and apocryphal. I could write a book of stories about Bill. Many are now part of football legend, but these are true, told to me by Bill, so you may not have heard them.

Bill had not been in charge of Liverpool for very long but that did not prevent him from believing he would make the club one of the most successful in the world, such was the implicit belief he had in himself as a manager. On a trip to Scotland he called in at Easter Road, the home of Hibernian who were managed at the time by his brother Bob. Bill arrived unannounced and, looking for Bob, found his way into the home-team dressing room. There he found two youth-team players cleaning it out. One was Mick Cullerton (when I became manager of Port Vale in 1965 he was one of my first signings). The other was John Blackley who went on to enjoy a fruitful career as a centre-half with Hibs. Blackley was making a poor job of sweeping the dressing room floor and Bill, without saying who he was, immediately took control.

'Jesus Christ, son. That's no way to sweep a floor,' said Bill, taking the broom off the lad and proceeding to show him how a floor should be swept. 'You sprinkle water on the floor to stop the dust rising. Then you sweep with a backward motion towards you. Like so. Get it?'

Bill handed the brush back to John Blackley, but the lad continued sweeping as half-heartedly as he had done before, pushing the broom away from him.

'No, no, no!' exclaimed Bill. 'Sweep towards you. That's the proper way to do it.'

Blackley, annoyed at this stranger having come into the dressing room and giving orders, threw the broom to one side.

'Who the hell are you?' asked the piqued junior player.

Bill stood back aghast.

'Who am I?' said Bill flabbergasted at not being recognised. 'I'm the best bloody manager *you'll* never play for!'

In the days before every hotel room had its own TV set, Liverpool were staying in a favourite hotel of Bill's in Porthcawl prior to a midweek European game. The night before the match Bill told the players they could watch a world championship boxing bout on TV and that they should make their way down to the TV lounge after their evening meal where he and Bob Paisley would join them. When Bill entered the TV lounge he was astounded to find the entire Liverpool team sitting watching *Coronation Street*. When he asked why, his captain Ron Yeats pointed out two elderly ladies seated at the front who had beaten the team into the lounge and turned on the TV to watch their favourite soap. Bill marched to the front of the lounge and bid the ladies good evening.

'Ladies,' he went on, 'there is some fine boxing on the television tonight.'

The two old dears continued watching *Coronation Street*.

'It's not me wanting it, it's these young boys,' said Bill, pointing to his players. 'That's the trouble with young people today. They expect to get everything too easy.' The ladies nodded in agreement. 'Not like when we were young, eh ladies? Young people today don't realise what we went through. A depression in the thirties, then a world war.' The two ladies nodded their heads in complete agreement. 'And what did we lay our lives on the line for?' asked Bill before answering his own question. 'So people like these young boys here could be free from persecution. Free to live in an open and honest democratic society.'

The ladies looked quizzically at Bill, wondering what on earth he was getting at.

'You *do* believe in democracy, don't you ladies?' asked Bill.

'Oh, yes, of course we do,' chorused the two old dears.

'Good!' said Bill, clapping his hands together. 'Then let's have a vote on whether we're watching the boxing or *Coronation Street*!'

Bill was one of the greatest characters I ever met in football. His passion and commitment knew no bounds. During one typically combative game when we came up against each other for Preston and Blackpool, I was moved to say to him, 'Sometimes I think you'd tackle your own grandmother.'

'That's where you're wrong, Stan,' Bill replied. 'She'd have more sense than to get in the way!'

16

—— o ——

Thoughts of Going Home

S easons 1950–51 and 1951–52 were bitter-sweet. On the plus side, I felt I was playing some of my best football for Blackpool, a view shared by the sports journalists of the day, yet I made just one appearance for England after October 1950 until October 1953. Another disappointment was the 1951 FA Cup. At the age of 36 I was again on the losing side in the final, this time to Newcastle United.

The 1950–51 season started in grand style, Blackpool winning 4–1 at newly promoted Tottenham Hotspur in front of 64,978. Spurs had won the Second Division Championship the previous season and, despite the sound hammering we meted out to them in the opening game, eventually went on to finish the season as First Division Champions.

Spurs played a type of game that became known as push and run. In essence, it involved players receiving the ball, passing it, then running into space for the return. The name suggests it was very much in keeping with the frenetic British way of playing football, but in fact it was a purist passing game that demanded not only skill but an inordinate amount of fitness and stamina on the part of the players. It was an innovative style developed by manager Arthur Rowe and it worked. Not only were Spurs crowned champions, they were the highest scorers in Division One and had one of the best defensive records. Only runners-up Manchester United and mid-table Burnley conceded fewer goals.

The inspiration in this Spurs side came from Ron Burgess, Alf Ramsey, Eddie Baily and right-half Bill Nicholson. Bill eventually took over the manager's seat and led Spurs to a league and Cup double in 1961 and to British football's first-ever success in European club football when Tottenham beat Atletico Madrid in the European Cup-Winners' Cup of 1963. Bill Nicholson must have had lungs like sides of beef because in the push and run team he seemed to cover every blade of grass on the pitch, helping out in defence and being a key figure in just about every attack. That takes some doing week in and week out, especially on heavy winter pitches which were a feature of English football at the time. Bill Nick's physical capabilities were matched by a high level of skill and vision. As with Matt Busby, Bill's prowess as a player of some note has been overshadowed by his achievements as a manager. Although understandable, I feel that has been to his detriment; he was a very fine player indeed.

Blackpool as a team were still in the transitional stage. Finishing third in Division One in 1950–51 was testimony to the good players that formed the basis of the side and to the fact that manager Joe Smith brought in new players of real quality. The highlights for me were a 2–0 win at Sunderland in front of 56,000; a pulsating 4–4 draw at

Arsenal watched by over 55,000; and, although we were beaten 4–2, a thrilling match up at Newcastle United where a massive crowd of over 61,000 enjoyed an end-to-end game in which, if my memory serves me well, there was not one intentional foul.

Our form in the New Year was super – in 17 league matches up until the season's end, we lost just three and those defeats came in the last four games when Wembley was beckoning and we had injuries to key players to contend with. My understanding with Stan Mortensen reaped dividends. He was over his injury problems and back banging in goals. Morty finished the season with a total of 34, a great tally considering he missed six matches due to niggling injuries.

Three players who came into the side were to have a profound effect on our fortunes in the coming years – Jackie Mudie, Bill Perry and Allan Brown.

Jackie Mudie joined the club as a 16-year-old, but he did not make his debut until he was 19, scoring the only goal of the game against Liverpool in March 1950. In the 1950–51 season, this slightly built lad made the inside-right position his own. He was only five feet six tall but remarkably good in the air, due to his impeccable timing. Many times I looked on in wonderment as he beat a six-foot plus central defender to a cross.

Jackie became a very close and trusted friend of mine right up until his sad passing in 1996. Often I used to bully him on the pitch. Even before he got the ball, I'd say, 'Jackie, when you get that ball, don't hang about. Give it to me as quickly as you can,' and he always did. Forwards, particularly wingers, like to get the ball early, the earlier the better so progress can be made before a defence has time to re-group and get organised. That way maximum damage can be done. Jackie's superb close ball control – he could kill a ball and lay it off with one touch – was an integral part of my success at the time. That and his speed of footwork bamboozled even the best of defenders. He practised his art with all the nous, craftsmanship and skill at his considerable command. His reading of a game proved him to be a cerebral player. His quick and accurate passing opened and spread defences effortlessly. He was also a busy player who would pop up here and there. Just when a defender thought he had him in his pocket, with a sudden turn and burst of speed, he would disappear.

We had our ups and downs, our arguments, but they were always quickly forgotten, as they should be between true friends. In 351 appearances for Blackpool, Jackie scored 154 goals, a diminutive but dazzling inside-forward whose friendship I miss dearly.

Bill Perry arrived in England from South Africa in 1949 wanting to pursue a career in football. Both Charlton Athletic and Birmingham City were keen to sign him but Joe Smith, who could sell corner cupboards to Eskimos in igloos, sold him Blackpool Football Club.

Like Jackie Mudie, Bill had made his debut for Blackpool in the previous season but established himself in what had been our problematic outside-left position in 1950–51. Bill was quick and his considerable strength and beer-barrel chest meant he was very difficult to knock off the ball. He had an eye for goal as well as making goals but, to be brutally honest, we carried him when first he came into the team. Bill didn't make an immediate impact but Joe Smith persevered with him at outside-left and Joe's faith in Bill's ability reaped benefits. In 1955, he became the first South African to be capped by England since Gordon Hodgson in 1921 and in a career at Blackpool that spanned 13 years he made a total of 434 appearances. After his indifferent start at Bloomfield Road, Bill developed into a fast, tricky winger and a tremendous servant of the club. He still lives in Blackpool and on the occasions when we do meet up, his wit and charm never fail to engage me. 'The original champagne Perry' Joe Smith used to call him.

If any player was smitten with bad luck it was Allan Brown. Twice he sustained bad injuries that prevented him from taking a deserved place in the FA Cup finals of 1951 and 1953 when his goals had played a significant part in us reaching Wembley. Allan was the original 'Bomber Brown', a powerhouse of a forward and the hardest trainer I ever came across. Joe Smith signed him for what was then the considerable fee of £27,500 from East Fife in December 1950 and he made an immediate impact on his debut in a 2–2 draw at Charlton Athletic. Not only was Allan a good goalscorer, he was a good goal-maker and his robust style and immense strength proved a real handful for even the most granite-like of defenders.

That Allan liked to mix it on the pitch was an understatement. I remember the Sunderland centre-half Ray Daniel once telling me that playing against Allan was 'like taking on Joe Louis with all the speed of Roger Bannister and the precise skill of a brain surgeon'.

In training he had no equal. In every task we were given, Allan applied himself fully and more. He would do press-ups with one hand behind his back. On runs he would always be first back and when training was over, would do half an hour on the weights. 'Allan, you must have muscles on your muscles,' Joe Smith would say and he wasn't too far wrong!

My favourite story about Allan concerns his Blackpool debut away to Charlton Athletic in December 1950. Allan had only been at the club for a couple of days and was down to play at inside-left. He didn't really know anyone and was not familiar with our style of play so it was surprising to me when manager Joe Smith made no mention of Allan's role in the team in what passed for his pre-match team-talk. As we prepared to leave the dressing room, I turned to Allan, wished him good luck and said, 'The boss hasn't told you what he wants you to do out there, so just play your normal game.' Allan looked at me, smiled and said, 'Don't worry Stan, I know what's expected of me. Get a goal and see how fast their right-half can limp!'

He scored 68 goals in 157 league matches. Some were bread and butter goals, but a good proportion were spectacular power efforts from distance. His ability to score pile-drivers prompted Harry Johnston to nickname Allan the 'Master Blaster' some 25 years before Stevie Wonder came up with the term.

With these three added to what was already a good squad with quality in depth, Blackpool enjoyed a period as golden as the legendary sands were contrived to be in the minds of the million or so tourists who visited the town every summer. Unfortunately, the First Division Championship was always to remain elusive.

Hand-in-hand with our championship challenge in 1951, another exciting FA Cup culminated in us reaching the final for the second time in three years. Charlton were beaten in the third round after a replay; then we overcame Stockport County in the fourth and Mansfield Town in the fifth. The Mansfield game remains in my memory because, for all they were Third Division North opposition, I hardly got a kick! Mansfield were managed at the time by my former Stoke City colleague Freddie 'Nobby' Steele. Freddie knew me well and had done his homework for this game. I was tightly marked by two, sometimes three, defenders and when I did get the ball, they seemed to know what I had in mind to do, obviously information fed by Freddie. I didn't shine but we overcame Mansfield with goals from Jackie Mudie and Allan

Brown. Allan was our lone scorer in the sixth round when we squeezed past Fulham before a full house of 33,000 at Bloomfield Road. The semi-final against Birmingham City was played at Maine Road before a crowd of 73,000 – a goalless draw. The replay was at Goodison Park in front of another crowd in excess of 70,000. Goals from Morty and Bill Perry sent us to Wembley. We were ecstatic.

Between the semi-final replay and the final there were nine league matches to play. We continued in good form but our opponents at Wembley, Newcastle United, endured a terrible sequence of results. No surprise then that we arrived at Wembley the bookies' favourites and although I wasn't over-confident, I felt we had enough quality in the team to win and for me at last to pick up an FA Cup winners medal.

The run-up wasn't plain sailing. Allan Brown damaged knee ligaments in a league game against Huddersfield Town in the final run-in to the season. Allan was replaced by George McKnight who, while not the player Allan was, I knew could come in and do a job. Unfortunately, just before the Cup final George also damaged knee ligaments, in a league game against Sheffield Wednesday. Joe Smith drafted in Bill Slater, an England amateur international who had had a run at inside-left earlier in the season until the arrival of Allan Brown. Perhaps the occasion was too much for him, but on the big day Bill never performed and at times during the final, seemed lost. But our defeat was not down to him. Bill went on to become a fine defender with Wolverhampton Wanderers and, in addition to playing at amateur level for England, had the distinction of representing his country in the Olympics and in the 1958 World Cup, winning 12 caps at full international level. Bill's presence was historical in one sense – he was the last amateur player ever to play in an FA Cup final.

Newcastle were the better side on the day and try as Harry

Johnston, Morty and I might, we couldn't turn the game around in our favour. The first half was a pretty even affair. To my mind, we had the better of the chances but never made one tell. Our ploy was for our defence to push up quickly to try to catch the Newcastle forwards offside. This worked well in the first half, but it proved our undoing after half-time. Five minutes into the second half, Chilean George Robledo played a wonderful defence-splitting ball. With our defenders pushing on, Jackie Milburn timed his run to perfection and raced away enjoying more space than Captain Kirk as George Farm came off his line in an attempt to narrow the angle. At one point, Jackie glanced over his shoulder to check that he was onside. He was, and faced with a one to one with George Farm, Jackie didn't miss such gilt-edged chances. He coolly side-footed the ball wide of George into the net and we were chasing the game.

Less than five minutes later, disaster struck us. Newcastle's Ernie Taylor received a pass on the edge of our penalty area and, with our defence thinking he would have a shot at goal, he cleverly back-heeled the ball back into the path of Jackie Milburn coming up from deep. Jackie never broke sweat nor step as he hit a searing 25-yard drive into the right-hand corner of George Farm's net. It was a goal fit to win any Cup final, an absolute cracker, and though we battled back and seized the initiative, Newcastle remained steadfast and survived our onslaught. I played my heart out in that game, at times cutting inside to have a pop at goal myself. I gave it my all, even during the latter stages, but on the day it simply wasn't enough.

Bill Slater also gave it his all but he was out of his depth and turned in a performance that didn't do justice to the fine player he turned out to be. Jackie Mudie never produced the scintillating form he had produced in the league and overall we seemed to lack the cohesion and teamwork that had been the hallmark of our league and Cup performances of that season. I collected my second losers medal and, descending the famous Wembley steps from the Royal Box, started to come to terms with the frustration of a second failure in an FA Cup final and the notion that at the age of 36, the odds on me collecting a coveted winners medal were lengthening with every passing season.

There is no sadder sight in football than the losers' dressing room after an FA Cup final. For many of us, it was our second experience of the empty void that follows defeat, lingering exuberance, verve and fervour but no outlet for it. So you go into an almost trance-like state. No one talks, no one has the energy to move. The mental and physical exertions take their toll so that 11 zombies sit forlornly around the dressing room. You don't think about your team-mates. You don't think that so and so could have done better with the chance he had or that a certain player may have been able to prevent a goal if he had closed down quicker. You just think about your own efforts in the game. 'Perhaps if I'd just cut that ball back earlier instead of hanging on to it' or 'If I'd only taken a split second to compose myself when I had that shot'. Such thoughts are quickly put to the back of the mind because reliving the game becomes too painful. What makes it worse is that the FA Cup final is often the last game of the season, albeit on this occasion we had one league game left of no consequence. So when you are desperate to play again to get the game out of your system, you have to wait over three months until the new season starts in August.

I sat drinking a cup of tea and looking around the silent dressing room. Skipper Harry Johnston sat sipping his tea, too – cup in one hand, the small box containing his loser's medal in the other, he simply stared at the floor in a trance. Eventually after ten minutes or so, he stood up, opened the box and, displaying all the emotion and indifference of a cricket umpire, gave his medal a cursory look before snapping the box shut and putting it in the top pocket of the jacket of his suit. Helping himself to a towel, Harry trudged slowly and dejectedly to the plunge bath. He was probably thinking that having picked up two loser's medals, at 32 his last chance for Wembley glory had also gone.

Morty, always the life and soul of the dressing room, was equally remorseful. I watched as he gingerly removed a boot and stocking to reveal a deep gash on his right ankle. Like the rest of us, he was physically and mentally drained. Usually after a game he would be asking trainer Johnny Lynas to come and look at such an injury, but not on this occasion. He simply limped off to the bath, his loser's medal still in its box and left on the bench where he had been sitting.

Eddie Shimwell was sitting exactly opposite me. At one point, he stared directly at me across the room. His face registered no emotion whatsoever. It was as if I wasn't there. His eyes had glazed over and he was miles away, completely wrapped up in his own thoughts.

Players came and went from the bath and shower area, but George Farm still sat in his goalkeeper's jersey and full strip, making no effort to move and get changed. Bent double, arms resting across his knees, his teeth seemed to be gnawing on the inside of his gums. Eventually, with a tired drawn-out sigh he uttered an expletive, stood up and slowly started to take off his kit.

Joe Smith came into the dressing room, said something about bad luck and being proud of us and that there would always be another day, but no one was really listening and Joe never asked for our attention. It was as if he too was on automatic pilot and was saying these things because it was expected of him. Bill Slater was tearful, Jackie Mudie not far off tears. Eric Hayward, a strapping giant of a man, sat with his head in his hands, occasionally sighing as he repeatedly rubbed his face with his sweaty palms. Wembley once again proved to be our shirt of Nessus, a gift which far from bringing joy, brought frustration, angst and sorrow. But although on the day we were as down and forlorn as any men defeated in battle, ambition must be made of sterner stuff. We drew strength from it and were galvanised into making one more collective effort at achieving Wembley glory.

I consoled myself in much the same way I did after defeat against Manchester United in 1948 by being pragmatic, believing it was far better to lose in a Wembley final than to be knocked out of the Cup in the third round. The final apart, we'd had a great Cup run filled with excitement and fun and I would never have had such times if we had been knocked out of the competition at the first time of asking. In my own way, I thought I had coped better than any of my team-mates with the disappointment of losing to Newcastle, but looking back, perhaps I was just as shattered as they were by the experience. By not showing my emotion at the time, the disappointment manifested itself within me in the form of indifference. I say that because in the following season, niggled by injury, I felt in limbo and seriously contemplated leaving Blackpool to try pastures new where I might enjoy the luck that is crucial to winning anything in football.

———— o ————

Season 1951–52 was a big disappointment for me. Out of the England set-up, after a good start to the season with Blackpool I picked up an ankle injury that allowed me play just two games from November until the season's end.

Blackpool finished ninth in Division One but we made a sad exit from the FA Cup at the first time of asking at West Ham United.

In common with all players, when injured I was always riddled with a mixture of frustration, disappointment and restlessness. I wanted to get back to playing as soon as possible but the ankle injury was a bad one. Muscular and tendon injuries can often be worse than breaks of the bone as they take longer to heal. Even in the latter stages, when the pain has subsided and you feel OK, you know there will be more weeks on the sidelines because there is a big difference between an injury having healed and the tendon and muscle being strong enough to put up with the rigours of a professional game of football. Ask any player from any generation and they will tell you, those last few weeks are the most annoying and frustrating.

There is also the danger of conning yourself into believing you are 100 per cent fit. Many is the player who has come back from injury and got through the first two or three games of his return no bother at all, only to suffer a relapse. Often this is to do with the player's psychological state and adrenalin. He feels fit, the buzz of being back on the practice pitch gets him through training and adrenalin gets him through the first couple of matches. Then, when the initial rush subsides, if the injury has not fully healed, he suffers a relapse and everyone starts to say he came back too soon or he is not the player he was prior to his injury. It was the case in the fifties and it is the case today. That is why, even though I wanted to play again as soon as possible, I was determined not to return until I was absolutely certain I was 100 per cent fit. I may have been erring on the side of caution but I was coming up to my 37th birthday and a surefire way of ensuring I wouldn't carry on for much longer would have been to come back too soon. As any player will tell you, the older you get, the longer it takes to shrug off an injury.

I threw myself into running the hotel with Betty. I was always an early riser so getting up at the crack of dawn to help out in the kitchen was no problem. After breakfast, I helped out with the cleaning of the hotel. I constantly monitored the stocks of food and re-ordered when necessary. As anyone who has run even a small hotel will tell you, your time is never your own. There is always so much to do. For a good part of the 1951–52 season, Stan Matthews the footballer became Stan the cook-cum-waiter-cum-stocktaker-cum-cleaner-cum-taxi driver and more – all in a day's work for an hotelier. It may appear quaint to today's top players, but believe it or not, I was considered very fortunate to have a hotel to run. For most players, the dream was to run a pub when they finished playing. This was an era when many league players, because of the long summer break and a low retainer wage, had no alternative but to take on a temporary summer job to make ends meet. The top players probably didn't need to, of course, because their summer retainer, although less than the maximum wage, was adequate to live on. I was paid a basic wage by Blackpool while injured and it was more than many players from other divisions in the Football League were earning at that time. I was considered well off and very fortunate indeed to have the hotel to fall back on, not only in the summer but particularly during this extended period of injury.

I exercised every day and did some training of one sort or another. The injury restricted me, of course, but from initial short walks along the front I gradually built up the training as the ankle healed until eventually I was doing a full-blown session at dawn together with exercises, ballwork, sprints and a long run along the sands in the afternoon. It paid off. When I did eventually report back to Blackpool for full training in the spring of 1952, I was not far off the mark fitness-wise and all I was really short of was match practice.

In what spare time I had, I made the occasional guest appearance on BBC Radio and committed myself to numerous charity dinners and cheque presentations for one good cause or another. I may have been out of the spotlight as far as football was concerned, but I never had time to wallow in self-pity, not that that was ever my style anyway.

Joe Smith embraced the 'If you can't beat them, join them' philosophy or 'Get them to join us' I should say. In October 1951, he signed Ernie Taylor, the architect of our Cup final defeat against Newcastle the previous April. At five feet four Ernie was even smaller than Jackie Mudie but he had a big presence both in the dressing room and on the pitch. In time, Ernie and I were to form a very good right-wing partnership with Morty switching to centre-forward. Ernie was a cheeky, confident player who on his day verged on the brilliant. Despite his slight build, he could ride even the most brusque of tackles with aplomb and he could crack open even the most challenging and organised of defences. He made a total of 237 appearances for Blackpool scoring 55 goals before the club allowed him to join Manchester United in February 1958 as a goodwill gesture following the Munich air disaster. His average of scoring a goal every four games does not do him justice as a player, for it was his prowess as a playmaker rather than a goalscorer that was his true forte. Added to his on-the-pitch vision was an acute sense of tactical awareness. Ernie knew exactly where the ball was going to go before he received it, and more often than not, short, sprayed or long, it came to me. He was our distribution unit and no matter how much opposing teams attempted to close him down, his joyous, effective artistry and ability to lose markers ensured he continued to man the engine room almost single-handedly.

Ernie hadn't been at Blackpool for a month before he came up against his old club, Newcastle United. How they must have rued the day they sold him because from start to finish he ran them ragged. His footwork was magical to a degree and his frenzied quality on the pitch belied the cool head he had on his shoulders. We gained some degree of revenge for our Cup final defeat, beating Newcastle 6–3 with goals from Billy Perry, Morty (2), Allan Brown, Cyril Robinson and Ernie himself. His own effort was a typical Taylor goal, draped in cheek. Following a goalmouth scramble, Ernie lost his marker, popped up at the far post and with the ball seemingly spinning away from him, raised a heel to bring it back in front of him and under his control. With everyone expecting a volley, Ernie lifted the ball over goalkeeper Ronnie Simpson, who had come to the near post, and the despairing leap of full-back Cowan on the line, and gently guided it just beneath the bar into the empty far corner of the net. Cool and confident under pressure, that was Ernie Taylor. His razor-sharp footballing brain and speed of thought processed situations quicker than a computer, giving you the impression he had far more time on the ball than he actually did. That was the mark of a truly wonderful player at the height of his footballing powers.

Ernie's ability to laugh at himself was just the tonic we needed in the dressing room. His diminutive size was often the cause of much hilarity, not only from jester supreme Stan Mortensen but from Ernie himself. 'The only player I know who when he pulls up his socks, blindfolds himself,' Morty once said. But Ernie made light of the fact he was vertically challenged. At one black-tie dinner in a good-natured jibe at my Saturday morning promotional appearances at Co-op stores, Ernie said he, too, had fixed himself up with an extra earner on Saturday mornings – renting a penguin suit and hiring himself out to stand on the top of wedding cakes alongside the wife of Wee Georgie Wood. He was great fun and played on the fact he wasn't the greatest of time-keepers by having a funny excuse every time he turned up late for training. 'I was cleaning out the budgie's cage when the door slammed shut on me,' was his excuse on one occasion. Ernie was a clever player whose performances merited far more than the solitary England cap he has to his name.

Manchester United were champions that year and Newcastle repeated their FA Cup success, beating Arsenal 1–0 in the final. England after a mixed set of results – three wins, two draws and another Wembley defeat at the hands of the Scots – gained a good victory in the Prater Stadium against a strong Austrian side. The game was notable for the performance of Bolton's Nat Lofthouse whose two goals, his second a brave solo effort during which he was injured, earned him the nickname of the 'Lion of Vienna'. England were roared on by a mass of khaki-clad servicemen stationed in Austria to help with rebuilding and rehabilitation after the war. I was sad not to be there.

The 1951–52 season was also notable for the fact that the first official game to be played under floodlights since an experimental match in 1878 took place at Highbury. A crowd of 44,000 saw Arsenal beat Hapoel Tel Aviv of Israel 6–1 in a friendly and the most satisfying aspect was that everyone did see it. The late Arsenal manager Herbert Chapman had been advocating the use of floodlights back in the 1930s. It shows how slow the FA were to accept innovative ideas that it took 18 years from when Chapman spoke out, and 73 years after the first experimental game under lights, for the idea finally to be put into practice. There was nothing new about the technology involved. Continental teams had been using lights for years but the FA had banned their use because, as they said in a statement, they feared 'clubs would be drawn into spending too much money'. This was a typical conservative stance from our FA.

During the time I was injured, I took to reading just about every book I could lay my hands on. One was *The Official 1951–52 FA Year Book*, which I still have. On page 31, the FA printed their reaction to and views on the growing campaign to stage European competitions for clubs, in particular an annual cup for the league champions of each European country. The FA did not warm to the idea. In their article, they worried about the effect such a competition would have on the Home International Championship, which they erroneously believed still had great significance in world football. The article went on to express concern about 'the problems in organising such a competition', especially the travelling. That suggests they were oblivious to the burgeoning commercial airlines that were making Europe 'shrink'. Their main objection to a European Cup, however, was that with a 42-game league programme and the FA Cup, the 'fixture programme was already seriously overloaded'. All I can say is the domestic fixture programme had been in place since 1919. If they really believed it to be 'seriously overloaded' why hadn't they done something about it? The truth of the matter was, even following the 1950 World Cup, the FA still believed our domestic game to be superior to anyone else's and they were reluctant to allow English clubs to enter any competition where it might be proved to be otherwise. Perhaps they thought if the myth were exploded, it would have an adverse affect on domestic attendances. Also, of course they were loath to allow English clubs to enter any competition, European or otherwise, that they did not control. I believe they felt their own shortcomings as administrators and officials responsible for the growth and development of football in this country would be exposed when set against the go-ahead and innovative ideas being put into practice on the Continent; their own position as head of football in this country would be undermined. So while other European football administrations got on with organising such competitions as the Mid European, Balkan and Mediterranean Cups, until the inception of the European Cup in 1955–56, which incidentally no English club was allowed to enter, our FA continued to bury its head in the sand. I believe this attitude had a detrimental effect on English football for years.

A brief look at *The Official 1951–52 FA Year Book* also convinced me that my idea of wearing streamlined, lightweight boots was right. The advert for boots that appeared in the book was for the 'Official Association Boot' called the Hotshot. This boot hadn't changed in decades and indeed among the advantages listed were 'reinforced hard toes', 'non stretch instep supports' and a back that came some two inches above the ankle. Made of 'best materials' they may have been, but they were not conducive to a game that was rapidly changing on the Continent and in South America. By coincidence, on the opposite page to the advert for the official Hotshot boot was an advert for Gymphlex tracksuits as worn by Blackpool. We were considered innovators in wearing tracksuits for training but the photograph is of interest to me now because it shows me sitting to the far left of the front row, next to manager Joe Smith, wearing my lightweight boots – the old and new world of football facing each other across the page, me in a Gymphlex tracksuit and custom-made lightweight boots, the FA promoting their Official boot that had hardly changed since I made my Stoke debut in 1932 as a 17-year-old.

One thing that had changed was the actual balls used in games. In the thirties there were two types used in English football – the Tugite which cost 24s.6d (£1.22) and the

Aged 46 I signed for Stoke City live on BBC's *Sportsview* programme, returning to my former club more than 14 years after Bob McGrory thought my best days were behind me. Looking on are Blackpool assistant manager Eric Haywood, Stoke director Albert Henshaw (who was personally to meet my wages) and Stoke manager Tony Waddington, a master of PR who delayed my debut a week so that it would be at home.
(Huston Spratt)

Skipper Bobby Howitt congratulates me after my return debut for the club against Huddersfield. A crowd of 35,974 watched the game – the attendance for Stoke's previous game was just 8,408.
(Huston Spratt)

Stoke practice match.

Training at Stoke took place on what was not much more than waste ground round the back of the Victoria Ground. (Stanley Matthews)

A proud moment. With daughter Jean at her wedding to Bob Gough in January 1963. The three of us regularly went to Stoke games together. (Huston Spratt)

Tony Waddington called football 'the working man's ballet'. In this game against Norwich City in October 1962 you can see just why. (Huston Spratt)

A crucial game in May 1963 against title rivals Chelsea. Ron Harris tries to tackle me from behind, but his rough-house tactics were countered by team-mate Eddie Clamp who made sure he dealt with me fairly for the rest of the game. (Popperfoto)

My last league game v. Fulham, 6 February 1965, a few days after my fiftieth birthday. A huge crowd turned out to watch my farewell performance. (Popperfoto)

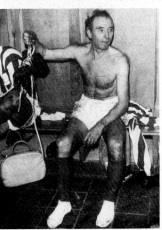

Hanging up my boots for good. My old photographer pal, Huston Spratt, came in asking for one last picture and I obliged. (Huston Spratt)

With my mother in 1965 just after I had been made a Freeman of Stoke-on-Trent. If it hadn't been for my mother I might never have been a footballer. (Huston Spratt)

Arriving at Buckingham Palace with my wife Betty to receive my knighthood. (Popperfoto)

A Dagenham girl piper leads me on to the pitch for my testimonial game in April 1965. Note the state of the pitch! (Huston Spratt)

A specially posed shot for the private collection of photographer Huston Spratt, prior to that testimonial game. After all the photos he had taken of me there wasn't one of us together, but as you can see I had had much more practice at posing than he had! (Huston Spratt)

Carried off the pitch at the end of my testimonial by Lev Yashin and Ferenc Puskas. (Mirror Syndication International)

Jackie Mudie welcomes me to Vale Park, where I had taken on the role of general manager. (Huston Spratt)

With some of the young players at Port Vale: Brian Wharburton, Paul Bannister, John James, John Bostock and Stan Turner. At one stage the oldest player in our forward line was just 18 – the youngest ever forward line-up in league football. (Daily Mirror)

At home in my den around 1970. My Footballer of the Year award is on the mantelpiece while a photo of Stanley Jr holding up his Wimbledon trophy is on the wall. (Popperfoto)

The first day at work on my autobiography with my friend Les Scott. (Les Scott)

Thomlinson 'T' ball costing 18s.6d (92p). The Tugite was more expensive because it was considered a superior ball – it didn't gather mud on heavy grounds – whereas the 'T', which did collect mud on a sludgy pitch, was favoured only when pitch conditions were firm. From March onwards, we invariably played with a 'T' ball. At this time of the season the pitches were rolled when still soft from the inclement winter weather and more often than not, due to the wind, dried out quickly. In a matter of weeks the conditions of pitches changed from being quagmires to being rock hard. As anyone who has played football at any level will know, playing on a bone-hard pitch in windy weather, the ball seems to be overly light and always bouncing up around your knees. To counteract this, trainers would soak the 'T' ball for 24 hours in a bucket of water, then insert another bladder, additional to the one already inside the leather outer case. From being light and balloon like, the ball took on all the attributes of one of those large concrete balls you see on the gateposts of stately homes. You knew when you had headed this ball, I can tell you. What's more, if rain fell during a game, as the match progressed the leather expanded so that the ball grew to almost beachball size. This is the reason why, when looking at photographs of footballers of the thirties with the ball at their feet, the ball often appears enormous compared with the balls used in football today. It says much for the general standard of skill that for all the cumbersome weight of such balls, the players still managed to produce football of high quality.

The standard weight of the ball was supposed to be 16 ounces (just under half a kilo), but the 24-hour soaking and the additional bladder probably doubled its weight. If the weather broke during a game and the pitch became muddy, the 'T' ball with its penchant for gathering clinging mud became heavier still. That was when the Hotshot boot came into its own.

The balls used in the 1950s, still very different from those used today, were a big improvement on those used in the thirties and forties. The most popular officially approved footballs were the Webber 'Premier', the 'Super Straight' manufactured by Stuart Surridge, and the improved 'T' ball. All three still needed to be dubbined to make them water resistant – footballs today are laminated – but the quality of the leather and their improved structure – several sewn panels instead of three pieces of leather stitched into a ball form – meant they kept their shape and weight irrespective of the weather.

My enforced and lengthy time out of the Blackpool team in 1951–52 did not result in me disappearing from the sporting headlines. A number of sports writers were of the mind I was finished, others questioned the wisdom of 'an ageing manager putting his faith in an ageing genius'. If I can give any advice to today's young footballers who suddenly find themselves being portrayed as stars by the media it is, don't believe it. If you do, you're lost. A bad run of form, a lengthy injury or a career near its end will result in you waking up one morning and finding you have nowhere near the number of friends you once thought you had, no ego-massaging publicity and your heart will be filled with bitterness and resentment. By virtue of the fact I never believed my good headlines, I never took on board the adverse publicity when it came my way, and I received quite a lot of such publicity during the 51–52 season. I knew I wasn't finished, far from it. I knew that once I got over my injury I could regain peak fitness and play for years. Of course I couldn't tell anybody that, just in case my inner belief was wrong and I fell flat on my face, so I simply got on with the job of trying to shake off the injury while in some quarters, the press penned their Matthews epitaphs.

It was during this period that through Tom Moss, a well-known comedian of the time, I was introduced to an osteopath from Bury by the name of Arthur Millward. I initially went to Arthur for treatment on the troublesome ankle injury. He cured it, but that was only part of the story. He also gave me a new lifescript. A vegetarian, Arthur had what for the time were radical ideas on diet. While not becoming a vegetarian myself, I did cut down considerably on my intake of red meat and took up a diet that he devised for me. In addition to encouraging me to eat lots of fresh fruit, vegetables and wholemeal brown bread, Arthur introduced me to Biostrath, malt and vitamins B1 and B2; also to what in those days were thought by many people to be cranky health drinks such as pure tomato and celery juice. This diet, coupled with the fact that every Monday I would abstain from all food for 24 hours to detoxify my body, played a significant role in maintaining my fitness through what in footballing terms were ageing years, and sustaining a career in the game far beyond what anyone but myself thought possible. Once over the troublesome ankle injury it was simply a matter of getting back to my training routine and sticking to the lifestyle guidelines suggested to me by Arthur.

Arthur Millward was years ahead of his time. The importance of a diet and fitness programme has really been realised only recently, yet there was I following one in 1952. I still do. But perhaps it was not so much a case of Arthur being ahead of his time as everyone else being out of step and taking time to catch up.

That prolonged spell out of the Blackpool team laid my spirits low. Although I didn't think so at the time, the disappointment of losing a second FA Cup final lingered like an unwanted guest at a party. All in all, it served to make me restless. Stoke City had a new manager, Frank Taylor, and seemingly in an attempt to kick start the club following a poor season – they had finished just one place above relegated Huddersfield and Fulham – Taylor made an inquiry about my availability. The thought of re-joining my old club was not unappealing. They were still in Division One and with Bob McGrory gone I felt there would be no repeat of the bad feeling and resentment that had resulted in my departure five years before. The Blackpool board, having taken into consideration that I was now 37 and had missed the majority of the 51–52 season, which I am sure they felt was the beginning of more injuries to come given my age, agreed to let me go as long as Stoke came up with the asking fee. I never found out what their idea of the asking fee was because as soon as Joe Smith got wind of the interest from Stoke, he put his foot down.

Joe went to see the Blackpool board and told them in no uncertain terms that I was an integral part of his plans for not only the forthcoming 1952–53 season, but for a number of seasons thereafter. He convinced them, as only Joe could, that I still had years left in me and, once he had done that, he turned his attention to me.

'What on earth are you thinking of, Stan?' he said, having called me to a meeting in his office. 'You missed most of last season with injury and that is bound to get you down. No player likes to spend the best part of a season sitting in the stands, especially you, who loves playing so much.

'I know what's got into your head. You think that we're destined never to win the FA Cup. Well, I don't believe that to be the case. If I did, I wouldn't be sitting here now.

'I have implicit belief in this club, in those lads who are your team-mates and, above all, I have every faith in you. You will bounce back better than ever before. A lot of people may think I'm mad, but even though you're 37, I believe your best football is still to come.

'Now, if you want to walk out on the team I have sweated blood to build and on the manager who believes you can play better than ever before, then so be it. But you'll be walking out on the manager who has faith in you even when you're full of self-doubt. Faith, Stan. It can tear down mountains, it can win wars and it can win FA Cups. Those who win do so because they never stop believing they can. This club hasn't seen better days. The better days are to come and we'll see them if you stick it out with us.

'The way to be nothing in football is to do nothing. After bringing you to this club, did I rest on my laurels? In the past couple of years I've brought in Bomber, Farmy, Mudie, Perry and little Ernie. All better players than those I had at the time. It hasn't happened yet but it will happen if we all stick together. I've never said this ever to a player before, but I'll say it to you. Don't go, Stan.

'I live the dream 24 hours a day, seven days a week. I'm not asking you to do that, just to believe in it. More importantly, believe in yourself and what you can still do out there where it matters, on the pitch.'

Joe Smith may not have been much of a tactician or organiser, but could always find the right words to inspire you. I looked at him across the desk and for a time didn't say a word. For his part, he just looked straight back at me. Joe, as I have said more than once, was a wily old bird. I couldn't make my mind up if his stirring words had come from the heart or, given his ability to flannel players into doing what he wanted them to do, if he was giving me the kiddums treatment. Eventually, I broke the silence.

'Tell the board I'm staying,' I said, still not absolutely certain of his genuineness but wanting to believe what he told me. With that I left his office, still a Blackpool player.

Joe's words, which I later decided had come from the heart, had a profound effect on me. I thought about the players in the team; they were all top-quality players and he was responsible for every one of us being there. I realised for the first time why Joe Smith had assembled such a team over the years, that there was an aim – to bring trophies, glory and success to the club, its players and the town; to provide every player with the crowning moment of his career. If he saw me as crucial to his plans, who was I to argue? Although we hadn't won anything up to this point, he had indeed built a superb team and I realised to walk out on it without giving it my best shot would be foolhardy. As it was to turn out, my decision to stay with Blackpool would have a profound effect not only on my career, but on my life.

17

———◦———

Through – but Phew!

Joe's faith in me, Arthur Millward's diet and the fact that I had overcome the ankle injury that had plagued me in the previous season all served to rekindle my enthusiasm. When the 1952–53 season kicked off at Portsmouth, I felt fitter than ever before and was raring to go.

A shirt-sleeved crowd of 44,000 in a sun-kissed Fratton Park saw goals from Bomber Brown and Morty give us a 2–0 win and the perfect start to the new season. We followed that with a home draw in a north-west derby against Preston North End; then in another derby we got the better of Bolton Wanderers by 3–0 and I managed to feature on the scoresheet. We whacked Aston Villa 5–1 at Villa Park but lost at Chelsea. A scintillating spell of form followed – we ran up four straight victories including a 5–2 win at much-fancied Wolves and an 8–4 home win over Charlton Athletic in which Bomber Brown scored a hat-trick, Morty chipped in with a superb opportunist goal and I featured among our other scorers. The excellent sequence of results made our confidence soar and the spirit in the dressing room was sky high. I was hitting a good vein of form, enjoying my football again and the unrest I had experienced just weeks before had totally evaporated.

In October, however, I picked up another injury in a game against Spurs at White Hart Lane. It was a muscle injury, bad enough to keep me out of the side until 10 January when I returned for our third round FA Cup tie at Sheffield Wednesday. Despite spending two and a half months on the sidelines, my spirits remained buoyant. There was the frustration of not being a part of the team and the annoyance that injury had once again beset me, but at no time did I feel down. I just couldn't wait to be fit again and take my place once more in a team that was playing so well.

The FA Cup had real status in the fifties. For a start, it was the only opportunity for the majority of players to tread the famous Wembley turf. There were no play-off matches in those days. No club would ever dream of hiring the stadium to stage big games and there were no other cup competitions for league clubs that offered the opportunity of a Wembley appearance. The FA Cup final was the only fixture when league clubs could grace the famous stadium and, as it involved only two clubs, the competition took on all the importance of football's Holy Grail.

Although I'm all for the opportunities given today for clubs to appear at Wembley in play-offs or in the finals of subsidiary cup competitions, the fact that the stadium has lost its exclusive tag has, I feel, served to diminish its magical quality. To reach an FA Cup final in years gone by was not only a tremendous achievement in itself. The bonus for players and supporters alike was in savouring the rare opportunity of going to a stadium that was known to have a unique atmosphere, history seeping out of every brick. The fact that Wembley, as well as proffering glory, had also inflicted self-immolation on even the greatest of players, and that it would be heaven and hell on the same day for the two teams and their supporters, only added to its magical allure. In short, Wembley was seen as being very special. Only those whose efforts and skills had been of a sufficiently high standard to warrant the honour could display them on its hallowed turf. Winning the FA Cup was eminently more glamorous than being crowned Football League Champions.

Sheffield Wednesday was not only a tough comeback game for me, but a difficult FA Cup tie for the team as a whole. In Redfern Froggatt, Albert Quixall, Derek Dooley, Jackie Sewell – the world's most costly player at the time – Norman Curtis and Cyril Turton, Wednesday had players of real class. They were seen as very difficult opponents, especially on their home ground.

'It mustn't happen again,' Joe Smith told us before the match, referring not only to our previous meeting that season at Bloomfield Road when Wednesday had beaten us 1–0, but also to the past heartache the FA Cup had caused me.

'It's a tricky tie,' Joe said, 'but if we are going to go all the way and win it this year, someone has to beat the fancied teams and if we are to be worthy winners, it will have to be us.'

We stayed at Buxton for a few days prior to the match but I didn't join the squad. I was in Manchester having treatment for the muscular injury that had kept me on the sidelines. The treatment was precautionary. I had high hopes of being fit enough to play against Wednesday and following the remedial treatment, journeyed back to Bloomfield Road for a rigorous workout and fitness test. There were no problems, so I telephoned our Buxton hotel and told Joe Smith I was fit to play if he wanted me. 'You're in,' was all Joe said.

I was fit but Morty wasn't. His place was taken at centre-forward by Allan Brown. Jackie Mudie was doing his National Service with the RAF and although he was unable to secure his release to join the party in Buxton, he did manage to get a weekend pass, which meant he was available to play in the game itself.

It's funny how you can often remember moments from childhood that seemingly have no significance whatsoever. It's the same with football. For some inexplicable reason I remember the cover of the match programme for this game. It featured a picture of Wednesday's free-scoring centre-forward Derek Dooley heading goalwards in a game against Cardiff City. I can also recall, as the Blackpool team took to the field, our supporters greeting us with their own version of the song 'Yes, we have no bananas'. They had adapted it to incorporate my name and Morty's, Bill Perry's and Bomber's. It went along the lines of 'Yes, we have some foot-ballers', ending with 'And yes, we'll see you at Wem-blee. We'll see you at Wembley this year!'

Over 60,000 turned up to see the game. By four o'clock – kick-off 2.15 p.m., no floodlights – our campaign was still on course but Wednesday's wasn't. The match was played in atrocious conditions. Rain gave way to fog and the visibility was so poor the referee, Mr Jackson from Leeds, called for a white ball, which was a rarity in those days.

On 43 minutes we won a free kick. Ernie Taylor lofted the ball into the Wednesday penalty area where their keeper Ron Capewell, under pressure from Jackie Mudie, Bomber and his own defenders, could only punch the ball away. It fell to me. Seeing a gap beyond the cluster of Blackpool and Wednesday players struggling to get back to their feet, I simply lobbed the ball back over their heads. It sailed into the net just under the bar.

At the start of the second half, the fog was if anything worse, but a slight breeze got up and after 20 minutes or so, it cleared. On 74 minutes, however, Wednesday were level. Derek Dooley rose majestically to head a corner from Albert Quixall against our crossbar and before any of us could react, Jackie Sewell headed in the rebound.

With two minutes left a replay looked on the cards. Bomber had drifted on to the right wing near me and when I received a pass from George McKnight, I made as if to cut inside but flicked the ball back out on to the wing. Bomber took off towards the byline and sent over a beautiful cross in the direction of Bill Perry. Perhaps Bill was in two minds whether to head towards goal or lay it off. When Bill jumped, I thought he was setting himself up for a header at goal but he seemed to think better of it, twisted his body and headed back in the direction of Ernie Taylor. It caught Ernie with his back to goal, but he did his best impression of a spinning cotton spindle, in a flash was facing the goal and lashed a textbook volley into the roof of the net. Pockets of the large crowd frothed and bubbled with tangerine and white as the travelling Blackpool supporters went wild.

In a desperate attempt to claw back the game, Wednesday pushed ten men forward from the restart but although Derek Dooley fizzed a shot past George Farm's right-hand post, we held firm.

The post-match press reports were full of praise for our performance. I was singled out for special mention, though I felt it was undeserved. Bomber had been terrific. He had led the line well and his unselfish play had created opportunities for others. Harry Johnston was rock solid in a defence that had played extremely well and in Ernie Taylor and Jackie Mudie we'd had two gremlins as far as the Wednesday rearguard were concerned. Bill Perry was starting to repay the faith Joe Smith had shown in him and when Wednesday did create chances, they found George Farm in scintillating form in goal. It was a fine team performance in which every player had come up trumps.

Before the game I had indulged in a little kiddums of my own. Although I was convinced of my fitness, the newspapers had serious doubts about whether, after my long lay-off I could get through 90 minutes of what was expected to be, and was, a gruelling Cup tie. I was up against Norman Curtis whose ploy in past meetings had been to stick to me like glue from start to finish. I knew Harry Johnston was quite pally with Wednesday's Redfern Froggatt so, with this in mind, prior to the game I told Harry to pop into the Wednesday dressing room and tell Redfern that I was nowhere near fit and shouldn't be playing. Harry did just that, supposedly confiding in Redfern his concern about Joe Smith playing me after such a long lay-off.

'It's a crying shame,' Harry told Redfern. 'Stan can hardly walk, never mind run. He shouldn't be playing but Joe thinks of him as a bit of a talisman and that even an unfit Matthews on the pitch will inspire us, when you and I know that's codswallop. But Joe is the manager, so what can you say?'

It worked a treat. From the start, Curtis left me alone and concentrated on making himself available for Wednesday attacks. When such attacks broke down, the ball was quickly played to me and off I danced to my merry little tune.

Blackpool drew Huddersfield Town at home in the fourth round. Allan Brown continued at centre-forward in place of Morty. Huddersfield were in the Second Division but ended the season being promoted. Up to our FA Cup tie, they had conceded just six goals at home all season and were free scoring on their travels, which led me to believe they would be difficult opponents. I wasn't wrong.

Once again, we prepared in Buxton. We played a lot of five-a-sides and, to keep spirits up, Joe Smith even took us along to the local swimming baths where we were encouraged to play games of water polo and generally have fun.

On the Friday before the match, we travelled back to Blackpool but were not allowed home. We were booked into the Norbreck Hydro Hotel and, to our surprise, found Huddersfield Town were staying there as well. Probably because of this, on the Friday night Joe Smith said he was going to 'get us out of the hotel' and take us all to the cinema, though when we got there, in true Joe Smith fashion, we found we were paying for ourselves. It wasn't an issue, just another vehicle for Morty's humour who said on seeing Ernie Taylor and Jackie Mudie seated either side of the boss, 'Joe will have got them in at half price just so he can get them to buy his ice cream and Kiaora orange in the interval.'

On Saturday a gale was blowing in from the west and proceeded to deposit what seemed like most of the Irish sea on Blackpool prior to kick-off. Nevertheless, 30,000 people braved the watery and windy elements and were treated to an intense and pulsating Cup tie. Huddersfield kicked off with the wind at their backs and such was the pressure we were placed under I spent most of the first half helping out in defence, a rarity for me which prompted Eddie Shimwell at one point to say, 'Stan, you're playing so deep, be careful you don't end up with the bends.'

Having survived Huddersfield's first-half pressure, we spun the game around in the second half and laid siege to their goal. The terrible conditions made for some desperate defending but to their credit Huddersfield held out until the 83rd minute. Some 40 yards from goal, Tommy Garrett hit a speculative shot high in the air. To be honest, it seemed like a hopeful punt destined for the massed ranks of the Spion

Kop behind the Huddersfield goal but the wind got hold of it and the ball swerved and veered around in the mirk before dipping over goalkeeper Jack Wheeler's head and into the net. The game had been dominated by the two defences and if there was to be a goal in it, I always felt it would have to be something very special or else one that came as result of the conditions. Tommy Garrett was adamant afterwards that he meant his effort, though his proclamations had more than a touch of tongue in cheek about them.

Round five pitched us against Southampton who at the time were struggling near the foot of Division Two. We met them on Valentine's day but there was little in the way of love between the two teams. The newspapers had this one down as being our easiest tie to date, but Southampton, with only two away wins to their credit, belied their lowly league status and gave us a very difficult match.

Joe Smith was keen to continue the FA Cup pre-match preparation so we set off again for our hideaway hotel in Buxton. As it turned out, it was more hidden away than ever before. During the journey to Derbyshire, the north of England was swept by a blizzard and our coach driver had great difficulty in negotiating the roads. The last few miles into Buxton took us about two hours and when we finally did arrive I wondered how beneficial this break was going to be. The thick snow meant training in the grounds of the hotel was not possible, and with snowflakes the size of Royal Doulton dinner plates coming down thick and fast, Buxton was in danger of being cut off. Desperate to find us something to do, and with a perverse sense of irony, Joe took the players to Buxton ice rink, which, as you may imagine, prompted numerous comments from the players.

'Two bob to come here just to slither about then fall flat on our backsides,' said Harry Johnston. 'We could be doing the same on the hotel's drive and it would be costing us nowt!'

The following day, with the snow having stopped but the forecast promising more, news reached us that a snowplough had managed to clear the track on the railway line between Buxton and Manchester. Joe Smith immediately ordered us to pack our bags and check out, and within 15 minutes 13 players were sliding and slipping their way along the icy streets of the town in the general direction of Buxton station. We arrived at our Blackpool base, the Norbreck Hydro, two days earlier than expected, happy to have left Buxton's Christmas card scene behind us and immediately set about catching up on our training.

Come the day of the game, a light frost had descended on Blackpool but by noon it had vanished. The Bloomfield Road pitch was firm but very playable.

Southampton proved a difficult nut to crack. At half-time with the score at 0–0 it was anybody's game and the second half seesawed as both teams went in search of the all-important breakthrough. It came our way on 63 minutes. There seemed little danger for Southampton when Johnny Crosland sent a hopeful, cynics might say aimless, ball down the middle of the pitch. Bill Perry gave chase but the Southampton goalkeeper John Christie seemed odds-on favourite to reach it first. What followed was what sports writers like to describe as 'a defensive mix-up', managers bemoan as a 'lack of communication' and supporters, well at least those there that day, call 'an almighty cock-up'. A Southampton defender came across and in attempting to clear the ball succeeded in colliding with Christie. Bill's persistence paid off. Unable to avoid the two prostrate Southampton players, he collided with them but the loose ball broke at his feet, he stretched out a leg and hooked it towards goal. The ball had little in the way of momentum behind it and seemed to take an age as it agonisingly bounced and bobbled goalwards. The Blackpool fans behind the goal watched on tenterhooks, uncharacteristically silent; they drew a collective breath as it neared the goal giving the impression they were trying to suck it over the line. With the whole of Bloomfield Road hushed and all eyes focused on Bill's snailpace shot, the ball eventually trickled over the line and came to rest just three or four inches into the goal. A terrific roar ripped around the ground as the Blackpool supporters gave vent to their nervous tension and I joined my team-mates in backslapping Bill.

It was what the newspapers called 'a scrappy goal'. In many ways, they were right but as Bill said after the game, 'They count just the same as a 35-yard thunderbolt,' and of course, he was also right.

It wasn't our style to kill the game and sit on our lead, so we pressed forward in search of a second goal to put the issue beyond doubt. Harry Johnston once told Archie Ledbrooke, a sports reporter with the now defunct *Sunday Graphic*, 'When we have scored one goal, we are never satisfied. We go looking for a second. When we have got that, we're still not satisfied. We can't sit back and defend, it's not our way. So we push on looking for a third and more often than not we get it. That's why we lose a lot of games 4–3!'

There was more than a grain of truth in his light-hearted response to Archie's question about our style of play. Having taken the lead, we took the game to Southampton only for them, with six minutes remaining, to equalise through a bullet of a header by their centre-half Henry Horton from a Peter Sillett free kick.

Although we had not lost, we had failed to beat a side struggling to preserve their Second Division status and that resulted in a very despondent Blackpool dressing room after the match. What's more, the way Southampton had equipped and applied themselves made me think we were in for a very tough game at the Dell.

Blackpool supporters, though obviously disappointed, quickly rallied to our cause. Blackpool received around 800 tickets for the replay, scheduled for the following Wednesday afternoon. Every ticket was snapped up within hours of going on sale and come the day several 'football specials' left from Central station, jam-packed with tangerine and white bedecked supporters. A number of supporters took the unprecedented step of flying to the replay, taking advantage of a special package deal on offer from the club in association with the Lancashire Aircraft Corporation. Six planes took off from Blackpool Airport and if my memory serves me well, the cost was £8 10s. (£8.50), a princely sum for the time, even though it included ham and tomato sandwiches for the journey! It shows how forward-thinking Blackpool were in those days, as befitted a club which at the time enjoyed the sort of status in football that Manchester United and Arsenal enjoy today.

It may seem odd that the game was played on a Wednesday afternoon but before the introduction of floodlights such a fixture arrangement was the norm. Many shops had half-day closing on Wednesdays and those still tied to work either swapped shifts or came up with some excuse to be off on the afternoon of a match. The most common was to attend the funeral of a relative. That provided numerous jokes for the comedians of the day, including my old pal Tom Moss whose forte was to turn such gags on their head when Blackpool weren't playing well by saying such things as, 'Stan, can I be excused from going to the match this afternoon? My grandmother has died – again!'

Wednesday afternoon it may have been, but the Dell was packed to capacity and from our point of view I can describe the game in three words – we were lucky. Southampton took the lead in the first half and nothing seemed to go right for me. The Southampton left-back Peter Sillett played me very well and I struggled to make any impact at all upon the game. At half-time Joe Smith told us, 'The team that wins the FA Cup is the one whose players have the biggest hearts. Come on! This is not a game for fancy footwork and party pieces. We've got to roll our sleeves up and fight. We've played poorly so far, but we all have the ambition to win and ambition never looks back. So put the first half out of your minds, get out there and work, work, work to pull this one off.'

As we took to the pitch I got hold of Harry Johnston and said, 'Skipper, I'm not getting any room. I'm going to roam about this half, is that OK?' Harry still made those decisions rather than Joe. I felt we had to do something different; our pattern of play was predictable in the first half and when that happens, you have to change your gameplan. Harry didn't give it a second thought. He told me to do it and as luck would have it, it paid off.

Free from the attentions of Sillett, I prodded and probed from midfield, went on runs on both wings and managed to pull the Southampton defence about so that they lost their shape and composure. From the off, my roaming seemed to unnerve them and not long after the restart we had not only equalised but scored a second to give us the lead. Bill Perry took the credit for our equalising goal. With a typical burst of speed, he panicked the Southampton defence and from his cut-back ball, home centre-half Henry Horton sliced the ball into his own goal. Two minutes later, with Southampton still reeling from our equaliser, I linked with Bill, Jackie Mudie and Ernie Taylor to create a chance for Bomber. When the ball was eventually played into his path, he hit one of his master blaster efforts into the roof of the net from just inside the penalty area. It knocked the stuffing out of Southampton and, with the home crowd subdued, we tightened our grip on the game to, if not exactly cruise, then steer a steady course through choppy waters and into round six.

During our Cup run, we managed to maintain reasonable form in the league. Without ever putting real pressure on Arsenal, Preston, Wolves and West Brom, who were embroiled in a dramatic fight for the title that went to the final day of the season, we did enough to keep in touch of the leading pack, yo-yoing between fifth and seventh position. At times, we were only three or four points adrift of the top spot. It all made for an exciting and enjoyable season. Arsenal were still *the* team to beat in the league and their consistent form meant they were the bookies' favourites for the FA Cup, so there were groans all round when listening to the draw on the wireless we heard we had drawn them at Highbury in the sixth round.

The only team to have reached round six from outside the top flight was Gateshead. Everyone wanted them at home but the little north-east club drew Bolton Wanderers at their Redheugh Park ground. Far from being given a favourable tie the general feeling among the players was that we had the toughest draw. For my part, I was more than happy. I was always on my mettle, irrespective of the opposition and size of the crowd, but a full house of 70,000 at Highbury was the ideal draw as far as I was concerned. I loved a big stage on which to display my skills and derived great satisfaction from pitting my ability against the very best players in the game. In the likes of Jack Kelsey, Alex Forbes, Ray Daniel, Joe Mercer, Jimmy Logie, Arthur Milton, Don Roper, Cliff Holton and Doug Lishman, Arsenal possessed players of real quality, the majority of whom were top internationals. Oh yes, Arsenal suited me down to my streamlined, lightweight size sevens.

On the Monday before the Cup-tie, we were in London for a league game at the Valley against Charlton Athletic. We lost 2–0 but the real downside was an injury to centre-half Johnny Crosland, who pulled a thigh muscle.

Jackie Mudie was still managing to play for Blackpool while at the same time fitting in representative games for the RAF as part of his National Service; two days before playing for us against Arsenal, Jackie played for the RAF against London University. It meant our sixth round tie against the Cup favourites was to be Jackie's seventh game in a fortnight – another example of the number of matches played even then.

We didn't prepare for the Arsenal match by going to Buxton; instead, Joe Smith took us a few miles up the road from Blackpool to St Annes. It was hardly away from it all, especially as it was only a brisk walk from my hotel. We took to the waters, such as they were, in the form of the brine baths in Lytham, trained on the sands and in the evenings played table tennis. A number of players added spice to the games by entering into little wagers on the outcome. The camaraderie and spirit among the team was high and when Morty joined us with the news that the specialist had informed him he would be fit to play again in two weeks, Joe Smith's joy knew no bounds. He went completely overboard and bought us half a shandy each. 'I don't know whether I should drink it or have it preserved in a glass case,' said Harry Johnston. 'Either way, I think we ought to get in touch with Valentine Dyall' – a reference to the popular radio personality of the day who presented amazing stories of mystery and the unexpected.

Joe wasn't as mean as the lads liked to make out, though he did know how to work the system and was not very forthcoming when it came to money for the players. At the start of the season, every player was given £2 10s. to cover the cost of a new pair of boots. On learning that everyone else had received their boot money, I knocked on Joe's door.

'What do you want boot money for?' he asked, tetchily.
'You don't pay for your boots, you get them for nowt from
the Co-op.'

I explained that I had to pay to have my special boots
made at their factory out of my own pocket.

'That's as maybe,' he said, 'but more often than not all
you do is slip the foreman at the factory a box of fags.'

I didn't have a clue how he knew about that. I told him I
still had to fork out for the cigarettes.

'Wholesale price, not cost. You get them via Harry
Johnston's newsagent and tobacconist shop.'

Again he took me aback. How on earth did he know
about that?

'You're getting twenty quid a week from the Co-op, more
than anyone earns here, including yourself. That's more than
enough to cover the cost of a single pair of boots.'

In the end, I had to refer to the fact that the boot money
was written into my contract and had been since the day I
signed for Blackpool.

'Whose daft idea was that?' Joe asked.

'Yours,' I told him.

So he agreed to pay me the £2 10s. saying, 'You've diddled
me again, Stan.'

As I left the room I thought about what he knew about
my arrangement with the Co-op and in particular with the
factory foreman.

'Is there anything you don't know about me, Boss?' I
asked.

'Only one thing. How at your age you still manage to be a
world-class player and run rings round players half your age,'
said Joe, smiling. 'Dunno how you do it, I'm just glad that
you do.'

As I closed the door, I was smiling, too, especially when I
heard him shout after me.

'Having new boots won't make you play any better, you know!'

We set off for London from Central station on the Friday morning. Reserve-team player Dave Frith, who had deputised well for right-back Eddie Shimwell when Eddie was injured, travelled with us. Harry Johnston was to replace Johnny Crosland at centre-half with Ewan Fenton taking over at right-half from Harry in the only change from the team that had beaten Southampton.

We stayed at a hotel in Southampton Row and that evening went to see the Crazy Gang, featuring Bud Flanagan and Chesney Allen, regale a packed theatre with their own brand of offbeat humour and fine singing.

On the morning of the match, we went for a short stroll around the streets leading off from our hotel before taking a light lunch and heading off for Highbury. The streets around N5 were chock-a-block with supporters as our coach made its cautious way to the stadium. On arriving we learned that the 5s. (25p) and 6s. (30p) turnstiles had been closed at one o'clock and that thousands of fans were going to be disappointed. All-ticket games were rare at the time and I remember feeling sorry for the many Blackpool fans who had made the overnight journey and would arrive at Highbury to find the ground full. The only recourse was the spivs who, I was told, were asking £5 for a 12s. 6d (62p) ticket for the seats in the stand.

You only had to look at the match programme to know that Arsenal were a cut above the rest. Most match programmes of the day comprised some eight pages all told, rarely contained photographs and, apart from the all-important team line-ups, consisted of pen pictures of the opposition, a note from the home-team manager and the current state of the fixture list and league table. Arsenal's programme by comparison was stylish and informative, running to 16 often 20 pages. It contained pictures of their last game as well as of the opposition, guest articles from leading sports writers and not a single advert. The club's directors, like those of Tottenham Hotspur, believed it was undignified to carry commercial messages in a programme that was seen as the official voice of the club. Times have changed!

In the FA Cup at this time, when there was a colour clash, both sides played in their second strips. We wore white shirts and black shorts. Arsenal's second strip was normally yellow shirts and white shorts but they took the field in black and white striped shirts and white shorts. I had never seen Arsenal play in such a strip and never saw them wear those colours again. Perhaps this was the only occasion in their history when the Gunners wore shirts akin to those of Newcastle United.

Highbury was heaving. Huge rafts of fans swayed at the Clock End like massed poppy heads in the wind as we kicked off with a watery thin sunshine in our eyes. The first half was tight. From the off, Lionel Smith and Joe Mercer were keeping close tabs on me so I started to roam as I did in the previous round against Southampton, at one stage swapping wings with Bill Perry.

Irrespective of which wing I took to, the Arsenal defenders tried to position themselves to jockey me inside. As a winger, you don't want this to happen. Your aim is to get down the flank to the byline where you can pull the ball back or make a telling cross. By allowing defenders to jockey you inside, although you're heading towards goal, you are also going into the area of the pitch that is the most congested. Invariably it means you run into trouble and your chances of making a telling pass that will cause the opposition problems are nowhere near as great as they are if you can feed the ball from a wide position where you have room to manoeuvre.

There was nothing to choose between the two sides when the half-time whistle blew but straight from the restart Arsenal proceeded to put us under a great deal of pressure. We weathered the storm and spurred on by Harry Johnston, took the game to them, winning a succession of corners. I continued with my roaming, but wherever I went three, sometimes four, Arsenal players converged on me whenever I received the ball and it was all I could do to keep possession never mind set up a chance for our forwards. Such close attention meant I often had no option but to play a simple ball back to Eddie Shimwell or Ewan Fenton in the hope that they could work something by exploiting gaps left by the players I had drawn around me. It wasn't constructive football on my part, but I was content to do it because it meant we kept possession of the ball and while we had it, Arsenal couldn't inflict any damage on us.

With 13 minutes remaining, we made the breakthrough. Bomber won the ball on the halfway line and rode a couple of tackles as he made good progress down the middle before looking up to see little Ernie Taylor alongside him to his left. Bomber rolled a beautifully weighted ball for Ernie to run on to. For all his slight build, Ernie could really connect with a ball. He hit it first time on the run and sent a seering shot wide of Arsenal's goalkeeper Jack Kelsey. The net ballooned and the stanchions juddered as if an elephant had just leaned against them. Seconds later Ernie disappeared under a mound of white shirts as we gleefully offered our congratulations.

With the clock against them, Arsenal stepped up a gear and we found ourselves on the back foot, but I felt we would hold out. However, Arsenal's pressure paid off for them and they equalised with a goal that would definitely not be allowed today but was perfectly legitimate at the time.

The Arsenal right-back Joe Wade hit a long ball into our

penalty area that had more than an air of desperation about it. George Farm with plenty of time to weigh it up came off his line and collected it, hugging the ball safely into his chest. There seemed to be no danger but just as George's feet touched the ground, two Arsenal players charged into him as if he was a rugby full-back under his own posts taking a garryowen. George was sent flying and the ball broke from his grasp. Hurtling backwards, he made a valiant effort to twist his body and reclaim the ball with an outstretched hand but it fell to Jimmy Logie who lashed it into our net. Highbury erupted. We didn't complain. Such challenges were part and parcel of the game at the time. I stood with my hands on my hips, not wanting to believe what had happened. I glanced up at the clock situated to the rear of the massed terracing. It told me there were just under five minutes of the game remaining. To have victory snatched from your grasp at such a late stage in a match is always a bitter disappointment, but we were still in the Cup and, although time was running out, still very much in this game. After all, I reasoned, it only takes a second to score a goal.

From the kick-off we went on the attack. I received the ball on the right and was suddenly aware of Jackie Mudie coming around me from my rear and overlapping down the flank. I rolled a simple pass into his path, Jackie kept going and played a low ball into the Arsenal penalty area. It was one of those balls that is very difficult to defend. The Arsenal rearguard turned to face their own goal, with the ball having been played in behind them. Kelsey came diving out to collect but seemingly from nowhere, there was Bomber. Kelsey's momentum carried him straight into Bomber's legs but despite being poleaxed Bomber managed to get the all-important touch. As the ball skidded towards the empty Arsenal net, Bomber suddenly lurched forward, his large frame skidding across the greasy turf. When he eventually stopped, he didn't move. We raised our arms in celebration. It was the perfect retort to Arsenal's equaliser. Within a minute of them scoring, we were back in front, but our celebrations were over almost before they had begun. You can always tell when a player is badly injured because he doesn't roll around on the pitch. Today, players may roll about in a melodramatic way after a challenge, but then players never turned on the dramatics even after a heavy tackle because they knew they would be the subject of much derision from team-mates and spectators alike. It was immediately apparent to us all that Bomber had sustained a bad injury. He was as strong as a bull, nothing fazed him, but having scored the all-important goal, he didn't even raise an arm to acknowledge the cheers of the Blackpool supporters. He simply lay motionless.

The game was held up for some time and Bomber was eventually lifted on to a stretcher and taken from the field. To their credit, the Arsenal fans broke into spontaneous applause, partly to acknowledge the efforts of the two trainers and the St John Ambulance men who had attended to Bomber, partly to acknowledge his efforts in the game. Down to ten men, we held out for those remaining few minutes to secure a famous Cup win.

I shook hands with the Arsenal players and referee Arthur Luty from Leeds who'd had a superb game. Apart from the injury to Bomber, I'd hardly noticed Luty was on the pitch, which is always the hallmark of a top-class official. The exhilaration of winning was completely diluted when we entered the dressing room to be told that Bomber had fractured his left leg just below the knee.

Bomber's goal was typically brave but he paid a high price for his courageousness. We had made it to the semi-final, one game away from another Cup final appearance but Bomber wouldn't make it to Wembley, even if we did. There had been no outstanding individual performances in the game as far as we were concerned. Victory had been gained through good solid teamwork and, of course, the bravery of Bomber Brown. On the train journey home, skipper Harry Johnston said, 'If I had known what the consequence would be of Bomber's challenge, I would rather he had ducked out and settled for a replay.' That sentiment gained wholehearted agreement from all of us, but I doubt whether Bomber would have gone along with it.

We met Tottenham Hotspur at Villa Park in the semi-final on 21 March. The only downside to the run-in to this game was the miserly ticket allocation for Blackpool and Spurs supporters. Was it ever thus? Both clubs received an allocation of 20,000 tickets. Given the capacity was 68,221, that meant that just over a third of the tickets were finding their way to heaven knows who. I can never understand it, especially for semi-finals which to all intents and purposes are private parties for the two clubs concerned. The ticket allocation was nowhere near our average home attendance and certainly not anywhere near that of Spurs. White Hart Lane averaged over 44,000 for every home game. The spivs, who would sell you tickets for the end of the world if such an event was ever to happen, had a field day.

We trained at Bloomfield Road in the week leading up to the semi-final, leaving Blackpool on the Thursday morning for a hotel on the outskirts of Leamington Spa. The team posed for a photograph alongside the team coach as we prepared to leave Bloomfield Road. The only person missing from the line-up is me because I had to answer the call of nature and by the time I rejoined the group, the photograph had been taken and the photographer gone. So much for so-called star status!

On the day of the game, given the ticket allocations, the spivs raked it in at the expense of the genuine supporters of both clubs. It annoyed me that those who organised our game projected an image as pious guardians of football, totally against black market tickets, yet their very actions helped the spivs our FA claimed were a cancer on the game.

As far as team selection for this game was concerned, a fit again Stan Mortensen replaced Bomber Brown in the only change to the side that had beaten Arsenal. From the start, Spurs displayed their intent, launching wave after wave of attack but it was us who managed to get into the driving seat. The game was only seven minutes old when Ernie Taylor won a corner on our right. As I prepared to take the corner, I was, of course, looking for Morty but saw he was tightly marked. I suddenly noticed that Bill Perry had drifted in from the left wing and taken up a good position to the left just beyond the penalty spot. With corners I did one of two things – float the ball into the area or drive it. I decided to drive this one hard in the direction of Bill who made ground before rising virtually unchallenged to send in a header that crashed down into the net off the underside of the bar. It was a collector's item. In all the games I had played with Bill, I rarely saw him have an effort at goal with his head. However, he put this one away with all the confidence and technique of Tommy Lawton which left me wondering why the heck he hadn't done it more often.

Spurs continued to attack as the second half got under way, but we had our moments. I was linking well with Ernie Taylor and we created a number of openings without succeeding in adding to our solitary goal, but the fact that we were creating chances encouraged me. The second half was only five minutes old, however, when Spurs got their equaliser.

The Spurs inside-right Les Bennett sent in a low cross from their right wing. Eddie Baily met the ball but very cleverly stepped over it and let it run. It totally wrong-footed our defence and as they struggled to recover, Len Duquemin swept the ball past George Farm. Game on.

That goal lifted Spurs and they came at us in no uncertain fashion. For a time it was a case of all hands to the pump but having survived their onslaught we began to play ourselves back into what at this stage was developing into an absorbing encounter and classic Cup tie. For half an hour the game seesawed as play lurched from one end of the field to the other. No sooner did we break down a Spurs attack than we ourselves went on the offensive, only for them to break us down and regain the initiative. From its cagey start, the game had gradually become flowing and intoxicating but for all the gusto and zest displayed, the quality of football remained high and had a packed Villa Park roaring their approval. Both teams were intrepid. With Wembley just one step away, we went in search of the goal that would do it. There are occasions when a game of such import enters its final moments and you sense both teams are ready to settle for a draw. It is as if they have mentally agreed to live to fight another day rather than for either to have the heartache of losing out in the final stage. It wasn't the case in this game. Referee Arthur Ellis was checking his watch but we were still going at it hammer and tongs. For all the continued endeavour, I thought we were destined for a replay but suddenly, out of the blue, we scored.

Alf Ramsey, who'd had a superb game in the Spurs defence, beat Bill Perry and Jackie Mudie in a race for a loose ball. Hindsight is a wonderful thing, but from Alf's point of view he should have sent the ball into the crowd. As Joe Smith used to tell us, 'When in doubt, put it out. I've been in football for thirty-odd years and in all that time, I've never seen a goal scored from Row G.' Perhaps if it had been earlier in the match Alf would have opted for safety first and sent the ball into the terraces. But the game was in its final minute, tiredness was taking over, and perhaps he wasn't thinking as clearly as he normally would. Whatever the reason was, Alf decided to push the ball back to his goalkeeper Ted Ditchburn. Sensing an opportunity, Jackie Mudie struck like a viper. He took to his toes, sprinted past Alf who had ground to a halt and within moments had the ball at his feet and the Spurs goal in his sights. Realising the possible disastrous consequences of his action, Alf tried to recover but Jackie was away before he was out of the starting blocks. There's a golden rule when you have the ball at your feet and you're confronted with a one on one situation and that is 'over him or round him, but not through him'. Ditchburn spread himself well in an attempt to give Jackie as little view as possible of the goal, but Jackie coolly slipped the ball round Ted Ditchburn's spreadeagled body and we were Wembley bound.

The travelling Blackpool supporters went berserk. In the days before the segregation of fans, on the heaving brownish grey terraces huge pockets of tangerine and white exploded like marigolds suddenly coming into bloom. Jackie Mudie disappeared from view as the entire Blackpool team, with the exception of George Farm, descended on his back. Out there on the Villa Park pitch under a charcoal grey sky in the heart of Birmingham, we had suddenly found Elysium. THROUGH – BUT PHEW! ran one newspaper headline, wonderfully encapsulating our victory with an economy of words.

After the game, I made time for a few words with Alf Ramsey, who was understandably very down. Alf later said that the greatest game he was ever involved in was not as manager of England when we won the World Cup in 1966, but this semi-final. 'It contained everything a great game of football should contain,' he said. 'Twenty-two talented players playing to the very limits of their considerable abilities, displaying artistry, craft, stamina and strength in equal and bountiful measure to produce football at its very best. For all we lost and the fact our defeat was in no small way down to a mistake of mine, it was the finest game of football I was ever involved in.' Alf, forever the gentleman, went on to add, 'On that day, I didn't have the problem of playing against Stan Matthews, I had the honour of being taken to the cleaners by him.'

I can't go along with such words, especially as for most of the game he was up against Bill Perry while I was on the opposite wing. I mention it simply to illustrate what sort of man Alf was. Even in defeat, he retained dignity, grace and an overwhelming respect for the opposition and their efforts; a chivalrous man if ever there was one. Later in life, he never really received the accolades due to him for leading English football to its finest hour.

18

---◆ o ◆---

Cup Fever in
Blackpool

As usual, there was a lengthy wait from the FA Cup semi-final to the day of the final itself. As before, we had nine league games to play over a six-week period and while every player is worried about picking up an injury that may result in him missing out on the big day, the knowledge that an FA Cup final appearance beckons makes for a happy end of season. Allan Brown of course was to miss out. Left-half Hughie Kelly was also injured, during our 3–1 league win over Liverpool. Hughie's place was to be taken in the final by reserve-team player Cyril Robinson. Although he had been with us for four years, Cyril had played only two games that season due to our good form and the stiff competition for places in the half-back line. Two other players unlucky not to be named in the line-up for Wembley were Johnny Crosland and Jackie Wright. They were travelling reserves and as such would miss out on a medal of any sort after having come into the side at various times during the season and given sterling performances.

I always enjoyed the run-in to a season, knowing that I had English football's biggest day out to look forward to. For a few weeks at any rate, the pressure of having to play another big Cup tie is removed. You're there; that's all that matters to players, club and supporters alike. You bask in the glory of being one of the two teams to have made it to the final of the world's oldest and greatest club cup competition. You don't worry about the day itself – that will come soon enough, time enough to worry then. It is a great time to be a footballer and I loved every minute of it.

The 1952–53 season ended with Arsenal clinching the Division One Championship for a then record seventh time. They won it on a Friday night, beating Burnley to overtake Preston North End who had already finished their season. Arsenal's 3–2 win gave them the championship on goal average as both they and Preston had finished on 54 points, with Wolves on 51 points in third place and West Bromwich Albion fourth on 50. Arsenal notched up a highly commendable 97 goals in their 42 league matches, indicative of the all-out attacking style of play in vogue at the time. No fewer than nine First Division teams clocked up 70-plus goals in the season including Manchester City who rattled in 72 yet still finished only one place above Stoke City and Derby County. They were both relegated.

It saddened me that what had been a great season for me at Blackpool turned out to be a disastrous one for Stoke City, which proved to me that my heart was still there with my home-town club. If I had returned to Stoke, I would now be faced with the prospect of Second Division football. If it had not been for Joe Smith's intervention, I probably would have gone back to the Victoria Ground. Who knows if my presence could have made a difference to their fortunes. I doubted it. One or two of my former team-mates such as Frank Mountford, Harry Oscroft, Johnny McCue and Jock Kirton were still there but with the exception of McCue they were ageing and the new players who had been introduced, with all due respect, were not of the quality of those they had replaced. I couldn't help thinking that someone or something was looking out for me and channelling me in the direction I had been chosen to go.

The season was tinged with tragedy for Sheffield Wednesday's Derek Dooley who had battled so well against us in the third round of the FA Cup at Hillsborough. Derek broke his right leg against Preston North End in February when, like Allan Brown, he challenged a goalkeeper for a fifty-fifty ball. Unfortunately, gangrene set in and Derek's right leg had to be amputated. In Wednesday's promotion season the year before, he had scored 46 goals in only 30 games. Not the most elegant of forwards, he was, however, big and strong. If you can imagine a large fridge-freezer being swung at you from the jib of a crane you have some idea of what it was like to compete against Derek in the air for a high ball. Still only 23, he had scored 16 goals in 29 First Division games up until his accident. I am sure he would have had a highly successful and enterprising career as a player. Derek went on to prove he was not only physically, but mentally and emotionally strong as well. He coped magnificently with his situation, never at any time displaying any form of self-pity. Every time I met him, his cheerful personality and warm disposition never failed to impress me and make me feel better about life in general. Today he is still involved in football as commercial executive at Sheffield United. This is a man whose talents on the pitch were considerable but who has proved he has a lot more besides goalscoring to offer the game of football.

I was determined to make it third time lucky in the Cup final. My experience taught me to take in every moment of the build-up and the day, irrespective of the result, so I could savour it for a lifetime. I have often been asked for advice on how to approach the day by players lucky enough to be about to play in an FA Cup final. It has always been the same – savour and remember everything because it is over all too quickly and you might never get another chance to go back and relive it. I felt I was lucky, damned lucky, to be going back for a third time. I would be 39 next birthday and felt as fit as ever, but the clock was ticking against me. It would probably be a last chance to win the one thing I had set my heart on, an FA Cup winner's medal. Win or lose – and I had it in my head that this time we would win – I was determined to enjoy every moment.

Every player who has appeared in an FA Cup final could, I am sure, write a book just about the build-up and the day. The excitement builds and builds, not only among the players, club officials and supporters but the whole town. Those who had never set foot inside Bloomfield Road and had no interest in football were gripped by Cup fever simply because their town was the focus of national, and to some extent world, attention and they did not want to see it fall flat on its face. The town and its entire population were under the media spotlight and great pride was taken in it. As the day drew closer, shops were adorned in tangerine and white, each one trying to outdo the other. What had started out as a mild inflammation before turning into an enjoyable malady had suddenly developed into high fever, fuelled by the frenetic scramble for tickets.

Concerned that on previous occasions many tickets had found their way into the hands of the spivs, the FA issued a statement which read: 'The Committee had always been aware of the importance of distributing Cup final tickets fairly through authorised channels and of preventing them from falling into the hands of profiteers. Any club or person proved to have sold a ticket at an enhanced price will be debarred from receiving a ticket for at least five years.'

At last it seemed the FA were going to do something about ticket distribution. Genuine supporters were at last to be given a fair deal. You can imagine the despair and outrage when the FA later announced that each club was to receive just 12,000 tickets. The capacity at Wembley was 100,000 which meant the vast majority of tickets, 76,000 of them, were going, well I don't know where but certainly not to genuine supporters of the two finalists. It made my blood boil to think the FA were distributing 76,000 tickets to whom they thought fit, many of whom I knew would attend just that one football match in the year. Tickets would be given to people who weren't even interested in the final and they would find their way into the hands of the spivs who would make a lot of money at the expense of genuine supporters. It made a mockery of the FA's statement about 'the fair and even distribution of tickets' and of wanting to clamp down on ticket touts. It appeared to me that the FA were using the greatest day in our football calendar to ingratiate themselves with the makers and shakers of society and the blazer brigade. Did they not realise that by allocating 76,000 tickets to people not connected with either Blackpool or Bolton Wanderers they were in fact creating a black market and fertile ground for the spivs? I couldn't make my mind up if they were dunderheads or simply didn't care about the genuine supporters who were the lifeblood of the game. Either way it was a totally unacceptable state of affairs. The situation has improved but is still not right today. The FA Cup final while being a showpiece should be a grand day out for the players, officials and supporters of the two clubs concerned and not a beano for the sycophants of the FA. End of story.

The miserly allocation of 12,000 made the scramble for tickets in Blackpool more frenetic and manic. A fortnight after our semi-final victory over Spurs, I called into the club office and was told they had received over 40,000 applications for tickets. Blackpool had a considerable number of season-ticket holders, particularly on the terraces, so it meant many loyal supporters who had committed money up front were going to be disappointed never mind our many regulars who paid on a match-by-match basis at the gate. The applications continued to flood in to such an extent the club had to issue a statement in the *Evening Gazette* asking fans not to send any more. With four weeks to go, the club had over £10,000 to be returned to unsuccessful applicants.

When our ticket allocation finally arrived, the circumstances were like a pantomime. The FA had informed the club that the tickets would be on a certain train due in at North station from Euston. However, when the train arrived, there was no parcel of tickets on board. The story of the missing tickets was picked up by the press who had a field day. 'The Great Cup Final Ticket Mystery', as one newspaper dubbed it, made headline news. The club, if not exactly panicking, was very concerned and after a series of phone calls to the FA was informed there had been a delay in sending out the tickets which would arrive the next day on a train due in at Blackpool Central. The tickets duly arrived and passengers at Central station stood about dumbfounded as a porter wheeled the brown paper package down the platform on a trolley flanked by a bevy of reporters and photographers with cameras trained and flash bulbs popping in the direction of a seemingly mundane brown paper parcel.

More farce ensued when it was discovered that Field Marshal Montgomery of Alamein had, according to one newspaper, pledged his support to Bolton Wanderers. As Monty was a Freeman of Blackpool it caused a right old furore. The Mayor wrote to Montgomery expressing his concern and received a reply from him on notepaper from the White House in Washington. It was to the effect that as he was a Freeman of both Blackpool and Bolton, as well as being President of Portsmouth FC, contrary to reports he would be strictly neutral as far as this FA Cup final was concerned.

As befitted the man all the players looked to for guidance and inspiration, skipper Harry Johnston was elected chairman of the players' organising committee. An appearance in an FA Cup final did not usually result in players being paid any money by the club above or beyond their normal weekly wage, so in the absence of a bonus, the players' committee drummed up cash to be distributed among the squad. I believe the work of these committees was perfectly justified in those days, though I find it hard to justify the fact that they still exist today when many of our top players are millionaires, or at least enjoy a weekly wage into five figures.

Harry organised an FA Cup celebration dance that took place in the Tower Ballroom on 15 April. Around 3,000 people paid 4s. (20p) each to meet the team and enjoy entertainment provided by George Formby, Richard 'Stinker' Murdoch, Norman Evans and Frank Randle, big stars of the day. The music was provided by Reginald Dixon who played the Wurlitzer organ accompanied by the Tower band bedecked in tangerine and white. It was the town's way of saying 'well done'. Everyone thoroughly enjoyed the evening, including me, and I surprised everyone by staying until the end which at 2 a.m. was way past my normal bedtime!

The committee also generated money for the players fund

by negotiating a deal for us to wear Aqua Peers raincoats supplied by King's, a local gents outfitters situated in Church Street. Whenever we attended a function or fund-raiser we were obligated to wear the raincoats. The fact that the duration of the deal coincided with a spell of dry weather was neither here nor there. I did wonder what comments we provoked when those around us were in shirts and sports jackets and we stood about in belted raincoats.

How on earth our supporters managed to track down a good proportion of the 76,000 floating tickets I do not know, nor what they paid for them, but come the day, over twice as many people as the official ticket allocation made their way down to Wembley to guarantee we were going to have great support on the day. By way of consolation for those supporters unable to get their hands on a ticket, the BBC announced that this final was to be televised in its entirety. Not many people had TV sets, but that announcement ensured sales soared overnight in Blackpool and I dare say Bolton as well.

The fact that it was a derby match was overshadowed by the human interest story concerning my appearance in the final. I never realised that, after my two unsuccessful attempts, there were so many people who wanted me to win an FA Cup winner's medal. I later learned that practically the whole nation wanted Blackpool to win just so I could collect the medal I had wanted for so long. To this day I am still deeply moved by the affection shown to me by so many people but I have to emphasise that at the time I was not fully aware of its true extent. Many people wanted me to win because they thought at 38 I'd never get another chance.

We left Blackpool on the Friday morning on the ten o'clock train bound for Euston. Harry Johnston stood on the platform and gave a statement to a reporter from the *Evening Gazette*, simple and to the point – 'it's been a hard journey, make no mistake about that. No club reaches the final without a struggle. But now that we're there, rest assured, to a man, we'll give it everything we've got.' In a scene reminiscent of *Brief Encounter*, Harry boarded the train, enveloped in steam, and left the reporter standing on a platform that due to the constant residue of steam seemed to be made of black glass as our train pulled away. I had taken a seat next to Morty and gazed out at the backs of buildings, backyards and small gardens. We were on our way to Wembley.

I remember thinking as we left the outskirts of Blackpool behind, if ever there was a year for us to win the Cup, this was it. It was coronation year and the Queen and the Duke of Edinburgh would be in attendance, her first major engagement as our new monarch. It was a great year to be British and a great year to be from Blackpool. Mount Everest had been conquered for the first time and a local climber, Alfred Gregory, had been a member of the summit assault party. Squadron Leader Neville Duke had broken the sound barrier for the first time by flying a Hunter jet over Blackpool promenade and Blackpool's own George Formby was Britain's number one entertainment star. Could we top what had been a great year for the town by returning with the FA Cup? This was also to be the year Gordon Richards would at last win the Derby, on Pinza. I wondered if in 30 hours' time people would be referring to it as the year in which Stan Matthews finally got his coveted FA Cup winner's medal.

19

— ◦ —

The
Mortensen Final

Saturday, 2 May 1953. We arrived at Wembley from our base at the Edgewarebury Country Club in Elstree some two hours before kick-off. There had been heavy rain, but the skies had cleared and Wembley was enveloped in golden sunshine as I walked out on to the famous Cumberland turf with my Blackpool team-mates for the obligatory 'soaking up of the atmosphere'. Morty as usual had something funny to say. Looking up at the blue skies and bright sun he turned to me and said, 'Thank heavens that deal Harry pulled off with Aqua Sports didn't involve us wearing the raincoats today.' That eased the tension we had all been feeling on the drive up to the stadium.

In the centre circle the massed bands of the Scots and Irish Guards, resplendent in their red tunics and towering busbies, played 'I'm a Lassie From Lancashire', a diplomatic choice considering the geographical position of both teams. The Wembley terraces like great concrete Alps were already filling with supporters of both clubs, sporting their favours. Rattles and ribbons, scarves and shirts, hats and headscarves in tangerine or blue and white adorned the stadium as the early arrivals hung over the crash barriers. Below the royal box it was as if Jackson Pollock's palette had been thrown across the flower beds. Every conceivable colour of herbaceous border plant vied for attention. Behind each goal there was a perfect crescent of sawdust, a sight unique to Wembley but the point of which I never understood. The emerald green turf, still wet from what had been almost 48 hours of continuous rain, was soft underfoot and in the bright sunshine dazzled the eyes.

As I gazed around Wembley with my team-mates, I felt the pressure. For my mind was on that second death-bed promise I had made to my father. As well as promising to look after my mother, I had said to him that I would win the FA Cup for him one day. I have never spoken publicly about this before, but I had never forgotten it. In his final minutes on this earth that was his dream for me, and now I had to make it come true. I knew how fortunate I was to have been given another chance, but this was probably the last one. I knew I had years left in me as a player, but another Cup final appearance? As I walked back towards the dressing rooms the magnitude of the day and the occasion rested heavy upon me. To everyone else it was a great day, a carnival occasion. For me, it was the final of finals and in more ways than one.

In the dressing room, the mood was of quiet confidence. Even Morty was totally focused. Joe Smith as usual didn't say too much. 'Go out and enjoy yourselves. Be the players I know you are and we'll be all right. We'll win it and remember, whatever happens, you're my boys and I'm proud of every damn one of you.' The sound of 100,000 muffled voices singing 'Abide With Me' seeped into the dressing room with its towering glass-pannelled windows, bringing a moment of reverence. The voices trailed away and were followed by a tumultuous cheer which was pierced by the harsh sound of the buzzer indicating we had to assemble in the tunnel.

Joe Smith, in a brand new suit, donned his trilby and walked towards the door. Skipper Harry Johnston, ball in hand, fell into line behind him. George Farm stood behind Harry and the rest of us followed. As he opened the dressing-room door, Joe turned to us.

'We dream brave dreams, eh? So be brave, lads,' he said. Joe swung the door open and out we walked into our destiny.

Bolton lined up alongside us in the tunnel. The most striking thing about them was their shorts which seemed to be made of black satin. We all jiggled our arms and stomped our feet for a moment in an attempt to rid ourselves of nervous tension. Then the attendant at the mouth of the tunnel gave Joe and the Bolton manager Bill Ridding the nod and we commenced the walk that would take us from the gloom of the tunnel into blinding light and the cauldron that is Wembley.

As soon as the supporters caught sight of Joe, Bill Ridding and the two crocodiles of players behind them, bedlam broke loose. The stadium immediately filled with a cacophony of noise, an alarming, volatile sound that sent a shiver through my entire body. The terraces undulated. I looked over to where the Blackpool fans were in the main situated. It was if someone from up on high had suddenly tipped a gigantic box of tangerines down on to them. The atmosphere was nerve jangling as only Wembley in full cry on Cup final day can be.

Joe Smith walked proudly at the head of our line. He had been a captain in the Cup finals of 1923 and 1926. His team? Bolton Wanderers. Behind him, Harry Johnston also had a special personal reason for wanting to win. His mother had died in January and the one thing he wanted to present to her from his career as a footballer was an FA Cup winner's medal. Like me, he had known disappointment twice. Harry was 34 and he knew that this might well be his last chance. I knew exactly what he was feeling and what thoughts would be racing through his mind.

'More things are wrought by prayer than this world dreams of' – I prayed that come a quarter to five my team-mates and I and every Blackpool supporter would be able to testify to the efficacy of that belief. Ever since we had removed Tottenham Hotspur from the competition in the semi-final it seemed that football followers in this country and elsewhere had been entreating the gods to look favourably on Blackpool.

I had slept a perspiring sleep the night before, now I was ready for what I saw as my ultimate challenge. I had always liked the big occasion and they wouldn't come bigger than this. On the walk to the centre line I hoped and prayed I'd be equal to it. Most players, myself included, had rolled up their sleeves. Not much of a breeze would reach the pitch and the atmosphere was going to be hot and stifling. The teams veered to the right to line up for the national anthem and presentation to the Duke of Edinburgh. Ernie Taylor was to my left.

'Good luck, Stan,' he said.

'Good luck, Ernie,' I replied.

For a split second we looked at one another in the way comrades at arms do before battle, nervous at the prospect of not knowing. Sensing the moment was awkward, Ernie gave an anxious smile before we both turned to await the arrival of the Duke of Edinburgh. The teams were as follows:

Blackpool: George Farm; Eddie Shimwell, Tommy Garrett;

Ewan Fenton, Harry Johnston, Cyril Robinson; Stan Matthews, Ernie Taylor, Stan Mortensen, Jackie Mudie, Bill Perry.

Bolton Wanderers: Stan Hanson; Johnny Ball, Ralph Banks; Johnny Wheeler, Malcolm Barrass, Eric Bell; Doug Holden, Willie Moir, Nat Lofthouse, Harry Hassall, Bobby Langton.

As the game got under way I told myself, 'This is the one. Don't blow it, Stan, because this is it!' No sooner had I run the thought through my mind than Bolton delivered a blow to the body of huge proportions. From the kick-off they went straight on to the attack with the ball finding its way to Harry Hassall on the left-hand side of our penalty box. I was tracking back to provide extra cover when Hassall switched the ball across the edge of the penalty area to Doug Holden. Seeing that we were closing him down, Holden laid the ball back into the path of Nat Lofthouse who was steaming up just to his left. Nat hit a low, powerful shot that bounced across the glistening turf.

George Farm dived to his right and was down quick enough but Nat's angled drive shot across his body and through his outstretched hands. The ball reared up one last time and the net shivered. What seemed to be the sound of thunder swept down from terraces alive with blue and white. There were only 75 seconds gone on the clock and we were behind. I hadn't even touched the ball.

I looked at Eddie Shimwell. He was staring in disbelief at the ball now nestled in the back of our net. His shoulders dropped and he momentarily closed his eyes and let out a deep sigh. Opening his eyes, he glanced momentarily up to the sky and shook his head before turning to us all, clapping his shovel-like hands together and shouting, 'Come on! Let's pick ourselves up!' Harry Johnston was also clapping his hands together. 'Heads up!' he shouted. 'Get those heads up and let's get at them!'

Without being reckless we took the game to Bolton because we had no alternative. The quicker we could pull back the deficit the better it would be. Jackie Mudie tried a shot at goal but didn't connect cleanly and his effort gave the Bolton keeper Stan Hanson no problems. From Hanson's clearance we won possession and back we came. The Bolton centre-half Malcolm Barrass headed a cross from Jackie Mudie clear with Morty and Ernie Taylor lying in wait as we buzzed around their penalty area looking for an opening.

Ernie Taylor started to play me into the game. I was shouting for the ball at every given opportunity and although I managed to put a few crosses into the Bolton penalty area nothing came of them, primarily because big Malcolm Barrass was dominating all proceedings in the air. But the fact I was getting the ball into the danger area gave me confidence. After the initial excitement, the game degenerated for a time into a tough and sometimes dire battle for midfield dominance. Both sides staged attacks without ever succeeding in making a telling final ball. After a quarter of an hour or so, Bolton's left-half Eric Bell fell awkwardly following a challenge from Jackie Mudie and left the pitch for a while, returning with his left thigh heavily strapped. He took up a position on the Bolton left wing which told me straightaway that they were effectively down to ten men.

Bolton still came forward and caused problems. Ewan Fenton had a pass cut out by Barrass who played a long ball upfield to Nat Lofthouse. With all of us racing like mad to get back and cover, Lofthouse played a neat one-two with Moir but fortunately George Farm had read the situation and came off his line to close Nat down. Under pressure from George, Nat didn't have time to control Moir's return pass and hit a hasty shot that evaded George's lunging body only to come back into play off the foot of the post and rebound to the Bolton inside-left Hassall. As Harry Johnston said later, 'It was the moment I discovered adrenalin was brown.' With George Farm racing back, Hassall fired his shot in the direction of our gaping goal. It looked a certain second for Bolton. Suddenly, like the American cavalry arriving at the last moment, Eddie Shimwell came racing into the six-yard box and launched himself. Left leg out-stretched like the jib of a small crane, among 100,000 people I heard him grunt and strain as he stretched every sinew of his body and his momentum carried him airborne in the direction of the ball. Sliding across the turf Eddie managed partly to block Hassall's shot with the toe of his boot and the ball bounced some 12 inches away from goal.

I'm not too clear about what happened next – there was one almighty scramble as players from both sides descended on the loose ball. In the scramble for possession, Ewan Fenton had been barged to the ground but when the ball spilled from the mêlée in his direction he managed to extend a boot and hook it away for a corner. Bolton corner or not, I sighed with relief. At least the few seconds it would need for them to take the corner would give us some respite and the chance to regain our composure.

Concerted pressure on our part paid off in the 35th minute. Tommy Garrett met a goalkick from Hanson with his head and sent the ball back in the direction from which it had come. Jackie Mudie won possession and turned to send Morty away. I'd seen Morty practise bearing down on goal with the ball at his feet countless times. It was like watching a fish practise swimming – a sway here, a jink there, a drop of the shoulder and all done with the most rhythmic beauty that never for a moment necessitated him breaking stride or sacrificing pace. Within seconds he was past two defenders and into the Bolton penalty box – head up to pick his spot; head down to ensure he didn't get any height on the ball and wham! Morty's shot took a wicked deflection off Hassall, richocheted past a wrong-footed Hanson and clanked against the metal stanchion in the corner of the net. Wembley erupted once more as the man in heaven doused the terraces with thousands of tangerines yet again.

We were back in the final, but not for long. Four minutes later, Hassall floated a centre-cum-shot towards our goal. I'd seen George Farm collect such balls effortlessly on many occasions, they were meat and drink to him. However, this time as George took to the air, arms outstretched, Bolton's inside-right Moir joined him. Whether Moir's sudden presence made George take his eye off the ball for a second I don't know, but he flapped at thin air and the ball sailed over the pair and into the top right-hand corner of our net. The blue and white of Wembley bounced into celebration and our ears were assailed by that awful noise of opposition supporters heralding a goal that your inbuilt defence mechanism tries to blot out by focusing your immediate attention on the grass, the goal or the back of a team-mate's shirt, anywhere but the rejoicing terraces.

At half-time we sipped our tea and listened to Joe. He wasn't panicking. He didn't rant and rave and he didn't berate anyone. He simply told us to keep 'playing our normal game'. Joe did tell me, however, that he thought I had been dropping too deep and I should push on more in the second half and that Ernie Taylor should work to get me more of the ball.

Once Joe had said his piece, Harry Johnston got to work. He told our defence to be more compact and tighter as a unit. He reiterated Joe's point that Ernie Taylor should play me into the game more and that Ewan Fenton should do likewise. As for Morty, Harry was brief and to the point – 'Get in their box and make a bloody nuisance of yourself.'

As for the threat of Lofthouse, Harry would get tighter on Nat and, 'Let him know I'm there.' That was something for Harry to say because of all the centre-forwards he played against the one Harry never relished playing was Nat Lofthouse, but then which defender ever did? Nat was like a bull, strong, pacey and very difficult to knock off the ball. He was a barnstorming centre-forward with class and the desperate look of a haunted man who knew his job would be to run head first into a brick wall if called upon to do so. Nat in full flight was an awesome and frightening figure for defenders. In saying he would take the responsibility of dealing with him, Harry demonstrated to us all he was leading from the front.

'Eddie, Tommy, Cyril and me, we will deal with the rough and tumble and win the ball. You lot who can play, do your bit,' said Harry. 'We've got the ball players to win this Cup, so let's get out and bloody well win it.'

The second half started where the first half left off with both teams playing open football in search of a goal, us to pull it back, Bolton to kill off the game. I started to wander and from a deep position on the left, set off on a mazey run before releasing Bill Perry who was pulled up for being offside. I was becoming more involved in the game now and the runs I had been making convinced me I had the beating of the Bolton defenders. I felt confident and had high hopes of us creating an opening for the equalising goal but on 50 minutes my heart sank.

Hanson found Ball with a long throw from his goal and the Bolton right-back's long delivery into our half was put out by Harry Johnston for a throw-in. From the Bolton throw-in, Holden crossed deep into our penalty area. With

Harry Johnston and Nat Lofthouse wrestling each other to such an extent neither could get near the inviting cross, Eddie Shimwell took to the air with the injured Bell. Injured he may have been, but Eric Bell managed to edge in front of Eddie to direct a downward header past George Farm's despairing leap and into the far corner of the net. The Bolton fans went into ecstasy as a limping Bell disappeared under a cloud of white shirts.

At 3–1 to Bolton, it looked pretty grim. I couldn't believe it. In the build-up to the game all the portents for us had looked good but now we found ourselves staring down the barrel of a gun. A third Wembley defeat loomed. The odds were now against us, so I buckled down, determined to give it everything I had. There were less than 35 minutes remaining but, as I have always maintained, it only takes a second to score a goal. I made a concerted effort to pick up my game and give it a real go. Looking about the pitch I could see I wasn't alone. All my team-mates, far from being despondent and throwing in the towel, were still buzzing.

Moments after the restart, Ernie Taylor flew into a tackle on Wheeler and came away with the ball at his feet. That seemed to exemplify the fight that was still in us and raised everyone. If we were going to go down, it would be with all guns blazing. Then again, if we all contrived to give it our all, who knows? Football matches can be turned on their head by a simple pass or a hopeful shot.

Morty had a good chance but blasted wide. Then only the outstretched leg of Barrass denied him as he bore down on the Bolton goal. The pressure was on Bolton and I believed the outcome of the game would depend on how well we kept the pressure turned up and how well they coped with it.

With 24 minutes left, Harry Johnston ordered Jackie Mudie to go wide on the left and brought Bill Perry, who hadn't been seeing much of the ball, inside. This was in the hope that Bill's pace and dashing runs from deep could disrupt the Bolton defence. It was a tactic that paid off almost immediately. With the Bolton defenders tight on Bill Perry, Ewan Fenton found Ernie Taylor who in turn fed the ball to me wide on the right. I went into overdrive. I took myself past Ralph Banks and, as Wheeler came across to close me down and with the Bolton defence thinking I was going to cut inside, I whipped the ball across the penalty box to the far post. I grimaced when I saw Hanson in the Bolton goal reach up but instead of collecting cleanly, he fumbled the ball and it fell towards the post under the ever-watchful eye of Morty. Morty always followed up such crosses in the hope a goalkeeper might spill the ball. As he used to say, 'Always expect the unexpected.'

Morty was on to the loose ball in a flash and although under pressure from two Bolton defenders who contrived to whack him from either side as he slid in, his determination was total and he managed to toe poke the ball off the inside of the post and into the net. Whether conscious of the fact or not, and I doubt whether he was, he had adhered to the words Joe Smith had said as we left the dressing room at the start of the game. Morty had gone in where boots and elbows were flying to give us a chance of rescuing the Cup final. It was indeed a brave goal.

Morty stood up dazed and groggy. Now it was the turn of the Blackpool contingent on the terraces to celebrate and they did so unreservedly. We still had a way to go, but we were back in it.

While Morty received attention from our trainer Johnny Lynas, I had a few words with Ewan Fenton. 'Give me the ball at every opportunity,' I told Ewan. 'I've got the beating of them down this wing. They're rattled now. So come on, give it to me.' Ewan, his face a stream of perspiration and grimacing from the physical effort he had been exerting, in an attempt to conserve even the energy it takes to say a few words, said nothing and merely nodded his head.

The game now developed into a titanic battle. Time was running out and our efforts on occasions not only verged on the frantic but had an air of desperation about them. It was do-or-die and we were determined to press forward while not giving any quarter at the back. There was a sickening thud as Tommy Garrett challenged Lofthouse for a high ball and their heads clashed. No sooner had Tommy hit the ground than he was up on his feet and sprinting after the loose ball, the trickle of blood from the resultant cut above his eye polka dotting his tangerine shirt. I thought to myself, 'We want this. We really do want it and maybe more than them.'

When you're chasing a game, time flashes by. When you're in the position Bolton were in, each minute seems an eternity. In chasing a game, you must remain calm and collected in order to think straight, but in throwing so many men forward, risks have to be taken. We were in constant danger of Bolton breaking away and scoring a goal that would put the issue beyond doubt. That was our dilemma. Bolton still had the lead but we had the game by the scruff of the neck. We poured forward sometimes leaving alarming gaps at the back but what else could we do with time ticking away?

Ernie Taylor and Ewan Fenton supplied me with pass after pass. I was playing the game of my life, pulling out every trick I knew, working the ball into the penalty area in the direction of Morty, Ernie Taylor and Bill Perry at every given opportunity. But to our frustration and angst an equaliser just wouldn't come.

With two minutes of normal time remaining a cross from Eddie Shimwell was headed clear and in challenging Jackie Mudie for the ball a Bolton defender conceded a free kick some 20 yards from goal. Morty stood over the ball with Ernie Taylor. I heard Ernie say words to the effect that he wanted Morty to lay the ball off to him so he could work the ball into the box, but Morty had other ideas. As the Bolton defence lined up, Morty told Ernie he could see a gap and was going to go for it. Ernie at first tried to dissuade him, feeling it was far better to keep possession than try a hopeful shot. Morty was adamant and I watched from my vantage point wide on the right as Ernie nodded to indicate Morty should have a go.

Morty walked back some five or six paces. The Bolton defenders were shouting to one another to ensure every one of our players in and about the box had been marked tight. An uncharacteristic hush descended on both sets of fans as they waited to see what Morty would do. He took a moment to compose himself, then he drew a deep breath and ran up to the ball. With a sniper's eye trained on the narrow gap he had seen, Morty gave it everything he had. With a bass-like thud, the ball took off like a missile.

I watched for the split second it took the ball to travel the 20 or so yards to its destination. It flew past the lines of tangerine and white-shirted players. Such was the power and accuracy behind Morty's effort, Hanson in the Bolton goal hardly moved a muscle. The top right-hand corner of the Bolton net billowed. We threw our arms aloft and took to our toes to offer our thanks and congratulations to the man who had scored a hat-trick for us in the Cup final and brought us back from the dead.

The referee Mr Griffiths from Newport indicated there would be four minutes of injury time. We poured forward yet again. Bolton for their part were happy to boot the ball anywhere as long as it alleviated the pressure. At one point, when the ball ran out on to the cinder track I was amazed to see Joe Smith leap from his seat, run after it and throw it back, so eager was he for us to keep the pressure up.

A minute of injury time remained. What happened then no scriptwriter could have penned because no editor would have accepted a story so far-fetched and outlandish. Ernie Taylor, who had not stopped running throughout the match, picked up a long throw from George Farm, rounded Langton and, as he had done like clockwork through the second half, found me wide on the right. I took off for what I knew would be one final run to the byline. Three Bolton players closed in, I jinked past Ralph Banks and out of the corner of my eye noticed Barrass coming in quick for the kill. They had forced me to the line and it was pure instinct that I pulled the ball back to where experience told me Morty would be. In making the cross I slipped on the greasy turf and, as I fell, my heart and hopes fell also. I looked across and saw that Morty, far from being where I expected him to be, had peeled away to the far post. We could read each other like books. For five years we'd had this understanding. He knew exactly where I'd put the ball. Now, in this game of all games, he wasn't there. This was our last chance, what on earth was he doing? Racing up from deep into the space was Bill Perry. 'Head over it Bill, don't blast it. Don't blast it!' I said to myself.

I was doing Bill an injustice. The 'Original Champagne Perry' was as ice cool as the finest vintage in the coldest of buckets. He coolly and calmly stroked the ball wide of Hanson and Johnny Ball on the goalline and into the corner of the net. From 1–3 down it was now 4–3! Those in the seats took to their feet, those on the terraces and already standing, leapt into the air as Wembley erupted.

Perhaps it was down to the fact I swallowed hard to get some saliva into my dry mouth, or that the sudden eruption of sound was momentarily too much for my eardrums; maybe it was a combination of the two. For a brief moment, although conscious of the pandemonium that had broken out about me, I didn't hear a thing. I watched the ball hit the back of the net, looked back at Bill as he raised his arms and was for a split second rendered totally deaf. I looked at my team-mates jumping for joy and the only noise was a low, droning buzz in my ears. It was as if I was dreaming it. Swallowing hard again, my ears suddenly popped and were immediately assailed by the loudest and most resounding roar I'd ever experienced in a football stadium. It burst from the terraces and roared down and across the pitch like some terrifying banshee.

Having regained my feet, I watched as every player bar George Farm made a beeline for me. Morty's arms were outstretched his face beaming as he sprinted towards me; Bill Perry had an ecstatic smile on his face, his head going from side to side as if in disbelief; Ernie Taylor skipped and jumped as he ran in my direction, punching the air with a fist and yelling 'It's there! It's there!' Harry Johnston, who always left his part top set of dentures in a handkerchief in his suit pocket, unashamedly bared his gums to the world. I felt Ewan Fenton's wet and clammy arms across my face as his hands ruffled my hair. It was all I could do to keep my feet as my team-mates mobbed me.

When I eventually extricated myself I glanced up at the Wembley scoreboard and felt a quick rush of adrenalin. Was I wrong? The scoreboard read, Blackpool 4 Bolton Wanderers 4. 'No,' I thought, 'I'm not wrong. It's them!'

Bolton restarted the game but there was little time left. Their final attack ended with George Farm beating Holden to a through ball. As George prepared to play the ball upfield, a long shrill blast of Mr Griffiths' whistle brought the game to an end. I couldn't believe it. We had done it. From 3–1 down we had come back and snatched victory from not just the jaws but the epiglottis of defeat. At 38, and after 23 years in football, I had my FA Cup winner's medal at last. George Farm, probably because he'd had least running to do, reached me first and wrapped his arms around me. Then the others came, a wall of tangerine pulled me into its sweaty body. Out of the corner of my eye, I was amazed to see the arms of a suit. The arms belonged to Joe Smith, the 'ageing manager' who had put his faith in what the newspapers had dubbed 'an ageing genius'. He was the one person who for all my advancing years had never stopped believing in my ability, the manager who had persuaded me to stay and live out 'his dream'.

The Bolton players, despite their disappointment and heartache, were generous in defeat. They shook my hand and offered their congratulations. I was happy for them when they won the Cup in 1958, with a team including Nat Lofthouse and Doug Holden, so, they had had their day at Wembley.

We had been faced with a Herculean task, in coming back from 3–1 down. Our excitement, relief and joy knew no bounds. I was fourth in line as Harry Johnston led us up to the royal box to accept the Cup from Her Majesty the Queen.

'Well done, Mr Matthews,' said Her Majesty. 'It was very exciting.'

'Thank you, ma'am,' I said and extended my hand to receive a winner's medal.

As I descended the steps of the royal box, I opened the little box I had been presented with. 'You little beauty,' I said to myself as I gazed at the medal, as bright and as gloriously golden as the sun that had presided over what had been the most wonderful afternoon of my career. Back on terra firma, I took the medal out of the box and looking up to the heavens, held it high.

'There it is, Dad.'

In all the previous Cup finals there had been no lap of honour. The victors merely walked back to their dressing room after receiving the Cup. We broke with such po-faced and killjoy tradition. Harry Johnston grabbed the microphone connected up to the Wembley PA system and with stewards looking on aghast took centre stage.

'Your Royal Highness,' announced Harry, 'ladies and gentleman, on behalf of the players from both sides I call for three cheers for Her Majesty the Queen. Hip, hip . . .'

Every man, woman and child joined in. Whether officialdom wanted it or not, there was little they could do about it as Wembley cheered the nation's new monarch who responded with a beaming smile. That done, Harry put the microphone to one side and, in another break with Wembley protocol, was immediately hoisted high. Jackie Mudie and Morty lifted me on to their shoulders and with Harry and I holding the Cup with one hand each, we posed before the small army of photographers as flash bulbs popped like champagne corks. From my elevated position I watched the Bolton team trudge sadly back to the tunnel. What a grim finale for them. My heart went with them.

Once the press photographers had secured their shots for the Sunday morning editions, I joined George Farm in following Harry Johnston back around the cinder track in the direction of the tunnel and our dressing room as the cloth-capped and headscarved supporters cheered us wildly every step of the way. I still did not fully realise, as in the heat of the moment one never does, the true enormity and magnitude of our victory. History has deemed it to be the greatest ever FA Cup final.

Our dressing room provided a haven from the tumultous noise and celebration but, high on adrenalin and pure exhilaration, my team-mates whooped and hollered in turn as they entered the room. The FA Cup was filled with champagne and for only the second time in my life, and the first time knowingly, I imbibed alcohol and savoured our moment of glory.

As I've said before, I was never one given to great celebration, but that is not to say I wasn't overcome. Having taken my turn in drinking from the Cup, I flopped down on to the bench under my peg to rest my weary limbs, have a cup of tea and try to bring some tranquillity to my fuddled brain and racing nervous system. In any game, but especially one of this magnitude, my mind is totally focused, blocking out thoughts of anything else. You enter another world where the events of the game are all you know. You are constantly appraising and assessing, deciding what to do. Such a concentrated and concerted mental effort leaves you drained. Once the game is over, tiredness and fatigue set in.

For 90 minutes-plus all I had known in the world had been that Cup final; my concentration had been total. It is a mental state you have to achieve if you want to be a winner. How close you are to it can mean the difference between being a champion and being nowhere. It's true of all sports. Golfers I am sure know this only too well. Take the British Open Championship of 1999, when Frenchman Jean Van de Velde blew a three-stroke lead on the final hole at Carnoustie. No one knows what Van de Velde was thinking as he set about playing that final hole but I should suspect his mind was elsewhere and that proved his undoing. To be winner or a champion you not only have to give it everything you have physically, you have to be supremely mentally atuned to the job to the exclusion of all else. I had reached that elevated mental state in this game and as my team-mates celebrated, I found myself enjoying the moment but doing so as an onlooker as my body and mind tuned down.

One by one we crossed the corridor and entered the Bolton dressing room to offer our commiserations. Usually players only say 'Well played, you did well' when they have won. They rarely say such things when they have lost. However, the Bolton players for all their deep disappointment were generous to a man.

'We know how you're feeling,' said Morty. 'One of us had to lose and we know what it's like to lose here, we've done it twice. Why can't we both win?'

The Bolton captain Willie Moir, held his hand up to indicate Morty should say no more.

'Thanks, lads,' said Moir. 'If we had to lose, there's no team we'd have preferred to lose to. It was a terrific effort on your part. I think you might have made history today.'

At the post-final dinner at London's Café Royal, we arrived to find Bolton had booked their post-match banquet at the same hotel, so the sporting spirit between the two parties carried on into the evening. In our banqueting room, cheers swept up to the rafters when our chairman Harry Evans entered the room proudly holding the FA Cup aloft. Following the dinner came the speeches. Referring to my efforts and Morty's historic hat-trick, Joe Smith said, 'Cometh the hour, cometh the Stan and I had two of them.' Joe went on to say, quite rightly, that our victory was 'all down to team effort in which every player had played his part to the full'.

The following day, the Sunday newspapers brandished my name in their headlines: WIZARD STANLEY MATTHEWS MADE THIS HIS FINAL TO REMEMBER, *Empire News*; MAGNIFICENT MATTHEWS, *Sunday Chronicle*; MAESTRO MATTHEWS, *Sunday Express*; STAN'S FINEST GAME, *Sunday Pictorial*; STAN MATTHEWS INSPIRES GREATEST CUP VICTORY, *News of the World*.

To be honest, I found the whole thing one great embarrassment. Our victory was a team effort but if any one player deserved to make the headlines it was Morty who in scoring a hat-trick in a Wembley FA Cup final had created football history. Yet in all the editions of the Sunday and indeed Monday newspapers, it was my name that featured in the headlines. Can you imagine a player scoring a hat-trick in an FA Cup final today and his name not appearing in one single headline in the newspapers? If there was a downside to our victory, that was it as far as I was concerned. The man whose three goals had been all-important in us winning the Cup had his efforts tucked away in the columns dealing with the match report. It was monstrous and I felt Morty had been denied his moment of glory. Even now the game is referred to as the Matthews final and every time I hear the words spoken I cringe with embarrassment because, quite simply, it's not true. Of all the things I have wanted to say in the writing of this book, that has been paramount all along. Now I hope people will take an objective view of the game, give Morty the credit he so richly deserves and begin to refer to it for ever more as the Mortensen final. Nothing would give me greater satisfaction.

In addition to scoring a hat-trick, Morty had in fact created our fourth and winning goal as I came to realise after the game when he and I were sitting next to one another in the plunge bath.

'Morty, what were you doing when I made that final cross?' I asked. 'I pulled the ball back thinking you would be there. But you weren't. I looked up and saw you running away to the far post. I thought we had this understanding?'

'We do, Stan,' said Morty. 'But when I saw you about to make the cross, I was tightly marked. Maybe I could have had a shot at goal, maybe not. If I had managed to fire off a shot, the chances were it would have been blocked. So I peeled away to the far post, took a couple of their lads with me and shouted for Bill to run into the space.' Clever or what? Morty spurned the opportunity of perhaps scoring four goals in a Cup final by creating a better opportunity for someone else. He had put the team and Blackpool before personal glory and gain, such unselfishness and devotion to teamwork was the mark of the man. The Matthews final it never was – it was Morty's final and no amount of copy from so-called eminent football writers, or the passing of time, can ever convince me otherwise.

On the Sunday afternoon, a few of us went for a walk in a nearby park. A group of schoolboys having a kickabout recognised us and asked us to join in, so for a few minutes we happily kicked a ball around with these lads. Who they were I don't know, but I am sure it gave them a thrill. The game was changing and becoming more professional, but players were still accessible to the fans. It doesn't happen today. FA Cup winners are whisked off to their hotel hideaway from where chauffeured cars take them to their out-of-town mansion-like houses and ne'er the twain shall meet. I understand the need for privacy but I do feel that in distancing themselves from ordinary, genuine supporters, many of today's top players are missing out. The lack of communication fosters mistrust and the players never get to understand their fans. Such distancing can also lead to a grossly inflated sense of one's own worth which, as well as being misplaced, can be dangerous. It can make certain players vulnerable. Hence we have a young player and his popstar bride seated on thrones at their wedding, a situation as sad as it appears crass. Footballers are footballers when all is said and done, and the fact that you can put in a half-decent cross or bang a ball into a net 20 or so times in a season and get paid handsomely, sometimes obscenely, for doing so is no reason to believe you are someone extra special on this earth. For all those headlines in the aftermath of the 1953 Cup final, I certainly didn't. I simply felt I had been very lucky and while thanking the good Lord for the gifts he had given me, remained of the opinion that I was better than no one and no one was better than me – an attitude I feel that has helped me throughout my entire life to gain a better understanding of myself and others.

We left London on the 10.40 a.m. train from Euston on the Monday morning. There was no doubt our victory had been well-received by the nation in general – as our train travelled north, we noticed tangerine and white ribbons were tied to the telegraph poles that flanked the railway line. We slung the Cup up on the luggage rack. Halfway home and with many of the players snoozing I left my seat next to Morty to go to the loo. Walking down the centre aisle I passed skipper Harry Johnston. His head was bowed and at first I thought he was deep into some novel he was reading. On passing him, however, I saw that he was holding open the small box and was staring down at his winner's medal. He was miles away and never looked up. When I came back, he was as I had left him. Perhaps his thoughts were of his mother, maybe he was running the game through his mind. I was going to say something, but thought better of it. Harry was a marvellous captain; Blackpool was his only club. His tough tackling, gritty determination and fine qualities of leadership both on and off the field had seen us through many a game, that Cup final in particular. He was a hard man, not given to too much sentimentality, but I felt he was experiencing very sentimental thoughts at that time. That's what winning the FA Cup can do to a man.

We were given a cigarette lighter each by the club by way of a bonus for beating Bolton. For some reason I never did receive mine but that didn't bother me. A cigarette lighter is hardly the ideal presentation gift for a professional footballer, especially someone particular about fitness and health. To this day, I have never smoked a cigarette or cigar in my life.

After the Cup final a story circulated around Blackpool for quite some time involving an elderly man and his grandson, a young man in his early twenties. I don't know if it's true but I'd like to think it is. The elderly gent and his grandson were both season-ticket holders at Blackpool. Grandfathers, as we know, are the best liars in the world and this old gent assailed his grandson with tales of how he and an old pal would travel to matches together and saw all the classic games and footballing greats such as Sam Hardy and Charles Buchan. Being season-ticket holders, both qualified for tickets for Wembley but a fortnight or so before the Cup final, the grandfather passed away. With his own father having no interest in football, the grandson decided to trace his grandfather's old pal, who had moved to Southport. If his grandfather couldn't go to Wembley, who better to take his place than his old pal with whom he had attended so many great games?

The grandson managed to track down his grandfather's old pal and, though despondent to hear the news of the death of his friend, he agreed to take his place on the trip to Wembley. Come the big day, the grandson went to collect the old boy from his home in Southport. A shock awaited him. His grandfather's old pal was blind, and had been all his life. The grandfather had accompanied him to all those games of yesteryear and given a running commentary on the action taking place on the field.

After overcoming his initial surprise, the grandson felt great pride that he should now be taking his grandfather's place, taking his old pal to Wembley where he too would attempt to give a commentary on the entire proceedings – Blackpool back from 3–1 down to win the Cup, with the equaliser and the winner in the last two minutes of the game; a hat-trick from Mortensen; and the 38-year-old

Matthews along with another old timer, skipper Harry Johnston, collecting winner's medals at long last. Apparently on leaving Wembley stadium, the grandson and his new friend were like every other supporter that day – stunned into silence because every drop of emotion had been drained right out of them. It was some time before one of them managed to speak and it was the grandfather's old pal.

'I've been blind all my life, but I'll tell thee what, lad,' he said, turning to the grandson, 'after that, I've seen it all now!'

I was reminded of this story a few years back. It formed the basis for a radio play and I am not ashamed to say, it moved me to tears. In the comfy confines of my den at home, it brought it all back to me, the whole atmosphere surrounding the build-up to the final and the game itself. For a time I was transported back with Morty, Ernie, the 'Original Champagne Perry', Harry Johnston and dear Joe Smith. I can't remember the name of the author, but whoever it is, I thank you.

20

---◦---

Trying to Catch the Galloping Major

The press turned to extolling my virtues as an England player once more. The fact that I was going on 39 didn't matter to them. I was in their view a must for the forthcoming England tour of South America, even though I hadn't been selected in the original squad. I still felt fit enough to play at international level, though not on the tour of South America. I was concerned about the muscle strain for which I had received a pain-killing injection just before the Cup final and felt the best antidote would be rest.

The pressure on the FA from the press was relentless and, sure enough, I received a belated call-up to the England team. Unfortunately, I had to convey my apologies. It wasn't sour grapes on my part because I hadn't been originally included. I just thought not resting would aggravate the muscle problem and therefore I'd be of little or no use to the England squad. I made the decision as much for the benefit of England as myself.

As it turned out, England didn't do too badly on the tour. They drew against Argentina in a game that was abandoned after 23 minutes because of a downpour, won against Chile and lost to Uruguay. On the way home, a 6–3 win over the United States went some way to erasing the awful memory of the 1950 World Cup, but also rekindled the misplaced belief that British was best in the minds of the selectors.

Walter Winterbottom was doing his best to create a team but still had to battle to get his views and opinions across to selectors who contrived to make any England side something of a Heath Robinson affair. Each selector had his own agenda when it came to choosing players for England and the team was still selected one position at a time on a show of hands. It was an archaic system completely at odds with Walter's idea of playing a combination of players from one club to exploit their familiarity and understanding of one another. This selection system, anachronistic even in the early fifties, goes some way towards explaining why, in 1953–54 in the first four internationals, there were no fewer than 13 changes to the England team. In November 1953, however, the FA had the lesson that British was not best brought home to them in no uncertain manner when England played Hungary at Wembley.

I had played in the two previous internationals, a 4–4 draw against a Rest of Europe XI – a game marking the 90th anniversary of the Football Association – and our 3–1 win over Northern Ireland. My form for Blackpool was good, so it came as no surprise when I heard I had been selected to play against the Hungarians. This was the match in which many England players found themselves strangers in an alien world. On a misty grey afternoon at Wembley, England were clinically and effectively put to the sword. It was our first-ever defeat on home turf against Continental opposition but, more importantly, the game served as a watershed in British football. How we approached and played the game and how we perceived ourselves, would never be the same again. Far from being the masters, on this day we were shown to be the pupils as the Hungarian team, who the press dubbed 'The Magical Magyars', won a thrilling encounter by six goals to three. To my mind, the result did not truly reflect their overall superiority on the day.

Hungary were unfamiliar opposition but not an unknown quantity. They had won the Olympic title the year before and since 1945 had won over 80 per cent of their matches. I had seen in our 4–4 draw with the Rest of Europe that they possessed players of bewildering class. Yet we took to Wembley that day with four changes to the forward line from our previous international and little in the way of a gameplan other than the selection of four Blackpool players – myself, Ernie Taylor, Harry Johnston and Morty – which, we were told, 'would provide some adhesion and co-ordination in our play'.

In the dressing room before the game, there was no mention of how to counteract Hungary's deep-lying centre-forward Nandor Hidegkuti. Even at half-time after this sublimely gifted player had ravaged us, still nothing was said about him and no one was given the specific job of picking him up, a bad mistake in my opinion.

The result gives an insight into our performance – we scored three but conceded six. We played well enough in attack, but we were woefully weak in defence and midfield. Our defensive shortcomings were exposed to the full and a few players who were favourites with selectors, I believe primarily because they said the right things before games and at the post-match banquets, were seen not to possess sufficient quality to play at this level. To be fair, I doubt if even the most accomplished of defenders could have lived with Hungary on this day, but nevertheless, the performances of some players against Hungary did not prevent them going on to win future England caps, one player in particular going on to amass a bountiful supply.

It has been said that genius is 1 per cent inspiration and 99 per cent perspiration, a trite remark that when set alongside the Hungary team of 1953 does not bear up. Hungary worked hard but it was their imaginative play in which they made the ball do the work that touched them with genius. The orchestrator of their triumph was a portly player who the press had dubbed the 'Galloping Major', one Ferenc Puskas. Puskas would merit a place in anyone's team of all-time greats. He played for the crack Hungarian side Honved, but didn't enjoy his best days until he joined Real Madrid when past 30. His small, stocky physique belied his precocious talent and breathtaking brilliance. With a left foot that caressed the ball as Romeo would the cheek of Juliet, he was the epitome of that age-old scrap on the football field between true class and impudence. That magical left foot of Puskas cut a swathe through the England rearguard. At Gil Merrick's left-hand post he pulled the ball back from the byline with the sole of his foot and the incoming Billy Wright tackled the Wembley atmosphere and nothing else. Geoffrey Green summed it up perfectly the next day in *The Times* when he said, 'Billy Wright rushed into that tackle like a man racing to the wrong fire.'

At half-time and 4–1 down, the game was more or less over as far as England were concerned. In the second half we came in for more of the same. Hungary were combining two styles – the British all-running cut and thrust and the short passing game of probing infiltration much favoured at the time by the South Americans. It was an imaginative combination of exacting ball control, speed of movement and esoteric vision that knitted together to formulate a style of football that was as innovative as it was productive. For decades it had been believed that the continentals' downfall was their inability to shoot intelligently. That afternoon another myth was laid to rest. Outpaced and outmanoeuvred we were skittled as six goals hit our net and once again Wembley witnessed football history being made.

The England side that was selected was not a poor one, given the standard in the country at the time. The team that took to the field was an acceptable one and we had our moments. I felt I gave a reasonable account of myself but we were always chasing the game in every sense of the word and long before the final whistle the glory of our footballing past had been laid to rest. Geoffrey Green in *The Times* said, 'We have our Matthews and our Finney certainly [Tom did not play in this game] but they are alone.' I found it flattering that Green should set Tom and me apart but I also found it ironic. Tom Finney and I had been the only two players back in 1950 who had to some extent seen it coming and had wanted to stay on in Brazil to learn from the teams we could watch there. The fact that we weren't allowed to was neither here nor there; on the broad front, Tom and I couldn't have changed anything. We just implemented one or two new ideas into our individual games. It was the fact that no one from the FA or the England management stayed on to watch the remainder of the 1950 World Cup that was so significant. The pompous and ill-conceived idea that nothing could be learned from those teams had been our undoing on the international front. England were left behind and that state of affairs lasted until 1966, and has done intermittently ever since.

The 'British is best' attitude held in the early fifties does not exist today, of course, but back in 1953 this 6–3 defeat brought the bitter realisation that we had fallen behind in footballing terms. England quite rightly could be proud of its past but what the Hungarians had shown us in no uncertain terms was that we should enjoy the past but look to the future. However, hard lessons were not immediately learned from this game. In the return in Budapest in May, England were butchered by seven goals to one. I didn't play but if I had it wouldn't have made any difference, so far ahead of England in footballing terms were those Hungarians at the time.

Over the years I became very good friends with Ferenc Puskas who kindly agreed to play in my testimonial match at Stoke City in 1965. Not only is Ferenc held in high esteem by those who played against him and those fortunate enough to have seen him at full gallop, but also by later generations.

In the early 1980s, George Best and Denis Law were coaching young footballers in Australia. Everyone wanted to be in a group being taught by either George or Denis, so you can imagine the disappointment of one group of lads who were put under the charge of a large, heavy-jowled man so overweight his stomach spilled over the top of his tracksuit bottoms.

On the first morning of the coaching course, this man had been the subject of much derision from the young Aussies placed under his leadership. The boys made rude comments about their coach's weight, the fact that he spoke broken English and laughed aloud whenever he ran after the ball. Come lunchtime, anarchy had befallen this group with the boys taking no notice of their coach whatsoever. They kicked balls about aimlessly between one another and their coach was unable to restore order and get them back in line.

As George and Denis walked across the playing fields towards the clubhouse they saw what was going on and detoured to join the group. The boys immediately flocked around George and Denis happy to hang on to every word they said. George didn't say much. He simply lined up ten footballs some 20 yards from goal, gathered the boys around him and invited the coach to address the first ball.

'OK, boys,' said George. 'There are ten footballs here. How many times do you think your coach can kick them from here and hit the crossbar?'

Various numbers were called out, but one lad in particular loudly proclaimed 'None! He won't be able to see the balls for his belly!'

Extending an arm towards the balls, George invited the coach to try his luck. The boys looked on slack-jawed as one after the other each ball crashed against the crossbar some 20 yards away. When it came to the final ball, the coach flicked it up in the air, caught it on his forehead and let it rest there for a moment before flicking his head to one side and catching the ball on his left shoulder. Jerking his body to one side, the ball fell, only for the coach to catch it on the heel of his left boot. He flicked the ball into the air again and produced a perfect volley that had so much power behind it, it left the crossbar reverberating. Ten out of ten! The boys broke out into spontaneous applause and cheered.

George and Denis turned away as the gaggle of young Aussies gathered around their coach wanting to know how he could do such a remarkable thing.

'What's ya name, mate?' asked the loud lad.

George Best spun around. 'To you, son, he's Mister Puskas!' said George, wagging a finger at him before heading off for his lunch with Denis.

———○———

I was out of the England side for the games against Scotland, Yugoslavia and the return with Hungary, but my form with Blackpool had been good enough for the press to once again call for my re-instatement for the World Cup. We finished fifth behind champions Wolves but had exited from the FA Cup on my return to the Potteries when we were deservedly beaten 2–0 at Port Vale. The 1953–54 season, though providing Blackpool with no further silverware, had been highly enjoyable. I felt as fit as ever, certainly fit enough to take on the very best of a World Cup.

Blackpool had been there or thereabouts in the race for the First Division Championship for most of the season, but a run of bad results from 21 November to 23 January when we didn't win one single game in ten league matches, cost us dear. Even a final run-in during which we lost only two of our last 13 league games failed to haul us back into contention. But all-in-all it was a satisfactory season that provided our supporters with several thrilling encounters, most notably a 4–1 away win at Manchester City where I uncharacteristically appeared on the scoresheet twice (the only goals I scored all season); an exciting 4–4 draw down at Portsmouth; and home wins over both Manchester United and Liverpool. In the Liverpool game, Morty took his season's goal tally to 22 in 32 league matches, reinforcing his reputation as one of the country's top post-war goalscorers.

Our game at Cardiff City in front of 45,508 I remember well, but only because it provided another example of Joe Smith's clever psychology. In our previous match we had played poorly losing 3–2 at Bolton Wanderers. In the dressing room afterwards, Joe glowered at us. He didn't have to say anything to make us feel uncomfortable, his stony stare did it. After a minute or so of silence in an atmosphere that would have made a dentist's waiting room seem like a good place to be, he finally spoke.

'Seeing that out there, has made me as happy as the day is long,' Joe said quietly, 'the day in question being midwinter's day somewhere up in Greenland. I have something to tell you all, something very important. But emotions are high immediately after a game, so better to wait until Monday.'

That is all he said. When he had left the room we were all

agog to know what he wanted to tell us. Were new players coming in? Were some of the old hands being eased out? We just didn't know.

Come the Monday we all trained like men possessed, each and every one of us wanting to prove we were good professionals totally committed to the Blackpool cause, just in case he had any doubts and was thinking of bringing in replacements. At the end of the session, Joe gathered us around him.

'Good work today, lads,' he said. 'We still must have words though, but it can wait until tomorrow.'

The agony was prolonged for another 24 hours. The next day we applied ourselves in training as we had done the day before and at the end Joe once again said he had something 'important to tell us all, but that it could wait'. We carried on like that for the rest of the week. The entire team giving everything in training, those whose contracts were due for renewal running round with all the enthusiasm of 16-year-olds. At the end of each day's session, Joe simply said the same – 'What I have to say is of vital importance to each and every one of you, but it can wait.'

Come Saturday, we sat in the away team dressing room at Cardiff's Ninian Park on tenterhooks.

'Right,' said Joe, looking around the dressing room for absentees. 'Where's George Farm? I want everybody to hear this.'

'In the foyer giving out complimentary tickets to some friends,' said Harry Johnston.

'Well go and tell him to get back in here and sharpish,' said Joe.

With George Farm back in the dressing room and everyone else present and correct, Joe said his piece.

'Listen, lads, what I have to say is vitally important. No one, no one do you hear, must not adhere to this today, otherwise there will be trouble and I mean big trouble.'

We sat in silence not knowing what on earth was to come. Was he about to tell us he was going to resign?

'As soon as the referee blows his whistle . . .' He paused. By now we were all as attentive as runners under a starter's pistol, '. . . to end today's game, you *must* dash back into this dressing room and get changed straightaway. No shower. I've checked with the timetables and there's only one train out of Cardiff for home tonight and that is the five o'clock. We *must* be on it.'

With that he turned on his heels and headed towards the dressing room door, turning to face us as he opened it.

'Oh, one more thing. Let's be two goals up at half-time, so I can enjoy my cigar in the second half!'

We were all left amazed. All week we had been expecting bad news. Joe had strung us along, getting the best out of us in training and ensuring we were mentally focused in the aftermath of our shoddy performance at Bolton. It worked. A Bill Perry goal gave us a 1–0 win and, yes, we did catch that five o'clock train out of Cardiff.

On the general football front, the directors of Bradford Park Avenue did their best to add credence to the claim that what directors know about football can be written on a piece of confetti when they whittled down to two the applicants for their vacant manager's job. They chose Norman Kirkman who quit before 1954 was out. After managing Bradford, Norman became a baker, an estate agent, an aircraft worker, an insurance representative and a sales executive. The man the Bradford board rejected? Bill Shankly. On such decisions rest not only careers but the fortunes, or in the case of Bradford Park Avenue misfortunes, of clubs.

— ○ —

England set off to Switzerland with high hopes of doing well in the World Cup. We had lost the two internationals immediately preceding the competition, one of which was the 7–1 trouncing in the return game with Hungary, so I was somewhat surprised to say the least when I heard that Walter Winterbottom and the selectors had decided to stick with the same defence for our opening World Cup game against Belgium. Changes came to the forward line, my recall in place of Peter Harris being one of four. The only forward to remain in his position from the Hungary game was Tom Finney at outside-left.

The new-fashioned forward line did their bit. We scored four times with two each from Nat Lofthouse and Ivor Broadis. We also conceded four. It seemed to me that we hadn't learned a great deal from either our first venture into the World Cup in 1950 or those two telling games against the Hungarians. I think an attitude still prevailed among many in the FA that the two defeats at the hands of Hungary were 'one of those things' – a one-off that curiously had happened twice.

The press said I had an outstanding game against Belgium. I think I did OK, but then again so did all the England forwards. It was in defence that we were once again found to be so sadly lacking. Individually, our defence were good players. That was the problem – they played as individuals and not as a collective unit. Football was changing and while there was ample scope for individual talent to express itself, the top international teams were now becoming well organised, particularly at the back, something I never felt England were. In our second game, against Switzerland, changes were made to the England defence. Billy Wright was moved to centre-half with Billy McGarry of Huddersfield Town coming in at right-half. With respect, Billy had never been a great distributor of the ball, a prerequisite of any good international right-half at the time. However, he was a great competitor had not bad in the air, so to move him to centre-half made good sense.

I had picked up an injury against Belgium so had to sit this game out, my place against Switzerland being taken by Tom Finney, with the vacant outside-left berth going to Jimmy Mullen of Wolves.

In World Cups, games against the host nation are always tricky and a temperature on the pitch in excess of 100 degrees added to our problems, but goals from the Wolves pair of Dennis Wilshaw and Jimmy Mullen saw us safely through to a quarter-final clash with Uruguay, who in qualifying from their group had beaten Scotland 7–0.

Uruguay were one of the fancied teams in the competition and a side I rated very highly, but I was confident England had enough quality in the side to beat them. That we didn't wasn't down to lack of effort on our part. Indeed, we matched the Uruguayans for skill and technique for much of the game. We lost 4–2 and it has to be said that our goalkeeper Gil Merrick had had better games. When a goalkeeper makes errors he usually does so with catastrophic results. Outfield players can make elementary errors and get away with them; not so a goalkeeper. Uruguay's first goal was a soft one which crept in past Gil at his near post and I am sure it rattled him. When your goalkeeper is not playing with confidence or dominating his penalty area, the whole team senses it. It unnerves you. You are afraid to make a mistake for fear of the opposition going on the attack and scoring another. We had such tension in our play and although we were on top for the last 20 minutes, we couldn't take our chances and England exited from the World Cup.

I was very disappointed. It was my last chance to demonstrate my skills on the greatest stage football has to offer. I was, however, more disappointed from the point of view of the team. For all the chopping and changing and poor performances against Hungary, I felt we had the team to go all the way to the final. Against Uruguay, Billy Wright had been outstanding at centre-half, our defence had played well, but there is no legislating for goalkeeping errors. I felt sorry for Gil, he was a decent goalkeeper, but on the day I am sure even he would agree, three of the Uruguayan goals could be put down to him. But that's football.

Hungary were the popular favourites to win the World Cup. They had beaten Korea 9–0, West Germany 8–3 and had also accounted for Brazil and Uruguay both by 4–2 scorelines. In the final they came up against West Germany again but having scored an amazing 25 goals in four matches they came unstuck after racing into a 2–0 lead. German organisation and determination, seen so often in subsequent World Cups, was on show for the first time and in a thrilling final, West Germany were surprise 3–2 winners.

In terms of goals, this tournament was the most prolific of all World Cups – 140 goals scored in 26 games – so there was no argument from those lucky enough to attend that they had not been royally entertained and received value for money.

———— o ————

In the ensuing years, I was engaged in a constant unspoken battle with certain sportswriters who were quick to write me off as too old every time I had an off day. No matter if I had produced very good form for Blackpool in the previous six or so games, one so-so performance would bring the barbed pencils into action. As you get older, it takes that little bit longer to shake off injuries, even minor ones. In 1954–55 I missed just eight league games for Blackpool, but every time I was sidelined certain journalists would write to the effect it was down to my age and I couldn't take the knocks or pace of the game any more. It was all balderdash, I can tell you.

The fact that younger players at Blackpool – and, let's face it, they were all younger – such as Bomber Brown, Roy Gratrix and Dave Durie missed more games than me due to injury that season seemed to matter not one jot. The problem was compounded by the fact that irrespective of how well I played for England, if we lost I was the first to be dropped.

The constant reference to my age irritated me. I felt very fit and I was certainly still producing the goods in matches. Opponents certainly didn't take playing against me lightly. In fact, my performances aroused interest among other clubs, including Arsenal. In 1954, following a game at Highbury, I was approached by the Arsenal manager Tom Whittaker who said he wanted me to sign for the Gunners. The maximum wage limit was still in force, of course, and I pointed out to Tom that such a move could never be in my interests financially. In the first place, I was on the maximum wage at Blackpool so there was nothing to be gained by moving. Also, a move to a London club would mean moving house and property prices in the south east were far in excess of what they were in Blackpool. Tom understood the problem and explained that should I agree to sign for Arsenal, in addition to receiving the maximum wage, I would also be put on the wage bill of a catering company to do promotional work for them, although I would never be required to do any such work. This additional wage would, he told me, more than double my weekly wage income and as he was happy for me to continue my arrangement with the Co-op, I would be financially far better off. As for a home, I could keep on my current house in Blackpool and live in a 'club house'. Arsenal would buy it and I would vacate it when the time came for me to leave the club. It was a tempting offer, Arsenal were a big club, as far as I was concerned, but the move was never really on. I was very happy at Blackpool and therefore I politely turned down Tom's offer.

Such an approach was against the rules at the time and consequently I couldn't tell anyone about it and I never have until now. But the fact that a club of the stature of Arsenal were willing to pay so highly for my services confirmed my own belief that I still had years in me at the top and helped me ignore adverse comments about my age.

I have to say the criticism levelled at me was not unique. At the time, individual players came in for far more criticism from the press than they do today. Nowadays you find directors and managers are the subject of harsh words; rarely is a player lambasted for a performance. In the fifties and indeed throughout the thirties and forties, sportswriters were quick to fire a broadside at any player they felt had had a bad game and believe you me, such criticism could be so harsh it made you wilt at the knees. In the mid fifties I was still very much in the spotlight off the field as well as on it, some publicity self-generated through my promotional appearances for the Co-op. Some, however, I never knew about until the magazine or book in question hit the news-stands.

Players, myself included, were very naive when it came to what nowadays would be called our image. My face cropped up on the front of all manner of football annuals, cigarette cards, give aways with comics called something like 'Play the Stanley Matthews Way', even advertisements for products for which I was never paid. It never occurred to me that I could be making money out of such things. Whenever I saw my face on a football annual or peering out from the corner of a pack of sweets, I just thought it was good publicity; it never crossed my mind that I could be charging the company for using my name and image. Today players earn thousands of pounds in that way; not so in my playing days. I don't begrudge the money today's players receive for endorsing products. Why should a company make money off the back of the efforts of a player and the player receive nothing in return? It's not right, but that was the way it was in my day.

The fact that my name and image cropped up here, there and everywhere caused one or two reporters to question my commitment to the game. I had been in football in excess of 25 years and thought that alone was testimony to my great love for and commitment to it. One incident following a game at Spurs brought the barbs out.

I had not travelled with Blackpool to London on the Friday. Instead, I had gone to Ipswich for a Saturday morning promotional appearance as part of my deal with the Co-op. I arrived at White Hart Lane at two o'clock. Some reporters saw me dashing into the players' entrance and proceeded to ask around for the reason for my late arrival. We lost the match 2–0 and the following day a couple of newspapers ran a story along the lines of 'What right has Stanley Matthews to be tiring himself out going to Ipswich to sign autographs at a Co-op when his main commitment is to Blackpool?'

Such stories peeved me but I found the best way of dealing with it was to shake hands with the reporters concerned the next time I bumped into them, to be very pleasant in my conversation and emphasise how fit and keyed up I was for our next game. It usually worked. That way I could bite one of the hands that fed me and make it feel like a manicure. With some football writers, the only flair they showed was in their nostrils, but experience had taught me not to get on the wrong side of any sports reporter, irrespective of their talent or lack of it, for words and the truth. Most of all, I learned to take whatever they wrote with not a pinch but a packetful of salt. That way I kept not only a level head but my sanity. As Sam Goldwyn once said, 'Never pay any attention to your critics, don't even ignore them.'

—— o ——

The influence of the Hungarians was starting to filter through into the English game. At Manchester City, Don Revie was fulfilling a role not unlike that of Nandor Hidegkuti, playing as a deep-lying centre-forward. This system was tried when the Football league played the League of Ireland in Dublin in the autumn of 1954. We ran out convincing winners by six goals to nil, but rather than Don Revie, the player who caught my eye in this game was a young inside-forward from Fulham by the name of Johnny Haynes. He went on to become England captain, of course, but also made his mark in English football history as the first £100-a-week footballer when the maximum wage limit was abolished in 1961.

My own performance in this game was good enough to earn a recall at international level. I was named an outside-right for England's game against Northern Ireland in Belfast on 2 October. Don Revie continued in the role of a deep-lying centre-forward but although we won comfortably enough, with Don getting one of our goals, I didn't feel the system worked particularly well. That was in some way down to me. Don played very close to me and rather than complementing each other, we got in each other's way. I would receive the ball and, as is my wont, set off down the wing aiming to make a telling cross into the penalty area but often found Don out on the wing alongside me. What was the point of giving the ball back to Don? There wasn't any, so I tried for an early ball into the penalty area for Nat Lofthouse or Johnny Haynes, making Don to all intents and purposes superfluous. I was all for trying new systems, but new gameplans had to be suited to the players in the team at the time, and I felt

Don's role as a deep-lying centre-forward, which had worked well for his club, wasn't suited to England just then. This view was seemingly shared by Walter Winterbottom and the selectors because for England's next international against Wales the following month, they dropped not only the idea but Don himself.

Don wasn't the only change for the game against Wales. Although we had won in Belfast, no fewer than seven changes were made. Chelsea's Roy Bentley came in for Don Revie at inside-right and justified his inclusion by scoring all three of our goals in a 3–2 win. West Brom's Ronnie Allen replaced Nat Lofthouse at centre-forward and Sunderland's Len Shackleton came in at inside-left for Johnny Haynes. I received excellent write-ups for my performance against Wales which, for a time at any rate, served to quell the stories that I was too old for international football.

The victories over Northern Ireland and Wales did much for the confidence of the England team but the jury was still out on how England would perform against top-class continental opposition. We supplied the answer in our next international, at Wembley in December against World Cup holders West Germany.

West Germany fielded a side far different from the one that had won the World Cup. Only three players who had played against Hungary – captain Posipal, Kohlmeyer and Liebrich – appeared at Wembley. Nevertheless, our winning margin of 3–1 was a highly creditable performance and it did much to restore national pride in English football. I enjoyed myself immensely in this game. The German centre-half Liebrich later wrote in his memoirs that my performance in this game placed me 'at the very peak of international players, akin to Maradona or Beckenbauer'. Praise indeed, though the passing years may have allowed him to gloss over the errors I remember making during the game itself! The English press were also full of praise for my performance but in fact it was a fine all-round team performance. Still, with my fortieth birthday less than two months away, I was delighted to receive such write-ups. I had been up against a good full-back in Kohlmeyer and had led him a merry dance. I never felt fazed by the fact that some players I was up against were 20 years my junior.

As a point of interest, the West Germany team that day included Uwe Seeler, a young forward who would go on to become something of a German footballing legend and a thorn in England's side in the 1970 World Cup. Also in the side was Jupp Derwall, a classy inside-forward and a wonderfully gracious man who at 27 was in his prime as a player. He eventually succeeded Helmut Schoen as West Germany's national team manager and enjoyed considerable success in that role.

Len Shackleton, who was happy to be dubbed 'The Clown Prince of Soccer' because of his extravagant and often eccentric behaviour on the field, had a superb game against the Germans but was never picked for England again. Len was unpredictable, brilliantly inconsistent, flamboyant, radical and mischievous; in short, he possessed all the attributes of a footballing genius which he undoubtedly was. But such a character would not go down well with the blazer brigade who ran English football and had such an important say in the selection of the England team. Len would often say or do something to upset authority and I believe this predilection of his to shock was something the FA and England management were always uneasy about, and thus they never warmed to him.

Outspoken comments about coaching and his contempt for officialdom didn't endear Len to the England hierarchy and, despite his undoubted genius, this most talented of inside-forwards won only five caps in what was to all intents and purposes a fine footballing career with Bradford Park Avenue, Newcastle United and Sunderland.

Len was a continuous exasperation and affront to the conventional and the conformists of English football, of whom there were many. He even made fun of fellow professionals not blessed with his considerable talents. In one game for Sunderland, having beaten a full-back, he put his foot on the ball and pulled the cuff of his shirt sleeve back, implying he was checking his wristwatch and not taking any notice of events on the field. Then, as the full-back came roaring in for a second bite of the cherry, he dragged the ball back with the sole of his foot, to the delight of the Roker Park crowd but to the great annoyance of the opposing full-back who rightly felt he had been made a fool of. The full-back in question tackled fresh air. Len slipped away with the ball at his feet and rubbed salt in the wound by arrogantly gesturing with his hands that he was taking a cup from its saucer and sipping tea.

The supporters loved such showmanship, but the authorities and opponents felt he was going too far, not in showing off his superior skills but in allowing full rein to the impish side of his character and showing lesser players to be foolish by comparison. Like George Best and Paul Gascoigne, Len Shackleton often displayed a cheerful disregard not only for authority but for his own career.

Len played to the gallery and in so doing, fully demonstrated what I have always believed about football – that it is not only a superbly dramatic and exciting game but can be a wonderfully clever one. For long periods in a match, Len would be quiet, often contributing little, but the two or three minutes when he turned it on and did something unpredictable and outrageous would be the moments of the game that provided the supporters with a golden memory to cherish for ever. As one supporter once told me, 'Two minutes of Shack's genius is worth the admission price alone.' Indeed it was, but the difficulty of fitting such an individual and inconsistent genius into a team's playing system was Len's Achilles' heel, certainly at international level.

Len Shackleton's talents were extravagant in the extreme, he was inordinately clever and, despite playing to the crowd, I never saw him being selfish to team-mates. He was no mean goalscorer himself, and made many a goal for his fellow forwards, a fact that only those who had the pleasure of playing alongside him now seem to remember. For all his individuality, he did buckle down to team play when the mood took him, especially in his time at Sunderland. However, in the latter stages of a match when it was evident the game was either won or lost, it was as if he said to himself, 'Stuff this for a game of soldiers,' and he would proceed to amuse himself and the crowd. To apply himself fully to a gameplan or a task for 90 minutes seemed beyond him. His capacity to shock and entertain in equal measures won him that dubious title, 'The Clown Prince of Soccer', which I feel belies his true genius.

Your reaction to Len Shackleton, saint or sinner, depended on what sort of person you were and how you viewed football. In the final minutes of one game, with Sunderland coasting to a victory over Leicester City, he waltzed through the Leicester defence and sold the oncoming goalkeeper a great dummy. With the Leicester goalkeeper scrambling in his wake, Len took the ball to the goalline, stopped it dead and called over his shoulder to the scurrying goalkeeper, 'Come on, have another go, it's not over the line yet!' That's a typical example of Len Shackleton's superior skills and arrogance which amply illustrate why he was known among his fellow professionals as the 'Player's Player'.

On his retirement from football in 1958, Len became a

football writer, most notably for the *People*. He was also a fully qualified boxing referee and for a short time in the mid seventies, was a director of Fulham. That eminent sports writer John Moynihan memorably described the club as being, 'A Saturday afternoon team, offering a feeling of animated recreation rather than solid professionalism. A side of happy, sometimes comic, triers watched by garrulous actors, serious actors, pantomime players, band leaders, stuntmen and starlets in tweeds, black leather, pink ankle-length knickers, baggy overcoats over armour-plated suede and with cheroots between thumb and first finger.' Rather than Len's appointment as a director of a football club, it was his all too brief association with Fulham that was the surprising thing. Given Moynihan's description of the club, I felt Len would have been at home there.

———— ○ ————

At Blackpool we didn't enjoy the best of domestic seasons, finishing a lowly nineteenth in Division One, only three points ahead of Leicester City who occupied the second relegation spot. Luck plays an important part in football and up until Christmas, if it wasn't for bad luck, we wouldn't have had any luck at all. In September, for example, in front of a crowd in excess of 50,000 at Molineux, we outplayed Wolves hitting the woodwork three times but lost 1–0. In the following month, a series of bad results continued when we went to Bramall Lane, played Sheffield United off the park but lost 2–1 with Harry Johnston scoring two own goals. Things did pick up in the New Year. There were notable victories over Leicester City, Everton, Burnley and Manchester City, the latter by six goals to one, and a creditable 0–0 draw at title-chasing Chelsea in front of 56,000. All of that thankfully helped us to pull clear of the relegation trapdoor.

In the FA Cup we had a ignominious exit at home in round three at the hands of York City from Division Three North. To be fair to York City, 1954–55 was the season in which they very nearly became the first-ever Third Division team to reach an FA Cup final. They went on to beat Spurs and only succumbed to Newcastle United 2–0 in the semi-final after a replay. The amazing thing about York's FA Cup run was that they did it without a manager. Jimmy McCormick left the club in September 1954 and the club didn't replace him until they appointed the former Charlton Athletic goalkeeper Sam Bartram as manager two years later in 1956. Without a manager, York not only reached the FA Cup semi-final but just missed out on promotion to Division Two. Make of that what you will.

The season ended on a personal high note as far as my international career was concerned when in April 1955 England beat Scotland 7–2 at Wembley. At the time, it was the heaviest defeat suffered by Scotland in the Home International Championship. The Scots had been beaten 4–2 by Hungary at Hampden in December, a result that, given England's two trouncings at the hands of the same Hungarian team, was seen as a moral victory. Scotland fielded all but one of the team that had performed so creditably against Hungary and although I was confident of an England win, the margin of our victory surprised even me. Don Revie was recalled to play what today we would call a midfield schemer's role and he linked up with me in a much more positive way than he had on his international debut against Northern Ireland.

Despite the plaudits England had received for our performance against West Germany, there were seven changes for the game against Scotland. The inconsistency of selection was by now par for the course, irrespective of how England had played in the previous international. I never knew what the line-up for the following game would be and was just pleased to be included. Chelsea's Roy Bentley, having scored a hat-trick against Wales and another goal against West Germany found himself out of the side against Scotland.

The newspapers bestowed the honours for England's then record victory over Scotland on me and, I have to admit, when the Wembley crowd rose to applaud me off the field, I was very moved. Again, however, I have to emphasise this was a fine all-round team performance, marked by four goals from Dennis Wilshaw and by the international debut of an 18-year-old who impressed me greatly, Duncan Edwards of Manchester United. I had been playing professional football before Duncan was born and my age was the cause of much good-natured humour among my England team-mates who made such comments as 'Stan's National Insurance number is 3A' and 'Stan's the only player whose car is insured against Viking raids'. There were also requests for me to tell them what football was like when players had to wear pill-box hats and there were no crossbars just rope strung out between the goalposts. I took it all in good part. As it turned out, I had another 11 years at the top in football and outlasted just about every one of them!

The domestic season ended with Chelsea, managed by my old England team-mate Ted Drake, as First Division Champions. Chelsea were hard-pressed all the way by Wolves, Portsmouth and Sunderland who all finished on 48 points, four points behind Chelsea whose 52 was the lowest total ever to win the First Division Championship. Chelsea were only 14 points ahead of Blackpool and we just escaped relegation, which goes to show how tight the First Division was that season. It was one of the most competitive seasons I had ever known in football. There wasn't much to choose between any of the teams in the First Division and there were many thrilling encounters.

Chelsea's success as English league champions brought them an invitation to compete in the newly formed European Cup. The club accepted and were drawn against the Swedish side Djurgaarden but the FA intervened and put pressure on Chelsea to withdraw. In the opinion of the FA, the newly formed European competitions were merely an inconsequential distraction from the really important business of our domestic league, an opinion I might add that was totally out of step with that of many clubs and players.

This is not to say the game wasn't developing; it was, albeit slowly. In the summer of 1955, the FA lifted the ban of Sunday football, which allowed thousands of people who worked or went to matches on Saturdays the opportunity to play organised football themselves. The FA's line at the time was that while it would not recognise or organise Sunday play for amateur players, participants would not be suspended. It was a move forward.

The FA and the Football League stipulated that no match in which a Football League club participated could be televised without the League management's permission and so league football remained absent from our screens until the sixties. The view taken was that televised football would have a catastrophic effect on attendances, and this was a view held until the late eighties when the power in the game swung away from the football authorities to TV companies and it became evident that rather than having an adverse effect on attendances, televised games played a significant role in increasing interest in football.

In 1955 there were 36 league clubs with floodlights but perversely the FA and Football League had hitherto allowed floodlights to be used only for friendly games and, what's more, deemed that players should not be paid for such matches. In the summer of 1955, the FA ruled that postponed league matches could be played under floodlights along with replayed FA Cup ties, but only up to the third round proper. Why the clubs who had invested on floodlights were not allowed to use them for league games and FA Cup ties, especially replays from round three onwards, when the competition was played in the heart of the British winter and daylight hours were short, is beyond me. Suffice to say this was another example of the nonsensical way the game was run by two governing bodies that were old-fashioned, autocratic and personally proprietorial. Their suspicion of any change in football had as much to do with their lack of vision and understanding of how the game was developing as it did a fear that any new development would result in a reduction of their powers.

— o —

I spent part of the summer on tour with England but there wasn't much to write home about. Although I was enjoying a renaissance on the international front, England lost their opening match of the tour 1–0 against France. This was followed by a 1–1 draw with Spain in Madrid and a 3–1 defeat against Portugal in Oporto. The chopping and changing of the England team continued. For the game against France, two changes were made to the team that had demolished Scotland only a month before. More changes were made in the subsequent games against Spain and Portugal and although I felt I had given a good account of myself in all three games, the fact that England had not done well on tour made me feel, given my age, that I would be made a scapegoat. I was only partly right. When the new 1955–56 season got under way and England met Denmark in Copenhagen in October, I was one of no less than eight changes to the team that had played in the previous international against Portugal! Continuity, it seemed, was not high on the list of priorities of the England management and selectors at that time.

On returning from tour with England, I accepted an invitation to coach in South Africa. This was the first of what would turn out to be annual visits over the next 25 years. With Joe Smith's permission, I did all my pre-season training in the township of Soweto where I was coaching black youngsters. I enjoyed my time there so much, I didn't arrive back in England until the day before the new 1955–56 football season started. I joined the Blackpool party at our team hotel on the Saturday morning for our opening fixture against Arsenal at Highbury. When I arrived, Joe Smith was sitting in the hotel lobby and immediately rose to his feet when he saw me.

'Where the bloody hell have you been?' he said.

'South Africa,' I replied. 'I rang and told you, but you never listen.'

'When did you get back?'

'Last night.'

'Are you match fit?'

'Yes.'

Joe turned to reserve-team player John McKenna who had been sitting alongside him.

'You're not playing,' said Joe, to the bewilderment of McKenna and not a little embarrassment to myself. I felt for the lad, who had obviously been keyed up for his big day only to be rejected in such an offhand manner.

The game against Arsenal was considered one of my best ever for Blackpool. Ernie Taylor, Bill Perry and Morty scored our goals in a 3–1 victory to give us the perfect start to the new season. I was feeling refreshed after my trip to South Africa and my confidence was sky high. At one point in the second half I stood for what must have been ten seconds with my foot waving over the ball and not one Arsenal player was prepared to come and try to take it off me. As a player, you know when you are having a good game and have the opposition rattled when they begin to switch things and allocate a different player to mark you during the course of a game from the one originally given the responsibility. This game began with me being marked by Lionel Smith. He gave way to Walley Barnes who was followed by Alex Forbes, then Joe Mercer and eventually near the end, Don Roper.

Jackie Mudie is on record as saying that this was the greatest game he ever saw me play. The Arsenal manager Tom Whittaker was quoted in the press the next day as saying, 'I've never seen him play so well. At over 40 years of age, it's a miracle.' I wouldn't go so far as to say I agree with Jackie's comment about it being the greatest game he saw me play. I enjoyed the standing ovation the Arsenal supporters gave me when I walked off the pitch and just thought, 'Not bad for someone knocking on 41 who has spent all his pre-season playing and coaching teenagers in Soweto.'

21

— o —

The End of my England Career

For the next three years I was in and out of the England team while Blackpool launched concerted efforts to win the league championship without ever doing so.

In October 1955, I played for England in a 1–1 draw against Wales at Ninian Park but missed the next three internationals. On the domestic front, Blackpool finished as runners-up to champions Manchester United. That opening-day victory at Arsenal set the scene for the rest of a season in which Blackpool enjoyed some memorable results. Sunderland were beaten 7–3 at Bloomfield Road, Aston Villa 6–0, Charlton Athletic 5–0, West Bromwich Albion and Newcastle United by 5–1 scorelines and we rattled in four against both Everton and Huddersfield Town.

It wasn't bad going considering we had lost Morty through injury in October. It meant he missed the rest of the season and he decided after spells with Hull and Southport, to retire from playing and concentrate on the sports shops he owned in the town. Morty's position at centre-forward was taken by Jackie Mudie, with Jackie's position at inside-left being shared for various spells by Bomber Brown and Dave Durie from our youth team. In 15 league matches, Dave gave ample evidence of his promise by notching 14 goals.

Joe Smith was slowly dismantling the side that had won the FA Cup. Older players such as Harry Johnston, who had retired, and Eddie Shimwell were replaced by younger players. In addition to Dave Durie, this season marked the emergence of Jimmy Armfield at right-back. Jimmy went on to become Blackpool's most capped player, winning 43 caps for England. He played 568 league games for Blackpool which remains a club record to this day.

Jimmy hailed from Denton in Manchester. He represented Lancashire at rugby but chose football as his career. He signed for us as an amateur in 1951, turning professional in 1954. Jimmy was an excellent full-back who got on with his game in a quiet and unassuming manner. He had no airs or graces and though he was never a robust full-back and had no great flair, his reading of the game and ability to win the ball ensured he made the number two shirt his own. His strength was his tackling; his timing was immaculate. When he first came into the side, I never thought he used the ball well. His passing it seemed to me was poor. But he worked hard at his game and improved with every match to the extent that he became one of the best distributors of the ball I can ever recall playing with at Blackpool. He was without doubt a fine full-back and one of the nicest guys you could ever wish to meet.

On retiring in 1971, Jimmy was appointed manager of Bolton Wanderers. He moved to Leeds United in 1974 and guided them to the European Cup final. When he left Elland Road, he went to work as a broadcaster for BBC Radio for whom he still works, combining it with an advisory role with the FA. We talk often on the telephone swapping football news and it is always a delight to hear from one of the really good guys to have graced the game. Jimmy has come a long way since his days as a raw young full-back with Blackpool and deserves all the success that has come his way, though he might not thank me for recalling one particular incident that I bet he has long since forgotten.

It was Boxing Day in 1955 and we were at home to Huddersfield Town. Jimmy had replaced Eddie Shimwell at right-back in October. He enjoyed a continuous run of some dozen games in that role and was just beginning to feel his feet and come to terms with the fact he was a first-team regular, enjoying the confidence that such a position brings. Joe Smith had noticed this and didn't want Jimmy to become over-confident but he wasn't sure how to deal with the situation. Joe wanted to keep Jimmy on his mettle, but felt if he were to give him a chat about the problems that could lie ahead when this unknown quantity was known to opposing teams, Jimmy's confidence could take a dive and the effect of that would be as detrimental as over-confidence. Jimmy had done well but skipper Harry Johnston believed that he had had a fortunate start because his opposing winger, rather than bearing down on him, invariably spent much time shackling me. Harry used to wind young Jimmy up about this. On more than one occasion as we sat soaking in the plunge bath after a game, Harry said, 'Jimmy, I think you should give Stan half your wages. That winger you were up against today spent half the game tracking Stan about.'

As we were about to get changed for the Huddersfield game, the situation Joe had been looking for suddenly presented itself when young Jimmy made to leave the dressing room.

'Where are you off to?' asked Joe.

'Reception. To hand out complimentary tickets for my family and friends.'

'Sit yourself back down and get changed,' said Joe. 'If your family and friends aren't prepared to pay to see you play, who the hell do you think will?'

Job done.

———○———

Manchester United under Matt Busby were worthy league champions in 1955–56 and Matt won his battle with the FA for the right for United to compete in the European Cup the following season. The inaugural European Cup took place in 1955–56 without champions Chelsea, although Hibernian competed under the Scottish banner. Matt Busby was, as I have already said, a visionary. He saw the great potential that European competition offered and wanted United to be part of it. Happily in the face of what was initially strong opposition from the FA, he stood his ground and won the day.

Matt had developed a youth policy that at the time was second to none. His young charges were dubbed the Busby Babes and included players such as Duncan Edwards, Bobby Charlton, Wilf McGuinness, Jackie Blanchflower, Dave Pegg, Roger Byrne, Dennis Viollet, Bill Foulkes, Eddie Colman, Liam Whelan, John Berry, Ray Wood and Tommy Taylor. To my mind, they were the most exceptional crop of youngsters ever to have been assembled at a British club and of those I have mentioned, only three – Tommy Taylor, Ray Wood and John Berry – cost Matt any sort of a fee. The Munich air crash of 1958 was to claim the lives of eight of Matt's brilliant youngsters, including Geoff Bent, the reserve left-back. I still see one or two of the others, most notably Wilf McGuinness and Bobby Charlton. Wilf was a fine wing-half whose career was cut short by injury. He has developed into a very funny and accomplished after-dinner speaker. Bobby I often come across at official FA functions.

Wilf was very humorous, sometimes unwittingly so, as a youngster. During one encounter between United and Blackpool, Wilf was given the job of marking Jackie Mudie who, on the day, had too much experience and guile for the young Wilf. Time and again, Jackie would feint one way only to set off in the opposite direction and lose Wilf. By half-time Jackie had notched two goals and as the teams headed toward the dressing rooms for the half-time cuppa, a number of United players started to express their concern at the fact that Jackie Mudie had scored twice.

'Don't blame me for those two goals,' said Wilf defensively. 'When Mudie scored them, I was nowhere near him!'

The advent of the first European Cup did a lot to open people's eyes to the fact that there was much to be admired in football beyond our shores. Slowly but surely, the inward-looking attitude that had prevailed in British football began to diminish, especially when people saw Real Madrid. Real won the first European Cup by beating Reims of France by four goals to three. It was the first of five consecutive European Cups for the Spanish giants; they seemed unbeatable. Real had some of the best players in the world in their ranks. They had a superb goalkeeper in Alonso who was later replaced by the equally competent Argentinian, Rogelio Dominguez; the gifted Santamaria and captain Jose Maria Zarraga; Frenchman Raymond Kopa who was a prolific goalscorer; the flying winger Gento; the cunning Rial; artisan Del Sol; and, to my mind, one of the greatest players ever to grace the game, a true footballing genius, Alfredo Di Stefano. As if that wasn't enough, in 1959 Real added Puskas to their ranks. It was like adding 120 lbs of the finest icing sugar to what was already an overly rich and sumptuous cake.

Unbeknown to them at the time, Real served as a catalyst for the European game. Many continental teams played a very flat, patient game, but Real changed all that. With their swaggering, explosive style and predeliction for attacking in waves, they set the standard for entertaining football and did so to the highest level.

The two leading lights of that great real team were Alfredo Di Stefano and Puskas. Both kindly agreed to play in my testimonial game at Stoke in 1965 and I formed lasting friendships with both players. Di Stefano played as a deep-lying centre-forward and was to all intents and purposes the hub of the Real team around whom everything turned. He was a player of serious expression who radiated character and intelligence; an extraordinary player who could size up any situation in a flash and act accordingly. His mastery of the ball was complete and his great powers of acceleration took him with consummate ease past usually bewildered opponents. Off the ball, he would glide ghost-like into excellent positions; on receiving the ball, he would bring the team-mates around him into the picture. The Real players played instinctively to Di Stefano, which was no more surprising than a theatre cast playing to Lord Olivier. He preserved the balance and dictated the tempo and just as Olivier could out-act anyone, Di Stefano could outplay all around him.

At the end of the 1955–56 season, the first-ever European Footballer of the Year award was introduced and, to my complete surprise and embarrassment, it was given to me. I couldn't believe my performances warranted such a prestigious award but, for all I felt others were more worthy, it is something I look back on with great pride.

Having been out of favour in the England set-up for the best part of 1955–56, my form for Blackpool once again brought calls from the press and public for my re-instatement and I found myself recalled for the game against Brazil at Wembley in May. I was delighted to be back on the international scene and particularly pleased at the prospect of pitting my wits against the Brazilians whom I admired so much. It turned out to be an extraordinary match. Brazil fielded several of the team that had reached the World Cup quarter-final two years before and the new players formed the nucleus of the team that would go on to win the World Cup in Sweden in 1958.

I was up against the Brazilian captain Nilton Santos. He and right-back Djalma Santos formed a formidable full-back pairing. They were fast, aggressive and not only fine defenders but superb all-round ball players in what we now call the Brazilian tradition.

England ran out 4–2 winners and I was in my element. The Brazilians possessed remarkable skills but they were not as tactically efficient as they would be in winning the World Cup in 1958. I had a hand in all four England goals and afterwards that brilliant inside-forward Didi paid me what I consider to be the ultimate compliment when he told me, 'Stan, you play more like a Brazilian or Argentinian than you do a British player.'

It was as exciting and entertaining a game of football as I had ever played in. The Brazilians gave dazzling virtuoso performances without really gelling as a team and I think that was the telling point in England's victory. Manchester United's Tommy Taylor and Sheffield United's Colin Grainger scored two goals apiece. Grainger was known as 'The Singing Footballer'. He had a decent crooning voice, good enough to secure a recording contract and numerous cabaret appearances. He could have made a career out of singing but it was the right voice at the wrong time. Colin was a crooner in the Dickie Valentine mould and that style was soon to become old-fashioned with the advent of rock 'n' roll, so his career as a popular singer never really got out of the starting blocks.

My performances against Brazil produced a wealth of plaudits from a press no doubt smug at the fact that they had called for my return and I had performed so well. To a paper they called for my inclusion in the England team that were due to tour Sweden, Finland and Germany that summer. However, I had already committed myself to another coaching trip to South Africa and therefore had to declare myself unavailable. I knew at the time this would not do my future chances with the England team much good, especially as I would be 42 on my next birthday. It was a shame but when I accepted the invitation to coach in South Africa I wasn't part of the England set-up and didn't think a recall was on the cards. Still, I set off for South Africa in good heart. England had beaten world champions West Germany and much-fancied Brazil and I had played a role in both victories. It reinforced what I had always believed – there was plenty of life left in the old legs yet.

——— o ———

For a couple of years I had realised that I didn't have to do as much training to be match fit. Some players train harder as they get older in order to keep up their level of fitness, but after 35 years of intense training, man and boy – and I am sure I did far more than any other player – I realised I just didn't need to do as much. I still got up early in the morning and indulged in a session of stretch exercises and sprints, but overall I cut back, even on training at Blackpool. I knew my own body and thought that after 25 years of rigorous daily training, I needed to do top-up training sessions only, as my general level of fitness was now almost ingrained into me. In football then as now, the vast bulk of training to ensure a player is fit for the season is done pre-season. That is when the really hard work is done. The daily training sessions that follow are of a much lighter variety with perhaps one intense session every three to four weeks. With my trips to South Africa I was missing the pre-season work at Blackpool but I can say in all honesty, it did not have a detrimental effect on me. Besides, playing against teenagers in the Soweto township was no cake walk, believe me. So with the fifties coming to a close and remarkably finding myself still at the top in football, I tempered my commitment to training without it having any undue effect on my level of fitness.

I may have been fit but there's not much you can do about injuries. After a good start to the 1956–57 season, I picked up an ankle injury during our 3–0 win at Manchester City in late September that was to dog me throughout the season. I played intermittently thereafter, clocking up just 14 more appearances, and they came in little bursts of three or four games.

The Blackpool team had changed much. George Farm was still there in goal but only Ernie Taylor, Jackie Mudie and Bill Perry remained as regulars from the side that had won the FA Cup. Hughie Kelly and Ewan Fenton were still with the club, but their appearances were spasmodic as Joe Smith, position by position, sifted out the old guard and replaced them with new blood. I knew my time would come some day, but despite the injury, Joe showed no indication whatsoever of letting me go. I have to say, that pleased me immensely; I was still enjoying my football to the full and far from diminishing my enthusiasm for the game, the passing years merely made me thirst for it more. I couldn't imagine a better life for me than that of a footballer and I was determined to carry on as long as I could. A player knows within himself when his appetite for the game has gone. He knows when he can't do the business any more. He doesn't need the press or anyone else to tell him. His legs are the first to let him know, but I felt as fit as ever I had been and I can only put that down to a lifetime commitment to training, my healthy lifestyle and diet, and the chemistry my body had been blessed with.

Blackpool finished a creditable fourth in Division One in 1956–57 emphasising once again our status as one of English football's leading teams. My appearances were limited to just 25 in the whole season because of injury, but the games in which I did feature I fully enjoyed. I always loved going to London to play the big teams from the capital and, as luck would have it, in between spells on the sidelines I managed to play against both Chelsea and Arsenal in the capital with both games ending in draws. Those games in London were watched by the England selectors and I did well enough to earn a recall into the England team for what was to be my international swan song.

England had done well on their summer tour in 1956, and one would have thought, given that and my age, I would not get a look-in at international level again, but with a selection committee given to aligning themselves to popular opinion (I always thought, to lift the burden of criticism from their shoulders), I knew there was always a chance of me regaining my England place. I wasn't wrong.

I was picked to play against Northern Ireland in October 1956 and, despite my ankle injury, managed to play in all seven internationals that season. England remained unbeaten, which pleased everyone especially as the games against the Republic of Ireland and Denmark were qualifiers for the 1958 World Cup in Sweden. Having played in all these games, I nurtured high hopes of playing in another World Cup but, as it was to turn out, the game against Denmark on 15 May 1957, which England won 4–1, was to be my very last in an England shirt.

The selectors and Walter Winterbottom had for over a decade pondered over whether myself or Tom Finney should occupy the outside-right berth. Tom was an outstanding player and, as such, their quandary had been solved by the fact he was so versatile; Tom could play in every position in the forward line. It meant a place for Tom could be found in the England team, while I continued in my natural position of outside right. In the summer of 1957, however, the selectors and Walter Winterbottom decided Tom would be best suited to outside-right, which would allow them to include the talented Manchester United winger David Pegg at outside left.

I was greatly disappointed not to play in the World Cup but could have no complaints. I was 43 and having made my debut in 1935 I had enjoyed 22 years as an international and won 54 caps, not including wartime internationals. Who knows if it might have been more? No other player had enjoyed such a long England career, but that does not detract from the fact that I felt the selectors were wrong and I wasn't alone in that opinion.

The press called for my re-instatement, but this time their words went unheeded. What pleased me more was that team-mates like Tom Finney in *Finney on Football*, were saying, 'If I were England's sole selector, Stanley Matthews would have been in the 1958 World Cup party to Sweden.' Tom's opinion is always one I have respected greatly and if he felt I was good enough, and not too old, that was good enough for me. I still felt I had plenty to offer and if England didn't think so, fortunately Blackpool still did. With the lessons that had been meted out by Hungary, and the emergence of fine teams in the newly introduced European competitions, most notably Real Madrid, British football in the late fifties underwent a modernisation.

Managers realised there were different systems to play. Players were bought or groomed to fit whatever system a team adopted. Wolves had success with a long-ball game; West Ham were laying the foundations for what would be called their Academy; Manchester City adopted a style not too dissimilar to Hungary's by playing Don Revie as a deep-lying centre-forward; and at Blackpool, we played what in many respects was a 4-4-2 system with myself and Bill Perry playing wide on the wings but coming up from deep.

Training which for decades had been stereotyped also changed. The days of players turning up every day, doing a few laps of the cinder track, then going back in for a shower and a Woodbine were consigned to the past. Many managers and trainers attended the newly established FA Coaching Centre at Lilleshall where from Walter Winterbottom and others they learned the tactics of the top continental coaches such Helenio Herrera of Barcelona, Inter Milan and Roma. Players started to adopt lightweight kit, an idea I had picked up from the Brazilians in 1950. They were leaner, fitter, more mobile and looked the part. The attitude to the game became more professional. Teams realised the importance of warming up properly before a game. The use of weights became part and parcel of a player's training as managers saw the need for physical strength as much as fitness and stamina. Ball work was introduced into daily training to a level hitherto unknown.

I welcomed these new ideas though, at the risk of sounding pompous, I had been practising many of them for the best part of my life. If British football was to compete with the best in Europe and the world, we needed to get our act together so I was all for the new professionalism that came into the game in the mid to late fifties. With any new and worthwhile ideas, however, there comes a point when it can go wrong. In many respects this happened in British football and it has been the case for many years.

There was, of course, a need for coaching and a better level of fitness, but the movement towards that has, over the years, gone too far. The emphasis on coaching individuals and playing to a system has become so great, it restricts players. Many teams nowadays play to too rigid a system and as a result the more talented players do not have the freedom to express themselves and develop to their full potential. I look at the dugout during a game today and often see a manager, his assistant and sometimes anything up to three coaches at various times, all shouting instructions to players. I want to jump up and say, 'For heaven's sake, just let the players get on with it.' Such a barrage of advice from the touchline, no matter how well meaning, in my opinion serves only to prevent a player from playing his game and in many respects just confuses him. How can a manager in the dressing room prior to a match tell players, 'Go out and play your natural game' and then proceed to bellow instructions about what he wants them to do once they are out there on the pitch? I once saw an England international game where, in addition to Kevin Keegan and coaches Les Reed, Derek Fazackerley and Arthur Cox sat on the England bench, there was also goalkeeping coach Ray Clemence. Ray was a superb goalkeeper in his day but I couldn't help wondering why he was there during the game. If the England goalkeeper, which on this day was David Seaman, with his level of experience doesn't know what he should be doing, it's a bit late to be telling him during the course of an international match.

The move towards 'greater professionalism' has also served to stifle players' characters. It's a common complaint nowadays that football does not have the characters it once did. Little wonder when players function within rigid systems and any effort on their part to entertain the fans or introduce a little humour into a game is seen as unprofessional. Today any player who attempts to bring humour to the proceedings or to do something extravagant, runs the risk of being branded a buffoon and not taking his job or role within the team seriously. Paul Gascoigne is a recent case in point.

Manchester United took Europe by storm in 1956–57. United played their preliminary round against Belgian champions Anderlecht at Maine Road, which had floodlights. They won 10–0. The Anderlecht captain Jef Mermans, an old pal of mine, was prompted to say, 'Why don't they [the England selectors] pick the whole side for England? The best teams from Hungary have never beaten us like this.' Indeed they hadn't. United eventually reached the semi-final where they gave British football some degree of pride by drawing 2–2 with the great Real Madrid. Unfortunately, it was not enough as Real won the home leg 3–1. United were out of the European Cup but in reaching the semi-final and in giving Real two really tough games they had displayed to everyone that British football was no longer isolated and inward-looking. The football we played was industrious, what Real played was art, but United's performances in Europe showed that progress was being made to fuse the two, which was Matt Busby's ultimate ambition.

——○——

Joe Smith still showed no inclination to move me to one side in 1957–58 and I enjoyed another profitable season with Blackpool. We finished seventh. We were never in the hunt for the championship, eventually won by Wolves, but for a club based in a provincial seaside town, it was another satisfactory season.

The interesting thing about this season was how many actual results the First Division produced. There were very few draws. We won 19 and lost 17 of our 42 matches with just six ending in a draw. Twelve of the 22 teams in the First Division drew eight or fewer of their 42 games. The emphasis was very much on winning matches and that produced goals galore. Wolves, Preston and Manchester City all scored in excess of 100, with Spurs and West Bromwich Albion both finishing in the high 90s. Blackpool averaged two goals per game and even Sheffield Wednesday, who finished rooted to the bottom and were subsequently relegated, scored 69. It all made for entertaining football which the supporters loved, even if some of the new coaches in the game balked at the fact they had teams that 'leaked' goals like a sieve.

1958 was the year of the Munich air disaster. In February, the plane carrying the Manchester United party back from a European game in Belgrade crashed in a blizzard when attempting to take off from Munich airport. Over half the 40 people on board lost their lives, including several United players and my old England colleague and dear friend Frank Swift who had been covering the game in his new career as a sports journalist. Among the other journalists to lose their lives was Don Davies. Under the pseudonym 'The Old International', Don produced sports reports for the *Manchester Guardian*, as it was then known, and for the BBC. Don had a preoccupation with the arts that was reflected in his sports writing. He was without doubt one of the very best, a man whose personal example was a source of constant encouragement and cheerful inspiration to many, no matter how humble they deemed themselves to be. On Don's death it was found that he had scribbled the following quotation in his notebook:

> He loved great things, and
> thought little of himself;
> desiring neither fame nor
> influence, he won the devotion

> of men and was a power in their
> lives: and seeking no disciples,
> he taught to many the greatness
> of the earth and of man's mind.

No one knows in what context Don Davies intended to use that quote. It comes from a memorial tablet to Richard Lewis Nettleship, a tutor of Balliol College, Oxford, which can be found in the college chapel. In many ways it is applicable to Don himself but it also serves as a pertinent and thought-provoking maxim to any aspiring sports person today, particularly any budding Premiership footballer. The quotation expresses a sentiment I have attempted to adhere to throughout my career and as such it has special meaning for me as, for reasons we were never to know, it obviously did to Don.

For Blackpool, 1958 was a watershed year because Joe Smith left the club after 23 years in charge. It still isn't clear whether Joe left of his own accord or was pushed, but leave he did and, to my mind, the day he cleared his desk, Blackpool said goodbye to the best manager they have ever had in their history. Perhaps the fact we had not repeated our great FA Cup success of 1953 and had not won the First Division Championship despite being there or thereabouts, prompted the Blackpool directors to look for a new man to take the helm. Maybe, after 23 years at Bloomfield Road and now subject to bouts of ill-health, Joe simply felt he had had enough. Whatever the reason was, his departure saddened me.

He was, as I have said so often, a wily old bird. Never a great tactician, or even a reasonable one, he was nevertheless the best manager I ever had the privilege to play for. Joe brought out the best in me because he allowed me to play my natural game. I will always be grateful for his support and belief, especially when I look back to those moments when situations contrived to make me doubt myself and my own ability. When the Blackpool board agreed to my transfer to what was then a declining Stoke City, he stood firm and wouldn't let me go. The fact that I stayed to enjoy Blackpool's, and my, finest hour was all down to Joe and I like to think my performance in that 1953 Cup final went some way to repaying the faith he always had in me.

Joe was a great psychologist who could kid an average player into believing and performing as a good one, and a good player as a very good one.

He signed some very good players, and that's the hardest part of a manager's job. Joe did it time and again. As I have said before, a manager doesn't have to tell good players what to do, they know. His team-talks may have been brief but some of his words have stayed with me – in persuading me to stay on at Blackpool and reject the offer from Stoke City: 'They're not the team you knew, Stan. They're like a pair of knickers with no elastic. They just won't stay up'; following a 4–0 defeat at Aston Villa in 1952: 'That was a difficult game to play in, lads. But believe me, the pain you went through was nothing compared to the pain I endured having to sit and watch what you lot dished up out there'; referring to a report in the *Daily Graphic* that in every game one in ten professional footballers would turn in a below-par performance that didn't merit them picking up their wages: 'Look around you. If you think the rest of the team did OK, then it's you'; after a disappointing FA Cup exit at the hands of York City: 'Someone told me that to be a football manager you have to have the patience of Job. But Job never had to manage this club.'

Although I didn't know it at the time, Joe's departure was to precipitate my own. The incoming manager Ronnie Suart did not have such a benevolent attitude towards me and my style of play. Ronnie wanted me to stay out wide on the wing, which I was never happy doing because I felt I would not be so involved in the game and see the ball so often. I didn't carry out Ron's instructions to the letter, so as a new decade dawned, I found my appearances in the first team limited.

In 1958–59, I avoided serious injury but played in 19 league matches only. The following season I didn't make the team for the start of the season at home to Bolton and with Arthur Kaye, a signing from Barnsley, and local lad Stephen Hill vying with me for the outside-right berth, I managed just 15 first team appearances, 11 of these coming in the final 15 games of the season. I was recalled at outside-right in February and would like to think I justified my inclusion with some decent displays. We enjoyed a run of nine matches in which we won six and lost only one, although that was a 6–0 drubbing at home by Manchester United. Mudie and Perry were still regulars. In full-back Jimmy Armfield, centre-forward Dave Charnley and centre-half Roy Gratrix, Blackpool possessed a spine to their team which had real class. George Farm still ruled supreme between the goalposts although a young goalkeeper called Tony Waiters was beginning to push him. Eventually, Tony pushed George out of the team and went to fulfil his true potential by winning five caps for England at a time when English football had some of the best goalkeepers in the world.

The final run-in to the season was disappointing. We failed to win any of remaining six games and given that I was far and away the oldest member of the team, the general opinion was, I had had my day. Fortunately there was one man who didn't think that was so. His name was Tony Waddington and the club he managed was my home-town club, Stoke City.

Although in the following season, 1960–61, I was to

figure in the majority of Blackpool's games, it was evident Ron Suart and I didn't see eye to eye and he figured the time had come for me to leave the club. Given that I was not in his favour and first-team opportunities were spasmodic, I was of that opinion myself.

Blackpool as a club and a team had changed, as had football in general. We were still a competent First Division outfit. While not setting the league table alight, we had never been among the perennial strugglers at the bottom. In Joe Smith's last season in charge, 1957–58, we finished seventh. Since 1947, when I had joined Blackpool, that is 11 seasons under Joe Smith, we had finished out of the top-ten teams in the First Division twice. We had played in three FA Cup finals, winning one, and in 1956 had finished runners-up in the First Division. Considering the club's core support, which given the size of the town was far less than most First Division clubs, it was a successful period under Joe.

In 1958–59, under Ron Suart, we finished eighth and in the final season of the decade, 11th. In 1960–61, the club just managed to stave off relegation, finishing one place and one point above relegated Newcastle United. The days of Blackpool being a leading English club were over. The club were still in the First Division, but in the ensuing years Blackpool found themselves for ever battling it out around the lower reaches of Division One until finally, in 1967, Ron Suart's last season, the club were relegated.

The inference from this might be that I thought Ron Suart was not a good manager. I wouldn't say that, though he was no Joe Smith. Ron brought some decent players to the club, but football was changing yet again. As a provincial town club, following the abolition of the maximum wage, Blackpool found it hard to attract the top players. Like the Prestons, Huddersfields and Burnleys of this world, Blackpool went into decline. Financial circumstances played a key role in their change of fortunes on the pitch.

To date, with the exception of one fleeting appearance in 1970–71, Blackpool have never regained their position in the top flight. That saddens me greatly. It's a great town with great people who, on the football front, frankly deserve much better than the poor fayre they have had to endure in recent times. I hope Blackpool will undergo a renaissance one day and recapture their glory days. Should they do so, no one will be more pleased to see them re-establish themselves at the top in English football than me.

22

---○---

Fifties
Favourites

British football in the fifties went through a golden then traumatic period, followed by one of introspection and self-appraisal which in turn led to transition. There was also much to be admired. Football was industrious and workmanlike but still highly entertaining. The level of skill was good, although at the very highest level it lagged behind the top club and international sides of the world. They were establishing new standards which, to all intents and purposes, are still the benchmark today. Between 1950 and 1960 British football underwent a metamorphosis, but the fifties still produced its fair share of great players, most notably Tommy Finney of Preston North End and Nat Lofthouse of Bolton Wanderers, both dear friends, although their careers began in the 1940s.

---○---

The trams would hiss like ganders as they made their way

out of town towards Deepdale, the home of Preston North End. They were jam-packed full of men in hairy overcoats and caps the size of pie plates who smelled of Woodbines and Friday night's best bitter. During the week these men toiled away in the textile factories or at the local aircraft works. Come Saturday afternoon, however, they left their crackling hearths, babbling wireless and wives called 'Mother' and headed in their thousands to Deepdale, the place where their hero lived. His name was Tom Finney.

There can't be many players who played for their club in a Wembley Cup final then had to wait five years before making their league debut, but that can be said of Tom. It is an extraordinary fact but as footballers go, there was never anything ordinary about Tom Finney.

As a 20-year-old, he came in to the Preston side for the 1941 Wartime Cup final against Arsenal. Three days later he joined the Eighth Army in North Africa and spent the rest of the war fighting Rommel. Suffice to say, Rommel lost. It was not until 1946, after being de-mobbed, that he finally played his first official league match for his beloved Preston. Less than a month later, he won the first of his 76 caps against Northern Ireland.

Tom exploded on to the British football scene like one of the heavy artillery shells he had administered in the deserts of North Africa. As a player, he was happy operating on either wing. He could also drop into midfield to mastermind a game and, when asked, to play as an out-and-out centre-forward. He was a striker of considerable note, as a career total of 187 goals testifies. He took all the corners, the free kicks, throw-ins and penalties and, such was his devotion to Preston, I reckon he would have taken the money on the turnstiles and sold programmes before a match if they'd let him.

On the pitch he made ordinary players look great and

helped the great players create the magical moments that for years would be sprinkled like gold dust on harsh working-class lives to create cherished memories that would be recalled to grandchildren on the knee. If greatness in football can be defined by the ability of a player to impose his personality on a match and dominate the proceedings throughout, then Tom Finney, for club and country, was indeed a true great. His delayed spurt, lengthened stride, his ability to beat a man then cut in and shoot and, above all, his cunning use of the ball with both feet, posed insurmountable problems for even the best defenders.

The sight of one man dictating the fortunes of a team is one of football's greatest and rarest spectacles. To dictate the pace and course of a game, a player has to be blessed with awesome qualities. Those who have accomplished it on a regular basis can be counted on the fingers of one hand – Pelé, Maradona, Best, Di Stefano and Tom Finney. Looking back, it is remarkable how often I believed Tom would contrive to win a game for Preston and no less remarkable how often he obliged. He didn't always fall into his best vein immediately. Often at the start of a match there was a feint hint of hauteur, almost condescension in a demeanour not dissimilar Raich Carter's. But after a few minutes, having sized everything and everyone up, he would get down to realities and with scintillating speed of foot, draw a cordon behind him and impose his considerable talents and skills on a game in no uncertain manner.

Preston played football in what we called the Scottish style. They held the ball close before distributing it to feet. It was a style that demanded accurate passing, which suited Tom, a player of thoughtful, careful passing, along the ground. As a winger, Tom was more direct than me. He was lightning quick and to see him in full flight, bearing down on jittery defenders, was one of football's finest sights. Even at international level, he was equally at home on either wing, in midfield or at centre-forward. The only problem he posed for managers, was where to play him.

In 1952, the Italian side Palermo came in for him. At a time when he was earning around £12 a week, they offered him a £10,000 signing-on fee, £130 a month plus bonuses, a villa and a sportscar. Tom went to see the Preston chairman to discuss the matter. The chairman huffed and puffed when he read the offer from the Italians and told Tom, 'Tha'll play for us, or tha'll play for nobody.' Tom stayed and saw out his career with his home-town club, clocking up 433 league matches between 1946 and 1960.

He was voted Footballer of the Year in 1954, the year in which Preston lost the FA Cup final to West Bromwich Albion, and again in 1957. He was awarded the OBE in 1961 and a CBE in 1992.

Tom is still known as 'The Preston Plumber' because he combined football with running his own plumbing business in the town, something which was often the cause of much humour even to Tom himself. In 1957, when I had been replaced in the England team supposedly to enable Tom to play in his best position of outside-right, he was selected at outside-left for the game against Wales. Brian Douglas of Blackburn made his debut at outside-right and Johnny Haynes of Fulham was at inside-left. It was Johnny's fourteenth cap, but up to this game his England appearances had been intermittent and he still lacked confidence. Following the 4–0 defeat of Wales, during which Tom had talked and nurtured the young Haynes, Johnny, ever the gentleman, felt he had to thank Tom.

'You talked me through that one,' said Johnny. 'If there is anything I can do for you, Tom, just say. I owe you.'

'Come to see me tomorrow afternoon,' said Tom. 'I'm putting a bathroom in at a house in Preston and my labourer's gone sick!'

Tom lives with his wife Elsie in Preston and is still revered. But the best way of summing him up is to recall a story as told by Michael Parkinson. Assigned to interview Tom, Michael stopped off at a newsagent's near Tom's home to ask for directions. Having established that Michael was a journalist and had come to interview Preston's most famous son, the newsagent volunteered his own piece of Finney information.

'This is a fact about Tom Finney that not a lot of people know,' said the newsagent. 'Tom is still the same hat size as he was when he was 16!'

Not so useless a fact as you might first think, as Michael Parkinson, like many others, was to find out. It was a fitting testimony to the modesty of a footballing genius who throughout his life has shown how a true hero of football can also be the most unassuming of gentlemen.

— ∘ —

If ever you need proof that values in football have changed over the years, it is that Nat Lofthouse's greatest moment came not when he scored both goals to win the FA Cup for Bolton in 1958, but when he scored in a friendly for England. Today most international friendlies hardly raise the enthusiasm you'd have for watching a fishfinger defrost. In 1952, it was a different story. Every international match England were involved in took on the magnitude and significance of a World Cup game.

The setting was post-war Vienna, as depicted in that masterpiece of British *film noir*, Carol Reed's *The Third Man*. If the gnarled and seasoned campaigner Jackie Milburn was Harry Lime, then Nat was Joseph Cotton's naive pulp writer who overcame the obstacles of his own making to champion a cause.

England had played Italy a few days before in Florence and Nat had gone there expecting it to be a straightforward game like those he was used to in the English First Division. But as he found out, it was a lot more cynical and calculating than that. The Italians were well organised and knew all the tricks necessary to put him off his game. The match ended in a 1–1 draw with Ivor Brodis getting the England goal. Nat, very much in the Alan Shearer mould but more bull-like, mixed it with the Italian defenders but, all in all, didn't do himself justice.

Austria was the next game on the England itinerary and it was in this game that Nat really made his mark. He was dubbed the 'Lion of Vienna', a wholly appropriate epithet. Vienna in 1952 was rubble-strewn with gutted buildings and a thriving black market. It was a city of divided rule and when the England team finally arrived in the British controlled zone, Nat managed to negotiate a devilish telephone system to put in a call back to his wife in Bolton. Nat's wife was in a tizzy. She told him she had read an article by Desmond Hackett in the *Daily Express*. Hackett, in the light of Nat's performance against Italy, was calling for him to be sent home and for Newcastle's Jackie Milburn to be played at centre-forward against Austria instead.

Walter Winterbottom and the England selectors stuck by Nat and he repaid them handsomely. The game was played at the Prater stadium, which at the time was smack bang in the middle of the Russian-occupied zone. Austria were considered to be one of the very best teams in Europe at this time and in players such as Ocwirk, Dienst and Huber they had world-class players. The Austrians had scored a staggering 57 goals in their previous 13 internationals. To say England were going to have their work cut out was an understatement. For his part, Nat was determined to pull out something special in order to resurrect his international career, but he couldn't have chosen tougher opposition in which to do it.

It has been said that the British treat war like a sport and sport like a war, and there was a large contingent of British soldiers in Vienna at this time. In the days leading up to the game, the frugality of life in post-war Vienna was forgotten as all conversations centred around the match and the patriotic pride that rode on it. The city took on an electric atmosphere and with the British forces present, home and away fans had three days to argue and stew together before the big showdown.

As Nat and the England team took to the pitch they looked up at the terraces and saw thousands of Tommies who had been allowed leave from the British zone and access to the Russian one. Nat told me the presence of the Tommies made him feel it was like a home match and the vocal support of those British soldiers gave him a tremendous lift.

With the game only minutes old, Nat made the perfect start. He fired low and hard from 20 yards, the ball bounced a few times and deceived the Austrian keeper to put England ahead. This was a speciality of Nat's which Spurs' Eddie Baily used to call Nat's 'Barnes Wallis' after he of dambusters fame.

Sheffield Wednesday's Jackie Sewell sent the Tommies delirious with a second goal but the Austrians soon showed their mettle and by half-time the scores were level. England were fortunate to go in on level terms. After a slow start, the Austrians really put their game together, laying siege to the England goal, and only some desperate defending on the part of our lads restricted them to two goals.

Back home in Bolton, Nat's wife sat by the hearth listening to the game on the radio, Raymond Glendenning's rich, fruity voice competing with the static crackle of the airwaves.

It was touch and go if England could escape with the draw. Then with ten minutes remaining, Gil Merrick in the

England goal, collected a near-post ball and immediately looked up to spot Nat's bulky frame cruising across the halfway line. As the players of both sides began to make their way out of the England penalty box, Gil gave the ball an almighty throw. It sailed through the air and bounced just inside the Austrian half with Nat in hot pursuit. An Austrian defender unable to keep pace with Nat gave him a wicked blow to the face with his elbow. Nat staggered for a moment but kept running and, ignoring the pain, upped his pace. His eyes were focused on the ball he had managed to toe poke in front of him.

The Austrian right-back had come across to cover and, with Nat one pace ahead, the two sprinted towards goal, Nat continuing to nudge the ball ahead of him. Eventually, probably in desperation because Nat was uncatchable, the right-back made a lunging tackle. His right boot caught Nat's heel as he was in full flight and although Nat staggered for a few paces, he quickly regained his balance and kept on going as the Austrian goal loomed ever closer.

The Austrian goalkeeper came racing off his line to narrow the angle and as he did so, Nat pushed the ball a little too far forward. The packed stadium held its breath. It was touch and go who would get to the loose ball first, with the Austrian keeper looking favourite. Blood streaming from his nose from the earlier elbow, Nat drew on his reserves of strength and dug in. With one almighty effort, he produced a last burst of speed, reached the ball and, as the Austrian keeper hurtled into his shins, managed to toe poke it goalward. Nat was well and truly poleaxed by the keeper's challenge and it was apparent to everyone present as he lay motionless on his back that he was injured.

'I were reet down and out,' Nat told me later. 'I knew I had hit it true, but I never knew it had gone in till I heard them Tommies roaring. I were in reet pain, but hearing them British lads cheering, I looked up at the heavens and felt elated.

'Jimmy Trotter [England trainer] came out to me and as he applied the magic sponge said, "Nathan, lad, you've never scored better – and you never will." '

That is the story of how Nat Lofthouse became known as the 'Lion of Vienna'. The strength, determination and bravery he showed were typical of the man. At the final whistle, Nat was chaired off the field on a sea of khaki. The Tommies took him back to the British barracks where Nat tells me he had a few drinks, purely for medicinal purposes to nullify the pain in his nose and leg. From there he was taken to the sergeants' mess before, late into the night, ending up in the privates' mess for what he still says was the finest night of his life.

By some strange irony, it was an unapologetic Desmond Hackett who, in the following day's edition of the *Daily Express*, coined the phrase the 'Lion of Vienna' and so he was, and so he is and there is now a pub in Bolton to prove it.

Nat was a vigorous and bustling centre-forward, thought by many to be a bit too physical. To my mind, he was one of the best centre-forwards of the fifties. Like Tommy Finney, he was a one-club man. When his career was ended in 1960 through injury, he had made 503 appearances for Bolton scoring 285 goals. In 1953, the year Blackpool defeated Bolton in that never-to-be-forgotten final at Wembley, he scored in every round of the Cup, including the final itself. He was voted Footballer of the Year that season and no one deserved it more than he.

In 1958, post-Munich, with the country wanting Manchester United to win, he scored the two goals that won Bolton the Cup, proving sentiment has little place in the order of things as far as football is concerned. Nat's second goal of that Cup final is still talked about today. The United goalkeeper Harry Gregg had the ball in his hands following a cross when Nat came steaming in and shoulder charged Harry and the ball into the back of the net. It isn't allowed today but the shoulder charge was part and parcel of the game at the time and not even Harry Gregg complained. Football may be faster nowadays, but it is not as physical. I often wonder how Nat would fair if he were playing football in the Premiership. With his barnstorming, physical style he probably wouldn't be on the field for ten minutes, yet in a 500-game career for Bolton he was never sent off. Opponents, Harry Johnston for one, never liked playing against Nat, but they accepted his robust, physical style as being a part of football at the time. No defender to my knowledge ever complained because to do so would have brought ridicule. For his part, Nat came up against some mean and tough centre-halves of whom in the fifties there were plenty, but for all the bone-crunching and clattering he endured, he never whinged either. That was the way it was back then.

In 33 games for England – it should have been more – he scored 30 goals. The mind boggles to think with such a record what value would be placed on Nat Lofthouse if he were playing today.

I still see Nat, especially when Stoke City meet Bolton Wanderers and at sporting dinners and FA and Football League functions. Our friendship has deepened over the years. Whenever it is time to go, without fail Nat makes a beeline for me. As I watch him walk away, with those broad shoulders and bulky frame, it's probably just my imagination, but it's as if I can hear the theme from *The Third Man* playing in the background.

———○———

It is impossible to mention all the players whom I admired during the fifties. Tom Finney and Nat Lofthouse were true greats, but there were others who touched greatness. One of these players was John Charles of Swansea, Leeds United, Juventus, Roma and Cardiff City. He was an international before he was 18 years of age and a player of seductive passes, power, grace and style. Equally at home at centre-forward or centre-half, he was a player of gentlemanly self-control, never given to complaint or retribution no matter how shabby the provocation. A giant of a man who could sprint, leap, shoot and head like no other player of his day, he would shake off opponents like a dog shakes water off its back; but for all his gargantuan stature, he could tame a ball with such a deftness of touch you would have thought his boots were made of gossamer. For years he strove to tip the scales in Leeds' favour before eventually his talents were recognised by Italian giants Juventus to whom he was transferred in 1957 for a then British record fee of £65,000. John helped Juventus win the Italian *Serie A* championship three times and the Italian Cup twice. Diligent, loyal, classy, hard-working and supremely versatile, he was the Admirable Crichton of Welsh football.

Bert Trautmann is another I must mention. Was there ever a player with a more remarkable story than his? He was one of British football's most unlikely heroes, a German prisoner of war who stayed on in England to sign as a goalkeeper for Manchester City, the club he served so well until his retirement in 1963. He had the strength of character to overcome the initial wave of anti-German feeling that met him at every ground he played at in his early days with City. In the 1956 FA Cup final against Birmingham City, he played the last 15 minutes of the game in great pain, not realising his neck had been broken in a dive at the feet of Birmingham's Peter Murphy. He was voted Footballer of the Year in 1956 and the Manchester City fans showed just how much they thought of him when over 47,000 turned up for his testimonial in 1964. I had the privilege of being asked to play in that game, which enabled me to pay my own respects to an outstanding goalkeeper and one of the warmest and most endearing people I ever met in football.

I also admired George Young, captain of Rangers and Scotland. A player of imposing physique with a devastating tackle, he had the gift common to all great defenders, that of being comfortable on the ball. He was courageous, indefatigable, a player who could quickly assess situations and act accordingly. He was at his most awesome when wearing the dark blue of his beloved Scotland, a hero right out of the pages of John Buchan.

Sam Bartram kept goal for Charlton Athletic for 22 years and 582 league games. He defied the stereotype of red-haired players because he was always cool, calm and collected during games. Jimmy Seed, the Charlton manager, was so used to putting Sam's name down first on his teamsheet that, it was said, he continued to do so for weeks after he'd left in 1956 to manage York City. Sam was the best goalkeeper never to win a cap for England.

Joe Mercer was an England colleague but a tenacious adversary in his Arsenal shirt. He began with Everton in 1932 but, having lost his place in 1946, was transferred to Arsenal with whom, in my book, he enjoyed his best years even though he had passed 30. Despite his frail physique – Harry Johnston used to say you'd have to tie knots in Joe's legs to give him knees – he was a strong and relentless tackler. Footballer of the Year in 1950, following his retirement from playing Joe went on to manage at Sheffield United, Aston Villa, Manchester City and Coventry, also serving as England's caretaker-manager in between Sir Alf Ramsey and Don Revie.

At Manchester City, Joe teamed up with Malcolm Allison to great effect. Together they led City to the First Division

Championship in 1968, the FA Cup in 1969 and both the League Cup and European Cup-Winners' Cup in 1970. Joe, like Joe Smith, wasn't given to big team-talks. Often he would just tell his players, 'The grass is green, the sky is blue, go out and rejoice in the fact you are professional footballers.' More often than not, Joe's teams did exactly that.

Forget the successes and tribulations of his managerial career, Tommy Docherty was a fine wing-half for Celtic, Preston North End and Arsenal. His reputation now is as a high-profile manager in the sixties and seventies, but I remember Tommy as a robust, no-nonsense right-half who, although he will no doubt deny it to keep his reputation intact, possessed a high level of skill, winning 25 caps for Scotland.

Tommy began his footballing life with Celtic in 1948 but soon moved to Preston where he stayed until 1957 before moving to Arsenal then to Chelsea initially as a player-coach. On the pitch he was here, there and everywhere, an electric eel of a player and just as slippery to pin down. He didn't mess about, that's for sure. Tommy was a tough, tenacious tackler who would leave inside-forwards of delicate constitution as rattled as a shutter in a cyclone. Once he had won the ball, however, as he invariably did, he would use it intelligently and to good effect. Very rarely did I see him give the ball away. With his short cropped hair and flint-like features, he gave the impression of a man permanently helping the police with their inquiries, but his physical demeanour belied a clever and calculating football brain.

Even in his formative years at Celtic, Tommy was a force to be reckoned with. One of my favourite of his stories concerned a centre-half for Glasgow Rangers called Willie Woodburn who was so hard in his play the Scottish FA finally banned him *sine die*. Every player in the Scottish League was at best wary and at worst afraid of playing against Willie, – every player except the young Tommy Docherty. Tommy feared no one either by reputation or deed and whenever he came up against Willie, Tommy gave as good as he got, often coming out on top. This riled Willie who just couldn't come to terms with the fact that he had met someone he couldn't intimidate verbally or physically. The way Tommy told it, he once happened to be in Glasgow and he went along to the funeral to pay his respects to his old adversary. Some weeks later Tommy met another former player at a sporting dinner and the conversation got around to Willie Woodburn.

'I hear you went along to Willie's funeral,' he said.

'Aye,' said Tommy, shaking his head sadly.

'Tell me, Tom. Willie had the reputation of being a right so and so in his playing days. Did he ever mellow over the years and become more amiable?' he asked.

'Put it this way,' said Tommy. 'I went to pay my respects at the cemetery and the inscription on Willie's headstone said "Just what the hell do ye think you're looking at?" '

It wasn't true, of course, in more ways than one, as I later heard that Willie was still alive, but it showed how Tommy would never back down.

One player I feel I must mention in the context of the fifties although his crowning glory came in 1960–61, is Danny Blanchflower. Born in Belfast, Danny began his career with Glentoran before moving on to Barnsley then Aston Villa but it was only when he was transferred to Tottenham Hotspur in 1954 that his innumerable talents were fully appreciated. Danny was a thoughtful player and an inspirational captain who played as he talked, lucidly and fluently. With his sliderule passing and cool demeanour, Danny didn't play on football pitches, he graced them. Somehow he was always available to team-mates, a magnet for the ball which he used with all the art, intelligence and craftsmanship at his considerable

Doing a final check on my boots before a game for Blackpool in 1955. After the World Cup in 1950 I had decided that this sort of boot would give me an edge for speed. In today's world of million pound boot sponsorship deals, it may surprise you to learn that I paid to have these handmade. (Popperfoto)

One of these boots today. They are so light and flexible you can fold them up and put them in your pocket. Each pair would last me on average no more than two games.

Warming up before Stoke's game against Charlton Athletic in September 1962. The match ended 6–3 and was the beginning of a run that set the platform for our promotion at the end of that season. (Huston Spratt)

Leaving my house on my fiftieth birthday, 1 February 1965. It was a cold and frosty morning. (Allsport)

At the World Cup in 1986, the year after I had played my last ever game (against a Brazilian Veterans side). (Colorsport)

I continued to watch Stoke play as often as I could after retiring – the love of the sport never deserted me. (Allsport)

When I met Mila during Port Vale's tour of Czechoslovakia in 1967 I knew I had found the true love of my life. (Stanley Matthews)

With my daughter Jean at my eightieth birthday party. (Stanley Matthews)

Greeting Ferenc Puskas at the same party. He is a true star of the game.
(Stanley Matthews)

Eddie Clamp, my on-the-pitch
'minder' in my latter days at
Stoke. (Stanley Matthews)

With Gary Lineker in 1996. We shared the same proud record of never having been cautioned or sent off during our entire careers. (Daily Mirror)

Formally opening the Britannia Stadium in August 1997. After knowing the old Victoria Ground for nearly 70 years it was a wrench to leave. (Daily Mirror)

An evening of football legends held in London in May 1999. (Stanley Matthews)

With Michael Owen and Les Scott during the shooting of Michael Owen's football skills video in the summer of 1999. (Stanley Matthews)

In 1995 Mila and I were invited to join a committee working on the 2002 World Cup in Seoul. Football gave me so many wonderful opportunities to travel the world, and that I could do so in the company of Mila made it all the better. (Stanley Matthews)

command. He was cerebral, articulate and persuasive to the point you thought you were on the pitch next to a high-flying barrister. My only regret is that I never had the honour and pleasure of playing with him as my wing-half. What a creator and prompter of a wingman he was! Danny projected his mind where other players projected their bodies; played the game as constructively and intelligently as he thought and talked about it.

After retiring, Danny turned to journalism and was asked for his thoughts on the news that a current First Division player was to write his autobiography – 'Every player who has played at the top thinks he has a book in him – and in 99 per cent of cases that is the best place for it.'

In 1960–61 he led Spurs to the league and Cup double, the first time it had been accomplished in the twentieth century. The following year, he held the FA Cup aloft again and the year after that he became the first captain to lead a British team to European success when Spurs demolished Atletico Madrid in the European Cup-Winners' Cup final. The significance of that result has now been forgotten, but it was a landmark in British football. After years of failure in European competition, Spurs showed that British clubs could not only compete with but beat the best in Europe. Spurs' success begat Celtic, Manchester United and all that followed in the 1970s and 1980s, and the player who held the reins of that rampant and stylish Spurs side was Danny Blanchflower – the most inspirational of captains and one who practised what he preached, that leadership is action, not position.

23

───◦───

My Final
Bow

I n 1961–62, it was obvious to me that Ron Suart felt
he had found my heir apparent in Steve Hill. I had no
gripes. I was going on 47 and given that football had
become faster and more competitive, I realised that a
manager might not fancy a winger who had been playing
league football before the rest of the team were born.

I started out the season in the Blackpool reserves but,
following injury to Steve Hill, came back into the side on
30 September in a 4–0 win over Chelsea. I was retained for
the next match, at Arsenal, which we lost 3–0 in front of a
crowd of 42,000. It was my last appearance in a Blackpool
shirt. I remember thinking at the time that it would be
fitting if my last match for Blackpool was against Arsenal at
Highbury. I always enjoyed playing against them and
Highbury had given me so many wonderful memories.

Even in those two games, Ron Suart was at pains to tell
me to stay out wide on the wing and wait for the ball. I

didn't but it wasn't so much a case of an old dog unable to learn new tricks as the fact that I had been playing professional football for 32 years and felt I knew how best I could contribute to a team. No manager I had ever played for before at club or international level had ever told me to do that. Were they wrong?

Ron Suart had made it known that he would happily release me if I wanted to continue playing, which I told him I did. I didn't have a clue what I was going to do next and it was my old Blackpool team-mate, Jackie Mudie who came along to rescue my career.

Jackie had been transferred to Stoke City, who were wandering up and down the nether regions of the Second Division like a dog which had lost the scent. Their manager Tony Waddington, who had joined the club in 1960, was in the embryonic stages of building a team he hoped would win Stoke promotion back to the First Division. Waddington did not have the money for big-name signings. His idea was to build a team from the promising youngsters Stoke had on their books at the time combined with seasoned professionals with a reputation for class coming to the end of their careers who he could therefore pick up for a song. Jackie Mudie was one of the first seasoned players Tony Waddington signed and he told Waddington that, in his estimation, I still had a few years left in me and would do Stoke a job at outside-right.

The press got hold of Stoke's interest and were not enamoured to say the least. Many sports writers ridiculed the very idea of me continuing to play. In the *Daily Express* Desmond Hackett wrote, 'Don't do it, Stan. Retire with pride – now!' Jackie Mudie rang me up about it and at one point said, 'Maybe he's right and I'm wrong, Stan.'

'No,' I told Jackie. 'Remember what Desmond Hackett said of Nat Lofthouse before that game against Austria in Vienna?'

Tony Waddington rang to reassure me my age was not an issue. He wanted me back at Stoke because he thought I could do well for them and he had the full backing of his board, especially vice-chairman Albert Henshall. When a manager singles out a specific director as being in support of a player his club are wanting to buy, it's not an indication that the other directors aren't in favour; it's a surefire sign that the director in question is the one putting up the money. So with the intimation that all were in favour of my return to Stoke, I was only too happy to sign and the quicker the better.

A meeting was arranged with the Blackpool directors, I thought to rubber-stamp the deal but not a bit of it. After 14 years at Blackpool, during which I felt I had contributed in no small way to the club's achievements and therefore merited a free transfer enabling me to continue my career elsewhere, the board amazed me by asking Stoke City for a fee. The fee was put at £3,500, not a lot even in 1961 but it could have been a stumbling block for cash-strapped Stoke. I respectfully asked the Blackpool board if there was any way, given my years of service to the club, they could waive the fee, but was told in no uncertain terms, 'No'. One director, Mr Marshall, enraged me. Drawing himself up in his chair he admonished me for asking if the fee could be waived as if I were an impertinent schoolboy, concluding by saying, 'You forget. As a player, we made you.'

For one of the few occasions in my life, I saw red.

'You – made – ME?' I said, totally flabbergasted. 'As a small boy I was getting up at six in the morning to train and practise my skills and I continue to do so to this day. When I came here, this club had only a few hundred season-ticket holders. Now it has over 12,000. Self-appraisal is no guarantee of merit, Mr Marshall, that I know. But my presence in the team helped Blackpool become, for a number of years, the biggest draw on the road. With their share of the gate revenues, this club has done very well out of that financially. So don't you sit there and tell me, YOU made ME!'

Mr Marshall sank back in his seat, shocked I should imagine at my unaccustomed anger. The rest of the board shifted uncomfortably and chairman Albert Hindley said, 'Now, now. Let's not have words about this. I'm sure some compromise can be reached.'

No compromise ever was reached. Blackpool stuck out for the £3,500 and got it. I was a little chagrined to say the least. In the first instance, following the abolition of the maximum wage in 1961, I was on £25 a week at Blackpool whereas my team-mates were on between £30 and £35 – hardly a recognition of the part I had played in their success over the past 14 years. Secondly, I had been troubled by a niggling knee injury which Blackpool knew about but, it transpired, hadn't told Stoke about. To ask for a fee for a player who had given 14 years' loyal service to the club and who was now 46 years old with a dodgy knee seemed a bit rich to me.

Stoke were a struggling Second Division team strapped for cash and their offer to me made me realise I had been underpaid at Bloomfield Road. After outlining Stoke's money problems and taking into consideration my age, Tony Waddington said that the best he would offer me was a two-year contract paying £50 a week with an extra £25 appearance money. I sat there and tried to keep my one good knee from knocking against the dodgy one. It was double my Blackpool wage and with another £25 appearance money it meant for every game I played at Stoke I'd pick up three times what I was on at Blackpool. I felt I could do Stoke a job, but because of his honesty and sincerity, I couldn't let Tony Waddington commit himself to such a deal, especially as I was worried about my knee.

'No, make it a one-year contract renewable,' I said. 'That

way you'll protect yourself and the club. As for the £25 appearance money. What are you afraid of? That I'll sign, train every day of the week and not turn up on matchdays?'

So I signed for Stoke for £50 a week for a year on a contract that would be renegotiable after 12 months. I was quite happy to turn up at the club, sign on the dotted line and be done with it without any fuss. But Tony Waddington had been talking to a producer at BBC Television and they wanted to feature it on the popular midweek sports programme *Sportsview*. Even though the nature of my job had kept me in the public eye for 30 years, I was then, as now, not given to fuss or courting publicity. My initial reaction was to say no to the TV signing, but Tony Waddington said it would be good publicity for the club who for years had been out of the main spotlight of football. So I agreed to sign for Stoke City 'live' on television in front of millions of viewers. At the signing, which was introduced by the programme's host Peter Dimmock, vice-chairman Albert Henshall stood behind me with Tony Waddington to my left. Before the ink was dry, Tony leaned in to me and said, 'Welcome home, Stan. For years this club has been going nowhere. Now we're on our way.' Nobody realised at the time how prophetic his words were to prove.

A friend of mine told me I had been foolish – I should have told Tony Waddington I wanted a five-year contract at £100 a week because the club would get that money back and more in increased gate revenue. I had spent some of the previous summer playing in Canada for £100 a week and knew for a fact that Ron Suart had used my name on at least one occasion to fix up a lucrative friendly fixture for Blackpool. In the close season, I had also been playing and coaching in South Africa and it was there I received a telegram asking me to return to play in a friendly in the Republic of Ireland. I contacted Ron Suart and told him it was impossible. In fact, I was under no obligation to return because I was out of contract; I told him that, too. Ron said that Blackpool were to receive a good fee for appearing in this friendly but a key part of the deal was that I would play. Given I had 14 happy years at the club, I felt obliged to help Blackpool out and play. So I knew my name still had worth in football.

As it turned out my friend was spot-on about the increased gate revenue, but my decision to go back to Stoke wasn't about money. My passion and love for the game were the motivation. I wanted to continue playing and at a decent level. Stoke City were offering me the opportunity and that was great as far as I was concerned. The fact that Stoke were to pay me twice the money I was on at Blackpool was already icing on the cake. I felt it would have been ungracious of me to ask for more. I had also warmed to Tony Waddington. I felt he was genuine and sincere, not only in his dealings but in what he wanted to achieve for the club and people of Stoke who are, after all, my home-town folk.

It was Tony Waddington who described football as the working man's ballet. Even now, in an era of excessive ticket prices, executive boxes, corporate entertainment, debentures and all-season-ticket stadiums that have resulted in many fans, for decades the bedrock support of clubs, being priced out of football, it is still an apposite, poetic and relevant description.

I thought my debut was to be at Home Park against Plymouth Argyle but Tony Waddington had other ideas. He wanted to put my debut on hold until the following week, when Stoke had a home game against Huddersfield Town. It was a great marketing ploy on his part. By delaying my debut until Stoke's next home match, Tony hoped to attract many stay-away supporters who he believed would turn up not only to see me play but for the additional reason that for the rest of their lives they could say, 'I was there when Stanley Matthews made his return debut for Stoke.' Only 8,409 had turned up for Stoke's previous home match against Preston North End. When I took to the field at the Victoria Ground on 24 October 1961, I couldn't believe my eyes. The terraces were packed – 35,974 had turned up to witness my return. I was filled with a mixture of humility and delight. The delight for the most part was for Tony Waddington and the club's directors who, in having faith in my ability and paying me a decent wage, had been rewarded in full. The club would indeed get back what they were paying me and more. The day could not have gone better. I was up against Ray Wilson, who later left Huddersfield for Everton and was a member of the 1966 World Cup winning side. As a full-back Ray Wilson was a class act but I felt I gave a decent account of myself. Stoke ran out 3–0 winners and I enjoyed the bonus of having laid on one of our goals. What a start to my second spell at Stoke!

There was still a long way to go in the season, some 27 games but the omens were good. Prior to my arrival, Stoke had been floundering in the lower reaches of Division Two but results suddenly picked up and we finished a respectable eighth. Although attendances never matched the Huddersfield game, they regularly topped a healthy 20,000, more than double what they had been prior to my return, and this put some much-needed revenue into the club's coffers. Tony Waddington spent the money very well indeed, continuing his policy of bringing good-quality, seasoned players to the club as he strived to create a side capable of winning promotion to Division One.

The newspapers had made much of my return to Stoke and in general the coverage was good, the consensus being that 'the magic was still there'. Skill, as I have said before, never leaves you; age is the enemy of footballers. I knew in myself that my fitness was such that I could go on playing for another three or four years at least, and having a concerted run in the first team at Stoke, rather than tiring me, served only to improve my match fitness. I was coming up against players half my age and younger but I felt it had no adverse affect on me or my game. I knew I could contribute to Stoke's cause as much as anyone in the team and decided that when the inevitable day arrived when that was no longer the case, I would retire. What's more, I wouldn't need anyone to tell me when that day had come; the first person to realise it would be me.

I thoroughly enjoyed 1961–62. After protracted spells in the Blackpool reserve team, my career had once again picked up. I felt very fit and more than capable of playing well in a game that was becoming increasingly faster.

Tony Waddington's policy of mixing talented youngsters with seasoned pros who could do him a job for two or three years was starting to pay off. Before my arrival, Tony had signed goalkeeper Jimmy O'Neill for £2,000 from Everton. Jimmy already had 17 Republic of Ireland caps and having made 201 appearances for Everton in the First Division, had proved himself a reliable keeper with a very safe pair of hands. Stoke had two talented young full-backs in Bill Asprey and Tony Allen and another youngster, Eric Skeels, at left-half. Eric went on to play a club record 606 games for Stoke, not bad for someone who had written to Tony Waddington's predecessor Frank Taylor asking for a trial. Other youngsters who were knocking on the door at the time included Alan Bloor who, like Eric Skeels, went on to give Stoke City tremendous service, Alan Philpott and wingers Keith Bebbington and Gerry Bridgwood. Of the old stagers, in addition to Jackie Mudie, Jimmy O'Neill and myself, there was a versatile forward called Don Ratcliffe.

Don was a local lad who had signed for Stoke in 1950 but had not become a first-team regular until 1957. He could play in any position in the forward line but to my mind was best at outside-left. Don was a big favourite with the Stoke fans and also with his team-mates because his tremendous sense of humour lightened up the dressing room on many occasions and played no small part in engendering a great spirit among the players.

Like Joe Smith, Tony Waddington was a wily bird and used my name to attract other seasoned players to the club. The first to arrive, some three months after me, was Dennis Viollet, who signed in January 1962. Dennis, a survivor of the Munich air crash, joined Stoke from Manchester United. A lot of First Division clubs had been after his signature and in signing him for £22,000, Stoke had really pushed the boat out as far as they were concerned. It was to prove, however, money well spent.

Dennis was a superbly gifted player with a keen eye for goal. He possessed a clinical and imaginative football brain, boundless energy and excellent all-round technical ability. There is no player around like him now, though I see some similarities in the play of Teddy Sheringham. Sheringham, like Dennis, is an uncomplicated provider and a more than occasional goalscorer. Sometimes maligned and often under-rated, Sheringham's admirers like Dennis's are usually to be found among his fellow professionals. Teddy Sheringham gears his play to the good of the team and shares with Dennis that most enviable of reputations, being 'a player's player'.

People have said that I enjoyed my swansong at Stoke City. Let it also be said that I had a marvellous orchestrator in Dennis Viollet and a wonderful accompanist in Jimmy McIlroy. Good inside-forwards are born with their gifts and without doubt Dennis was blessed. There were moments in games when the ball came to him and it was as if a spotlight had fallen on him and every other player on the field was in shadow. Your eyes were drawn to him as he engineered a space to work in, then proceeded to conjure up his own special brand of magic, stroking the ball rather than kicking it to team-mates. Only when the ball had left his feet did you then see the opening as it glided across the turf just in front of a galloping forward and the course of the game would be changed. Short pass or long pass, it was always the right pass when it came from Dennis. He knew when to hold the ball and when to release it. More importantly, who to release it to. Dennis never made a pass simply to get himself out of trouble or to hand over responsibility to a team-mate. Every pass was constructive, a creative arrow that would in a split second turn defence into attack. He wasn't the quickest of players but he more than made up for that with his speed of thought. Rarely, in all my years of playing football, did I come across such a quick-thinking player. Dennis Viollet made the ball do the work. That he did so well for Stoke was down to him, of course, but also because in the seasoned players about him, Dennis found team-mates whose anticipation could match his speed of thought and ability to change plans. He was a truly wonderful player and, to my mind, much under-rated.

In 1961–62, Ipswich Town, who had been promoted from Division Two the previous season, were the surprise champions. My old England team-mate Alf Ramsey was their manager and I don't think it any exaggeration to say he had worked a minor miracle at that club. Alf was a very good motivator and an even better strategist. Ipswich played fresh and fluent football, which proved the undoing of the so-called big-city clubs such as Spurs, Arsenal and Manchester United and they eventually pipped Burnley for the championship. A year or so later when teams had latched on to Ipswich's style and found ways to counteract it, they found life much tougher, but in winning the First Division Championship in 1962, Ipswich Town gave hope to all clubs who didn't have big budgets at their disposal. That's an indication of how football has changed over the years. Ask yourself what are the chances these days of a team with the suffix Town winning the Premiership.

Alf's employers at Ipswich Town were the Cobbold family who owned breweries in that part of the country. Teams may not have relished a trip to Portman Road because they would invariably return pointless, but they did enjoy the hospitality for which Ipswich and the Cobbolds were renowned. The Cobbolds knew how to entertain, that's for sure, and the drink would flow as if their brewery needed the bottles back. The Cobbolds' bonhomie and inclination for having a good time was in sharp contrast to the personality of Alf Ramsey, a quiet, studious and unassuming man who rarely imbibed and was to partying what Lionel Blair was to rugby league. Yet they got on famously, a case of opposites attract if ever there was one. I remember Alf telling me how, on his first day as manager in 1955, he was taken into the boardroom and offered a glass of wine by John Cobbold who then informed him, 'This is the first and last time you will be offered a drink in this boardroom.' John Cobbold threw two keys at Alf and said, 'From now on, you can come in here and help yourself.' But Alf told me that in all his eight years of managing the club, he never did. Knowing Alf as I did, I believed him.

John Cobbold was a great character with a ready wit. After Ipswich had won the championship, he was interviewed by Peter Wilson of the *Daily Mirror*. Knowing the Cobbolds, liking for celebration whatever the occasion, Peter Wilson opened the interview by saying, 'John, First Division Champions. I suppose for the directors of the club this has been one long season of wine, women and song?' John Cobbold replied, 'I can't remember us doing much singing.' They don't make them like the Cobbolds any more.

Jimmy Greaves returned to English football after a none too happy sojourn in Italy with AC Milan. I think Italian football had been an anathema to Jimmy, although he continued to score goals there. Spurs manager Bill Nicholson paid a then British record transfer fee of £99,999 to bring Jimmy back to England, the Spurs board refusing to make him Britain's first £100,000 footballer not because they thought such a fee to be ridiculous but because they didn't want Jimmy to have that added burden. He was *however* such a great player, I doubt if it would have made any difference to him. To my mind, Jimmy had his best days with Spurs, although he was some way down the road career-wise. A phenomenal goalscorer with tremendous ability, Jimmy was the most mercurial of inside-forwards who had the distinction of scoring on his debut for every team he played for. He scored 357 goals in 517 First Division matches, about 356 of which seemed to be scored from in or around the six-yard box. He was the most exciting and entertaining player of this era. I was a great admirer of his style and panache and later of the way he overcame deep personal problems, most notably his much-publicised fight against alcoholism. He is one of British football's all-time greats.

Talking of great goalscorers, this was the season a young Middlesbrough centre-forward with a record of 197 goals in 213 games for the club left Teeside for Sunderland. He continued to score prolifically for them until injury curtailed his career on Boxing Day 1963. He was renowned in footballing circles for having very forthright ideas about football and the way it was played, ideas that were as pronounced as the self-belief he displayed in his own not inconsiderable ability. His name was Brian Clough. I first came across him when I was playing for Stoke. Talking to him after the match, my first impression was that he was arrogant because he came across as someone who, for all his youth, knew it all. Yet as our conversation progressed, I came to the conclusion that under that swagger and self-assertiveness, he had some great ideas about football and although I wanted to dislike him, I found I couldn't. When the conversation turned to the FA and what they were doing for football and players in general, he didn't mince his words. 'They do bugger all,' he said with a wag of his finger, 'and they don't start till noon.'

———— o ————

I spent the summer of 1962, as had become the norm for me, coaching in South Africa and I returned to Stoke City fresh and fit and raring to go. Tony Waddington was a clever manager. I had a name in football but by signing other experienced players he ensured I didn't have to carry the burden of the attraction and appeal of the team by myself. He exploited my appeal to the maximum, not only for publicity and eye-catching headlines but in persuading other players to join the club. I didn't mind this one bit. In fact, I felt flattered to think one of the reasons players wanted to sign for Stoke was for the opportunity of playing alongside me.

One such player who arrived in the summer of 1962 was Eddie Stuart. Eddie was a rugged, no-nonsense centre-half who had helped Wolves win the First Division Championship in 1954, 1958 and 1959, as well as the FA Cup in 1960. Eddie was a hard player, but he tackled fair, which I liked. He gave 100 per cent with a little bit on top. Highly competitive, he was a dominant figure both on and off the pitch and Tony Waddington immediately made him captain.

Eddie was a man of awesome physique, not so much a product of the Wolves footballing academy as a force of nature. A restless powerhouse of a man, he would be in the eye of any storm on the pitch, which more often than not was of his making in the first place. As a captain, he was very much in the mould of Eddie Hapgood. With fists clenched he would urge players on to explore the very limits of their mental and physical capabilities. I can't ever recall him getting on to me, however, which I'd like to think was as much down to the fact that he knew I was giving it my all as it was respect for my reputation and senior status in the team. Eddie was very good in the air but he could also play a bit as well. With the ball at his feet he would power his way out of defence, cutting a swathe through opposing forward lines before playing one of his famous three-yard balls to a team-mate. 'Don't ask me to be creative,' he used to say. 'Creative to me is passing to someone with the same coloured shirt as I'm wearing.' Given his prowess as rock solid centre-half, that was good enough for me and everyone else in the team.

The 1962–63 season started disastrously for us. We lost our opening fixture at Leeds United and didn't record our first win for another six games when, on 12 September we beat Charlton Athletic 6–3 at the Victoria Ground. Dennis Viollet scored four in this game with our other goals coming from Don Ratcliffe and the promising young left-winger Keith Bebbington. This result proved to be the turning point in our season. The convincing margin of victory sent confidence soaring and with each game this curious combination of a team went from strength to strength, remaining undefeated until Leeds once again got the better of us on 15 December, ending an unbeaten run of 18 league games. During this run Tony Waddington added another seasoned player to our ranks. Eddie Clamp had seen service with both Wolves and Arsenal and was a player I had encountered on numerous occasions. There was only one player I knew to be tougher than Eddie Stuart and that was Eddie Clamp. Stoke now had the two hardest players in the Football League in their team. Clampy could also play. 'I may not be an artisan,' he said, 'but you'll find I'll always pass to a red and white shirt.' Eddie was actually doing himself an injustice. He may have been a renowned hard man whose tackling would make legendary Liverpool defender Tommy Smith's look namby pamby, but he possessed superb close ball control, was a fine passer of the ball and his penchant for getting forward added an extra dimension to our attacks. Eddie joined Stoke in September 1962 and I immediately warmed to him. Experience had taught me what a hard and rugged player he was, but what I didn't know before was that Eddie Clamp was a most wonderful man with a heart as big as a bucket in which he carried nothing but love for his fellow man.

'It's in me head that the hardness is,' he used to tell me. 'And then only on matchdays and against opponents who get naughty.'

On his first day at Stoke, Eddie sat down in the dressing room next to me and was rarely to leave my side for the duration of our stay at the club.

'Stanley, there's some naughty players about who think the way to stop you playing is to kick you up into Row G. I know that for a fact, 'cos I was one of them,' Eddie told me. 'For donkey's years, you've been kicked black and blue and have never retaliated because you're above all that. Well those days are over now 'cos I'm going to look after you.'

And Eddie did just that. Eddie Clamp became my minder on the pitch and, along with Jackie Mudie, my closest friend.

It has often been said, usually by those who have never got to know me, that I was a bit of a loner and, due to my out-and-out professionalism and devotion to my career, I never mixed well with team-mates or joined in their fun and frolics in the dressing room. This is not only untrue, but in this spell with Stoke City the very reverse was the case. I was often the catalyst for fun and games. Eddie Clamp could make me laugh like no other player I had ever met. He was a great storyteller and his animated antics, wonderful facial expressions and hilarious delivery never failed to send me into hysterics. Win, lose or draw – and at this point in Stoke's history, we were back to winning – Eddie could be depended upon to lift our spirits with his jokes and hilarious stories from his playing career. It's a pity the sporting after-dinner circuit took off in the eighties when Eddie was suffering from ill-health because he would have been perfect for it. I am sure he would have been one of its leading lights.

In March 1963, Stoke were battling it out for one of what was then only two promotion places to Division One. Ourselves, Chelsea and Sunderland were neck and neck; Middlesbrough, Leeds United and Huddersfield Town were hard on our heels and ready to capitalise on any slip-ups. It was in this month that Tony Waddington went out and brought the player whom I believed would be the final piece in our promotion jigsaw, Jimmy McIlroy. Like Dennis Viollet, Jimmy was a marvellous inside-forward. In fact, I am given to saying that as far as inside-forwards go, he was the complete article. Jimmy started his career with Irish club Glentoran in 1950 but such a marvellous talent was quickly spotted and he joined Burnley for whom he played 437 games, helping them to the First Division championship in 1960 and to the FA Cup final in 1962. As a person, Jimmy was genial; as an inside-forward, he was a genius. When play was congested in the middle of the field, up out of the trapdoor would spring Jimmy. A will-o'-the-wisp player, he glided rather than ran about the pitch with the ball seemingly hypnotised on to the toe of his left boot. A sudden drop of a shoulder and a flick with the outside of his boot, the ball would leave his foot at some acute angle and another rearguard was breached. On releasing the ball, it was as if Jimmy disappeared into the ether. He would re-emerge inside the opponent's penalty area, take the return pass and pass again; this time into the net. I say Jimmy passed the ball into the net because more often than not that is what he did. His cool, calculating brain enabled him to size up the situation and choose his spot. Not for him the robust shot into the roof of the net; Jimmy simply guided the ball between the outstretched hands of the goalkeeper and the post. He succeeded in doing so 150 times during his career.

In my time in football, I'd come across players who, it was said, could make the ball talk. Jimmy could make it sing an aria and, along with Dennis Viollet, he made life easy for me at Stoke City.

With a good experienced goalkeeper in Jimmy O'Neill and strength down the middle in Eddie Stuart and Eddie Clamp and a still lethal goalscorer in Jackie Mudie at centre-forward, Tony Waddington had built a side in the classic way, with a strong spine. Around that there was the class of Viollet and McIlroy who orchestrated proceedings and on either wing, feeding all and sundry up front, myself and the other old hand, Don Ratcliffe. Despite the youth of the other regulars in the team – Bill Asprey, Tony Allen and Eric Skeels – Stoke had the oldest average age of any team in British senior football at that time. It was a constant source of humour in the dressing room, especially to Eddie Clamp. It was a case of old jokes for old hands and, believe you me, Eddie knew them all – when this team goes, Prudential goes; our original National Insurance stamps are more valuable than penny blacks; Waddo doesn't have to worry about this team chasing girls when we play away

– even if any of us still had the energy to catch them we couldn't remember what we were supposed to do; I started playing in the days when the only automatic sprinkler system for a pitch was the club cat; Stan, I can remember the days when it was stairs you took three at a time and not Biostrath tablets.

My favourite Clampy joke in this vein was when a young reporter from the local press, the *Evening Sentinel*, asked Eddie how old he was.

'Put it this way, son,' said Eddie. 'You've heard of that great old actress Dame Edith Evans?'

The cub reporter confirmed that he had.

'Well,' said Eddie, 'if I was 20 years younger, I'd marry her mother!'

Football has a habit of kicking you in the teeth just when you think all is going swimmingly. Jimmy McIlroy's debut for us was in March when Stoke travelled to play Norwich City. It turned out to be a nightmare. Nothing went right for us and Norwich were in scintillating form. We lost 6–0. We just didn't play. Jimmy was on the right and Tony Waddington quickly realised he had made a mistake. Jimmy favoured playing at inside-left and although you might think it shouldn't make any difference to a player of his standing and experience, Tony wanted to get the very best out of him. For our following game against Grimsby Town, Tony moved Jimmy back to his favoured inside-left position and switched Dennis Viollet from inside-left to inside-right. This simple change worked wonders. Grimsby were beaten 4–1 and we were not beaten for the next ten games, a run that put us right back in pole position in Division Two.

Easter as usual was a crucial time – three games to be played in four days, two of them against our closest rivals for promotion, Sunderland.

The first encounter at Roker Park was played on Good Friday. I had picked up an injury and had to drop out of the team, my place being taken by young Gerry Bridgwood. A crowd of 62,138 turned up, a fantastic attendance for a Second Division game. It ended all square at 0–0, so neither side had gained ground.

The following day we travelled to Cardiff City. The rest had done me good. Over 30,000 turned up at Ninian Park to see what was a close and tight match. Dennis Viollet scored the only goal to consolidate our position at the top of the league. We played the return game against Sunderland on the Easter Monday and, I have to say, we had a bit of luck, which all teams need if they are to be successful.

Dennis Viollet gave us the lead, his 21st goal of the season. Sunderland equalised and just when it seemed a draw was the most likely outcome, we were awarded a penalty late in the game. Put it this way, I'd seen penalties not given for such challenges, but up stepped Dennis and coolly tucked it away to give us the points. Sunderland had had strong appeals for a penalty turned down earlier in the game and probably came off the field feeling a little hard done by, but that's football.

The fact that luck seemed to be running for us together with the three points gained at our nearest rival's expense encouraged me to believe we really could win promotion. The prospect of playing in the First Division again thrilled me. The newspapers dwelt upon it in great detail on a daily basis for the remainder of the season. Rarely was I out of the headlines as the debate raged about whether I could still make an impact in top-flight football. Tony Waddington loved it. The publicity I was getting put Stoke City on the football map again and the crowds continued to roll up in their tens of thousands at the Victoria Ground. The players were happy, the manager was happy, the directors were happy and the fans were happy – that doesn't happen simultaneously very often in football!

A crowd of 42,366 watched our home game at the Victoria Ground against Sunderland. This meant a staggering 135,000 people had watched Stoke's three matches over the Easter period and this in Division Two. The days of 8,000 crowds watching Stoke were definitely a thing of the past. The increased attendances meant the club was quids in. It was great.

The winter of 1962–63 had been one of the most severe on record. In certain parts of the north of England, the first snow had fallen in late November and didn't disappear until early April. The Big Freeze as it was called played havoc with fixtures. The season set a record for postponements, over 400 in England and Scotland. In January 1963, only three third round FA Cup ties out of a total of 32 were played; 14 Cup ties were postponed ten times or more. The Lincoln City–Coventry City game was postponed 15 times while Blackburn and Middlesbrough didn't resolve their tie until 11 March. On 9 February, only seven games were played in England and the 57 English and Scottish games that were postponed remains a record to this day.

As a result of the severe winter, the football season was extended. Like all other clubs, Stoke had some catching up to do and in the last four weeks of a season that was to end on 22 May, we crammed in seven league games. Following our Easter Monday victory over Sunderland, we wobbled: A 3–3 draw against Huddersfield Town was followed by defeats against Middlesbrough, Newcastle and Scunthorpe United, the only consolation being Sunderland and Chelsea also dropped points.

On 11 May we travelled to Chelsea for what both teams knew would be a crunch game, what in those days we called a four-pointer – two points gained from a victory would, to all intents and purposes, be worth four points as they had been gained at the expense of a close rival.

Chelsea were the complete opposite to Stoke City. We were by and large a team of ageing players while they were a team of fashionable young starlets. The contrast was reflected in the managers. Tony Waddington was low profile and softly spoken; Chelsea, suffice to say, were managed by Tommy Docherty.

In the dressing room prior to the game, I sensed my team-mates were tense. This match could make or break the promotion aspirations of either side. It would be gung-ho stuff and despite all the invaluable experience in the Stoke team, I think at the back of our minds we worried that this young Chelsea side could run the legs off us if we weren't careful. We changed in almost complete silence, which was very unusual. Experience told me that should this atmosphere prevail we would take it out on to the pitch and it would transmit itself into our play with possibly catastrophic consequences to our promotion hopes. What we needed was some hilarity to lift the tension so I set about egging Eddie Clamp to get up and tell us a story from one of his big games of the past. Within two minutes of him taking to his feet, the atmosphere changed. Eddie, centre stage, began to recall a tale concerning a Wolves visit to Manchester United for a game vital to the championship hopes of both teams.

'Wilf McGuinness was making his first-team debut for United that day. Wilf sat in the United dressing room like a nervous jibbering wreck, not only because he was making his debut but also because he knew he would have to mark Peter Broadbent.

'Now Peter was one hell of a player. A stylish inside-forward but a gentleman and a sportsman, like our Stan here. So the United trainer, Jimmy Murphy, clocks Wilf, all nerves and trembling, and goes and sits next to him.

' "Wilf," says Jimmy, "You're up against Peter Broadbent today."

' "I know, Jimmy. He's a great player and a great sportsman," says Wilf all a tremble.

' "That's as maybe," says Jimmy. "Now you come from a home with just your mum and your little sister don't you?" says Jimmy.

' "Yes, just me mum, me sister and me," says Wilf.

' "And this being your debut, you want that winning bonus really badly don't you, Wilf?"

' "Yes, I do," says Wilf.

' "I know that, son," says Jimmy. "With your winning bonus I know you plan to buy your mother a new dress. Well, that Peter Broadbent, he's going out there today and he's going to do his utmost to stop you getting that winning bonus. Peter Broadbent doesn't want your mother to have that new dress. Your mother has brought you up well, she's worked hard and made sacrifices for you and your sister. She deserves a nice dress but this Peter Broadbent doesn't want your mother to have it. He's going to take it away from her. Are you going to let him do that?"

' "No, Jimmy. I won't let him do that," says Wilf, getting all angry and worked up.

' "And that little sister of yours," says Jimmy. "She needs a new pair of shoes for school, I know that. Now with your winning bonus today, you can buy her them shoes. But that Peter Broadbent, he doesn't want her to have them, Wilf. He wants to take those new shoes away from that little sister of yours. Are you going to let him do that, Wilf? Take shoes from the feet of a little innocent like that sister of yours, and a nice new dress from your hard-working and loving mother?"

' "No!" says Wilf, jumping up to his feet and going all red and misty with anger. "I'm not gonna let that Peter

Broadbent take the shoes from my sister or that dress from my lovely mother."

' "Then make sure you get out there today and take the ball off him, Wilf," says Jimmy. "Don't allow Broadbent to get that ball." In saying that, Jimmy pushed Wilf out of the United dressing-room door just as the teams were taking to the pitch.

'Just as Wilf emerges from the door of their dressing room, we are coming down the corridor and the first player he sees is Peter Broadbent carrying a ball. Now Peter, being the gentleman and sportsman he is, knows this is Wilf's debut so he stops and says, "Good luck today, young man." But Wilf, all hyped up, snatches the ball out of Peter's hands and shouts, "Gimme that ball, you heartless thieving bastard!" '

The Stoke dressing room erupted into laughter. The ice had been broken. Eddie was now in his element so I urged him on. He was quite a good mimic so I got him to do some impersonations of the team. While he was doing this, I slipped out of our dressing room to ensure some tickets I had left for two friends had been picked up. As I passed the Chelsea dressing room, it was silent. I didn't have to enter ours to know what sort of atmosphere was prevailing, I could hear the gales of laughter from down the corridor. It was a good sign.

When I took to the pitch behind skipper Eddie Stuart and goalkeeper Jimmy O'Neill, it was like going back in time. Stamford Bridge was packed to the rafters – 66,199 were crammed in cheek by jowl. Another 10,000 were outside unable to gain entry as the house full signs went up and the turnstile gates were locked.

Chelsea had two formidable full-backs in Eddie McCreadie and Ron Harris. Harris had already gained a reputation as a hard nut and basked in the nickname of

'Chopper'. Within two minutes of the game starting, I realised Ron Harris's reputation was not one of football folklore. Having received a pass from Dennis Viollet, I attempted to do what I always did on receiving the ball, spin off my marker. This had been a trait of our play in the Stoke team. Most of the players had been accustomed to playing the ball into space when they saw a colleague tightly marked, but I had encouraged my team-mates to play the ball to my feet. I could get the ball under control with one touch and while shielding it from my marker, turn and beat him. I'd been doing this for over 30 years. The added advantage was that it drew other defenders towards me and thus created space for my fellow forwards. I was in the process of spinning away when suddenly I felt a searing pain shoot up the back of my left leg. Chopper had done his bit and I was unceremoniously dumped on my backside. Game on.

Five minutes later, Chopper hit me again with one of his more humane tackles. He took me out just above my right knee. Robust tackling I could cope with and indeed expected, but Chopper's attentions were foul rather than fair. This carried on for 20 minutes or so and I began to wonder why they had bothered to bring a ball out on to the pitch. After one late tackle which ripped a large hole in my stocking just above the ankle, the referee eventually intervened. Chopper, young as he was, had all the patter off to a tee.

'That was very late, son,' said the referee.

'I got there as quick as I could, ref,' said Chopper all smiles. Unbelievably, the referee still didn't book him.

A couple of minutes later, I pushed the ball past Chopper and was thinking I had the legs on him when, from behind, my legs were taken from under me. I crashed awkwardly in a heap on the turf and in so doing injured my elbow. Grimacing in pain, I opened my eyes to see Chopper standing over me. As I lay waiting for our trainer to arrive on the scene, I thought a large cloud had passed over Stamford Bridge and blotted out the sun because it suddenly seemed to go dark. Adjusting my eyes, I saw the reason for the blotting out of the sun – Eddie Clamp.

Eddie had come across Ron Harris in the previous season when Chelsea had been relegated from Division One and he had been at Arsenal. During that encounter, Chopper had apparently been up to his usual tricks but Eddie pulled him back in line under threat of a visit to Charing Cross hospital if he didn't cease.

'Listen, you little sod,' snarled Eddie grabbing a handful of Chopper's shirt in a fist the size of a ham shank. 'If I see you clobber Stanley again, I'll take you out of this game. On a bloody stretcher. What I said to you last season at Arsenal wasn't a threat, sonny boy, it were a bloody promise and it still applies.'

At this point, the referee intervened uttering placating words such as 'Now, now gentlemen. Football's the game, not boxing.'

As Jimmy McIlroy and Don Ratcliffe led him away, Eddie came out with what to my mind is one of the greatest lines ever said on a football pitch.

'That's the trouble with you referees,' said Eddie, speaking over his shoulder, 'you don't care which side wins.'

With order restored and my treatment administered, the game got under way again. It wasn't a classic game of football, probably because there was too much at stake for both teams. It was tight and physical. I received a pass from Bill Asprey and made progress down our right when out of the corner of my eye I was aware of a blue missile hurtling towards me. I was just on the point of upping my pace in the hope of avoiding it when an almighty force ripped into my left thigh, the momentum of which whipped my legs from under me and thrust me head down towards the turf. My legs shot into the air, waggling about like the legs of Old Mother Riley and it was all I could do to stick out an arm to prevent my head hitting the ground first and sustaining some injury to my neck.

I turned my head in the direction from which the blue blur had come but saw nothing. Looking to the other side, I saw Chopper Harris taking to his feet. His Exocet tackle had taken me out almost thigh high. The referee was quickly on the scene but to my dismay, Chopper received only a booking. Eddie Clamp was nowhere to be seen. It was then that the unthinkable crossed my mind. Perhaps after having confronted Chopper and witnessed what he was capable of, Eddie had come to think in the light of self-preservation; it was better for him to take a back seat and keep his head down.

Play resumed with me limping awkwardly. I was battered and bruised but still on for this game; I knew we had to get a result from it. Fortunately, the more running about I did, the more the pain subsided, though I knew once the game was over and my muscles had returned to rest, the real pain would emerge.

Just before half-time, Ron Harris received a pass from centre-half Marvin Hinton and was bringing the ball out of the Chelsea defence. For all his rough-house play, Chopper Harris could really play and on the ball was as assured and stylish as the best defenders around at that time. As Chopper progressed up field, he gained speed and was some five or so yards from the halfway line when I saw Eddie Clamp, some 15 yards away, sprinting towards him and working up a great head of steam. Eddie was looking in the direction of Chopper, but his eyes seemed to be transfixed on some point in the distance beyond Chopper's shoulders. The closer Eddie came to Chopper, the faster Eddie ran and the more transfixed his eyes became until they eventually bulged from his head like golf balls. When he was about three yards from Chopper, Eddie took off. Airborne, his right leg jutted forward like a lance. As he completed his descent Eddie snarled like a Rottweiler in the last stages of rabies and let forth with a deep grunt before his right leg made impact with first the ball, then various parts of Chopper's anatomy. In TV cartoons whenever there is a fight, it is depicted by swirling blurs with arms and legs protruding at various times in a circular motion. That is the best way I can think of describing the result of Eddie Clamp's tackle. Chopper rose into the air as if he was on a highboard and diving into some distant pool below, only there was no grace to his movement. Legs splayed in the air, Chopper headed back to earth and carved out his own niche on that pitch with his chin.

Never in 30 years of football had I seen a tackle like it. Such had been the force behind Eddie's challenge, the ball had shot from under Chopper and out for a throw-in on the far side of the pitch, some twenty yards away and when the ball disappeared into the parked terracing, it had still been rising. Eddie's momentum had carried him under Chopper and beyond him, but no sooner had he applied the brakes than he was up on his feet and sprinting back to tower over what was now a motionless and prostrate Chopper Harris.

'I telt thee what would 'appen, lad,' said Eddie menacingly. 'Next time, they'll just slide a stretcher under thee and cart thee off to 'ospital. I'm a man who always keeps his promises.'

From that moment on, I never had another spot of bother from Chopper Harris for the remainder of the match. He settled down to play the football he was so eminently capable of and we enjoyed a testing, but fair, tussle until the final whistle.

The only goal of the game came from Jimmy McIlroy. Jimmy started a move which involved Dennis Viollet, Jackie

Mudie and myself and when I threaded the ball through a gap in the Chelsea rearguard, up popped will-o'-the-wisp Jimmy to pass the ball between the flaying arms of goalkeeper Peter Bonetti and his left-hand post to give us victory and the crucial two points.

The pummelling I received at the hands, or rather boots, of Chopper Harris ruled me out of Stoke's next game, a 2–1 defeat at Bury but I returned to the side for what was our penultimate match of the season, and final home game, against Luton Town. Results had gone our way, both Chelsea and Sunderland had dropped points and a win would ensure us the Division Two championship and promotion.

As it turned out, no scriptwriter could have written it better. We were leading 1–0 thanks to a goal from Jackie Mudie but Luton, who needed the points to avoid relegation, were causing us problems. Luton were making a fight of it and in the second half were still in with a chance of a point. Towards the end of the match, having moved into the centre of midfield, I latched on to a long through ball from Jimmy McIlroy. Having beaten one Luton defender, I headed straight for goal, the telltale click-clack of boots running through mud telling me two or three defenders were in hot pursuit. I took to my toes as the Luton goalkeeper Roy Baynham came out of his goal to narrow the angle, it was a simple job of feinting one way so he committed himself and going the other. Taking the ball wide of Roy I took a moment to glance up and see the open goal before side-footing the ball into the net.

All 34,000 Stoke fans went delirious. We were promoted. We were champions and I had scored the goal that clinched it. My only goal of the season! As I say, from my point of view, it couldn't have been scripted better but the great satisfaction for me was that despite my age and the fact my goal came late in the game, I had run some 40 yards with the ball at my feet and not one Luton defender had caught up with me. Retirement was certainly not on my agenda.

After the post-match celebrations, I gave numerous interviews to the press, one to Peter Wilson of the *Daily Mirror* who for a long time had been writing that I should step down gracefully from the game before I embarrassed myself. At the end of my chat with Peter I remarked on the fact that not for some time had he penned an article saying it was high time I retired.

After 15 years of continually writing that the time had come for you to pack it in,' said Peter, 'I finally gave up last September.'

Chelsea took the other promotion place on goal average at the expense of Sunderland.

I derived great satisfaction from Stoke's promotion season. Not only was I delighted for the club and its supporters, but I felt that over a whole season in a game that was becoming increasingly faster, I had proved I could still do it. I can't tell you what it felt like to know I had not been carried at any time by my team-mates in matches. Tony Waddington told me I had been a 'talisman to the team'. That's as maybe, but I felt I had justified my inclusion in what was a very talented side. If I had felt anything different, I would have retired. Young players, as Dario Gradi knows only too well at Crewe Alexandra, are inconsistent. Experienced players, however, rarely have a bad game. They may vary in their levels of contribution but overall they rarely fall below being good and I believed that I had played my part to the full in Stoke's success in 1962–63.

Money was becoming more important in the game than ever. With the abolition of the maximum wage, the top players were drawn to the big-money clubs who paid them accordingly. In 1962–63 Denis Law returned to British football after a spell with Italian side Torino. The fee Manchester United paid was £115,000, a new British record. Another English player, Joe Baker, also left Torino and signed for Arsenal for £80,000. The new big stars of football were signing for the big-city clubs. The days when the Boltons and Prestons of English football could hang on to world-class players because they would not be financially better off moving elsewhere were over.

Everton were crowned First Division champions with a side bought at such expense the newspapers dubbed them the 'Cheque Book Champions'. Four players alone cost a total of £200,000, which was considered very big if not crazy money at the time. 1962–63 set the tone for a situation in football that is more or less set in concrete today.

Manchester United finished only two places above relegated Manchester City and Leyton Orient but appeased their fans by winning the FA Cup, beating Leicester City 3–1 in an entertaining final. I was pleased for Matt Busby. It was United's first major triumph since the Munich air disaster and their first trophy since 1957 and it paved the way for the great success they were to have throughout the sixties.

To cap what had been a great season for me with Stoke City, I was voted Footballer of the Year.

— ○ —

Stoke went to Tottenham Hotspur on the opening day of the 1963–64 season and upset the form book, such as it is on the opening day of a season. Spurs had finished runners-up in the First Division three months previously and we beat them 2–1, both of our goals coming from Jimmy McIlroy.

Among the 41,000 who watched the game was Mel Hopkins. It was just like old times meeting Mel again; he had been a formidable opponent in the fifties. He was still at

Spurs, in the last throws of his career, and was playing out his contract in the reserves. Mel had been a fine full-back and as we chatted we reminisced about one particular encounter. When I was with Blackpool in the fifties, we went to White Hart Lane for a game in which Mel had been given strict instructions to man-mark me. Throughout the first half he stuck to me like glue. In an attempt to shake him off I changed wings, then played down the middle of the park, but it was all to no avail. Mel followed me everywhere. As we walked up the tunnel for our half-time cuppa I felt the need to answer the call of nature. Seeing a door marked 'Gentlemen' I was in the process of opening it when I felt the presence of someone behind me. Turning, I saw it was Mel Hopkins.

'For goodness sake, are you going to follow me in here as well?' I asked.

'My instructions were to follow you *everywhere*!' Mel replied.

We had a good laugh together about the incident but there is actually a postscript to this story. In 1998 I attended a sporting dinner in Cardiff. In my after-dinner speech, I recalled the tale of Mel's close marking and on delivering the punchline the audience seemed to laugh more than normal. I stood there bewildered as the laughter rather than subsiding, started to increase in volume. I just couldn't understand it. The more I stood there, the more the audience roared. Eventually I turned around and there behind me was Mel Hopkins.

'And I'm still following you now!' said Mel, to the further amusement of the diners. Mel was always a true gentleman and one of football's great characters and it delights me to say the passing years have not altered him one bit.

Following our opening-day success at Spurs, Stoke went to Aston Villa where we won 3–1, our goals coming from

Jackie Mudie and Peter Dobing who scored two. Peter was another of Tony Waddington's seasoned-pro signings. He had joined Stoke in the close season from Manchester City. Sadly from my point of view, I picked up an injury which plagued me for much of the rest of the season. My appearances were spasmodic and following an appearance at outside-right in January against Leicester City, I didn't feature again.

We finished in seventeenth position and there was never any danger of relegation. We also had the distinction of reaching the final of the League Cup, losing to Leicester City. So from Stoke's point of view, it had been a satisfactory return to the top flight.

Thoughts of retirement had started to loom large in my mind. I was beginning to pick up injuries and even the niggly ones which years ago I would have shaken off in a day or so were taking two or three weeks to dispel. Although still quite capable of getting through games in the First Division, my lengthy lay-offs meant I was not contributing to the team in the way I wanted to. With this in mind, come May 1964 I decided that the following season would be my last in English football. I went to see Tony Waddington and he was full of understanding, which I took to mean he felt I had made the right decision at the right time.

I had played my part in Stoke's renaissance and I derived great satisfaction from that. Stoke City were now back in the First Division commanding an average attendance of over 25,000; in fact, in their last three home games of 1963 the attendance was 35,153, 45,697 and 32,149. Happy days had returned to the club and I had been a part of them once again. I would be leaving a club enjoying relative success and not one struggling to survive or make ends meet. That provided me with great contentment.

I was not the only player to bow out. Tony Waddington's

policy of buying players who could do him a job for two or three years meant that Jimmy O'Neill, Eddie Clamp, Eddie Stuart and Don Ratcliffe were also ready to go. We had all served our purpose and accomplished the job we had set out to do. I felt there was much honour in our departures.

On the subject of honour, on 1 January 1965, I received news of the greatest honour that can be bestowed upon any British person – I was to be knighted for my services to football. To be honest, I feel uncomfortable about mentioning this and only do so at the behest of those who are advising me in the writing of this book, who tell me that to pass it over would mean the omission of a key part in my story. In not wanting to dwell on my knighthood, I don't want anyone to think that I do not value the honour bestowed upon me or that I have anything but the utmost respect for such a privileged title. However, the title has never rested comfortably with me, purely because I believe there are many others far more worthy – surgeons; doctors; aid workers who alleviate suffering and hardship; teachers in inner city schools; those whose work involves the eradication of life-threatening illnesses and disease; people whose lives revolve around the constant care of children or relatives stricken with mental or physical handicaps. I could go on. Suffice to say I believed then, as I still do now, there are far more just and worthy recipients of a knighthood than I.

In 1964–65, with either Peter Dobing or Gerry Bridgwood occupying the number seven shirt, I played out my career with Stoke City reserves. Not long after my birthday, however, injury beset both players and so it was, on 6 February 1965, at the age of 50, I was recalled to the Stoke City first team against Fulham for what would turn out to be my last-ever appearance in the English First Division. I went public with the announcement of my retirement and the only problem the club had was finding seats for all the sports writers who descended on the Victoria Ground. They came from all over the world and the press box couldn't cope.

So in front of 30,000 Stoke supporters and heaven knows how many journalists, I took to the pitch for my very last game in English football. The Fulham left-back that day was an old friend of mine, Jimmy Langley. Jimmy thought he was seeing out his career with Fulham, but in 1967 he enjoyed his swan song helping Queens Park Rangers win the first-ever League Cup final to be played at Wembley. Jimmy was 37 which meant our combined age was 87. It was said to be the oldest combined age of two directly opposing players ever to have been recorded in the First Division. Whether that is true or not, I'm not sure, but I do know it hasn't been beaten since.

Jimmy and I enjoyed ourselves immensely. There was much banter about age between us and the game seemed to fly by. Stoke won 3–1 but my joy at the result was tempered by the tears I was struggling to hold back as both teams formed a line of honour to applaud me from the field at the final whistle. The Stoke fans gave me a tremendous send-off, the terracing rang with applause and it appeared that everyone in the seats had taken to their feet to express their sentiments.

In the dressing room, I took off my boots and posed for a photograph for an old pal of mine, Huston Spratt, a photographer with the *Evening Sentinel*.

'How do you want it, Huston?' I asked.

'Can I have one of you hanging your boots up?' said Huston.

I duly obliged and hung my boots on the peg above my seat as Huston's camera flashed to capture the moment. My Stoke team-mates sang 'For he's a jolly good fellow', something I am sure you would never hear in a dressing room today. Even in 1965 it was anachronistic but as Tony Waddington kindly said at the time, 'It may be an old-fashioned thing to do, but its sentiment is wholly appropriate, Stan.'

Thirty-five years as a professional footballer had finally come to an end. Everyone said I was bowing out with my dignity intact, but deep down I felt I was retiring too early and could have gone on for another two years. But in wanting another two years on top of 35, I felt I was being greedy, so I attuned my mind to the fact that from now on my life would not be that of a professional footballer. It wasn't easy; I had known nothing else since the age of 15.

After what seemed like an age spent thanking well-wishers, I finally found myself alone in the dressing room. Just as I was leaving with my grip bag in my hand, I remembered my boots, which were still hanging up on my peg. I looked at them for fully a minute or so as all manner of thoughts ran through my head. I took one last look around the empty dressing room, switched off the light and closed the door behind me, leaving my boots still hanging on my peg. It seemed like the right thing to do.

═══ ○ ═══

I travelled to Buckingham Palace to receive my knighthood from Her Majesty the Queen accompanied by Betty, Jean and Stanley junior, who was making a name for himself as a tennis player. It was a marvellous day and for all I felt it undeserved, I enjoyed the occasion immensely. At the investiture Her Majesty asked, 'Are you still enjoying your football?' All I could think of to say by way of a reply was, 'Yes, Ma'am.' I had wanted to say something more profound, witty or amusing but words failed me. I have never been in the Oscar Wilde or Peter Ustinov class but I consoled myself by thinking that anything more than that may have been in breach of protocol and the last thing I wanted at my knighthood was to make Her Majesty feel uncomfortable. I'd met the Queen before of course; she handed me my Cup winner's medal in 1953. I had also met the Duke of Edinburgh on several occasions when he had been presented either to England or to Blackpool team line-ups, but this was different. Afterwards we talked at length and I found them to be eminently gracious and warm people, both with a very keen wit which, given their status, they have little occasion to display in public.

The Duke of Edinburgh is a Companion Rat of the Grand Order of Water Rats, an organisation primarily comprising people in entertainment and sport who have over the years raised millions for worthy causes. His Royal Highness wrote a letter to the King Rat, who at the time was comedian and chairman of Fulham Tommy Trinder, which resulted in me being initiated as a Companion of the Order of Water Rats. Tommy Trinder let me have the letter, which I had framed and to this day it has pride of place on my desk in my den.

My initiation as a Water Rat took place at the Grosvenor House Hotel in London with over a thousand people from the world of showbusiness in attendance. It was a marvellous night and I was thrilled to meet so many people from the world of stage and screen who were in fact heroes of mine. I sat next to Tommy Trinder whom I knew well. Tommy was one of football's great characters whose humour was as much in evidence off the stage as it was on it.

I have two favourite Tommy Trinder football stories and the first concerns that great British hero of World War Two, Viscount Montgomery of Alamein. Monty was a big football fan and for years was president of Portsmouth. Tommy Trinder was appearing in pantomime in Portsmouth in the mid fifties and was invited by Viscount Montgomery to attend a Portsmouth home match as his guest. After the match, Tommy was being entertained in the Portsmouth boardroom but was trying to keep an ear open for the Fulham result on the radio. Eventually he heard that Fulham had won 2–0, with both goals coming from their bright new starlet Johnny Haynes.

'You must look out for that boy Haynes, sir,' said Tommy to Viscount Montgomery. 'He's going to be a great player, he has everything and mark my words, one day he'll captain England.'

'Really?' said Monty. 'How old is the lad?'

'Eighteen,' replied Tommy.

'Eighteen?' said Monty, frowning. 'What about his National Service?'

'Ah, that's the only sad part,' said Tommy, thinking on his feet. 'He's a cripple.'

My second tale concerning Tommy occurred when Manchester United visited Fulham. Tommy was never one given to standing on ceremony and quite often you would find all manner of Fulham employees joining the directors for a post-match drink in the Craven Cottage boardroom. Joining the Fulham and Manchester United directors and their wives on this day was the Fulham groundsman. Tommy introduced him to the wife of the United chairman Louis Edwards. Now Mrs Edwards was a gracious and benevolent lady but of a somewhat delicate disposition. She had noticed that the Fulham pitch was in fine fettle for so late in the season and asked the groundsman how he managed to keep the grass so lush. The groundsman, honest as the day is long, told her that his secret was that in the close season before seeding it he would cover the pitch with barrow loads of manure. After a time, Mrs Edwards re-joined her husband who was still in conversation with Tommy, and Tommy asked how she had got on with his groundsman.

'Very well,' said Mrs Edwards, 'but I'd appreciate it if you could have a word with him about his language which I found a little distasteful. I asked him the secret for keeping the pitch so good and he said the word manure. Could you have a word with him? Ask him to use the word fertiliser instead?'

'You've got to be joking,' said Tommy, dropping his not inconsiderable jaw. 'It's taken me six months to get him to call it manure!'

— o —

Following that final game for Stoke, the directors informed me I was to be granted a testimonial in recognition of my 21 years with the club, even though it had been in two spells, 17 and four years respectively. Needless to say, I was delighted to be given this news. I didn't have a clue what I was going to do when I retired and had adopted the Mr Micawber philosophy that 'something would turn up'. The money generated from a testimonial game would ensure that no matter what life had in store for me, I would be financially secure for some time. Given I was a family man and had not earned any great amount of money from my 35 years as a professional footballer, this was one of my anxieties.

It was generally accepted at this time that testimonials were granted to players who had seen ten years' service with a club, or else had had their careers cut short by injury. However, even when a player had completed ten years with a club, he wasn't automatically guaranteed a testimonial. It was very much at the discretion of the board of directors and I knew of several players who had completed ten years and more with a club and left with only a 'Goodbye and good luck'. My father, as I have said, always brought me up to expect nothing in life and that way you are never disappointed. I had spent 14 years at Blackpool, was arguably their biggest attraction for a good part of that time, but never expected to be granted a testimonial, which was just as well because all I got was a 'Goodbye and good luck'. For Stoke City to grant me a testimonial was a great privilege and I set about the organisation of it along with a committee comprising good friends such as Peter Buxton of the *Evening Sentinel*, Edgar Turner of the *Sunday Mirror* and several Stoke City supporters.

Testimonials can be a contentious issue. I am fully aware that millions of people can give many years loyal service to a company and leave without so much as a thank you. However, a testimonial is the supporters' way of saying thank you for some magical moments that will live on their memories for ever. Why do people go to football matches? Well, one of the reasons is to see players perform in a way they are unable to. Just occasionally, the acts and actions of certain players are touched with the stuff dreams are made of. The supporter leaves the ground not only with golden memories but also with the reaffirmation that football played at its most creative and inventive best is a thing of beauty. That, combined with loyalty, is to my mind justification for a testimonial.

However, I have to be honest and say the idea of testimonials for today's top players rests uneasily with me. In the past, the money a player received from a testimonial would make him financially comfortable as at the age of 35, or 50 in my case, he started to look for a new career. No matter how hard it was finding a new job, provided the player in question was careful, the testimonial money would provide a safety net for him and his family. Nowadays, Premiership players, especially those at the very top, can earn in just one week twice the amount the average working person earns in a year. Our top players are millionaires. On top of five-figure weekly sums, they have lucrative endorsement deals that can net them anything from £500,000 to a million pounds a year.

I'm all for today's players earning as much as they can when they can. The one thing that hasn't changed over the years is the timespan of a footballing career; it is still relatively short. I'm also all for supporters wanting to show their appreciation of a player. But to expect someone on a tight budget to turn up at a testimonial in support of someone who is already a millionaire or not far short is, pardon the pun, a bit rich. Of course, supporters are not compelled to attend testimonials but I feel benefit matches for millionaires tax supporters' loyalty and, at worst, appear embarrassingly crass.

The players who came to Stoke for my testimonial on 28 April 1965 left me slack-jawed – from the old school, Ferenc Puskas, Raymond Kopa and Alfredo Di Stefano; from the new, Eusebio, Denis Law and Jimmy Greaves. Letters, cards and telegrams from well-wishers arrived from all over the world, from ordinary football supporters and from just about every Football Association aligned to FIFA. They came from the sportswriters with whom I had enjoyed a love-hate relationship and from those with whom it was simply love. They came from millionaire owners of global companies and from the poor of Africa. They came from players I'd had the privilege to play with or against and they came from royalty. The Duke of Edinburgh sent a most moving and gracious letter. The mail had to be delivered to my home in a large van. The first day there were seven bags, the next 13 and the day after that, which was the day of the testimonial itself, 20 bags of mail arrived at my doorstep. There were so many mailbags they couldn't be stored in the house. I had to stack them in lines on the patio. With such a mind-boggling amount of mail it was impossible for me to answer even a fraction of those who had conveyed their good wishes. So if you wrote and I never replied, may I take this belated opportunity to say a heartfelt 'Thank you'.

The night itself was a great occasion. The pre-match entertainment was a game between two sides billed as post-war favourites, one skippered by my old Blackpool captain Harry Johnston and one by old Arsenal adversary Walley Barnes. The vets lined up as follows:

Harry Johnston's XI: Bert Trautmann (Manchester City); Tim Ward (Derby), George Hardwick (Middlesbrough); Jimmy Hill (Fulham – now whatever happened to him?), Neil Franklin (Stoke City), Harry Johnston (Blackpool); Don Revie (Manchester City and Sunderland), Stan Mortensen (Blackpool), Nat Lofthouse (Bolton Wanderers), Jimmy Hagan (Sheffield United), Tom Finney (Preston North End). Reserve: Frank Bowyer (Stoke City). The idea was that Frank would come on at half-time. When half-time arrived and Frank asked who was feeling the pace and would like to come off to give him a run out, 11 hands went up!

Wally Barnes XI: Jimmy O'Neill (Stoke); Jimmy Scoular (Newcastle United and Bradford Park Avenue), Walley Barnes (Arsenal); Danny Blanchflower (Spurs), Jimmy Dickinson (Portsmouth), Hughie Kelly (Blackpool); Bill McGarry (Port Vale and West Brom), Jackie Mudie (Blackpool and Stoke City), Jackie Milburn (Newcastle United), Jock Dodds (Blackpool), Ken Barnes (Manchester City). Reserve: Arthur Rowley (Shrewsbury Town).

⎯⎯ o ⎯⎯

The main match, in which I was to appear, featured some of the greatest players in the world at that time. As is often the case with testimonials, substitutes came and went like fashion fads, but whatever the composition of either team, the 40,000 supporters who came to give me a terrific send-off were not short-changed. Every player who took to the field was a class act and some boasted the highest football pedigree it is possible to have and have since gone on to take their rightful place in the pantheon of the footballing gods. The teams were as follows:

Stan's XI: Tony Waiters; Jimmy Armfield (both Blackpool), George Cohen (Fulham); Johnny Haynes (Fulham), Bobby Thomson (Wolves), Denis Law (Manchester United); Stanley Matthews (Blackpool and Stoke City), Jimmy Greaves (Spurs), Bobby Charlton (Manchester United), Alan Gilzean, Cliff Jones (both Spurs). Substitutes: Brian Douglas (Blackburn Rovers), John Ritchie (Stoke City), Ray Wilson (Huddersfield Town and Everton), Roger Hunt (Liverpool), Kai Johansen (Rangers and Sweden).

International XI: Lev Yashin (Russia); Karl Heinz Schnellinger (West Germany), Wolfgang Weber (West Germany); Josef Masopust, Jan Popluhar (both Czechoslovakia), Jim Baxter (Scotland); Willie Henderson (Scotland), Raymond Kopa (France), Alfredo Di Stefano (Spain), Ferenc Puskas (Hungary), Eusebio (Portugal). Substitutes: Hans Tilkowski, Uwe Seeler, Hans Schäfer and Wolfgang Overath (West Germany), Francisco Gento (Spain), Kubala (Spain) and Van Den Boer (Belgium).

It was a great night and one I will remember and cherish for ever. Stan's XI lost 6–4 but the result was as inconsequential as the sense of occasion was great.

At the end of the game, the players formed a circle in the middle of the pitch, joined arms and with the 40,000 spectators sang 'Auld Lang Syne'. It sent a shiver down my spine and I was moved to tears. Lev Yashin and Ferenc Puskas hoisted me on their shoulders and I was carried by these two greats of football to the tunnel and the dressing rooms from what was my last ever match at my beloved Victoria Ground.

The huge task of organising such a testimonial was one that might well have taxed the FA, FIFA and the Football League themselves, yet it was all down to the work of a few friends and well-wishers. They tackled it with enthusiasm and the end result to my mind was nothing short of remarkable. Seldom, if ever before, had there been such a gathering of stars from football and the stage. The 40,000 crowd who turned up on what was a mean night of incessant rain and a biting wind ignored the elements and relished the footballing feast of a lifetime. Even hardened sports writers, of whom there were over a hundred, told me afterwards that never in their experience of watching football all over the world had they seen such an impressive gathering and it was true. Frank McGhee of the *Daily Mirror* and Frank Butler of the *News of the World* sat down and tried to work out the collective current-day value of all the players on show and gave up at £2 million, this at a time when the record transfer fee was around £150,000. Frank McGhee also tried to work out how many miles some of them had travelled and gave up on that, too. Money and mileage were incalculable on such a night of magic.

For the very last time people saw the sophisticated artistry of Tom Finney and Jimmy Hagan; the still lethal shooting of Morty, Jackie Milburn and Nat Lofthouse; the crunch tackling of Harry Johnston and Jimmy Scoular; the heading of Neil Franklin that mixed power, grace and style; and, the most blessed sight of all, burly Jock Dodds, one time of Blackpool and my old RAF pal, slower in pace but not in mind or reflexes, harassing all and sundry, appealing for justice and, as of yore, getting very little. The Stoke fans who meant and still mean so much to me, had the opportunity to seeing a cavalcade of the world's finest weave their own particular brand of magic across Stoke's famous, or infamous, sodden slough. It was as I had hoped it would be, a match in which all football's arts, artifices and crafts were displayed to the full. It was a wonderful night and a wonderful match – my last in a Stoke shirt, my last at the Victoria Ground, my last in British football. I had enjoyed 35 years as a footballer, 783 league and Cup games, 84 matches for England, two for Great Britain and 41 other representative games. I had scored 71 league goals, nine in Cup ties and 13 for England. I was the oldest player to have scored in the FA Cup, won a Cup winner's medal, played for England and in the First Division (Premiership equivalent). I was the first player to be nominated Footballer of the Year and the first European Footballer of the Year, the first to receive a CBE and the first to be knighted. What I had achieved in my career surpassed even my wildest dreams. On 28 April 1965 I bade goodbye to it all. It was a hearty and heartfelt hail and farewell to a career about which it was impossible for me to have any regrets.

24

——○——

Footballing Missionary

A s it turned out, I was not out of football for long. Jackie Mudie had left Stoke City for near neighbours Port Vale and in 1965 was acting as caretaker-manager following the departure of another former playing colleague of mine, Freddie 'Nobby' Steele, with whom I had enjoyed great days in my first spell at Stoke City in the thirties. Jackie persuaded the Port Vale board to take me on. He became player-manager and I took on the role of general manager. My position was unique in football because I was to be unpaid, an arrangement I was quite happy with. The testimonial had provided a nice nest egg and after the career I had enjoyed, I wanted to give something back to the game that had given so very much to me. It was, I was informed at the time, another first. In embarking upon football management, I had become the first manager in the history of the professional game to be unsalaried, though I was to be paid expenses.

Although delighted at the prospect of entering management, particularly with a club from my home city, I missed being a player and the day-to-day life that involved. I didn't just miss it, I missed it a lot and to be truthful all these years on, I still miss it now. Many former players say they don't miss the playing side at all because the enthusiasm and excitement had started to diminish and it was the right time to give it all up. I suppose when you are not really enjoying playing, or the daily routine of training, it is right and proper to hang up your boots, but I never felt like that.

To me, football is the greatest jewel in life and as a footballer, you are privileged to have the God-given opportunity of providing the right setting for it to shine. Sometimes its radiance will dazzle all who view it. How much more fortunate can you be? When George Best said he loved the game so much he would have played football for nothing, I knew he felt the same way about playing football as I do. Once the playing days are over, despite being grateful for having had the chance to play and to entertain and occasionally bring light, colour, drama and excitement into the lives of your fellow man, there is a great void to fill. I had been a footballer for 35 years and when it came to giving it up, it was a great wrench. It was the one time the longevity of my career worked against me. Having feasted for so long on the bountiful fruits playing football has to offer, for them all of a sudden to be denied me was devastating. I had withdrawal symptoms and occasionally still do.

Playing football helped form my character, personality, psyche and emotional make-up and thus helped mould me as a person. I discovered much about myself and life in general – when the going gets tough, the human mind can be tougher; there are no mistakes in life only lessons; in football, like in life, if you have your wits about you, you will learn more from failure than you do from success; to look after your body because if you do, it will look after you; by being generous in defeat and modest when victorious you bring dignity and grace to your life. Giving up playing was like losing the love of my life, which in many ways it had been. I went into management because I wanted to put something back into football for all it had given me, but also because I thought it was the next best thing.

I was looking forward to football management. As it turned out, it was instrumental in bringing about the greatest change to my life and the most joyous and fulfilling relationship I was ever to have the pleasure of knowing.

Port Vale were strapped for cash – was it ever thus? – with no money available for team strengthening, so Jackie and I set out a long-term strategy for the club based on youth. By finding talented schoolboys and grooming our own players at Vale Park, in time we would produce a conveyor belt of youngsters that would form not only the basis of one team, but the majority of future sides. To help improve the club's financial position, I planned for one or two promising youngsters to be sold off on an annual basis to larger clubs. The money from the sales would be used for wages to keep existing talented players happy, while the transfer of one or two players at the most per season would not have an immediate detrimental effect on the club's playing strength, because youngsters coming up would take the place of the outgoing players.

What you need in order to set up a really successful youth policy is time. Unfortunately, the Port Vale board weren't prepared to give Jackie and me that time, and my stint as a manager lasted for only three years. I thought the Port Vale directors were wrong to get rid of me before my plan had a chance to bear fruit, and the passing years have not changed my mind. For a club of Port Vale's stature and size, I thought

I was on the right track and feel heartened when I hear Dario Gradi say that what he has put into operation at Crewe Alexandra throughout his term of management is in many ways similar to what I had been hoping to achieve for Port Vale back in the sixties. I feel this is praise indeed for although he has never won a major trophy, Dario Gradi to my mind is one of the best managers ever to have graced British football. The successful youth policy he implemented at Crewe Alexandra has brought about a renaissance for the club. More pleasing is the fact that Dario's teams play wonderful football the way it was meant to be played, on the floor with grace, style and panache.

The early signs at Port Vale were encouraging. I combed North Staffordshire and South Cheshire for promising youngsters, but concentrated my efforts on those two hotbeds of football, the north east of England and central Scotland. Before long the Vale Park dressing rooms were ringing with the sound of Geordie and Scottish accents and I set about teaching the youngsters soccer skills and good football habits. Our first youth side reached the quarter-final of the FA Youth Cup, beating Coventry City on the way. It was a good sign, especially as many of that team were only 16 years of age and would therefore have another couple of years in the tournament. I wasn't worried about giving them a chance in the first team, either; I adhered to the maxim that if you're good enough, you're old enough and several made their debuts in the first team at 17 and a couple at 16.

A young Scot called Mick Cullerton enjoyed a meteoric rise. Mick was a bustling centre-forward who was to enjoy two spells at the club. He was a talented player with an eye for goal, so much so that Brian Clough and Peter Taylor signed him for Derby County. Unfortunately, Mick was competing with Kevin Hector, Frank Wignall and sometimes John O'Hare for the two striking roles at Derby, then a high-flying club, and although he scored nigh on 40 goals in one season for the reserves, Mick never made their first team and eventually returned to Port Vale.

A number of the youngsters I brought to Vale Park, including Mick Cullerton and a young Geordie called Stuart Chapman, eventually left to play part-time football with Stafford Rangers. With a full-time job and top non-league wages, they could earn far more than they could with a Fourth Division club, or indeed many a Third Division club. They turned out to be better players than many who plied their trade full time in the lower divisions of the Football League, a fact borne out by Stafford Rangers' phenomenal success in the seventies. They won the FA Trophy twice and beat several league clubs during lengthy runs in the FA Cup, at one time drawing a crowd of 34,000 to Stoke's Victoria Ground when they played Peterborough United.

Of course, there is always one lad who slips through the net and for me that was Ray Kennedy, who went on to find fame and fortune with Arsenal, Liverpool and England in the seventies and early eighties. Ray turned out to be a superb player, equally at home in midfield or defence and all I can say in my defence is he was a late developer! Actually, when Ray was at Vale Park as a youngster, he carried a fair bit of weight. I tried all sorts of things to reduce Ray's weight and increase his speed but all to no avail. Bill Cope our reserve team trainer even tried tying Ray's bootlaces together. It was an old trick, forcing the player to shorten his stride which often resulted in an increase in speed, but even this didn't work with Ray. In the end, I had to tell Ray what all young players hate hearing, that I was going to let him go. He burst into tears and my heart went out to him, but it was the right thing to do at the time. Happily, he went on to make a name for himself in football and what a name!

In 1968, it all came to a head. After three years without success the Port Vale board ran out of patience and we parted company. Of course, it wasn't as simple as that – the club were actually expelled from the Football League as well! I have never told the story before, but this is exactly how it all happened.

I had signed a schoolboy from the north east of England whose name I will not disclose for reasons that will become apparent. When he arrived in North Staffordshire, I arranged for him to continue his schooling at the nearby Moorland High School and put him in digs with a lady who had taken in a number of our youngsters. This boy wasn't naughty but he did have habits that were considered by many to be, for want of a better expression, unsociable. The landlady complained to me on several occasions about this lad's peculiar idiosyncrasies, in the end saying she could no longer provide a roof for the boy. The boy came from a poor background and his family were in no position to send him money, so the club provided the lad with a nominal weekly sum to cover his living expenses. The boy's headmaster found out about this and immediately complained. Paying schoolboys, though common in footballing circles at that time, was deemed illegal by the Football League.

When the Football League heard about the headmaster's complaints, the club were hauled across the coals and a full investigation was launched. It was found that Port Vale had been paying other youngsters and the club not only incurred a fine in excess of £2,000, which was a hefty sum in those days, but also incurred the most severe punishment that could be metered out to them – expulsion from the League itself.

The Football League announced this sentence on the club in the February, but it was not to be imposed until the end of the season, which meant we had to carry on playing in the knowledge that no matter how well we did as a team, we would be thrown out of the Football League come May. To the credit of the players in the team at the time, they buckled down and did a superb job as professionals, actually finishing higher in the table than when the punishment was announced.

At that time the Football League operated a system known as re-election. This involved the bottom four clubs in Division Four along with the best and most aspiring non-league clubs seeking votes from the other members of the Football League. The four clubs that polled the most votes would enjoy league status the following season. It was a far from ideal system and one that had become known as the 'old pals act' because the bottom four clubs were almost invariably voted back in. In short, with one or two notable exceptions, the Football League was a closed shop.

Port Vale having been expelled, we joined the three teams that had finished at the foot of Division Four and a handful of non-league teams in campaigning for votes from the other Football League clubs. For the first time in my life, I used my name and reputation for gain. I contacted the chairman of every club in the Football League, imploring them to vote for Port Vale. Come the re-election, Port Vale were voted straight back into the League, but the whole incident left a sour taste in my mouth and I turned my back on management in English football for ever.

My time with Port Vale had ended with a chastening experience as far as football management was concerned but it also resulted in the most special and wondrous thing that has ever happened to me in my life. In 1967, I took Port Vale on a tour of Czechoslovakia and while we were there, I met the true love of my life, the lady who was to become my dear and darling wife and with whom I would enjoy the happiest and most rewarding and contented years I have ever known.

Mila worked as a cultural attaché in Prague for the American Embassy. As a multi-linguist, she was seconded to the Port Vale party of 1967 as our interpreter and guide to that beautiful city. Part of Mila's brief involved taking the Port Vale party on a tour of Prague's historic landmarks and art galleries and while the players were polite, I knew they were not very interested. I was. As Mila told us the history of her city and acted as our guide through the galleries, I became at first enraptured, then enchanted before falling under her spell and becoming completely besotted with this beautiful woman. It was kismet. I had gone to Czechoslovakia on a football tour; the furthest thing from my mind was romance. Yet every time I bade farewell to this woman I found myself literally counting the minutes until I saw her again. I wanted to ask her out to dinner but I was married and so embarked on one almighty fight with my conscience. I was desperate to spend as much time with Mila as I could, yet knew that if we were seen out together people would talk and eventually the tabloid newspapers would get hold of the story. So I compromised. I asked Mila to dinner but I also asked the entire Port Vale team to come along as well and we spent a magical evening together in one of Prague's top restaurants, just Mila, me and 18 footballers.

When the time came for us to leave Czechoslovakia, I knew I was deeply in love with Mila and the subsequent letters we exchanged confirmed what I had hoped, that she was also in love with me. I couldn't believe it. At the age of 53 I found myself behaving like a love-struck teenager about this graceful and gorgeous woman some 13 years my junior. It was as with all new loves; Mila and I wanted nothing more than to be with one another every minute of every day. We ached when we were apart and immersed ourselves totally in our own little world, rejoicing in our good fortune at having found one another.

In the summer of 1968 with Port Vale having been re-elected back into the Football League, I left the club with only one thing on my mind – to spend the rest of my life with Mila. It wasn't easy, for anybody. At the time I was still married to Betty. I had not gone looking for love when I set foot in Czechoslovakia, but it had happened as these things do. It was the end of Betty and me as a couple. I hadn't planned it, it just happened. It's not right to go into any detail. All I hope now is that for everyone touched by what happened in 1968, by healing past feelings the ability to understand and forgive is strengthened and as such we can give thanks for the good times and trust in the present time.

Mila and I were planning to go and live in Malta, a country I had visited often and loved. Our plan was simple but in the August of 1968 it hit what seemed an insurmountable problem. Russia invaded Czechoslovakia. I watched the events unfolding on the TV news, riddled with anxiety and the awful fear that I might never see Mila again. I was beside myself with worry but I had underestimated her strength, tenacity and resolve.

Towards the end of World War Two, Mila had spent a year in a labour camp in Czechoslovakia after striking a Nazi officer who had tried to take advantage of her. She was only 19 but managed to escape from the camp and spent six months hiding in a forest, living off the land and sleeping rough. She eventually came out of hiding when she spotted an American patrol, to whom she offered her services as a guide and interpreter. Mila spent another six months with the Americans and when the war was over, was offered a job as a cultural attaché with the US Embassy in Prague. That resolve came to the fore once more in August 1968. Desperate to make our date, Mila persuaded a friend to drive her to the Austrian border where she bluffed her way through the

Russian checkpoint by dropping the names of senior ranking Communist officials in Prague and convincing the guards she was just visiting a friend across the Austrian border for the day. From Austria, she made her way to the home of a dentist friend in Dortmund from where she telephoned me.

It is no use trying to describe how I felt on hearing her voice and learning she was safe in West Germany. I flew to Dortmund immediately and for the entire flight sat with tears of joy and gratitude welling in my eyes. When we met, I held her as tightly as I could and swore we would never be parted again and we never were. From that moment on, Mila and I lived and travelled everywhere together and hand on heart I can honestly say that with each passing day I loved her more and every minute I spent in her company contrived to produce the most gloriously happy and contented time of my life.

We spent the ensuing years living at various times in Malta, South Africa and Canada. They were the countries we had homes in, but Mila and I travelled the world extensively as I took up one coaching job after another and continued to play in representative and exhibition games.

All in all, I spent every summer for 25 years coaching in Africa in countries such as South Africa, Nigeria, Ghana, Kenya, Uganda and Tanzania. I started those summer coaching stints back in 1953 and enjoyed my time on that continent immensely. I didn't go coaching there for money. I spent many years coaching in Soweto in South Africa and believe you me, there is not much money there for luxuries and a football coach during the fifties, sixties and seventies was definitely a luxury and, sadly, probably still is today. I embarked upon such trips to put something back into football. I felt a deep debt to the game and by coaching youngsters in the poor townships of the Third World I felt I was paying back in kind a game that had been so very good to me. If I had wanted to make money from coaching, I could have done. I had numerous offers from around the world including many from the USA, Australia, West Germany and Brazil but the rewards I obtained from coaching in townships in Africa were such that no amount of monetary reward could ever equal.

I had some extraordinary experiences during my time in Africa. In Ghana in 1956 I was crowned King of Soccer, a title I am proud to say I have to this day. The initiation was a real crowning as befits a king and left me not a trifle embarrassed. A witch doctor danced around me then spat on a football I had at my feet. I was then seated upon a throne, a crown placed on my head, and my clothes removed and replaced by traditional Ghanaian robes. I still have the throne. It isn't large or in any way pretentious; it's made of wood, stands about two feet high and bears a plaque on which are words relating to be my being crowned King of Soccer. It's in my den along with all my other treasures.

On another occasion, I was coaching in Soweto when I received an invitation to visit a school on the South African border with what was then known as Southern Rhodesia and is now Zimbabwe. At the time, a driver was assigned to me called Sam, who is best described as a likeable rogue. Sam used to drive me around Soweto in a Land Rover but more often than not, having completed a coaching session, I couldn't find him to take me home. After one coaching session just outside the township, I had been waiting two hours for Sam to turn up. Eventually a local teacher took pity on me and invited me back to his home saying he would walk down to the local bank and ask to use their telephone to call a taxi for me. When the taxi arrived it was Sam in my Land Rover! While I conducted my coaching sessions he had been moonlighting as a taxi driver in the Land Rover. I felt like Colonel Hall in the old American sitcom Sergeant Bilko; the Colonel never gets to use his staff car because Bilko is always hiring it out.

As the border was quite some distance away, I sent Sam on a reconnaissance trip to the school. It was a difficult journey on roads that became less and less detectable and downright dangerous. However, Sam came back with a good report of the school and gave me a strict set of instructions about what I had to do to keep danger to a minimum.

I made the journey by myself which I don't mind telling you I found more than a little disconcerting. However, after a full day's driving I finally arrived at a small village near the border where arrangements had been made for me to stay overnight in a hotel. I asked for directions to the hotel and was shown to a small building that contained three rooms. They were all empty and I had the choice of all three. If you have ever spent any time in the jungle, you will know there is no twilight. It's light, then it's dark, with no in-between. The room I chose was basic but clean. However, any thoughts of a good night's sleep after a day of arduous driving were quickly dispelled when the hotel manager visited my room and brought me a hefty stick. I asked him what the stick was for and he informed me it was in case snakes got into my bedclothes during the night. I made the immediate decision that if any snakes were to get into my bedclothes during the night, I wasn't going to be in there with them. I spent the whole of the night in a chair with my feet up on the dressing table and the stout stick by my side. I might have had more restless nights but I can't remember when. Apart from worrying about the snakes, as tired as I was after my long journey, I was kept awake for most of the night by all manner of horrendous noises. It seemed that all the creatures out there were intent on eating each other, and the screams, squawks and screeching that emanated from the pitch blackness were right out of a horror movie.

You know how it is when you sleep in a room for the very first time. There always seems to be a noise that is too short and too inconsistent for you to find out where it is coming from. I was awoken from my dozing by a chomping sound. When I sat up in the chair and took the stick in my hand, the chomping ceased. When I settled back down, it started again. It went on like that all night; whenever I stirred the chomping would cease, when I settled down again, it returned. Come daybreak I got up to discover about a foot of the slatted shutter at my window had been gnawed away. I had spent the night in the same small room as something that ate wooden shutters! What could it have done to my stick or, perish the thought, one of my legs? I shuddered at the very thought of what it could have been.

On leaving the hotel, I consulted the instructions Sam had given me. They told me to drive for exactly ten miles out of the village in a westerly direction until I reached a large palm tree under which was a direction post pointing back to the village from which I had come. There I was to park and wait for someone to come and collect me. I drove for exactly ten miles, saw the palm tree, parked up and waited and waited and waited. I must have sat on that road for about two and a half hours and in all that time I never saw a soul. I was beginning to get very anxious when all of a sudden, out of the jungle across the road, stepped a young man in a tracksuit with a rifle slung over his shoulder. Introductions over, he told me to follow a track that led off into the jungle, which I did. I must have driven for about seven miles though it seemed like 70 so dense and unyielding was the terrain. At times the undergrowth and overgrowth conspired to make the track disappear altogether but on I pressed under the helpful instruction of my young guide. I was just on the point of thinking I had been set up and was about to be kidnapped by guerrillas when suddenly the jungle fell away and there before me was a vast low plain of grassland and about a mile away, a small school. When we got there, I was greeted by an incredible sight. Small boys and girls ran from a wooden building, formed two lines and cheered as I made my way to the front door where a rather formidable and smart-looking headmaster stood with the broadest grin I had ever seen. He extended two very long arms.

'Mr Matthews. You came. You came. You came to our little school. For that, may God bless you, sir,' and he clasped me to his chest.

Such a warm and sincere welcome made me feel quite emotional. As we stood talking, I glanced around. There didn't seem to be a village or a house for miles. In fact, I saw nothing but grassland and vague tracks leading from the school. We were in the middle of nowhere, yet there were 60 or so children turned out like new pins – smart, clean and all smiling. I felt very humble in their presence. The initial welcomes over, the headmaster walked me around to the rear of the schoolhouse.

'We have created a football pitch especially for you today, so you can show my girls and boys how to play football like you,' said the head.

There on a field of stubble was a makeshift football pitch. The lines had been made with small stones carried from heaven knows where because, as I say this, was grassland. The goalposts had been hewn from thin trees and although they basically formed a rectangle, the wood was oscillating and undulating. The centre point of what formed one crossbar seemed a good foot below the junction of the bar and the goalposts to which it was attached. As I surveyed the scene, I was suddenly aware that the excited din of the children had subsided. It was as if they were waiting for me to respond.

'It is not Wembley stadium,' said the headmaster somewhat apologetically.

'You're right,' I said. 'It's better. So let's get started straightaway.'

And we did. I spent the entire day with those 60 boys and girls coaching them in basic football skills. We didn't stop for a break at any time during the day and I only hope those children had half as good a time as I did, because I thoroughly enjoyed myself.

Come the end of the day, the headmaster invited me into his room saying he had a special surprise for me. The door of his office opened and in walked a little girl carrying a tray on which was a cup of tea on a saucer.

'Just for you, Mr Matthews,' said the head. 'To remind you that for all the miles you have travelled, you are still not too far from home.'

I set the cup, which had a chip in it, to one side and picked up the saucer, turned it over and saw that it was Royal Doulton, made in my home town of Stoke-on-Trent. There I was, thousands of miles from home, in a remote place and I was sitting drinking tea from a Royal Doulton cup made by one of my fellow townspeople. The headmaster was right, I didn't feel far from home at all.

I asked the headmaster about the remoteness of the school. He explained to me that its location had been chosen carefully. It was midpoint between several villages and all the pupils had more or less the same distance to walk to and from school each day.

'And how far is that?' I asked.

'Eight miles,' he replied.

I nearly dropped his precious cup and saucer. Each pupil had a 16-mile round walk each day in order to attend school! My upbringing in Stoke-on-Trent in the twenties was considered tough, but it was nothing compared to what these children undertook every day to attend their lessons. I felt very privileged to be in their company and that of a headmaster who, despite all the obstacles in the way, was totally dedicated to his work and his children. When I said goodbye and headed back to the village where I was once again to stay overnight, I felt very humbled indeed by my experience in that school but also very happy that through football I had been able to go there. If any of today's top players ever want to get their lives and careers into perspective, they should leave their comfortable homes and agents and offer their services abroad in a developing country as a coach to young boys and girls. Believe you me, it provides you with rewards that the most illustrious football career and the highest of salaries can never match.

In the seventies when Mila and I were living in South Africa and I was coaching in Soweto, I formed a team called Stan's Men. It was 1975 and apartheid was, of course, still very much in force in that country. I never had any truck with it and for years had happily stayed in Soweto on my visits there to coach. I simply ignored it and for the most part, I am relieved to say, those misguided people who inflicted it upon that beautiful country chose to ignore the fact that I flouted its rules.

Football is a beautiful game and for me one of its beauties is that it can break down all divisions, whether they be class, race, creed or economic. It is a game for everyone to be played by everyone together. I had seen and experienced what football could do for an individual and I wanted others to realise not only the possibilities that football can bring, but to get in touch with the possibilities that lay within themselves, irrespective of how hard and demeaning their lives were. If I could enjoy such rich benefit from football, I was determined to show others such benefits existed for them as well. Football teams are chosen on ability. The opportunity to develop your game should not depend on the colour of your skin or circumstances in life.

Stan's Men were a promising bunch of schoolboys. I formed the team as part of a programme sponsored by the *Johannesburg Sunday Times*. One day I asked them who their greatest football hero was and they told me Pelé. They asked me if I had ever played in Brazil and I told them my story of the 1950 World Cup and of England's 4–2 win over Brazil in 1956. The boys told me that their great dream was to go to Brazil one day and play football there, though they knew this would never happen. They would never be allowed by the government to travel outside the country. 'Besides,' one of them told me, 'we do not have the money.'

It was then I had the idea to take these boys to Brazil. I thought that no matter what life had in store for them, they would always be able to look back in the knowledge that their boyhood dream had come true. I told them of my plan and they were at first delirious, then anxious.

'It's such a high hope. Can it really happen?' one of them asked.

'Sure it can,' I said. 'In football as in life, if you aim for the ceiling, you will more often than not end up no higher than the floor. But aim for the sky and you just might hit the ceiling.'

For only the second and the last time in my life, I used my name and reputation to pull strings. I didn't have the money to take 16 young footballers to Brazil but I knew people who did. I contacted an executive of Coca-Cola and the team's sponsor the *Johannesburg Sunday Times*. Both companies agreed to put up equal amounts of money. The Brazilian airline Varig agreed to give us free flights so then it was just a matter of contacting people I knew in Rio de Janeiro who could provide us with opposition, accommodation and training facilities.

With the money in place and everything organised at the Brazilian end, all was going well until someone pointed out that as Stan's Men were not members of a proper league, and could only play friendlies against teams from official leagues, we therefore technically came under the jurisdiction of the South African FA. The problem was twofold. Not only would the South African authorities kick up about me taking a group of black youngsters out of the country, but the fact that we were technically under the jurisdiction of a Football Association that was barred from international football meant FIFA could step in and put the kybosh on the tour on the basis that we were breaking their anti-apartheid stance against the South African FA!

I was organising the tour along with other like-minded individuals including a great guy called Jack Blades, a sports journalist, and Jim Bailey, who founded and edited the African football magazine *Drum*. With the tour organised and the money in place we decided to go ahead anyway. By way of an 'out' we classified ourselves as an independent schools team, hoping that FIFA would turn a blind eye to such an obviously non-professional and non-senior side. The FIFA chief at the time was Joao Havelange and he must have heard about our impending tour as he was based in Rio, but as the day came closer for us to travel, we heard not a thing from FIFA. I learned later that Joao did indeed hear of our tour but decided to do nothing about it.

That left the South African authorities and here I took a bit of a gamble. I figured that if we turned up at the airport for our flight, the authorities would not prevent us from leaving the country because it would cause a major incident. With me in charge of the team, such an incident would get headlines throughout the world which I was sure the South African government did not want.

At the airport I was riddled with nerves but tried to overcome them by busying myself shepherding my young charges and allaying their obvious fears. Large, forbidding men in light blue suits and dark glasses with inscrutable looks on their faces watched our every move but, uncomfortable as it was, they never approached us. At any given second I expected us to be rounded up, hustled into vans and taken away to one of South Africa's infamous police stations but it never happened. My hunch about the authorities wanting to avoid a major international incident was right. It was much less trouble from their point of view to let us go to Brazil without the majority of the country knowing, and return in an equally low-key manner. After what seemed like an eternity at the airport, we eventually boarded the plane and only when we were up in the air did I truly relax. I couldn't believe it and neither could Stan's Men. We were on our way out of the country bound for Brazil, the first-ever black football team to tour outside of South Africa.

The reception we were given in Brazil couldn't have been better. We trained with some of the Brazilian national team including the heir to Pelé's crown, Zico, watched top matches at the Maracana Stadium and saw the sights, all courtesy of our Brazilian hosts. The quality of the Brazilian football was too much for my boys, however. We lost every game, the heaviest defeats being 10–1 and 8–1. I even turned out myself. I got through the game no problem at all, but those Brazilians were just too good.

At one point during our visit, I received a message at our hotel from the Great Train Robber Ronnie Biggs asking if I would call around and see him. In the course of my career I'd had the good fortune to meet quite a number of famous people not connected with football, but this was the first time I had been asked to meet someone infamous and agreed to his request.

I met Ronnie Biggs at his apartment in Rio. We had tea on the small balcony at the rear of his home and one of the first things he asked was, 'How are Charlton Athletic doing these days?' It turned out he had supported Charlton from being a small boy and had often seen me play at the Valley. Before answering his question, I did a deal with him. I told him I would fill him in on how Charlton Athletic were faring if he told me how he had managed to escape from prison. So I heard the story of the Great Train Robbery, the subsequent arrest and how he had paid various underground figures to steal him away from prison. It cost him a pretty packet moneywise, though I dare say much of that was illegally acquired in the first place. Once out of prison he was smuggled to the Continent where more money was demanded of him in order for him to make good his escape to South America. He eventually arrived in Brazil with most of his ill-gotten gains gone. When I met him, he was living a very simple life. His apartment was plain, unpretentious but comfortable and I listened intently as he told me hand on heart he had never hurt anyone in his life, or for that matter ever threatened anyone. I know the train driver was hit on the head during the Great Train Robbery and was never the same man again, but Ronnie told me he had nothing to do with that. He said the 30-year term he received was 'out of order' for the crime he had committed and that is why he escaped. I am anti-crime in every way, but I saw his point. Murderers have been sentenced to shorter prison terms.

I told him how Charlton Athletic had been getting on and we recalled some of the great Charlton players he had seen and I had played against such as Sam Bartram, John Hewie, Derek Ufton and Eddie Firmani. It was a pleasant afternoon and he shook my hand warmly when I left, saying what a pleasure and honour it had been to meet me. He waved me off as I descended the steps that led down from his apartment, and called after me.

'They was only gonna burn that money anyway, Stan. It's not like we nicked it off poor people or anything like that. We cocked a snook at the Establishment but did it on the front pages of the papers and the Six O'clock News on the telly. That's why they gave me 30 years.'

Or so they thought. I couldn't help thinking that for all he was a robber there was a warped sense of justice in the fact he hadn't served his full time.

When we journeyed home to South Africa after what had been an exhilarating tour in Brazil, the captain of Stan's Men, Gilbert Moiloa, came and sat next to me on the plane, thanked me, shook my hand and said, 'Stanley, you are a black man with a white face.' That was a great compliment to me on his part. Looking back on all the years I spent coaching in Africa, the time I defied apartheid and took those young players to Brazil stands out for me as a magic moment. I felt I really had given something back to football for all it had given to me.

During the seventies and best part of the eighties, Mila and I paid regular visits to England. I kept in touch with British football by attending games during those visits home, watching matches on TV, and listening to the BBC World Service. I saw and heard enough to make me realise that British football, as well as producing great players, was now also producing great teams that could not only compete with the best in Europe, but *be* the best in Europe.

In the sixties I marvelled at the skills of George Best. Although our careers overlapped by some two years, I never had the good fortune to play against Best, though I did have the pleasure of seeing him play at Old Trafford. With the passing of time, people's minds and memories have a habit of playing tricks. We are all susceptible to making out that past players were far better than those of today. Often our minds gloss over deficiencies and we make out a player to be better than he actually was. I like to think, however, that for all the passing years, my mind is still sharp, my memory still objective and clear. My assessment of players is how I saw them and when I saw George Best, I knew immediately that I was watching a football genius at work. Sport can be cruel. Football can make a man even more ridiculous than drink can. But there is no doubt in my mind that George Best's deeds on the football pitch have ensured his place as one of football's greatest ever players.

George was the first footballer to transcend the boundaries, enjoying fame and wealth beyond football. He was dubbed the fifth Beatle. His appeal found favour with those who thought Preston North End was just a railway station. George has known what it is like to live the life of a millionaire and he has known what it is like to play non-league football for a few pounds. He has even known what it is like to slop out in prison. But it is only as a great footballer that I would ever pass judgement upon him. Only his deeds on the football pitch remain imprinted in my mind – and what deeds they were!

I remember one particular game during which George displayed his true brilliance. It was against my beloved Stoke City in 1968 and against no less a goalkeeper than Gordon Banks. Stoke defenders John Moore, Alex Elder and Bill Bentley all had a go at George but with a drop of the shoulder and a sudden twist and burst of speed he left them panting in his wake. Tony Allen came across to supply cover but without sacrificing any pace, George flicked the ball between Tony's legs with laser-like precision and rounded Tony to collect the ball on the other side. It left him with a one-on-one with Gordon Banks.

Gordon, as you would expect of a world-class goalkeeper, did everything right. He came off his line quickly and remained upright to give George as little sight of the goal as possible. Faced with that situation against Gordon Banks, many a player paled but not George. With a shimmy that your sister Kate would have been proud of, George sent Gordon one way and the crowd in the Boothen End the other and with Gordon on his backside, he simply walked the ball into the net. For a moment I thought George was going to do what he always said he would do if he ever found himself in such a position – stop the ball on the goalline, drop to his knees and head the ball over the line. That he didn't I believe had more to do with the fact he did not want the Stoke defenders to suffer humiliation than the fear of a defender catching up with him.

It was typical George. He did what he had to do, but never rubbed an opponent's face in the dirt.

Stoke City were not a bad team in those days, but they had no one who could contain George either individually or collectively. A minute or so before the final whistle blew I left my seat to beat the crowds on the homeward journey. The commissionaire in the Victoria Ground reception attended every match but by the very nature of his job never saw any of the play. On my way out he asked me the score. 'Stoke 2 George Best 4,' I told him. It wasn't too far removed from the truth.

Many people say George retired too early, and compared with me he did. Then again, compared with me so did every player. George made his debut for Manchester United at 17 and bowed out at 28. He had 11 seasons at the top and many a celebrated player has had less. In those 11 years he came in for some rough treatment from defenders whose only response to his terrific array of skills was to leave their studmark calling card on his legs. It was the mark of the man, however, that for all the close attention and rough treatment meted out to him, George rarely reacted or missed a game through injury.

It's difficult to compare players from different eras. Footballers are only great in their own time. The game is constantly changing and players adapt their play to the order of the day. When George was in his pomp, the game was quicker than it was when I played and it has gradually increased in tempo ever since so that now Premiership football is played at breakneck speed. Today's players may be far fitter than those of the past, but in a quicker more direct game, some skills and technique have been sacrificed. However, the most gifted players would, I am sure, be able to play in any era. Skill and natural talent is all-enduring and transcends time. George had such an abundance of skill, he would make his mark on football if he was playing today.

Another mark of George's genius is that he took defences apart in an age of quality defenders. Defenders in the sixties were as hard as they were in the thirties, forties and fifties and, to my mind, definitely harder than those of today. There were players such as Liverpool's Tommy Smith; my old adversary at Chelsea, Chopper Harris; Billy Bremner, Jack Charlton and Norman Hunter of Leeds; Peter Storey of Arsenal; and Mike England of Spurs to name but a few. These were real hard men and George was not fazed by any one of them. The sixties and early seventies also had an abundance of top-quality defenders who although not of the overtly physical variety possessed many other qualities to compensate. I'm thinking of players such as Jimmy Armfield (Blackpool), Ray Wilson (Everton), George Cohen (Fulham) and Gerry Byrne (Liverpool) in the sixties; and Paul Madeley and Paul Reaney (Leeds), Mike Doyle (Manchester City), Colin Todd (Derby) and, of course, the golden boy of the West Ham Academy, Bobby Moore, in the seventies. These were all top quality yet not one could cope with George when he lived up to his name and was at his best, which was more often than not.

One aspect of George's play that impressed me and is often overlooked is that he was a good defender himself. To my mind, one of his strong points was his tackling; to all intents and purposes, he fulfilled the role of a wing-back in a great United team that included Denis Law and Bobby Charlton.

All great goalscorers have to be cool and calm in front of goal and when George had the posts in his sights it was as if he had ice in his veins. I remember seeing George score a tremendous goal at Old Trafford against Spurs. United were attacking the Stretford End and George had received the ball some three yards outside the angle of the penalty box on the United left. Two Spurs players, Cyril Knowles and Phil Beal, were on the goalline about a yard along from their respective posts. Spurs goalkeeper Pat Jennings, whom I consider to have been Britain's best-ever goalkeeper, had taken up a good position just outside his six-yard box facing George. In front of Jennings were three other Spurs defenders. I had the benefit of being seated in the stand and thus had a bird's eye view of the Spurs penalty box. I remember thinking, 'What can he do? There's nothing on for him.' With Bobby Charlton steaming up from behind and screaming for the ball to be rolled into his path, George swayed like a bird on a twig before casually flicking the ball off the muddy ground and leaning back slightly as if easing himself into his favourite armchair, then lobbing the ball towards the far corner of the Spurs goal.

The ball sailed over the heads of the three defenders immediately confronting him and the flaying arms of Pat Jennings. Phil Beal on the goalline jumped in an attempt to head the ball away. There was little more than the size of a football itself between Beal's head and the crossbar but George's lob was so precise, even though there was only a fag paper's width between the ball, the bar and Beal, it found the gap and sailed into the net.

That cold grey afternoon, Old Trafford lit up like a catherine wheel as all George's bountiful gifts burst into spectacular bloom. It was sheer brilliance and what further impressed me was, after having seen the ball sail into the net, George simply turned and walked away as quietly and unassumingly as the ghost in Hamlet. There was no sprinting towards supporters and gyrating of the hips, no running at breakneck speed and pushing away team-mates who approached to confer congratulations. Such over-the-top self-adoration was beneath the dignity of the man. George allowed himself a wry smile for a job well done, shook hands with that other great, Bobby Charlton, and trotted back to the halfway line for the restart. Suffice to say of the man who was to my mind the greatest player of the sixties and early seventies, if ever I were to be asked to name my all-time football team of greats, the name of George Best would be the first on my fantasy teamsheet.

The seventies seemed to have a profusion of finely gifted players whose individual skills were never fully appreciated at international level, players such as Rodney Marsh (QPR and Manchester City), Alan Hudson (Chelsea, Stoke and Arsenal), Tony Currie (Sheffield United), Stan Bowles (QPR) and Frank Worthington (more clubs than there are in the Working Man's Institute). They all impressed and, better still, entertained me. Yet those same players never seemed to impress the various managers of England in an era when we never saw an England team good enough to qualify for the World Cup finals.

I often hear the seventies referred to as the last golden era of football. This may have been true for many of the players, but it was certainly not a golden era for the supporters who had to endure appalling conditions at often decrepit stadiums. It was no good wearing any decent clothes, especially shoes. Hooliganism was the cancer of British football during this era, although it always irked me to hear the phrase 'football hooligan' – no true football supporter was a hooligan. The hooligan element I am convinced were thugs who happened to latch on to football to sate their misguided thirst for trouble and fuel the macho standing and adrenalin rush they derived from the group dynamics of being in a gang. These people were just hooligans; it so happened that after causing trouble at football matches they had the chance to melt away into the large crowds of genuine supporters, so football suited them fine. In the aftermath of Heysel, Hillsborough and the Bradford fire when the FA, Football League, the clubs and police worked together to combat the problem and introduced CCTV at improved stadiums, the anonymity the hooligans enjoyed was no longer possible. They subsequently drifted away from football almost completely in the late eighties and nineties and, thankfully, have by and large never come back.

— ○ —

I did come back however – to England, in 1989. After two decades of living abroad and coaching throughout the world, the pull of my roots became too strong, and Mila and I returned to the UK with a view to settling in Stoke-on-Trent.

I was 74 and unbelievably had played my last football match only four years previously. I had been invited to play for an England Veteran XI against a team of Brazilian Veterans in Rio de Janeiro. The Brazilians, who included such greats as Garrincha, Amarildo, Tostao and Jairzinho, were just too good for us and the English Vets lost 6–1. Considering I had started my football career in the era of

Dixie Dean and was playing against members of Brazil teams that had won the World Cup in 1962 and 1970, I thought there was no disgrace in defeat! During the game, I fell awkwardly and damaged my knee. It was an injury that led to me having a cartilage operation for the first and only time in my career. That operation reinforced the belief I had always held that I had been lucky in life. If I had sustained such a cartilage injury back in the thirties, my career as a footballer would have ended there and then. So, at the age of 70, I finally hung up my boots for ever. I thought it was fitting to do so after a game in Brazil. I had admired the Brazilian style of play so very much since I first saw them in action back in 1950. I had first played for England Schoolboys at the age of 13 and bowed out completely playing against former Brazilian World Cup winners at the age of 70 – not bad, I thought.

25

—◦—

Football in the
New Millennium

Mila and I bought a lovely old house in Stoke-on-Trent, and settled down to enjoy our retirement. As is the case with many a retired person, I found myself so busy I was left to wonder how I ever found the time to go to work. To begin with, we had a massive job on our hands to refurbish the house we had bought. It was old and in a very sad state of repair, but Mila took matters in hand and we eventually got it shipshape. Mila showed a great talent for interior and garden design and for all the practicalities involved but I was very much an onlooker. I am probably the most impractical person on this earth; I can't even rewire an electric plug. Fortunately, Mila more than made up for my deficiencies in this respect and the house became a home in every sense of the word.

I found I was in great demand to speak at sporting dinners and official FA and Football League functions. I am not the world's best at public speaking – I get by and that's about it – but people seem to enjoy hearing about my experiences playing with and against some of the greatest players to have graced the game and hearing about how football used to be.

As president of Stoke City, I go to practically all their home games. I receive numerous invitations to attend matches of every variety where I am often presented to the teams. These range from Cup finals and internationals at Wembley to local schoolboy and charity matches in Stoke-on-Trent and I do my very best to attend, whatever the occasion. I watch just about every game that appears on terrestrial TV and follow football avidly either by listening to the radio or by watching the Ceefax whirl around. Much has changed over the years, but one thing remains constant – I am still deeply in love with the game.

I believe football is currently going through another golden period, though sadly this time around not all clubs are benefiting. The money that has arrived from TV has definitely helped the game but more at the top than in the lower divisions. It took a series of disasters before stadiums and conditions for supporters in general were improved and the game rid itself of the hooligan element which besmirched its name in the seventies and eighties. I am all for better conditions and facilities for supporters and although the marketing johnnies tell us football is once more 'a family game' I think it is one of the biggest fibs currently being told. Football has rid itself of the hooligans, but how many ordinary working people can afford to take the family to a football match these days?

The money that has flooded into football has been a godsend to the game, but it is a double-edged sword. In recent years with the introduction of debentures, paid waiting lists for season tickets, executive boxes and the corporate culling of tickets for major games, football has suffered a rapid deterioration of its culture. Some stadiums are now all-ticket. Why? If the clubs who operate such a policy really cared about their supporters, they would do what the likes of Sunderland have done – put a ceiling on season-ticket sales and have several thousand seats available on a match-by-match basis for those supporters whose budgets do not run to paying out a hefty sum up front. Don't get me wrong; there is a place for executive boxes and pre-match corporate meals but many clubs, having worked hard to rid their stadiums of racism and hooliganism, are now simply practising economic bigotry.

The game must move with the times and many of the developments of the past decade in football have been for the good of the game. However, there is usually a downside to every good thing and while I'm in support of all-seater stadiums I do feel they have led to a pacification of the crowd and the loss of a sense of place and belonging. Time was when supporters had a favourite spot on the terraces. Meeting fellow supporters in the same spot every fortnight meant that going to a football match had a valuable social aspect to it. Of course, that still happens today if you have a season ticket; otherwise you have no control over where you sit. Football has lost its valuable sense of social occasion.

The pricing of matches, and indeed the cost of simply parking a car at the new stadiums, together with non-season ticket holders having a different seat for every game I feel has contrived to take the spontaneity out of football crowds. The wag on the terraces and the low earner with his two children for whom football is an escape from a harsh working life have to all intents and purposes been forced out of the game, especially at many Premiership clubs.

I have attended Cup finals and internationals at Wembley where supporters have been shepherded to sing along with 'The Three Lions' song which has been blasted out of the

Tannoy system, followed by a reminder that the song is still available on CD and cassette in the Wembley souvenir shop. This to me is evidence that the marketing people, unwittingly, have killed off the spontaneity of home-grown football songs which were as much part of terrace life in the forties and fifties as they were in the seventies and eighties. I am referring to songs that are good clean fun, not the abusive or obscene chants that prevailed for a number of years.

Football in the thirties and right up to the eighties served as a strong social glue. Many supporters left the pit shaft, shipyard, pottery or factory floor from a Saturday morning half-shift and headed straight to see their favourite team for a sense of escape as well as entertainment. Today, in the high-powered business world of football there is, I feel, most definitely a link between income and how often you are able to attend a match – the better off you are, the more games you can see. Conversely, the better off you are, the less important the role of football, the team and the club in your life. In my time as a player, I knew plenty of Stoke and Blackpool supporters for whom the club was the biggest focal point of their life next to their family. If their team had done well, they were happier with life, worked harder and in general their lot seemed not so bad. In short, they shared in the success of their club, it reflected upon them and their lives. Football played an important role. Ask yourself this. Does the supporter who can afford an executive box or regular corporate matchday entertainment and has watched his or her team lose 1–0 feel gutted on a Monday morning when they leave their comfortable house and two-car family to sit in front of a computer and look at share prices or what have you? I doubt it very much.

As I have said, there is a place for everyone at football and I am all for corporate matchday entertainment, executive boxes and season tickets which provide much-needed income for clubs, but not to the exclusion of those supporters who have for decades been the bedrock of clubs and for whom football is vitally important in their lives.

Football is enjoying a heady period. Millions of pounds continue to flood into the game from TV and the exploitation of the game's commercial potential, but I fear for a game that enjoys medium-term prosperity based on the fickleness of disposable income and rampant consumerism rather than what I and many others have – a deep-seated love and emotional attachment to football.

I do not envy today's top players their high salaries and lucrative endorsement deals. Good luck to them. What I do object to is players holding clubs to ransom as in the case of Nicolas Anelka at Arsenal in 1999. You may recall that Anelka, having joined Arsenal for a million pounds, wanted away. A number of continental clubs, most notably Real Madrid, were interested. Anelka's brother was acting as his agent and I am led to believe wanted Nicolas to move on. The asking price was, depending on which newspaper you read, between £15 and £20 million. The problem arose when Anelka's brother allegedly contacted Jean-Marc Bosman's former lawyer who suggested he might be able to buy himself out of Arsenal by paying the club the £1 million they had originally paid for him. This would leave Anelka, a top player, free to leave Arsenal with the club not able to receive a transfer fee. The money that Real Madrid were ready to pay Arsenal could then be paid in wages to Anelka. As it turned out, Anelka did go to Madrid and Arsenal did receive the fee they wanted for having spent time and resources developing a million pound player into one of Europe's best.

If Anelka had bought himself out of his contract simply by paying Arsenal back the fee they had originally paid for him, it would have had catastrophic repercussions. Small clubs such as Crewe Alexandra who buy young players cheaply, develop them and in several cases sell them on to bigger clubs could well go to the wall. The smaller clubs have already missed out on the big money flooding into the game, to deny them transfer fees as well for players they have put time and resources into developing into better players would be the last straw. Many small clubs would simply go bust and where would that leave our game? Anelka didn't buy himself out of his contract in the end, but that incident served as a warning shot across the bows of football's future.

The money that has come into the game from TV has of course enabled the top clubs to sign top players from all around the world, a situation that has played a significant part in the rich having become richer and the poor poorer. I think the foreign players that have come into our game have by and large improved it. But when I see a Premiership side taking to the field with just one British player in their ranks, I do feel the time has come to impose some restrictions on the number of foreign players in our game. Top foreign players can have a positive effect on young British players. The youngsters can learn a lot from them, particularly where technique is concerned, but given that our top clubs also sign the best young British players, I do worry for the future of English football and the England team in particular. The best young players sign for our top clubs at 15 or 16, but due to the influx of foreign players, with the possible exception of Manchester United, many find themselves still playing reserve team football at 20 and 21, and that will never help their development. In fact, it will curtail it and I am sure in the not too distant future sports writers will be asking why England cannot compete with the best international level.

Instead of TV money being used by Premiership clubs to buy foreign players and pay astronomical wages to even fringe squad players, I feel a small percentage of the money should be used for subsidising a part of a stand given over to senior citizens and those fans on low incomes who have supported the club usually through thin and even thinner. I suggest incorporating such a system throughout the Football League, so that irrespective of income or social standing, the local football club would indeed be the hub of the community. To inflict high admission charges for games and therefore exclude supporters whose loyalty to a club has been broken only through a lack of opportunity in life I feel is criminal. To paraphrase the lyric of that football song and the 1990s, football may be coming home, but it is in danger of coming to very nicely appointed homes only.

When I hear of clubs conceding to the outrageous wage demands of players who can trap a ball further than I could kick it, or the PFA having to step in and pay the wages of players in lower divisions, or directors boasting they are able to sell club shirts at ten times the price they cost to make, I sometimes think the Mad Hatter or Machiavelli is running football. But when I look back over my own career, I have to say it was ever thus. There were some great club chairmen and directors in my day whose reason for being involved with the local football club was multi-dimensional but rarely had anything to do with making money, unlike today. On the other hand, those directors and also many members of the FA and Football League officialdom treated players like serfs. As for what they thought of ordinary supporters, well, you only had to look around the tacky grounds and the facilities on offer and see how little development took place at our stadiums over 50 years to understand that.

Football now is very much a curate's egg. It appears to me that there are basically two roads ahead. One leads to a world where players cavort like happy foals in beautiful stadiums before row upon row of club-shirted supporters sated after a good dinner. The other road is bumpy and meandering and leads to a roadside eatery where football has overheated and lies burnt and encrusted on top of a very dodgy looking oven. I pray that what the future actually holds for this game we all love so much will turn out to be somewhere between the two.

In the eighties we had Heysel, Hillsborough and Bradford together with intermittent hooligan troubles, filthy terraces and rickety old stands. At a minute to midnight with a madman at the wheel, the Taylor Report forced football to turn the corner and there before it lay the Premiership, Sky TV and a whole host of advertisers and merchandisers with thumbs raised in the hope of a lift. They all rode together and now football is by and large enjoying balmy days. I just hope that football has not been blinded irrevocably by the light that shines from the crock of gold it discovered.

Strangely enough, I remain sufficiently optimistic to believe it hasn't, though I do feel that in order to survive, many of the lower division clubs will have to revert to being part-time. I don't think this is necessarily a bad thing. The Nationwide Conference League is flourishing and many of its players are better than those who ply their trade in the lower divisions of the Football League. As was the case with some of the players I had when managing Port Vale who went into non-league football with Stafford Rangers, a number of semi-professional players with good jobs are happy with the money they receive from part-time football. Their combined incomes are in excess of what they would earn in the lower divisions of the Football League. They have the security of a career and the more of their ilk there are in non-league football, the better the standard so the more they enjoy their football. So as the gap widens between the rich and poor of full-time football, there will, I believe, come a time when a number of clubs will have to go part-time in order to survive but far from being a disaster, it could have benefits.

There is much I admire about football today but at the risk of appearing negative there are a number of things that do annoy me, the fact that many supporters now mistake excitement for quality, for instance. Also, although TV has been marvellous for the game, I do think stopping managers and asking them for a comment as they leave the pitch or dressing room at half-time is an unwarranted invasion. At such times managers never say anything of note to the camera anyway because they have other things on their minds, like addressing their players. So why does TV bother?

I do feel that TV has burdened itself with too many pundits and commentators. A game can have a commentator and a summariser. Then we revert back to the studio where there are often three or four other people giving their views on the same match and the same incidents. Everyone feels they have to justify their being there, so we end up with too much analysis whereby simple things that have happened on the pitch are elevated into being marvellous things. Players of reasonable ability are portrayed as being good and good players as great. Through scoring one goal before the TV cameras, as Michael Owen discovered, a young player can be hailed as a star overnight. As it happens, I like Michael Owen as a player. I believe him to have tremendous ability, but that was also the case with Tommy Lawton and it took Tommy six years at 30 goals a season plus a goal a game for England before he was ever afforded star status in football and believe you me, by that time he had earned it.

I know not every commentator can be a David Coleman, Harry Carpenter, Henry Longhurst, Peter Alliss, John Arlott, Peter O'Sullevan or Brian Moore, but I do feel the standard of commentating is not as high as it was years ago. It is certainly not as objective. Commentators now repeatedly give a one-sided view of an incident. For example, if Manchester United score a goal, the whole emphasis is placed on the United build-up and how well each individual contributed. No mention is made of the mistakes made by the opposition, of their poor marking, poor sense of positional play or their inability to defend collectively. Conversely, if Manchester United concede a goal, the emphasis as far as the commentators are concerned, falls on the mistakes made by United players with not too much mention of the skill, technique and good work of their opponents.

As for football itself, I watched Liverpool play in the UEFA Cup recently. When you added together the 11 players on the pitch and the number of Liverpool substitutes on the bench, they totalled more players than Liverpool called upon in the entire 1978–79 season (15 players) when they won the league championship. That is one significant way the game has changed and that fact alone is not in need of any further reflection. It speaks volumes.

I look at the benches now and they comprise mini crowds in themselves. As well as the substitutes, there appear to be more coaches than Wallace Arnold owns and all manner of advisers and people in charge of this or that. I can see the day when someone will be on the bench whose sole job is to be in charge of tie-ups. It is getting that silly. Several years ago, Mila and I were invited to be the guests of the Dallas Cowboys at one of their games. On entering the Cowboys dressing room, I was amazed by the number of personal fitness coaches, advisers and the like. The backroom staff seemed to outnumber the players and in grid-iron football that's saying something. Mila also passed comment on this and I told her that I could see the day when this sort of thing would happen in British football. That day is here.

They are minor points of irritation. By and large I enjoy football as much today as I have ever done and I am delighted that it has undergone a renaissance since the early

1990s. Sometimes I fear for the future of the game but I also remain optimistic as we all should. Football is indeed the beautiful game and each generation will produce its Lawton, Carter, Mortensen, Greaves, Charlton, Best, Moore, Keegan, Dalglish, Ginola, Zola or Owen. They will be different because the way the game is played will be different, but the essence and spirit of football will always be the same. And when such players do come along and enthral, entertain and excite in equal measure, future generations will marvel as we did and, I hope, come to the same conclusion – that football, when played at its best, is the greatest of all games and has an important role to play in the best of all worlds.

I have no regrets about my career or my life but I do harbour one sadness. My darling wife Mila passed away during the writing of this book. Mila gave me true happiness in life. With her, I experienced the unmitigated joys of a true, sincere and loving relationship. I miss her dearly for we were, in the words of one writer, 'Two souls with but a single thought and two hearts that beat as one.' I feel therefore you will understand when I say this book is dedicated to you, Mila, the love of my life.

As time marches on and I sit old and grey and nodding by the fire, I find I spend much time looking back over my career and my life. The images that readily come to mind are not those of glorious victories in the big games, or the array of fine awards that have been bestowed upon me. It is the small things I remember most fondly, significant little gems that have all conspired to make my career and life the joy it has been . . . running down the wing with the ball for Blackpool and seeing Morty where I always knew he would be, running into a position at the near post . . . the on-the-pitch celebration after the 1953 Cup final win when, mobbed by tangerine shirts, I saw out of the corner of my eye the suited arm of Joe Smith around my shoulders... Eddie Hapgood standing on a railway station in pre-war Yugoslavia giving the finest and most heart-rending speech I have ever heard when replying to the question of what it was like to be a footballer... my father standing in the tunnel of a deserted Victoria Ground having come to take me home after the private training session that followed my disastrous game against Germany at White Hart Lane... Harry Johnston, the hard man, gazing at his Cup final winner's medal during our journey back to Blackpool... Eddie Clamp giving a one-man show in the Stoke City dressing room and the laughter that rang around the room as a result... a mud-splattered but beaming Tommy Lawton running towards me after our last-gasp winner against Scotland at Hampden... Mila's voice on the end of a telephone from Dortmund... 16 frightened boys clustered around me in an airport in Johannesburg and me trying not to show I was just as scared as they were.

Those images will remain with me for ever and a million and one others besides. In writing this book, I have told you how I saw it all and what I felt and experienced at the time. In telling my story, I feel you may have the advantage of me. As I have opened up and written from the heart, you will now know me.

I have no regrets about anything I have done in my career or life, but there is one thing I would have liked to have happened. Of course, it's impossible. I would have liked my father and mother to be around now to hear all the wonderful and complimentary things people so often say about me because my father would be very proud to hear such things and my mother would believe them.

I enjoyed a marvellous career and a great life and that is down to football and Mila. The game of football has changed greatly since I first started out back in 1930 but so too has life and society in general. I hope present and future generations will learn from looking back at the past. I only hope you have enjoyed hearing what I have had to say about football and my career. It's simply the way it was.

Epilogue

———○———

Sir Stanley Matthews
1915–2000

D oing easily what others find difficult is talent. Doing what is impossible for the talented is genius. Many is the footballer or supporter of a certain age who is willing to testify that he or she saw Stanley Matthews doing the impossible up and down some muddy touchline. Oddly, the only person to doubt such recollections was Stan himself.

In collaborating with him on his autobiography we referred to numerous press cuttings relating to his performances with either Stoke City, Blackpool or England. He was never comfortable with them.

'I was never that good,' was his frequent response.

We had known each other for some ten years, but had become particularly close in the eighteen months from the conception to the completion of his autobiography. We met daily and after the ritual glass of organic tomato juice and a chat about the previous night's football, we would set to work.

Stan, as he had been all his life, was an early riser. Our collaborations were over by eleven in the morning and without fail took place in his 'den'. The den, a room the size of an average lounge in a small semi, overlooked the short gravel drive that led to his house. In the bay window was his desk from which he answered the considerable volume of mail that arrived from all over the world on a daily basis. On the desk top, his prized possession: a framed letter from the Duke of Edinburgh thanking him for his contribution to football and good sportsmanship. We never sat at the desk to work. Stan preferred his favourite armchair to the left of the fireplace with me seated on the other side.

His memory was remarkable. As I guided him through his life story I was constantly taken aback by his ability to remember minute details not only of events that now have their place in football history, but of players and games long since forgotten by the majority. He loved working on his book and, after I had left him, he would give the morning's session more applied thought – more often than not ringing me at home to provide additional thoughts or anecdotes.

His professional career spanned generations. No other footballer can lay claim to a career of such longevity, nor one so star-studded and garlanded. That he waited until almost his 84th year finally to commit his definitive life story to book form, he said 'was purely and simply because I felt the time was now right'. Beforehand there had been subjects he did not want to discuss, or his involvement in books carrying his name was much less.

He was an avid reader of all manner of books but in writing his own story he became particularly interested in the autobiographies of other players. One day I told him a current Premiership player, still very much in his salad days, was to write his autobiography.

'On what?' Stan asked, his impish humour as ever veiling a certain poignancy.

With regard to his own autobiography, it was not the act of writing he found difficult, more the fact he had to write about himself. He was arguably the greatest footballer of all time. Gracious and dignified, he was a gentleman in the true sense of the word but, above all, he was as modest as a violet. Time and again we would reach a point in his story where he had created some landmark: the first Footballer of the Year; the first European Footballer of the Year; first to receive a CBE, first to be knighted.

'Do we have to mention that?' he would say, his face contorting with embarrassment. 'They made such a fuss and I never merited such.'

On telling him these events were integral to his story his response was always the same. 'OK. But let's play it down.'

It is no great thing to be humble when you are brought low, but to be humble in success or when praised as a great is in itself a great and rare attainment. It was the mark of the man. Even at the height of his prowess on the football field he remained low-key, quite simply because, as he once told me, 'Experience taught me, from the sublime to the ridiculous is often a case of just one step.'

It is not wealth, high profile or ancestry, but honourable conduct and noble disposition that make ordinary souls great, and such was the case with Stan.

As a footballer, he not only richly entertained but brought grace, dignity and nobility to football and thus the lives of the working folk who paid hard-earned cash to see him. To the end he was mindful of his responsibilities and conducted himself accordingly. A man of unyielding integrity.

For all his global fame, his humanity was always prevalent. On one occasion, we travelled to London together in my car for a meeting with our publishers. On our return I drew up outside his home and he immediately reached into his pocket and produced a little wad of notes.

'Here, take this for the petrol,' he said, pushing a little fold of notes towards me. I refused his kind offer.

We then spent two full minutes bandying the money to and fro. He trying to make me accept, I for my part flatly declining. In the end, he tried to open up the glove compartment to place the money in there, only he couldn't work out how it opened. Frustrated, he swung open the passenger door and leapt from the car with all the athleticism of someone 40 years his junior. In thanking me for my time, he threw the notes on the front seat.

I watched him through his front door. Satisfied he was safely inside, I took the money, got out of the car, and posted it through his letter box. I was just on the point of getting back into the car when I heard a squeaking noise, saw the letter box open and the money being pushed out.

It was typical of Stan. Self-willed, strong-minded, humorous, generous of spirit and, for all his fame, as down to earth as the folk who once adorned the terraces in the hope of seeing him sprinkle gold dust on to their harsh working lives.

For all his public appearances, he was by nature a private man, not one given to showing emotion or feelings. However, in his autobiography he wanted to write from the heart; to tell not only of the great players and games but to convey how he felt about them. In particular, he wanted to convey the feelings and emotions he experienced at important times in his private life and on such occasions as the 1953 FA Cup final, the Bolton disaster of 1946 and England's triumph over Germany in the Olympic stadium in Berlin in 1938. In so doing, he hoped the reader would be able to gain an impression and a feel for him as a person. How far he succeeded in this, only you the reader will know.

One aspect of his character I wanted his book to convey was his wonderful sense of humour. Stan was a very witty man and he loved people who made him laugh. In his playing days such people were Stan Mortensen, Bill Shankly, Nat Lofthouse and Eddie Clamp. In retirement he loved hearing the funny stories of former sports people who now work on the after dinner circuit, like Jimmy Greaves, Wilf McGuinness, Jack Charlton, Denis Law, Gareth Chilcott and Sir Richard Hadlee. 'They laugh that win,' said Shakespeare and, in his life, Stan did a lot of both.

Despite his elementary education, Stan was highly knowledgeable. Life taught him a lot but being an avid reader and a lover of art, he also taught himself much. Not only did his knowledge encompass sport, history and literature, it was full of surprises.

When first he decided to write his autobiography, our agent Julian Alexander of Lucas Alexander Whitley took us to meet several interested publishers. During one meeting a representative of one such company was outlining some books they had published recently.

'We did the Robbie Williams book,' she said, adding with due respect to Stan's octogenarian years, 'he's a contemporary pop singer.'

'I know,' said Stan. 'He used to be in Take That. Hasn't he done well since he went solo?'

Stan was very much a family man. A devoted and loving husband, father and grandfather. His family were very important to him. The fact he rarely mentioned them publicly was a sign of his protection.

He had two loves in his life. His first wife, Betty, and

Mila, whom he met in 1967. He found it difficult writing about this part of his life. Although Mila became the all-consuming love of his life, I felt there was still a love for Betty, for the times they had together. At one point there had obviously been much pain, but healing the heart is a gradual process of unfolding, one layer at a time, and I sensed that writing his autobiography helped him.

The sad passing of his beloved Mila in 1999 came as a devastating blow to Stan. In truth he was never the same person after it. He was grief stricken and only his sense of loyalty and obligation to those involved in the publication of this, his definitive story, saw him stick to the task in the months immediately following her death.

The book completed, Stan took off for a winter break in Tenerife and was due to return in February 2000 to help in its promotion when he had his untimely accident. His daughter Jean and son-in-law Bob flew out and brought him home. Even in hospital a few days prior to his death, he was still hopeful of returning to health and helping to publicise his book. Sadly it was not to be.

The fact that he had, at long last, not only written his story but told it in the way he wanted it told gave him great personal satisfaction. 'That's it, then,' he said on completion. 'All done and dusted. Like me.'

Stan played the game he loved, as he told me, 'In a time when football had a smile on its face.' That said, he was adamant that in his time football was a more physical game. Because of the player he was, he came in for some torrid treatment at times, but not once did he ever complain or retaliate. Of all his achievements in football, the fact that he was never cautioned or sent off was the single thing that gave him immense pride. His self-control was remarkable, indicative of a man who throughout his life kept his emotions in check. At times it was as if he had ice in his veins but, without exception, he always played the game with great warmth in his heart.

There are few things of which we can be certain in life, but of one thing we can be: we shall never see his like again. Throughout his playing career and in 'retirement', during which he coached across the world, he proved himself to be football's greatest ambassador. Pelé dubbed football 'the beautiful game' and beauty, they say, is in the eye of the beholder. This being the case, Stan did indeed leave us wonders to behold.

The pages which follow contain just some of the many tributes paid to Stan in recognition of what he gave to a game which, on his own admission, gave him so very much.

By way of a personal tribute, I make reference to a poem, the author of which is unknown. This anonymous poem is thought to have been written in the nineteenth century, but its true origins remain a mystery.

> Do not stand at my grave and weep;
> I am not there. I do not sleep.
> I am a thousand winds that blow,
> I am the diamond glints in snow.
> I am the sunlight on ripened grain,
> I am the gentle autumn rain.
> When you awaken in the morning's hush
> I am the swift uplifting rush
> Of quiet birds in circled flight.
> I am the soft stars that shine at night
> Do not stand at my grave and cry;
> I am not there. I did not die.

For fans of football the world over, and in particular those who saw him play or were fortunate enough to have met him, he never will. For his deeds on the football pitch have ensured the name of Stanley Matthews will not only be synonymous with all that is best about football but will live on for all time passing.

Les Scott
March 2000

In Tribute

You could kick him, do anything with him and he would never retaliate. He was the perfect example of self-discipline. I was very fortunate to play in the same team as Stan, even then I knew I was in the presence of pure footballing genius. Stan was the first real champion of football. He brought his sport into the modern era. He was a man who could reach for the stars and still keep his feet on the ground.

Jimmy Armfield

For me this man probably had the greatest name of any player ever, certainly in Britain. I don't think anyone since has had a name so synonymous with football in England.

Gordon Banks

He was a fantastic player. Respected throughout the entire world of football. Wherever you went in the world, they knew the name Stanley Matthews. He stood for everything that is good about the game. Football has lost its greatest player . . . Thank goodness television was already with us and I could watch him take on his opponents with his speed and skill. Almost no one in the game could stop him.

Franz Beckenbauer

All great players are in some way inspired and, without doubt, Stan had inspiration aplenty. I met him often at sporting functions, he was a gentleman and I was proud to be numbered among his friends. When I was a boy growing up in Belfast he was my hero. Over 40 years on, nothing has changed.

George Best

Sir Stanley was and always remains one of the all-time great footballers. He was not only one of the finest players this country has ever seen, he was also a model sportsman who played the game as it should be played, never booked or sent off once. Football fans the world over have this evening lost one of their heroes.

Tony Blair

Sir Stanley Matthews represented all the important values associated with the game of football and that was reflected in the great sense of loss felt by all age groups on the sad news of his death early into the new millennium. Those who were lucky enough to see him play at his prime can reflect on his wonderful individual skill and artistry. Those of us lucky enough to follow him into a professional football career can only marvel at the dedication and determination that enabled him to stay at the top level beyond his fiftieth birthday. While in recent times his affable style and continual modesty should be a constant reminder to the modern player that class counts both on and off the pitch. Sir Stanley Matthews really is a football legend.

Trevor Brooking, CBE

He was a lovely man and a great player. The way he beat people with the ball and the way he crossed it was really something. He was the best crosser I've ever seen – and he had to contend with the old heavy ball.

John Charles

I loved him. I loved Stanley Matthews. Magic, absolutely magical player. He just attracted people. You had to go and see him – magical player.

Sir Bobby Charlton

I grew up in an era when he was a god to those of us who aspired to play the game. He was a true gentleman and we shall never see his like again.

Brian Clough

He was without doubt a great, great player. As a child I was thrilled when I watched him. I knew then he was a legend and I was lucky later in life to meet him and, unlike some legends, he did not disappoint when you did meet him. Our country should be very proud of him.

David Davies

I hear some modern players being described as 'great'. They are not. They are good, some very good, but none are great in the way Stan was great. I was honoured to have played in his testimonial. It was a fitting tribute to a true legend of football.

Alfredo Di Stefano

In a game that has produced a number of truly great players, he was simply the best. A true legend of football who I am proud to say was a very good friend. I have never seen a player take the ball so close to a person and then send the defender the wrong way. Football will never see his like again, it is the end of an era. But he will live forever in the memories of those fortunate enough to have played with him or seen him play.

Sir Tom Finney

With Garrincha, Matthews was the best winger in international football. Nowadays there are no more players like him; wingers and wing-backs today. He was also a gentleman and had the joy of still playing into his fifties. He was lucky; I had to give up at 27 and I was jealous of him thereafter.

Juste Fontaine

Stanley Matthews was the sportsman everyone looked up to. He had everything – good close control, great dribbling ability and he was lightning quick. He was also an intelligent player, who knew how to pass the ball, and was an excellent crosser.

John Giles

When I was young, every boy interested in football aspired to be Stanley Matthews and I was no exception. I played with him and against him and was fortunate enough to be invited to play in his testimonial match at Stoke in 1965. He was quite simply *the* great footballer, *the* great footballing ambassador.

Jimmy Greaves

Sir Stan was a sporting legend who inspired generations of footballers. He was a great British sportsman, famous in the English game, but recognised the world over. Stan will be remembered for playing football with verve and dignity – a true sporting hero.

William Hague

More than any other player, Stanley Matthews represented all that was great about the Beautiful Game. He wore his country's shirt with pride, dazzled millions with his skill and epitomised sportsmanship, decency and integrity.

Kate Hoey

The last time I saw him he told me he thought he had retired from football too early. I was expecting a smile or a laugh, but he was serious. That to me summed him up. It showed how much he loved football.

Alan Hudson

He was a superstar, a super player – an absolute gentleman. He would have been great in any era. To me, Sir Stanley ranked alongside George Best as the best players there ever were in the game.

Emlyn Hughes

Sir Stan was always a true gentleman and someone that is synonymous with English football. He was always affable, kind and modest. That always struck me because we all knew just what a great player he was.

Gary Lineker

We will never see another like Stanley Matthews. For me, he was *the* great player. I always knew I was in for a good day for England when Matthews was on one wing and Tom Finney on the other.

Nat Lofthouse

Little could I have imagined that I would one day meet the hero of my schoolboy football annuals – the great Stanley himself. When I did, he greeted me as though the privilege was his – absurd. I had gone to Malta where he was living for a time and playing football, in his sixties, for I believe the Malta post office team. Nobody could get the ball off him and, remember, his opponents were a third of his age. I met up with him several times more recently and he was never less than absolutely charming. What an example to all who love the game of football. A true modest hero.

Desmond Lynam

Stan was a football man through and through. A man who was deeply in love with football and everything and everyone connected with the game. I only wish some of today's top players were like that.

Don Mackay

When I was growing up in Lewisham, he was undoubtedly the most famous footballer in the country. As a boy whenever Blackpool played in London, you queued for ages just to say you had seen Stanley Matthews play. He put 10,000 on the crowd. He will be remembered as the classic winger. He had incredible pace over the first five yards, which they say he developed training on Blackpool beach. I remember watching the 1953 final on television – it was fairytale stuff. Everybody wanted Stan to get his medal. It was very fitting that he won it in Coronation Year.

John Motson

On or off the pitch he had class. When he walked into a room my eyes suddenly turned to Stanley Matthews. I knew

I was looking at a true legend of football, one who loved the game as much as life itself.

Alan Mullery

The man who taught us how football should be played.

Pelé

They talk about legends but really he was *the* one and we were lucky enough to play with him week in, week out. We just used to give him the ball, get our heads down and run up the pitch because we knew exactly what he was going to do. The opposition knew as well, but couldn't stop him. That was why he was a great.

Bill Perry

He was one of the very few. A footballing great blessed with genius and possessing the highest virtue of them all – humility.

Ferenc Puskas

He was easily one of our greatest players. He would have played in today's game, he would have adapted. He had immense skill. He ranks alongside players like Pelé, Maradona and Cruyff – and he was one of ours.

Bobby Robson

He was a wonderful man and a true footballing legend who will be sorely missed by all.

Bryan Robson

I remember going to watch Sheffield Wednesday play Blackpool at Hillsborough in the FA Cup when I was 12 or 13 years old. There was over 65,000 there and we had all come to see Stan. Not only was he the greatest footballer we ever produced, he was a fantastic gentleman as well.

Jim Smith

He was a true star and hero of my generation. Quite simply he was one of the greatest, if not *the* greatest, footballer and sportsperson of all time.

Gordon Taylor

When I was very little, I loved following him. I always wanted to dribble like him. He and Garrincha were my heroes.

Rudi Voeller

It is not just in England where his name is famous. All over the world he is regarded as a true footballing legend.

Berti Vogts

I was at Wembley for the England–Argentina game when I heard the news of his sad passing. Wembley was stunned. The nation was stunned. We had lost our footballing great.

Dave Watson

Stan was very fit and the one thing he had was that he was very quick off the mark. He had a unique way of dribbling past people.

Sir Walter Winterbottom

Career Record

——o——

Sir Stanley Matthews

B orn Hanley 1 February 1915. England schoolboy
international v. Wales 1929. League debut for Stoke
City 19 March 1932. England debut 29 September
1934 v. Wales. Transferred to Blackpool May 1947 for
£11,500. Returned to Stoke City October 1961 in £2,500
deal. Awarded CBE 1956, knighted in 1965. Footballer of
the Year 1948 and 1963. European Footballer of the Year
1956. FA Cup winner's medal 1953, Runners-up 1948 and
1951. Division 2 Championship medal 1933 and 1963.

STOKE CITY

Season	League		FA Cup		Inter-League		Internationals	
	Apps	Goals	Apps	Goals	Apps	Goals	Apps	Goals
1931–32	2	–	–	–	–	–	–	–
1932–33	15	1	–	–	–	–	–	–
1933–34	29	11	4	4	–	–	–	–
1934–35	36	10	1	1	2	1	2	1
1935–36	40	10	5	–	–	–	1	–

1936–37	40	7	2	–	–	–	1	–
1937–38	38	6	3	–	1	–	6	5
1938–39	36	2	2	–	2	–	7	2
1939–40	3*	–	–	–	–	–	–	–

(Football League competition suspended during World War 2; replaced by regional tournaments as below)

1945–46	–	–	8	–	–	–	–	–
1946–47	23	4	5	1	3	–	1	0

BLACKPOOL

1946–47	–	–	–	–	–	–	2	1
1947–48	33	1	6	–	2	–	5	–
1948–49	25	3	3	–	1	–	5	1
1949–50	31	–	3	–	–	–	1	–
1950–51	36	–	8	–	–	–	2	–
1951–52	18	1	1	–	–	–	–	–
1952–53	20	4	7	1	–	–	–	–
1953–54	30	2	7	–	–	–	5	–
1954–55	34	1	1	-	1	1	7	–
1955–56	36	3	1	–	–	–	2	–
1956–57	25	2	4	–	1	–	7	1
1957–58	28	–	1	–	–	–	–	–
1958–59	19	–	6	–	–	–	–	–
1959–60	15	–	–	–	–	–	–	–
1960–61	27	–	1	–	–	–	–	–
1961–62	2	–	–	–	–	–	–	–

STOKE CITY

1961–62	18	2	3	1	–	–	–	–
1962–63	31	1	–	–	–	–	–	–
1963–64	9	–	4	1	–	–	–	–
1964–65	1	–	–	–	–	–	–	–

TOTAL	697	71	86	9	13	2	54	11

*Three matches played before competition suspended and not counted in total of Football League appearances. Matthews played in 69 Wartime League and Cup matches for Stoke City, scoring eight goals, and made 87 appearances as a guest for Blackpool, scoring eight goals between 1939–40 and 1945–46. He also made guest appearances for Airdrieonians, Glasgow Rangers and Arsenal. In addition, he appeared in 29 Wartime and Victory Internationals for England, scoring two goals. He represented Great Britain against the Rest of Europe on two occasions, in 1947 and 1955, and also played in the Bolton Disaster Fund international against Scotland in 1946.

ENGLAND INTERNATIONALS

1934 v. Wales (1 goal), Italy; 1935 v. Germany; 1937 v. Scotland, Wales (1), Czechoslovakia (3); 1938 v. Scotland, Germany (1), Switzerland, France, Wales (1), Rest of Europe, Norway, Northern Ireland (1); 1939 v. Scotland, Italy, Yugoslavia; 1947 v. Scotland, Switzerland, Portugal (1), Belgium, Wales, Northern Ireland; 1948 v. Scotland, Italy, Denmark, Northern Ireland (1), Wales, Switzerland; 1949 v. Scotland; 1950 v. Spain, Northern Ireland; 1951 v. Scotland; 1953 v. Rest of Europe, Northern Ireland, Hungary; 1954 v. Belgium, Uruguay, Northern Ireland, Wales, West Germany; 1955 v. Scotland, France, Spain, Portugal, Wales; 1956 v. Brazil, Northern Ireland (1), Wales, Yugoslavia, Denmark; 1957 v. Scotland, Republic of Ireland, Denmark.

WARTIME AND VICTORY INTERNATIONALS

1939 v. Wales, Scotland; 1940 v. Wales, Scotland; 1941 v. Scotland, Scotland, Wales; 1942 v. Scotland, Scotland, Scotland, Wales; 1943 v. Wales, Scotland, Wales, Wales, Scotland (1); 1944 v. Scotland, Scotland, Wales, Scotland; 1945 v. Scotland, Scotland (1), Wales, France, Northern Ireland, Wales; 1946 v. Belgium, Switzerland, France.

Index

Throughout the index Sir Stanley Matthews is referred to as 'SM'

Ajax 273, 329

Allen, Tony 512, 521, 570

Allison, George 104, 147, 210

Allison, Malcolm 61

Anelka, Nicolas 580–1

Anfield Road *see* Liverpool FC

Antonio, George 87–8, 232

Argentina 442

Armfield, Jimmy 470–2, 486, 546

Arsenal FC 65, 128–9, 148, 172–4, 210–11, 408

  1953 FA Cup tie v. Blackpool 393–402

  tactics 102–3

  see also Highbury

Asprey, Bill 512, 521

Astley, Dai 132

Aston, Johnny 283, 287, 288, 333

Aston Villa FC 21, 104, 129

  see also Villa Park

Attlee, Clement 216

Bailey, Jim 566

Baily, Eddie 342, 358

Baker, Frank 132, 194, 232

Ball, Johnny 421, 425, 430

Banks, Gordon 181

Banks, Ralph 421, 427, 430

Barnes, John 290

Barnes, Wally 545
Barnsley FC 104
Barrass, Malcolm 421, 422, 426, 430
Bartram, Sam 224, 463, 500
Bastin, Cliff 65, 121, 126, 129
Baxter, Jim 546
BBC 370, 414, 483, 569
 see also television
Beasley, Pat 143, 150
Beattie, Andy 90–1, 95–6
Bebbington, Keith 512, 518
Beeson, George 104
Belgium (football team) 216, 295
Belgrade 154–6
Bell, Eric 421, 422, 426
Benfica FC 178
Bennett, Les 402
Bentley, Bill 570
Bentley, Roy 342, 458, 464
Berlin, Olympic Stadium 115–24
Berry, John 472
Best, George 175, 178, 291, 446–7, 460, 569–74
Biggs, Ronnie 567–8
Bingham, Harry 228
Birkett, Ralph 73–5
Birks, George 274

Birmingham City FC 21, 183
black markets, ticket 396, 401–2, 410–11
Blackpool FC 1–2, 166, 194–5, 255–7, 268–78, 358–80, 447–50, 462, 464
 1948 FA Cup Final 279–92
 1951 FA Cup Final 363–7
 1953 FA Cup Final 417–39
 1953 FA Cup tie 393–402
Blades, Jack 566
Blanchflower, Danny 502–3, 545
Blanchflower, Jackie 472
Blenkinsop, Ernie 105
Bloomer, Steve 88, 170
Bloomfield Road *see* Blackpool FC
Bloor, Alan 512
Blunstone, Frank 169
Bolton Wanderers FC 219, 413, 419–38, 470
 see also Burnden Park tragedy
Bonnytown Golf Club 51–2
Booth, Albert 111

Booth, Harry 238–42, 247–9, 255–6

boots, football 337–40, 374, 394–6

Bournemouth FC 13–14

Bowyer, Frank 545

Bradford City FC stadium fire 219

Bradford Park Avenue FC 450, 460

Brazil 2, 334, 565–9

Brazil (football team) 273, 329, 335–7, 342–3

Brennan, Frank 276

Brentford FC 245–6

Bridgwood, Gerry 512, 537

Brighton and Hove Albion FC 195

British Open Golf Championship 434

Brodis, Ivor 451, 494

Brook, Eric 56, 66–8, 177

Broome, Frank 121, 128, 129, 157

Brown, Allan 'Bomber' 359, 361–3, 381, 384, 398–402, 407

Brown, Roy 232

Burbanks, Eddie 194

Burgess, Ron 358

Burnden Park tragedy 219–24

Burnley FC 29–30

Burrows, Horace 104

Busby, Matt 176–81, 291, 329, 472, 482, 534
see also Manchester United FC

Bussy, Walter 42

Buxton, Peter 543

Byrne, Roger 332

Camsell, George 171

Canada 332–3, 509

Capewell, Ron 384

Cardiff City FC 209–10
see also Ninian Park

Carey, Johnny 178, 285, 348–9

Carter, Horatio 'Raich' 48–9, 93, 96, 166, 175, 201

Chamberlain, Neville 131

chants, football 384, 579–80

Chapman, Herbert 173–4, 372

Chapman, Stuart 553

charity football games 326–7

Charles, John 168, 499

'Charlie' (Belgrade, 1939) 156–7

Charlton, Bobby 178, 290, 472–3, 546

Charlton, Jack 88

Charlton Athletic FC 568

Charnley, Dave 486

Chelsea FC 2, 103, 208–9, 464–5, 524–33
  see also Stamford Bridge
Chester, Charlie 326, 330
Chile 442
Chilton, Allenby 276, 286, 288
Clamp, Eddie 93, 518–22, 525–31
Clemence, Ray 182, 481
Clough, Brian 516–17
Co-op football boots 338–40
Coaching Centre, FA 480
Cobbold family 515–16
Cockburn, Henry 333
Cohen, George 546
Colchester United FC 278
Colman, Eddie 472
Colombia 231
commercial deals 337–40, 413–14
Communale Stadium 306
  see also Italy (football team)
Compton, Denis 196, 200, 304
Compton, Leslie 196, 329
Cook, Billy 135–6
Copping, Wilf 66, 68, 69, 104
Cox, Arthur 481
Craven Cottage *see* Fulham FC

Crewe Alexandra FC 552, 581
Crompton, Jack 286, 288
Crooks, Sammy 48, 122–3
Crosland, Johnny 389, 407
Cruyff, Johan 196, 329
Cullerton, Mick 552–3
Cullis, Stan 128, 107, 184, 200, 304
Cummings, George 144
Curtis, Norman 383
customs, working–class 22
Czechoslovakia 106, 305–6, 555–7

Daladier, Edouard 131
Dallas Cowboys 586
Davies, Don 483–4
Davies, Harry 44–5
Davis, Dickie 37
Dawson, Jerry 143, 145
Dean, Dixie 88, 132, 170–1
Dean Court *see* Bournemouth FC
Deepdale *see* Preston North End FC
Dell, the *see* Southampton FC
Denmark v. England
  (1948) 320
  (1957) 322
Derby County FC 166–7, 174–5, 408

Di Stefano, Alfredo 473, 474, 544, 546
Dickinson, Jimmy 545
Dickson, Bill 292
diets 334, 377
Dimmock, Peter 509
Dix, Ron 194
Dixon, Reginald 413
Dobing, Peter 536 537
Docherty, Tommy 501–2
Dodds, 'Jock' 189–91, 194, 545
Doherty, Peter 175–6, 191–2, 195
Dooley, Derek 383, 384, 385, 409
Dougall, Jimmy 142
Douglas, Brian 492, 546
Drake, Ted 65, 66, 67–8, 128–9, 171, 464
Drewry, Arthur 333, 340–1
dribbling 72
drugs 160
Duke, Squadron Leader Neville 415
Duncan, Dally 175
Duquemin, Les 403
Durham City FC 125
Durie, Dave 318, 470

Ealing, Harry 71
Eckersley, Bill 342
Edinburgh, Duke of 415, 420, 540

Edwards, Duncan 169, 464, 472
Edwards, Louis 181
Elder, Alex 570
Elizabeth II, Queen 415, 432, 433, 539, 540
Elland Road 190–1
    see also Leeds United FC
Ellerington, Bill 321
Ellis, Arthur 403
England tour
    (1938) 129–30
    (1939) 147–62
England v.
    Austria (1952) 494–7
    Czechoslovakia (1937) 106
    Germany (1935) 76–9
    Ireland (1938) 133–5
    Italy (1934) 64–9
    Scotland (1942) 200
    Scotland (1943) 200–1
    Wales (1937) 106
English, Sam 45–6
Estoril *see* Portugal v. England (1947)
Euro 96 262
European Cup 465, 472–3
Eusebio, Silva 544, 546
Evans, Harry 435
Evans, Norman 290
Everton FC 103, 183–4
    see also Goodison Park

Ewbank, Mr (FA treasurer)
301–3
expenses 301–3

FA Cup
1945–46 214
1948 Final (Blackpool v.
Manchester United)
279–90
1951 Final (Blackpool v.
Newcastle United)
363–7
1952–53 318, 382–405
1953 Final (Blackpool v.
Bolton Wanderers)
417–39
fan mail 107, 282, 544–5
Farm, George 317–19, 399,
403, 420, 421, 422–3,
424, 430, 431, 433,
477
Farrow, George 194
Fazackerley, Derek 481
Fenton, Ewan 398, 421,
422, 423, 425, 427,
428, 431, 477
Fenton, Ted 278
Ferdinand, Rio 291
FIFA (Fédération
Internationale de
Football Association)
150, 231, 251, 332,
566
Finan, Bob 194

Finney, Tom 233, 265,
266–7, 451, 452, 479,
489, 490–3, 545
floodlighting 372–3, 391,
465–6
Football League v. Scottish
League (1938) 132
Football Writers'
Association 281,
350–1
Player of the Year 280–1,
329, 492, 497, 499,
534
Footballer of the Year,
European 474
footballs 374–6
Forbes, Alex 329
Ford, Trevor 351–2
Formby, George 413, 415
Foulkes, Bill 472
Fowler, Robbie 160
France v. England (1938)
128–30
Franklin, Neil 229–31, 237,
257, 267, 296, 545
Fratton Park *see* Portsmouth
FC
Freeman, Tom 201–2
Froggart, Jack 321
Froggatt, Redfern 383, 386
Fulham FC 462, 540–1

Garrett, Tommy 421, 423, 428
Gascoigne, Paul 460, 482
gate receipts 171
Gento, Francisco 546
George VI, King 285
Germany 76–90
Germany (football team) 73
v. England (1938)
115–24
Germany, West (football team) 453, 458–9
Gilzean, Alan 546
Ginola, David 103 0
Glasgow Rangers FC 213, 305
Glendenning, Raymond 495
Glentoran FC 175
Gloucester, Duke of 140–1
goalkeepers 181–6
Goebbels, Joseph 118, 123
Goering, Hermann 118, 123
Goodison Park 292
see also Everton FC
Goring, Peter 329
Goulden, Len 122–3, 144, 152, 158
Gradi, Dario 552
Graham, George 102
Grainger, Colin 475
Gratrix, Roy 486

Great Britain v. Rest of Europe (1947) 251–5
Greaves, Jimmy 516, 544, 546
Green, Geoffrey 445
Gregory, Alfred 415
Gregson, John 318
ground safety 219–23
Gymphlex tracksuits 374

Hackett, Desmond 494, 497, 506
Hagan, Jimmy 200, 321, 545
Hall, Alex 104
Hall, Willie 133–7, 152, 153, 158
Hampden Park 19–20, 89–95, 140–5, 252, 255
see also Scotland (football team)
Hanson, Stan 421, 422, 425–30
Hapgood, Eddie 65–9, 84, 116, 118, 119, 143–4, 152–8, 196–8
Hardwick, George 266, 321, 545
Hardy, Sam 183
Harris, Peter 451
Harris, Ron 'Chopper' 527–32
Hassall, Harry 421–3

Haynes, Johnny 457–8, 492, 546
Hayward, Basil 195
Hayward, Eric 195, 268, 270
Henderson, Sir Neville 118
Henderson, Willie 546
Herd, Alex 177
Herod, Dennis 228, 257
Hess, Rudolph 52
Hewitt, Peter 257
Heysel stadium tragedy 219
Hibbs, Harry 182, 183
Hidegkuti, Nandor 443, 457
Highbury 67, 393, 396, 397
 see also Arsenal FC
Hill, Frank 104
Hill, Jimmy 383
Hill, Steve 486, 505
Hillsborough stadium fire 219
Hitler, Adolf 74, 116–17, 131
Holdcroft, George 183–4
Holden, Doug 421, 431 –2
Holland (football team) 329
Home International Championship 332, 373, 463
 see also individual matches

Hong Kong 313
hooliganism 575
Hopkins, Idris 132
Hopkins, Mel 534–5
Horton, Henry 392
Howe, Don 102
Howe, Jack 306
Hubbick, Harry 195
Huddersfield Town FC 113, 124–5, 386–7
Hughes, 'Whacker' 276
Hull City FC 184
Hungary (football team) 329, 442–6, 463
Hunt, Roger 546
Hurst, Geoff 181
Hutchison, Tommy 284

indiscretions 262–3
injuries 233, 367–9, 381–2, 477, 536
Ipswich Town FC 514–15
Ireland, Republic of (football team) 88, 133–6
Italy 64–9, 148–9, 305
Italy (football team) 60, 64–70, 305–6
 v. England
  (1939) 148–54
  (1948) 305–11
 see also Communale Stadium

Jack, David 172
Jackson, Alex 174
Jackson, John 232
James, Alex 172–4
Jennings, Pat 181
Jepson, Arthur 228
Johansen, Kai 546
John, Roy 55–7, 66
Johnson, Joe 90, 95, 96
Johnston, Harry 270, 271, 272, 385, 386, 392, 413, 414–15, 417, 419, 420, 421–2, 423, 424–6, 431, 432, 433, 438, 545
Jones, Bryn 147
Jones, Cliff 546
Jones, Sam 194
Joseph, Sir Francis 253

Kaye, Arthur 318, 486
Keegan, Kevin 133, 481
Kelly, Hughie 287, 288, 407, 477, 545
Kelsey, Jack 398
Kennedy, Joe 276
Kettering Town FC 10–11
Kirton, Jock 72, 176, 229
Kopa, Raymond 544, 546

Langley, Jimmy 538
Langton, Bobby 321, 421, 430

Law, Denis 178, 276, 446, 447, 544, 546
Lawton, Tommy 138–9, 144–5, 151, 254, 255, 265, 321
Le Saux, Graeme 160
Ledbrooke, Archie 390
Leeds Road *see* Huddersfield Town FC
Leeds United FC 104, 116 *see also* Elland Road
Leicester City FC 103
Liddell, Billy 300–1, 349–51
Liddle, Bobby 236
Light, Billy 87
Linfield FC 194
Liverpool FC 177, 349
Lofthouse, Nat 421, 422–3, 425, 426, 428, 432, 451, 457, 458, 493–8, 545
Logie, Jimmy 329, 399
Luton Town FC 89
Lynas, Johnny 331, 427

Maine Road 62, 200 *see also* Manchester City FC
Male, George 65, 69, 93–5, 104, 150, 152, 153, 157
Malta 149, 310–11

Manchester City FC 32, 61–2, 113, 175–6, 177, 185–6, 408
  see also Maine Road
Manchester United FC 103, 168, 169, 176–9, 333, 348, 482
  in 1948 FA Cup Final 283–9
  see also Busby, Matt; Old Trafford
Mannion, Wilf 168, 200, 254, 265, 321, 345–8
Marsh, Rodney 325
Masopust, Josef 546
Mather, Tom 19, 24, 35–6, 85
  see also Stoke City FC
Matthews, Arthur (brother) 13, 57
Matthews, Berry (SM's first wife) *see* Vallance, Berry
Matthews, Jack (brother) 13, 57
Matthews, Jack (father)
  wants SM to be a boxer 5–6
  gives SM financial advice 39–40
  encourages SM after 1935 Germany match 81–3
  dies 202–4

Matthews, Jean (daughter) 137–8, 539
Matthews, Mila (SM's second wife) 310, 555–8, 577, 587
Matthews, Ronnie (brother) 13, 57, 326, 327
Matthews, Sir Stanley
  admiration for Joe Smith 484–5
  Arsenal, declines invitation from 454–5
  Betty Vallance
    meets 26–8
    weds 51–2
  Blackpool FC
    joins 255–6
    leaves 505–10
  Bob McCrory, relationship with 98, 234–8, 241–6
  born 3
  and Burnden Park tragedy 219–24
  called before FA (with others) 301–4
  Co-op, commercial deal with 337–40, 454–6
  coaches in South Africa 467, 476, 559–64
  'combs his hair' in Turin 310–16

daughter (Jean) born
137–8
develops body swerve
32–3, 72
and dug-out advice 481
earns Division Two
winner's medal 44
and FA administrators
253, 302–4, 373–4,
410–12, 465–6
father dies 202–4
father's deathbed promise
204, 418, 432–3
favourite decade 169–70
final international game
321–2
Football Writers' Player
of the Year

(1948) 280–1

(1963) 534
and foreign players
581–2
and the future 578–87
Germany, disappointing
performance against
76–81
honoured by
Stoke-on-Trent
224–5
initial experience of
first-team football
41–2
injuries 153, 157–8, 576

international debut v.
Wales (1934) 54–6
in international
wilderness (1949)
323
irritated by reference to
age 454–5
and knighthood 537
last competitive match 2,
158, 575–6
last game for England
478–9
last league game 2,
538–9
learns golf 45–6
and match commentating
585–6
Matt Busby, praise for
176–81
meets King Carol's
gardener 161
Mila, meets 555–6
picked for England
Schoolboys 10–11
and players of today 133,
159–60, 297–8,
339–40, 437
plays for
England Schoolboys v.
Wales 14–19
Football League 52
plays in
1953 FA Cup final
418–39

Brazil (1985) 575–6
Canada 509
England schoolboy
    trial 10
England trial 47
Port Vale, general
    manager at 549–55
as racehorse owner 330
RAF
    joins 187
    leaves 207, 225
receives knighthood
    539–40
and referees 240
revered by National
    Union of Students
    293–4
runs hotel with Betty
    369
school days 7–21
scores first goal as
    professional 44
selected for England 53
selected for England in
    1950 World Cup
    332–3
skills on the ball 32–3,
    71–2, 101–3, 105–6
son (Stanley) born 213
Stoke City FC
    applies for transfer
        from 108–13
    asked to return to 378
    decides to leave 247–9
disagreement over
    bonus 85–6,
    98–9
joins 24
returns to 506–11
signs for 33–5
testimonial match 446,
    474, 542–8
works as office boy at
    25–31
and tackling 103–6
training routine 59–61
turns professional 33–4
as variety performer 326
and violent match v. Italy
    66–9
visits Blackpool with
    Betty 109–11
war years 187–204
yearns for FA Cup
    winner's medal
    414–15
Matthews, Stanley (son)
    213, 539
McCall, Andy 319
McCreadie, Eddie 527
McCue, Johnny 229
McGarry, Billy 451, 545
McGrory, Bob 36, 98, 210,
    217, 234–8, 274
    relationship with SM
        241–8, 255–8
McGuinness, Wilf 180,
    472–3

McIlroy, Jimmy 169, 513, 520–1

McIlvanney, Hugh 3

McIntosh, Willie 274

McKenna, John 467

McKnight, George 363, 385

McManaman, Steve 133

McNab, Sandy 144

McPhail, Bob 97

Mercer, Joe 61–2, 141, 151, 152, 397, 500

Meredith, Billy 214

Merrick, Gil 452–3

Middlesbrough FC 73, 75, 346–7

Milburn, Jackie 293, 320, 321, 342, 545

Millward, Arthur 377

Mitchell, Albert 246

Mitten, Charlie 287–8

Moiloa, Gilbert 569

Moir, Willie 421, 422, 424, 435

Molineux Grounds 132–4
  see also Wolverhampton Wanderers FC

Montgomery, Field Marshal Bernard 299, 412–13, 540–1

Moore, Bobby 181

Moore, John 570

Morris, Bill 142, 150

Morris, Johnny 288

Mortensen, Stan 199, 265–7, 269–70, 274–8, 545
  in 1953 FA Cup final 421–40
  injured in War 276–7

Moscow Dynamos 207–13

Moss, Frank 69

Mould, Billy 132, 194, 228–9

Mountford, Frank 229

Mountford, George 231–3, 246

Moyniban, John 462

Mozley, Bert 321

Mudie, Jackie 359–60, 384, 403–4, 421, 422, 423, 506, 545

Mullen, Jimmy 342, 452

Munich air disaster (1958) 169, 178, 186, 472, 483, 513

Munro, Alex 269, 271

Münzenberg 76–8, 115, 120–2

Murdoch, Richard 'Stinker' 413

Murray, Bill 37

Mussolini, Benito 64, 131, 148–9

Myott, Ashley 112

Nationwide Conference
  League 584
Nazi movement 74, 115–18
Nazi salute, England team
  forced to give 117–18
Newcastle United FC 85,
  330
  see also St James' Park
Nicholson, Bill 329, 358,
  516
Ninian Park 56
  see also Cardiff City FC
Northern Ireland v.
  England (1948) 320
Norwich City FC 195
Notts County FC 293

O'Donnell, Frank 97
O'Donnell, Hugh 189
Old Trafford. 136
  see also Manchester
  United FC
O'Neill, Jimmy 512, 537,
  545
Ormston, Alex 194, 232
Overath, Wolfgang 546
Owen, Michael 298, 585
Owens, Jesse 124

Pannaye, Joe 296
Parbleu (SM's racehorse)
  330–1
Parkinson, Colonel W. 194,
  248, 250, 255, 256

Parkinson, Michael 493
Payne, Joe 89
Pegg, Dave 472, 479
penalties 195–6
Peppitt, Syd 194, 232
Perry, Bill 359–60, 384–5,
  392, 402–3, 425–31,
  477
Peters, Martin 181
Philpott, Alan 512
Pope, 'Patty' 194
Popluhar, Jan 546
Port Vale FC 24, 549–57
Portman Road *see* Ipswich
  Town FC
Portsmouth FC 147, 323,
  381
Portugal v. England (1947)
  261–8
Powell, Ivor 188, 199
Preston North End FC 172,
  189, 323, 408,
  489–93
procedures, pre–match
  92–3
programmes, match 246,
  384, 396–7
Puskas, Ferenc 444–7, 473,
  544, 546

Queen of the South FC
  318
Queens Park Rangers FC
  188, 325

Quixall, Albert 383, 385

Raith Rovers FC 172
Ramsey, Alf 304, 321, 358,
    403–5, 514–15
Randle, Frank 413
Ratcliffe, Don 512–13,
    518, 521, 537
Real Madrid 273, 329,
    473–4
Reed, Les 481
Reid, Peter 290
Revie, Don 457–8, 463,
    545
Richards, Cordon 415
Ridding, Bill 419
Ritchie, John 541
Robinson, 'Bill' 230–1
Robinson, Cyril 407, 421
Robinson, Jackie 123, 126,
    128
Robledo, George 364
Roker Park 48
    see also Sunderland FC
Romania v. England (1939)
    158–9
Rous, Stanley 118, 153,
    264, 341
Rowlands, George *see*
    Antonio, George
Rowley, Arthur 545
Rowley, Jack 287–8

Sagar; Ted 182, 183–4
salaries *see* wages
San Siro, Milan 149–52
Schäfer, Hans 546
Schnellinger, Karl Heinz
    546
Scotland (football team)
    19–20, 90–7, 174
    v. England
    (1937) 90–7
    (1939) 139–46
    (1948) 299–300
    see also Hampden Park
Scott, Elisha 170, 182
Scott, Laurie 321
Scoular, Jimmy 545
Seaman, David 182, 481
Second World War
    187–202
    declared 163, 186
    League organisation
    193–4
    SM joins RAF 187
Seeler, Uwe 546
selection system,
    international 132–3,
    442, 466–67
Sellars, Harry 232
Sewell, Jackie 383, 385,
    495
Shackleton, Len 37, 272,
    321, 458, 459–62
Shankly, Bill 114, 172, 197,
    352–6

Sharpe, Ivan 125
Sheffield United FC 216,
    240–1, 409
Sheffield Wednesday FC
    104, 175, 383–5
Sheringham, Teddy 513
Shilton, Peter 181–2
Shimwell, Eddie 270, 271,
    272, 398, 420–6, 428,
    470, 471
Shorthouse, Bill 276
Skeels, Eric 512, 521
skills on the ball 32–3, 72,
    101–2, 105–6
Slack, Mr 10
Slater, Bill 363
Smith, Gordon 284
Smith, Joe 2, 249–56,
    268–72, 285, 419,
    448–50
  encourages SM to stay at
      Blackpool 378, 379
  entertains 'Willie
      Dugdale' 305
  leaves Blackpool 484–5
Smith, Lionel 397
smoking 438–9
songs, football 579–80
South Africa 313, 314, 467,
    476, 477, 559–64
South American tour,
    England's (1954)
    441–2
Southampton FC 388–91

Spiers, Cyril 210
Spratt, Huston 538
Sproston, Bert 116, 117,
    120
St James' Park 199, 331
  see also Newcastle United
      FC
Stamford Bridge 64
  see also Chelsea FC
'Stan's Men 564–9
Starling, Ron 95–6
Steaua Bucharest 273
Steel, Billy 255
Steele, Freddie 'Nobby'
    70–1, 86–7, 90, 232,
    245, 257, 362
Stein, Jock 172, 329
Stock, Alec 323–5
Stoke City FC 4, 70–1,
    227–39, 408, 506–38
  SM joins 3, 24
  SM works as office boy
      25–31
  SM signs 33–4
  camaraderie 70–1
  asks SM to return 378
  see also Mather, Tom
Stoke-on-Trent honours SM
    224
Strange, Alf 175
Streten, Bernard 321
strips, football 397
Stuart, Eddie 517–18, 521,
    537

Suart, Ron 270, 485–7, 505–6
Sudetenland 115
Summerbee, Mike 61–2
Sunderland FC 37, 47, 104
    see also Roker Park
Swift, Frank 47, 177, 182, 185–6, 264, 306, 321, 483
Switzerland v. England
    (1938) 124–8
    (1947) 259–61

tackling 103–6
Taylor, Ernie 370–1, 384, 420–31, 477
Taylor, Frank 258, 378
Taylor, Tommy 169, 472, 475
television 414, 465, 509, 581, 585
    see also BBC
Terry, Mr (headmaster) 10–12
Thomson, Bobby 546
Thornton, Willie 299
ticket allocation 396, 401, 410–14
Tilkowski, Hans 546
Tilson, Freddie 56, 171, 177
Torino FC plane crash tragedy 325–6

Tottenham Hotspur FC 357–8, 401–4
    see also White Hart Lane
Tower Ballroom, Blackpool 413
training routine 59–61, 480–1
transfer, from Stoke City FC, SM granted 247–9
transfer fees 147–8, 250–1, 256, 292–3, 516, 533–4
Trautmann, Bert 499, 545
travel to and from matches 40–1, 130, 190–2, 259–60, 301–4, 333
Tresadern, Jack 91
Trinder, Tommy 540–2
Trotter, Jimmy 91, 497
Turner, Edgar 543
Turton, Cyril 383

Uruguay 442, 452–3
USA (football team) 340–1, 442

Vallance, Betty 26–8, 37–8, 43, 49–52, 539
Vallance, Jimmy 26–8, 33, 45, 60–1, 89
Van de Velde, Jean 434
Victoria Ground *see* Stoke City FC

Vieira, Patrick 103
Villa Park 401–4
   see also Aston Villa FC
violence on the pitch 66–9
Viollet, Dennis 472,
      513–14, 518, 520
Voisey, Bill 215
vomiting, pre–match 93

Waddington, Tony 266,
      486, 506–7, 508–9,
      520, 521, 536–7
Wade, Joe 398
wages 1–2, 25, 31, 36–7,
      39, 153–4, 231, 454,
      582–3
   maximum 253–4, 292,
      457, 508–9
Waiters, Tony 486, 546
Wales 106
Wales (football team) 199
   v. England (1934) 54–6
Walker, Billy 172
Walker, Tommy 97, 114
Walsall FC 183
Ward, Tim 545
Wardle, Willie 319
Waring, Pongo 171
Water Rats, Grand Order of
      540
Weber, Wolfgang 546
Welsh, Don 122, 128, 158

Wembley Stadium 16, 263,
      285, 382–3, 417–18,
      442–4
Wenger, Arsène 102
West, Bromwich Albion FC
      15, 86–7, 113
Westwood, Ray 56
Wheeler, Jack 388, 426,
      427
Wheeler, Johnny 421
Whelan, Liam 472
White Hart Lane 76, 106,
      211
   see also Tottenham
      Hotspur FC
Whittaker, Tom 91, 153,
      454
Williams, Darren 291
Willingham, Charles
      Kenneth (Ken) 120,
      152, 158
Wilshaw, Dennis 452, 464
Wilson, Peter 515, 533
Wilson, Ray 511, 546
winter (1962–63) 524
Winterbottom, Walter 263,
      320, 321, 322, 340,
      442, 451, 458
Wise, Dennis 159
Wolverhampton Wanderers
      FC 21, 147
   see also Molineux
      Grounds
Wood, Ray 472

Wood, Wee Georgie 326, 330

Woodburn, Willie 276, 501–2

Woodley, Vic 93, 97, 142, 151, 182, 184–5

World Cup 60, 149–50, 176, 262, 273
1950, Brazil 332–44, 442
1954, Switzerland 451–3
1966, England 511

Wright, Billy 267, 296, 444, 451, 453

Wright, Jackie 407

Yashin, Lev 546

Yeovil Town FC 323, 324

York City FC 463

Young, Alf 122, 124, 127, 184

Young, George 500

Yugoslavia v. England (1939) 155–8

Zola, Gianfranco 103

Zurich, Hardsturm Stadium 126

Beating the Biological Clock
THE JOYS AND CHALLENGES OF LATE MOTHERHOOD

Pamela Armstrong

Babies change your life. They're hard work. They disrupt your sleep and devastate the body beautiful. So why are women leaving it later and later to have their children, when the natural difficulties of having a baby are compounded by advancing years?

There are a growing band of women in their thirties and forties who buck the trend. At the very time that most women are waving their offspring goodbye and facing an empty nest, these mature mums are putting their careers on hold and having babies.

Television presenter Pamela Armstrong, who had her first baby at forty-two, has spoken to many older mothers about the myriad trials, challenges and joys of later motherhood, and her book is packed with information and anecdotes drawn directly from the experiences of women themselves. Older mothers, with more to lose, often approach pregnancy with great zeal and commitment. They want to know everything; they want the truth and the very best for their unborn child.

The book covers everything from pre-conceptual care to the increasingly divisive issue of pre-natal diagnostic testing, and the statistical reality of handicap in later births. It reassures the older mother-to-be so that she can carry, bear and nurture her new born confident that she has made all the right choices.

NON-FICTION / SELF HELP 0 7472 5077 4